A NOTE TO THE READER

Thank you for reading this book. It took me a few years to turn a two-word inspiration into this story. I've tried to make it as accurate as possible; but, you know how things "happen." If you spot any errors or typos, or if you'd just like to share your thoughts or reactions, or just say "Hello," then please email me at any time. Really.

I'm thrilled when I hear from a reader about what they think about the story—pros and cons. It helps make the telling better for future readers. You can reach me at djkennebeck@emmaus-way.com.

Praise for *The Pivotal Pastor*

The church St. Mary of the Annunciation at Fremont Center in Lake County Illinois deserves to be documented and I am grateful to David for doing the hard work of recording its genesis. With thanks and appreciation.—Dirk Lohan, FAIA; Architect of the new church at St. Mary of the Annunciation; McDonald's Corporation Headquarters in Oak Brook, Illinois; and expansions to Chicago's Shedd Oceanarium, Adler Planetarium and Soldier Field Stadium.

This is a wonderful story about a former seminary student of mine – Ron Lewinski. It describes what can be accomplished with the kind of visionary leadership that Fr. Ron provided as pastor, working with a world-renowned architect and a faith community to expand a small country parish.—Sr. Agnes Cunningham, SSCM; S.T.D. Universite Catholoque de Lyon in Lyon, France. One of the first female theology instructors at a major Catholic seminary

I loved every minute of reading The Pivotal Pastor. My children have been parishioners at St. Mary of the Annunciation for about twenty years, so I have attended many events there. I will never again be there without admiring it in a very detailed way!—Ellen B.

This story will appeal to clergy and laity of other faiths who are curious about Catholic church architecture and liturgical norms. It will also appeal to anyone interested in architecture and design generally, land development project planning, fundraising, and leadership. -- Olga M.
I found this book to be engaging, well written, and a masterpiece homage to a wonderful pastor and the God Who drove his spirit!—Kathi B.

Every Deanery and every parish should have a copy and make pastors and parishioners aware of it when they are to embark on a building project. While reading, I experienced deja vu from my committee service when fundraising for our parish center. This book should serve as a 'blueprint', helping supporters prepare for their service.—Joyce F.

Really enjoyed the book. It walks through the whole process, starting with a vision that developed and matured into a plan with parishioner inputs and then was brought to reality. The first-hand accounts and details of discussions gave insight into the process that created such a beautiful building. It helped me understand the development and appreciate the meaning behind the architectural choices.—John B.

I had tears coming down my cheeks during much of the reading.... so many people, so many hours, so much leadership by Ron Lewinski... not many could have accomplished this.—Anonymous parishioner

Excellent! Fr. Ron Lewinski was a classmate of mine and a beloved friend. The Pivotal Pastor *is a great tribute to him.*—Fr. F.

This account digs into the leaders' and parishioners' personal and spiritual development in addition to the logistical and architectural difficulties. The powerful influence of religion, teamwork, and visionary leadership is demonstrated while honestly recounting the victories, setbacks, and breakthroughs that characterized the project. For readers who are interested in inspiring, real-life stories of spirituality, fostering community, and effective leadership, Fr. Lewinski serves as a tremendous source of inspiration regardless of which faith a reader follows. -- Jamie M.

The details that are captured and the way the story is told took me back 25+ years. Dave (the author) should feel very proud.—J. Riggio, Chair of the Planning Commission during the parish expansion

Lewinski is a testament to what it means to devote your life to the flock. The author writes a clean and concise narrative, and by incorporating photographs and other visual mementos of the journey, he brings the project of expanding the church physically to life. I enjoyed watching it all come together. -- Asher S.

This is a very comprehensive book with extensive details. It's well-written and flows with an engaging story. I'm finding it very interesting as I learn more about Fr. Ron and the process that unfolded during the building of the new church. I highly recommend it, especially for parishioners of St Mary of the Annunciation. Awesome book! —Tom W.

What sets this account apart is its meticulous attention to detail and unique access to [historical] materials. Through personal insights, anecdotes, and humor, the book brings to life the experiences of both the pastor and the parishioners involved in this transformative project. The Pivotal Pastor is a compelling and enlightening read for anyone interested in the intersection of faith, community, and leadership. I would not hesitate to recommend it. -- K.C.F.

I joined the parish in 2003, after the dedication of the new church. I really enjoyed reading the story about how it all happened. I appreciate that the author took the time to write this book. What a great tribute to Fr Ron! This book gave me a renewed sense of appreciation for the new church building.—Dustin Z.

My husband and I went to the Holy Land in 2013 with Fr. Lewinski. He was a different person outside of parish work. We really enjoyed being with him. We liked reading about how the church was built. We came to the parish a year later. It is interesting to learn what was involved. —Sheila B.

Get the companion volume:

Remembering Ron Lewinski includes remembrances of a nationally known priest by over sixty individuals. Ranging in length from two sentences to over four pages, each recollection provides insights into the pastor, priest, or man that the contributor knew. One contributor knew Lewinski for only a few hours, while others knew him for over six decades.

The collage of verbal portraits gives perspectives on Lewinski's ambition, dedication, sincerity, visionary leadership, sensibility, zealousness, and humor. Contributors include a childhood friend, teachers, parishioners, and fellow clergy from newly ordained priests to Cardinal Blase Cupich, Archbishop of Chicago.

The book is edited by D.J. Kennebeck, author of The Pivotal Pastor.

"A rich treasure of reflections from colleagues, superiors, parishioners and family members compiled in an easy-to-read, hard-to-put-down book. Gems of remembrances topped off by Fr Ron's own Christmas letter of 2016 (just a handful of months before his death) to his friends wherein his energy, imagination and resolve to continue on with the work of the Lord comes shining through!"—Jon and Sue M.

Visit www.emmaus-way.com/rr
for information and to order. ISBN: 979-8-9866668-7-7 (Paperback)

Comments? Questions? Corrections?

Contact the author at
djkennebeck@emmaus-way.com

Additional copies of this book are available from
www.emmaus-way.com/tpp

Discounts are offered for bulk purchases.
Contact sales@emmaus-way.com

For information about the parish of St. Mary of the Annunciation, and
additional information about Fr. Ron Lewinski, see www.stmaryfc.org or
write to them at 22333 W. Erhart Road, Mundelein IL 60060.
Inquire about a tour of the facilities.

ALSO BY D.J. Kennebeck:

Remembering Ron Lewinski

THE PIVOTAL PASTOR

*Ron Lewinski, Mission,
and St. Mary of the Annunciation Parish*

D. J. KENNEBECK

EMMAUS WAY LLC

Paperback version: ISBN: 979-8-9866668-0-8
Library of Congress Control Number: 2022913838
ISBN: 979-8-9866668-6-0 (epub)

Publisher's Cataloging-in-Publication data
Names: Kennebeck, David Joseph, author.
Title: The pivotal pastor : Ron Lewinski , mission , and St. Mary of the Annunciation Parish / D.J. Kennebeck.
Description: Includes bibliographical references and index. | Brooksville, FL: Emmaus Way LLC, 2022.
Identifiers: LCCN: 2022913838 | ISBN: 979-8-9866668-0-8 (paperback) | 979-8-9866668-6-0 (ebook)
Subjects: LCSH Lewinski, Ron. | Catholic Church--Clergy--Mundelein (Ill.)--Biography. | Mundelein (Ill.)--History. | BISAC BIOGRAPHY & AUTOBIOGRAPHY / Religious | RELIGION / Christianity / Catholic | RELIGION / Clergy | ARCHITECTURE / Buildings / Religious | HISTORY / United States / State & Local / Midwest (IA, IL, IN, KS, MI, MN, MO, ND, NE, OH, SD, WI)
Classification: LCC BX4705 .L49 K46 2022 | DDC 271/.5302/092--dc23

Front cover photo by Mark Segal, Chicago
Back cover photo and book design by David J. Kennebeck
Images are credited in the "List of Images"

Published by Emmaus Way LLC.
Printed in the United States of America

Rev. First Edition 2023 11 ...

Lord! who Thy thousand years dost wait
To work the thousandth part
Of Thy vast plan, for us create
With zeal a patient heart.
--From "Zeal and Patience" by John Henry Newman

PIVOTAL. VITALLY IMPORTANT:
vitally important, especially in determining
the outcome, progress, or success of something.

PIVOT. CRUCIAL PERSON OR THING:
the one person or thing that is essential to
the success or effectiveness of something.

--Encarta World English Dictionary, St. Martin's Press, N.Y. 1999

We all have a choice to either underscore the things that aren't going well and are missing in our lives, or we can pay attention to the signs of the Spirit among us. To choose the later compels us to praise the Holy Spirit who from that first Pentecost till this Pentecost day has enlightened the Church and kept it together. As we continue to add our chapter to the Acts of the Apostles, one thing we can be sure of is that the Holy Spirit is at the heart of it all and always one step ahead of us leading us into the future.

— Rev. Ronald J. Lewinski
May 23, 1999

LIST OF IMAGES

All images are from the author's archives unless otherwise noted.
(* indicates courtesy of St. Mary of the Annunciation parish)

CONTENTS

A TIMELINE OF MILESTONES CAN BE VIEWED AT
WWW.EMMAUS-WAY.COM/PROJECTTIMELINE

ACKNOWLEDGMENTS

The content of this narrative comes from multiple sources. I had kept for over twenty years a variety of printed material (newsprint articles, meeting agendas and minutes, and other paperwork) that helped flesh out and provide accuracy to the story. I also relied on photographs (print and digital) and audio or video recordings. Most 'dialog'—an individual's spoken words in quotes—came from these recordings. Archival material in electronic form (slide presentations, emails, document files, etc.) also helped inform the story. I interviewed dozens of individuals, both within and outside the parish. Finally, I relied on written correspondence between myself and individuals who knew Lewinski and between myself and Fr. Ron.

While preparing this account, I was very fortunate to have benefited in one form or another from many individuals.

I am most grateful to Fr. Lewinski's family, especially his sister Diane Ciesielski and her family. Their early acceptance of my desire to write this story, and their subsequent cooperation, often afforded me ongoing motivation.

I am awed by the insights provided by two teachers that Fr. Lewinski acknowledged as powerful influences in his life. I feel fortunate to have had a personal visit with Sr. Elaine Marie Klugiewicz, who was Fr. Lewinski's second- and third-grade teacher. Similarly, I hold dear a friendship with Sr. Agnes Cunningham, who was one of the first female instructors at Mundelein Seminary, where Fr. Lewinski studied in the late 1960s. She turned 99 this year (2022).

I am grateful to master architect Dirk Lohan for helping me understand some of his history and the project from his personal and architectural perspectives. The collective vision of Fr. Lewinski and Mr. Lohan, supported by their respective teams, resulted in the new church and campus at St. Mary of the Annunciation, as described in this story.

Thanks to Fr. Jerry Jacob, the current pastor at St. Mary's, and Deacon Howard Fischer, Director of Parish Operations, for granting me access to some parish archives.

Although a few people declined to contribute to my research, dozens of others helped inform my story by sharing memorabilia and personal recollections. I hesitate to identify those individuals explicitly for fear of overlooking someone and out of respect for their privacy. To those people, I say, "You know who you are," and know that I am immensely grateful for your help. You have not been forgotten or overlooked.

Though I did not have access to Fr. Lewinski's personal effects, the above sources have sufficiently informed the story to make it historically accurate and, hopefully, insightful for the reader.

I benefited in unexpected ways from people I had never met. (This digital age overcomes the traditional barriers of time and distance.) I'm grateful to Dr. Sophie zu Löwenstein and the Staatliche Schlösser and Gärten Baden-Württemberg, Salem Monastery & Palace, for pictures of the beichstuhls at Salemer Munster in Salem, Germany. Similarly, Meg Romero Hall, the Director of Archives and Records Center for the Chicago Archdiocese, was marvelously helpful—and patient—while fielding questions that kept cropping up during my prolonged research period.

Last, I'm grateful to my wife Isabelle, who afforded me precious time during retirement over years of researching and writing this story. She often accompanied me on interviews and provided support and encouragement. We share everlasting love.

I tried my best to ensure this account is accurate. While I owe many thanks to the individuals who helped me, I bear final responsibility for the content of this narrative.

By the way, the chapter title of "Prolog" is not misspelled. It is the spelling in Polish and German, so I thought it an appropriate way to honor Fr. Lewinski and Mr. Lohan.

—*D. J. Kennebeck*

INTRODUCTION

At first, I didn't want to write this story.

The initial inspiration flashed through my mind as rapidly as the mile marker sailed past our car on southbound I-57 in Illinois. My wife and I were returning home from the funeral of a friend and former pastor, Rev. Ronald J. Lewinski, in July 2017. The book you are reading resulted from that fleeting two-word inspiration: "Ron's story."

What did that mean? I imagine others who experienced a sudden inspiration and needed to interpret and act on it by themselves shared my confusion. At first, I thought it meant writing about—rather, a biography of—Ron Lewinski. I knew he had accomplished much in his seventy-one years of life on God's creation. So I tried to discern what I was being called to do. Not being a writer, I even read articles and a book about "writing biography." I decided I wanted nothing to do with it: too much time (three to five years or more), too much risk.

Besides, who was I to think I could write "Ron's story?" I asked, "Why me?"

I didn't want to begin a lengthy and challenging task. Still, I assessed what source materials I would need. I included newspaper articles and photographs I and others had taken during the six years of this story. Also, I'd want to read books and articles about subjects I was not knowledgeable enough to write about. I needed to identify and interview individuals whose life paths had intersected with Ron Lewinski or who knew of him. It would help to find audio or video recordings. I wanted to examine resources within the parish files and archives; and my private collection. I should ask for recollections of interactions with Lewinski or other people during the events recounted in this book. In short, it wasn't appealing; it seemed like a lot of work.

Over six months later, the idea was still nagging me. I kept responding, "Not interested," "It will take too long," "I don't have the skills," "I don't have time," and, of course, "Why me?" But the Spirit persisted. Then came Easter of 2018—a period of worship that had always been special to Fr. Lewinski and that he made special for countless others. I eventually surrendered. It is unnecessary and would be disrespectful to you for me to relate all the steps I've taken on the path from then until this point. But along the way, I realized "Ron's story" didn't mean a "story *about* Ron Lewinski." Instead, it meant "a story Ron Lewinski *wanted to be told*."

This is not **the** story of Fr. Ron Lewinski at the parish during his first term as pastor. Instead, it is **a** story about that. It is my account (with many thanks to those who have contributed to it). Several others took part in the effort to build church (both a building and parish ministries) with Fr. Ron a quarter-century ago. Each person has a story to tell. I encourage them to tell it.

At this time, two fine books relate the fuller history of the parish (herein referred to as "St. Mary's"), known as St. Mary of the Annunciation. One is the *Chronicle of St. Mary of the Annunciation* by Tom Wagner. Another is *Nothing is Impossible With God: the Story of St. Mary of the Annunciation* by John Gannon. Fr. Lewinski ensured both were available for the parish's sesquicentennial (150th) anniversary in 2014. I recommend them if you want to learn more about the interesting history of this parish, founded by German immigrant farmers during the end of the Civil War.[1]

Those books have wonderful stories about how in the late 1800s, parishioners moved the parish a few miles up the road, built a new church, and moved the cemetery—grave by grave (which took five years). They describe how another generation manually raised the church in 1930 to build a multi-purpose hall under it. They note how pastor Fr. Laukemper, that same year, led the parish into the future by changing the language from German to English, replacing kerosene lamps with electricity, and establishing a business school.

Fr. Lewinski's first six-year term at St. Mary's, beginning in 1996, added to this century-long legacy of change. It may be the most notable change. This book doesn't seek to retell the stories already told. It focuses on the period from 1996 to 2002.

During the parish's 150th anniversary celebration in 2014, I commented to Fr. Ron that the effort to expand the parish had been a mystical period.[2] He agreed. While "St. Mary at Fremont Center"—as it had been known—was not the only parish to undertake new construction, it was one of only ten to build a new church in the Chicago Archdiocese in the first decade of this century. During the last half of the 20th century, many Chicago Archdiocese parishes were merging or closing, but St. Mary's parish would expand and grow.

Like most parishes, especially those in large cities like Chicago, the campus at St. Mary's was landlocked. Most parishes are concerned about financing land acquisition and building construction. St. Mary's was no different. By the mid-1990s, many forces were pointing toward a need for the parish to grow physically and as a faith community.

Among these, the most obvious was a rapidly expanding population. The parish is near the middle of Lake County, Illinois. Population trends, by one estimate, projected growth exceeding 30% over the next quarter-century.

This increase in population required changes to supporting infrastructure. Implementing highway expansion created a catch-22 situation whereby more roads would enable further growth of existing and new neighborhoods.

The old church at St. Mary's is emotionally and visually appealing. This fact was not lost on many soon-to-be brides looking for a memorable setting for their wedding. St. Mary parish is part of a larger organizational structure, in this case, the Archdiocese of Chicago. It was important to the Archdiocese for this parish to have adequate space for worship and education.

It needed more facilities if the parish was to support new and growing ministries. The parish had limited meeting space: the church basement and the school gymnasium. This restricted the number of simultaneous meetings by even a handful of ministries. The parish's records reveal during Fr. Keusal's tenure (1983-1995), the number of households doubled.

In retrospect, one might summarize Lewinski's first term—the period of this story—as "Fr. Ron came to St. Mary and built new facilities"; but that would be a gross, and incomplete, understatement.

Observers of any effort to expand or grow a parish may have different interpretations. Their perspectives will filter and influence their view. An architect sees form, material, function, and even art. A builder sees materials, techniques, and engineering challenges. An artist sees light, color, focal points, and relationships between elements. A project manager sees milestones, due dates, dependencies, and the coordinated efforts of many individuals and teams. An organizational development specialist sees a sponsor, change agents, transitions, endings, and new beginnings. A priest sees norms, dogmas, liturgical relationships, and sacraments. The great marvel is that all these characteristics were part of the project. Like St. Paul's description of a body and its parts (1 Cor.), each stands distinct while combining with others to form the whole.

Part of my motivation to tell the story is my belief that ours was a unique experience for several reasons which I'll mention here, hoping not to give away too much of the story.

First is Lewinski himself. One can debate various aspects—pros and cons, of Lewinski and the project. But I believe he was the right person in the right place and time.

Second, the parish engaged a master architect, Dirk Lohan. It is important to build an attractive structure that will endure. The building should meet the functional and operational needs of the client at an affordable cost. It is also important the facility reflects the needs and values of the community that will use it. Lohan had several notable projects in his portfolio, but most were commercial or educational facilities. He had recently designed a synagogue. He wanted to design a church. St. Mary parish presented the opportunity. He invested himself professionally and spiritually in the effort.

Third, the project required both change and transition. By "change," I mean physical change focused on developing additional campus facilities such as worship, administration, education, and social spaces. Such change requires material and financial resources. "Transition" involves the psychological, social, and theological challenges of growing a small passive country church. It meant turning an inward-focused community to look outward. Management of both the change and transition facing the parish in 1995 required clarification and communication of a shared vision; leadership capable of aligning diverse people in a collaborative effort; a varied set of skills and knowledge; open communication; equal opportunity to take part; a comprehensive but flexible plan for realizing the vision; and substantial financial support.

Fourth, Lewinski enabled parishioners to explore and use their talents. He expanded the pastoral staff with skilled and dedicated people. He empowered the Pastoral Council and parish leadership. He encouraged the development of existing and new ministries. Many parishioners welcomed this opportunity to assume leadership or service roles. The community could benefit from everyone's time and individual talents. The parish would uncover hidden riches in highly skilled people who offered their expertise gratis or paid.

Fifth, among the registered parishioners were people who could share their time, talent, and treasure. The leadership offered various ways for parishioners to provide financial support. Although this was a rural parish, it had a healthy mix of young and old across the economic strata. The parish benefited because there were many resources—intellectual, physical, and financial—to help achieve success.

One can learn many lessons from the experience. While the specifics of the project are associated with St. Mary parish, there are elements of leadership (both clerical and lay); communication (interpersonal and inter-organizational); teamwork; empowerment, learning, negotiation, management, and other dynamics without regard to religious or cultural identification. I have not explicitly identified the lessons, but the mindful reader will recognize them.

Lewinski showed that responsibility does not equate to control. As a pastor, he bore ultimate responsibility for the welfare of the parish. He understood controlling everything is not the same as executing that responsibility. I believe the bulk of work done in a healthy parish represents a blend of responsibility and control between the pastor and the parishioners. Lewinski sought that balance.

The pastor preceding Lewinski, Fr. Eugene Keusal, had been at the parish for twelve years. During his term, he had witnessed population growth in the three communities—Mundelein, Grayslake, and Wauconda —surrounding the parish. He helped the parish achieve another milestone in its history by completing an addition to the school that included classrooms and a gymnasium/cafeteria. To his credit, he had been prudent with parish funds, accumulating a respectable amount for use by his successor.

Yet, St. Mary at Fremont Center in the 1990s was one of the last parishes in the Chicago Archdiocese still clinging to remembrances of how parishes existed before Vatican II. Of course, it was old: ancestors had established it in 1864. It had witnessed some dramatic and noteworthy periods of change during its lifetime, often due to progressive action—such as the school expansion—by either the pastor or the parishioners. Yet, it was a good example of what Thomas Legere meant when he wrote, "The spiritual renewal of externals in the Catholic Church envisioned by Vatican II is now [1983] largely in place.... But still, a void remains."[3]

I believe where there is no change, there is no life. By the 1990s, the parish's pace of change had slowed considerably. The threat posed to the parish was not being acknowledged by everyone responsible for doing so.

Many stories have a point called an "epiphany." It is when a character experiences a discovery, an insight, a moment that brings something hidden or unrecognized to light. It is a life-changing realization that changes the rest of the story. We've experienced it so often while reading a book or watching a movie that we readily accept it. We may sense something is wrong if an epiphany doesn't occur. But we don't always recognize it when it happens in real life. Lewinski arrived at "St. Mary at Fremont Center" parish shortly before the Feast of the Epiphany in 1996. Beginning then, life for the parishioners and himself would change in ways few would have imagined.

☩

The title of this book refers to Ronald J. Lewinski in the context of this story. But I believe every Christian pastor can be pivotal. Many are, and I think all should strive to be. Likewise, this is a story about six years in the life of a particular parish. I do not claim that only this parish could achieve what it did, nor do I offer the story as a perfect example of what can or should transpire. There are, I think, lessons to be learned about leadership, teamwork, communication, humility, prayerfulness, and other positive qualities of relationships between man and man, and man and God.

If you are a pastor, I hope you might read this book as a record of one pastor's experience and contemplate answers to the question, "What if that were me?" If you are a congregation member, how might you and others have responded to the vision the pastor in this book presented to his flock and their response?

The text contains references to Notes at the back of the book. I hope the reader will not ignore them. Some notes have background information to help answer the reader's questions, especially about the Catholic faith and practices. Some notes are humorous. Some are just citations. I hope you'll benefit from reading them.

History becomes more meaningful when specifics such as dates, places, and people are explicitly named. I identify people's actual names. Using fabricated names was more judicious in one instance. Similarly, a few citations are anonymous by request or at my discretion. Dates are determined from research materials.

Finally, this is a work of nonfiction based on my experience and information collected during my research. Any dialog between quotation marks comes from some printed or electronic historical source. Everyday conversations, and even formal presentations, can sometimes be challenging to follow when written verbatim because we speak differently than we write. So I have edited a few passages to be easier to understand yet convey what I believe was the speaker's intended meaning. Still, preferring to retain the original verbiage, I have avoided making grammatical changes (corrections). A few times, I have speculated about someone's thinking based on my personal experience with, or knowledge of, the individual(s) involved.

---

[1] There is also an earlier history, commissioned by Pastor Burke, written by Leonard J. Schmitt for the parish's 100th anniversary in 1964 while Lewinski graduated from high school. It is an unpublished, typewritten document about 40 pages long. Parish Archives.

[2] Sr. Madge Karecki, Lewinski's friend who worked in South Africa for two decades and was a former President of St. Augustine College in Johannesburg, observed, "He had studied sacramental theology in France. His vision was really sacramental, and that's what made it a mystical experience. I think that was a unique quality in someone building a new church: this entire vision of what the church *should* be in the sacramental rites, and going out and sharing." Personal conversation, June 3, 2022.

[3] Legere, Thomas. "Thoughts," p. 67.

PROLOG

In his adult years, Fr. Ron Lewinski could make a joke of it by saying that early in life, he had kicked the habit. Sr. Elaine Marie Klugiewicz pretended not to notice while she taught. She and her students were at a parochial school in the West Pullman neighborhood of Chicago in 1954. She had a quiet voice. She would stand as close to the students as possible to project it to her second graders. That meant standing immediately in front of a particular student's desk.

The student, young Lewinski, was a little short for his age. His feet didn't reach the floor when he sat at his desk. Like many a child, he would swing his feet back and forth. His feet were striking the cloth of the nun's gown. He was unaware he was "kicking the habit."

Sr. Elaine was Lewinski's teacher for third grade as well. She observed his intelligence and friendly personality. She believed he would "really amount to something" but she wasn't sure what.

✛

The 800-year-old church, Salemer Munster in Salem, Germany, is a fine example of Gothic architecture. Ornate stone columns ascend to support a ceiling sixty feet tall at its highest. Besides the main altar, there are twenty-six small altars. They are almost all named after a saint.

Wooden confessionals are found along—not in—the side walls. As a Protestant youth in Germany, Dirk Lohan knew them as Beichstuhls: "the confessor's chair." The sculptor had carved ornate figures around the perimeter. These Beichstuhls, and the inspiring building they are part of, were one of his "play areas" as a third-grade boy.

Young Lohan noted that the massive blocks of polished stone were cool. Despite the many windows, he later recalled the space being rather dark. There was one thing, especially, the boy would remember: the slightest sound he made would reverberate in the unoccupied church. Young Lohan marveled at the architecture of this beautiful space and pondered the effort behind designing and building it.[1]

✛

As adults, over four decades later, Lewinski and Lohan had become recognized leaders worldwide in their professions as priest and architect, respectively. At the turn of the millennium, they would combine their vocational experiences to lead a collaborative effort during a unique opportunity to build a faith community and a new church on thirty-three acres of Illinois farmland.

This is that story.

---

[1] "I could draw the plan of that church today because it was so impressive to me," said Lohan during a conversation on May 11, 2018. "To be in a building that you found impressive as a child makes you wonder 'how can that be done?' [The building] was something that I admired greatly."

IMAGE #1

REV. RONALD J. LEWINSKI

PASTOR AT ST. MARY OF THE ANNUNCIATION 1996-2014
(PHOTO CIRCA 2012)

IMAGE #2

DIRK LOHAN

ARCHITECT AND PRINCIPAL OF LOHAN ASSOCIATES
(PHOTO CIRCA 1990)

THE LITTLE WHITE CHURCH

1993

At the country farming parish, ladies in their kitchens baked fruit pies while cows in the barn prepared to compete with pies of their own. Each product raised money for "the little white church." In truth, the bovines' participation generated the higher revenue of the two. The organizers saw no need to inform the ladies.

Gently rolling farm fields of Lake County surrounded St. Mary at Fremont Center in northeastern Illinois. The parish hosted an annual Pork and Corn Roast. It was considered the largest such event in the state, drawing visitors from surrounding counties and nearby Wisconsin. "Roast" described how they cooked the hogs. It could also describe how attendees felt. It always seemed to occur on the hottest day of August.

A significant labor of love was needed to produce the Roast. Work on next year's event began within weeks of ending this year's. It required the time and talent of over two hundred volunteers. The final push occurred during the week prior. Workers erected a large two-pole tent to shade the standing-room-only crowd that would assemble for the morning Mass. Afterward, they rearranged the folding chairs around long party tables. Guests enjoying the meal and refreshments would later fill them throughout the sultry afternoon.

Dedicated volunteers arranged game booths. Others transported and organized weathered wooden picnic tables. A crew of adults and gleeful children shucked scores of corn. Green husks and silk hairs went on one pile, yellow cobs on another. As the piles grew, the glee shrank. An appetite-inducing scent arose from the occasional punctured corn kernels. Kitchen helpers prepared sides of sauerkraut, baked beans, and dinner rolls. Barbecue sauce, butter, salt, and other condiments would be available in the food line.

Organizers arranged booths to sell soft drinks, beer, and wine. Some men offloaded bales of hay from a flatbed. Others positioned them around the grounds for visitors to rest on. The hay bundles were also used for seating when entertainers performed on the temporary lawn stage. A few men showed exceptional dedication. They arrived the evening before the event and began cooking twenty hogs in open pit charcoal-fueled barrels, tending them throughout the night. In the morning, the aroma of roast pork permeated the air when volunteers carved the pigs for serving. Roasting and carving were difficult and dangerous tasks.

The Roast provided different types of amusement for children in the afternoon and adults in the evening. The youth enjoyed various children's games, pony rides, a bouncy tent, a petting pen for farm animals, and the quaint allure of tractors on display. Adults welcomed live musicians, including the renowned Beatles tribute band, "American English." Sam Leach (the original Beatles promoter) once called them "The Beatles Incarnate." The entertainment distracted people's minds from the heat and sometimes oppressive humidity. It also boosted refreshment sales.

Bingo was a popular option for those looking for respite from the hot weather. They conducted this longtime form of socialization in the school's air-conditioned gymnasium. Rows of long tables enabled players to sit close to family and friends or far away from strangers if desired. A corner of the gym closest to the washrooms attracted older folks. Young couples with strollers mingling with older adults was a commonly enjoyed sight.

The annual Pork and Corn Roast was the primary means of raising money to support the parish's K-8 school. An appetite-satisfying meal accompanied by a refreshment was the primary attraction. The Women's Club exchanged pastries for donations. Cows donated their pies for the same purpose through a game of luck called Cow Pie Bingo.[1] Enthusiastic players of "Bovine Bingo" insisted it was more exciting and entertaining than the indoor table version.[2]

Parish households included single young adults and married couples. Some had celebrated their golden wedding anniversaries. Observers driving past the little white church sometimes felt an attraction that held their gaze. Newcomers at services appreciated the friendliness and openness of the smiling individuals who welcomed them.

Parishioners often recalled with pride notable events in the parish's history. In 1930, their enterprising ancestors devised a way to elevate the church—then forty years old—to excavate a basement using man- and horse-power. Electricity replaced kerosene lamps. A progressive pastor started a business college for adults in a building that was otherwise a middle school. Many families saw multiple generations graduate from the small parish school that currently occupied a red brick structure.

Now in their seventies, many elders had lost their youthful ambition. Most had experienced a lifetime of change and challenge, including the Great Depression, World War II, the Korean War, Vietnam, and the civil rights movement. The Second Vatican Council, also called Vatican II, was the most significant event in their religious life.

Rome sent shock waves worldwide by convening the Council in 1962. The organizers invited people of various religious backgrounds and women to attend. This left numerous lifelong Catholics simmering with frustration. The Council clarified the responsibilities of the laity and the clergy. This resulted in angst and confusion among a large number of faithful.

Vatican II did not make significant doctrinal changes, but it made many revisions. Replacing Latin with the local dialect was the most obvious. Another was having the officiating priest face the congregation. For several laity, and some clergy, this change to the Mass seemed almost sacrilegious.

Other adjustments included clarification of roles within the Church hierarchy, from Pope through Bishop to lay people. The Council modified the hierarchy of responsibility within the Church. It encouraged the laity to participate more in worship and evangelization.[3] By the mid-1990s, three decades after Vatican II, one-third of Catholics worldwide had no experience of the pre-Vatican II Church before 1965. Embracing the Church in the post-Vatican II era was an invitation to all. But it became an impossible challenge for some.

Some believers quickly, even eagerly, adapted. Others refused to change. They searched for Latin Mass churches or left the Church. Most embraced and adjusted to changes when they understood them.

St. Mary parish had a number of younger people, several at some stage of raising a family. Parents regarded themselves as fortunate if their child was among the 220 students the school could accommodate. Several families had children attending nearby Carmel Catholic High School, across the street from Mundelein Seminary. St. Mary's enjoyed participation by people of all ages. Another Catholic church, Santa Maria del Popolo, was in the middle of nearby Mundelein. Then there was a third parish—St. Mary of Vernon—in neighboring Indian Creek. The presence of three "St. Mary" parishes in such close proximity often resulted in confusion by anyone not familiar with the area.

Naturally, members of the congregation had a range of opinions about their parish. Some could shock others if they were to express their genuine feelings. A placid facade hid growing frustration. Most parishioners were favorable, citing things like "People are personable, friendly and welcoming" and "We absolutely love it and would never go anywhere else." Yet, others would say, "I have been going to other parishes for Sunday Mass because our liturgy is so awful," or "It has always been slow and unprogressive," or, even worse, "The parish is stagnant."

If asked whether they would be comfortable speaking with the pastoral staff, some parishioners would ask, "Who is the pastoral staff?" Fr.

Keusal, the pastor from 1983 to 1995, was a good steward of the parish's funds—perhaps too much so. He, a secretary, and two maintenance men comprised a full-time "staff." This kept the personnel budget low but constrained the work the parish might be capable of doing if it had more resources. Fr. Keusal had encouraged a parishioner who worked in the office to become a deacon. Though a part-time staff member, parishioners respected him for his administrative and spiritual aid.

There was disagreement about taking part in decision-making. One mother entreated, "Let us show what we can do. Let us feel free to work, to make decisions, and know all we want to know about our parish. A good parent will teach their child, give them wings, and—believing they did a good job—let them go." Others might complain, "New ideas are not accepted or even heard," "Father assumes too much control," or "I would like to see more input from the parishioners."

In the early 1990s, parishioners' attitudes toward the parish varied from supportive to critical. The concept of "parish" can be perceived differently by people. Is it the pastor? Worship space? Parishioners? Campus grounds? One would hear perspectives from "Our pastor is invaluable" to "Our pastor is not a caring, compassionate person."

Parishes are communal entities, existing for a purpose beyond worship. Christian organizations confront a variety of the same challenges as public corporations and private companies. That includes leadership development. Was the parish's recruitment and training program of organization leaders working well? Many inquired, "What program?" A more critical comment was, "There's no empowerment of the lay leadership. Father feels he knows best. He has always been the final word on everything."

Even among those who considered their attitude toward their congregation as "positive," one might be told, "I see a need for stronger leadership from the pastor. To lead means to set standards, show the way and then delegate to the many who would like to be strong leaders themselves but feel their hands are tied." Another parishioner stated, "The pastor needs to be much more present to the people and the children of the parish. He should not be a figure in the background, but a leader working at making meetings, sacraments and so on, special."

Baptism, Confirmation, and Holy Communion are the sacraments most commonly conducted in any Catholic church. The Council fostered greater participation by the laity. One parishioner complained about this aspect of the Christian community at St. Mary's, even two decades after Vatican II. "Baptisms are 'hidden' away after Mass schedule rather than incorporating our newest member into the parish publicly." Still more emotional was a comment about Confirmation: "Make some changes in the confirmation program. Sr. Ruth, Mrs. Crane, and Kathy Brown spent eighteen months working on a program change. The pastor looked at it and said he liked things the way they were. Is it any wonder these ladies have left or want to leave?"

Most church ministries, like organizational projects, succeed due to the attitudes of those involved. Parishioners' opinions about St. Mary parish's ministry to the physical and spiritual requirements of its people varied. "Because of the number of communities served, this is hard to achieve," reflected a glass-is-half-empty attitude. This contrasted with a glass-is-half-full version: "The parish has a lot of talented people; all we need is to be made more aware of the needs of the community around us."

Before Vatican II, Catholics saw little need to evangelize and the Church seldom encouraged it. The most recognized names of evangelizers were Bishop Fulton J. Sheen and Rev. Billy Graham.

Ask, "In an ideal world, what would be the principal activities and programs at the parish in the future?" Responses would be, "I think things are fine," "I would not like to see St. Mary's go modern or American," "It is nice the way it is," and "It should be more conservative."

More hopeful comments included "Expansion of the school and parish with long-term or short-term goals being for a new church and an addition to the school," or "To create an exciting and vibrant community of people who come together to learn, pray, rejoice, and celebrate the Glory of our Lord. This might not always happen on parish grounds."

The social groups at the religious community were the Men's Club, Ladies Club, and a few ministries. Many parishioners wanted more, including a Welcoming Committee, Public Action to Deliver Shelter (PADS), Alcoholics Anonymous (AA), Phoenix Group, Respect Life, Young Adult Formation, altar girls (like altar boys), Outreach, a Religious Education Program (REP), Adult religious education, a "real" Choir, etc.

Some worshipers, however, didn't want more ministries. "There wouldn't be enough volunteers to serve." "I don't feel the need for other organizations." "How many more organizations do we need with poor attendance?" "Too many organizations now." Nine out of ten people who had been at the parish for over twenty-five years (and those between fifty-five to sixty-five) thought the parish had the "right amount" of activities. Meanwhile, most aged eighteen to twenty-five said the parish "needed more" functions. These comments leave one wondering what parishioners, and the pastor, thought about ministries—and the Church's mission.

Catholics often joke about the higher-than-normal attendance—usually standing room only—at Mass during Christmas and Easter. Catholics have a 'duty' to participate in these Holy Day celebrations.[4] They seem more rewarding than the "regular" Sunday Mass. What about daily Mass? Many attendees weren't satisfied.

About the pastor, some would say, "I would not be involved except for Fr. Keusal's ability to touch something very relevant to my daily life at each Mass I attend," and "Fr. Keusal does a wonderful job now."

But a common complaint was that "liturgies are stagnant; music is terrible." Others would say:

"Sermons are not very good."

"Sunday Mass is a ritual followed by obligation only; even celebrants act this way."

"Sermons and services are long and boring. We need more opportunity to participate, and better music."

"It seems that when St. Mary's gets a really good visiting priest, he becomes too popular, and we lose him real fast."

"There have been many times we have left before services begin when we see who is saying the Mass."

"I can't remember the last time I heard a liturgy at St. Mary's that left me feeling excited, content, or anything other than just blah."

"We attend other parishes. Our liturgy is outdated."

"It is impossible to sing in a 'dirge' mode constantly."

Not all parishioner opinions were subjective. Some physical shortcomings of the church include concrete steps up to the entry door and others below ground to the basement (front and back). There was also a wooden stairway to a side entrance. There were no ramps. The American Disabilities Act (ADA) became law in 1990, a century after parish founders built the church. The relative inaccessibility of St. Mary's —like most churches of its era—was apparent to those who found it a barrier. The remark, "Our church building is very inaccessible to physically disabled people. I know quite a few people finding it necessary to attend other churches" would not be surprising.

Often, the issue lies in thinking there is no issue. By the mid-1990s, St. Mary at Fremont Center was like the proverbial frog in hot water.

IMAGE #3

"THE PLATE"

THE MAIN CULINARY ATTRACTION AT THE ANNUAL PORK AND
CORN ROAST: PULLED PORK, SAUERKRAUT, CORN ON THE
COB, BAKED BEANS AND A BISCUIT.
ACCOMPANIED, OF COURSE, BY A REFRESHMENT.

---

[1] A "cow pie" is slang for large flat piles of cow dung. It is a very different sort of pie from fruit pies usually offered at a bake sale. During the parish's annual Pork and Corn Roast, cow pies also became a means of raising money by being part of a popular fundraiser called "Cow Pie Bingo." The prepared the cows the day before competition by ensuring they were well-fed. To play, a cow was let loose in a fenced area that is marked off in numbered squares. The cow determines the winner by making a "deposit" on one of the squares. Chances on each square are typically sold for a low dollar amount. The winner receives a predetermined amount such as $250 or 20% of the sales, whichever is less. The game is not without some risk, which any worker can tell you if they've been cornered by a choleric cow while preparing the ground for the next game.

[2] A notable exception occurred during Fr. Morrissey's tenure (1967-1983) when Bingo was illegal in the county. The parish devised a subsitute game named "Ducky." However, the similarity to Bingo was evident. One evening, the Sheriff and deputies arrived with lights flashing and sirens blaring. Despite a hasty attempt to "disguise the evidence," six men were arrested and Morrissey had to bail them out. "The specter of sheriffs arresting Catholics who were trying to raise money for their church and school probably didn't sit well with county officials, and it was not too long after that when Bingo was finally legalized in Lake County." —Gannon, p. 56.

[3] In *The Reinvention of Work*, Matthew Fox comments on ritual. "In Greek, the word *liturgy* means 'the work of the people.' Liturgy or ritual may be the human work *par excellence*. Ritual is the primary means by which a people get their inner houses in order, both as individuals and as a community. It is the primary tool by which macrocosm (our relation to the whole of the universe) and microcosm (our personal and more local relationships) come together, by which, as the Tao Te Ching puts it, we *Accomplish the great task by a series of small acts*."

[4] Such Catholics are known as "Convenient Catholics," "Submarine Catholics," "Two-Timers," "Chreasters," "C&E Catholics," "Poinsettie & Lily Catholics," "CEOs," and other unflattering terms. —https://en.wikipedia.org/wiki/Lapsed_Catholic

AN EPIPHANY

January 1996

Refreshment in hand, Lewinski stood observing parishioners. He wondered what they were thinking about besides Fr. Ron Lewinski, their new pastor. How did they feel about their growing parish and its future? He was in a parishioner's home with a group celebrating the Feast of the Epiphany just passed. The day began like a typical Midwestern winter morning with frigid conditions despite the bright sunshine. The snow would continue blanketing the ground because it would not warm up past freezing until the dinner hour.

He was casually dressed, absent a Roman collar, but everyone knew who "the new person" was. A couple next to him had also been observing the group. They took this opportunity to satisfy their curiosity by commenting on his appointment as pastor and the parish's future. He didn't seem troubled. "I wouldn't worry about it," he responded. Diocesan officials had sent him there to grow the parish and build a church. There would be time to do that. For now, he desired to get to know parishioners more intimately. He wanted to feel the community's pulse.

His method of learning was often simple observation. He noted how people related to each other via eye contact and physical proximity; their sense of comfort with others; whether they were restrained or talkative; what topics they discussed; to what extent and in what manner they would share humor in his presence; and where they might rank on the social hierarchy that is always a dynamic in such groups.

He appeared reserved, but he was receptive and open-minded. He sought to understand all perspectives when learning. He liked ideas and theories, but he preferred to rely on observations. The internal assessment he was conducting could cause him to seem distant, not present, absent-minded, or possibly aloof. Many people would have this misperception in the coming months until they got to know him. Some never did. His social interaction at gatherings was typically restrained. Yet, it wouldn't be unusual for him to return home feeling drained. Even he would describe himself as introverted.

One group of individuals in the parish had concerns about potential change that went beyond curiosity. They liked their quiet little parish as is. So had the prior pastor, Fr. Gene Keusal. Yet, the number of parishioners was increasing. The older population was comfortable with the status quo. As elders, they had learned that getting a new pastor can mean change. And change has the potential to be downright uncomfortable. As people age, such discomfort—whether physical or emotional—becomes something they prefer to avoid.

Some skeptical folks knew a fellow parishioner who had already become acquainted with this new pastor. As a member of one of the founding families, he was known to be a trustworthy friend. "What's he up to?" they asked. "What does he plan to do?" Their colleague, though he'd met the pastor and considered him "okay," didn't have answers. They were troubled by the uncertainty that lay ahead.

Another group was also concerned about the future but for the opposite reason. The source of their frustration was the complacency they had encountered before Lewinski's arrival. In fact, it was sometimes outright refusal by parish leadership to change. This group wasn't concerned about the potential for change; they were worried about the absence of change.

Neither group knew what to expect from the new pastor, and each group hoped it would be what they wanted. Satisfying two opposing goals is problematic.

✠

Personality profiles characterized Lewinski as an introvert.[1] He had never been a pastor before. Now, he became the religious leader at a parish in one of the largest U.S. Archdioceses.

He greatly disliked asking for financial contributions, whether as pledges, donations, or simple Sunday giving. He realized it took money to run a parish, but he was uncomfortable asking for it. He had a deep distaste for having *to ask for it repeatedly*. He also knew Catholics are notoriously less generous about "tithing" than other denominations. To his chagrin, he would discover that the parish held frequent fundraisers— over two dozen per year.

Many people outside the parish who knew him before his assignment regarded him as somewhat scholarly. Not long after getting acquainted with him, many recognized this characteristic. But being "intellectual" can look like being "aloof" or, when combined with introversion, being "withdrawn." Upon introduction, people perceived him as "friendly" but not someone they'd expect would convince a congregation to build a church.

As a young adult, Lewinski had been told by a college professor he would never be a good priest. He might as well drop out before failing at the Seminary. He never forgot that assessment. It would generate some self-doubt during his subsequent education.[2]

Lewinski was of moderate height, not tall enough to be accepted as a leader based on stature alone. He didn't project a television evangelist's charisma that would cause someone to reach for their checkbook. He turned fifty within weeks of arriving. Some would have considered him "past his prime."

This is the man the Archdiocese had sent to revive what Cardinal Bernardin called his "last country parish." Newcomers described the parish as welcoming and friendly. Yet, it was unsatisfying for many parishioners. For them, the liturgy was uninspiring; the music was awful; the staff was "unknown"; parents wanted a religious education program; and few people felt they could participate, much less lead. The parish was stagnant, if not dying.

The parish needed someone to fill the sails with the winds of change. A pastor who had previous experience leading such an effort. Ideally, a charismatic individual. Someone who could attract all ages, as the parish enjoyed a wide range of people. Maybe someone who would engage the children. Often, the students bring home daily news of what is happening in school and the church. Not all the parents attended Sunday services as regularly as they could. The parish could benefit from a newcomer who possessed these characteristics and others.

This quiet, aging, rural parish rested forty-five miles northwest of downtown Chicago. The Archdiocese sent an over-the-hill priest who grew up on Chicago's south side. He had worked at an Archdiocesan office in the city for a decade before arriving at this small parish.

They sent Lewinski to St. Mary's to strengthen the community, build a church, and expand the ministries. An introvert who seemed aloof, didn't like to ask for money, had been told by a professor he'd never be a good priest, and apparently possessed no personal charisma or obvious leadership traits.

What was the Archdiocese thinking?

---

[1] Traits and attributes are derived from personal observation and personality 'typing' of Lewinski using an established personality-typing tool in 2000. People like Lewinski comprise less than 2% of the population. Despite expressing self-doubt to others, he belonged among the most self-confident of people. He was a "builder," looking to the future rather than the past. He showed respect for others opinions, but "authority" resulting from rank did not impress him and did not restrain him from promoting his viewpoint. He was open to ideas others, and pursued them by sometimes inviting individuals who he knew disagreed with him to participate on a committee.

[2] Cunningham, Agnes. Letter from 2017 exhibited at Lewinski's funeral.

PREPARING VISION

1996 - First Half

Lewinski's column in the Sunday bulletin reflected on his experience and expectations during his first week at St. Mary's.

> Last Sunday, the feast of the Epiphany was my initiation into St. Mary Parish. What a joy and privilege it was to celebrate the Eucharist with you, to have the opportunity to introduce myself and to greet you after Mass. At the first weekend Mass on Saturday evening, I was very nervous. By the 11:45 am Mass, I was feeling very much at home. I could sense the faith and devotion of the community, your commitment to the Church and your love for the parish. I felt humbled by your warm and gracious welcome of me as your new pastor. Thank you for your kindness and good wishes.
>
> In the next few weeks, I hope to better acquaint myself with the systems in place in the parish, meet with the staff and faculty, review the records and files, and do a lot of listening. On Tuesday of this week, I hope to meet with the leadership of the parish so that I can get to know the leaders of the various ministries, committees, boards, and organizations, and they can get to know me. There are a few immediate issues for which I will seek their advice. I want to establish, right from the beginning, my firm belief in good communication, consultation, and teamwork.
>
> I hope to use this weekly column as one means of communicating with you and sharing a few of my own pastoral reflections. ... I welcome any ideas you might have to improve them.
>
> Thanks again for your sincere and gracious welcome. I am delighted to be here![1]

Lewinski did not hesitate to undertake his assignment. He and Archdiocesan officials were already discussing things. He found a basis for exploration among the parish materials he was reviewing. The March 10th bulletin carried a report of a Parish Council (AKA Pastoral Council) meeting. It included this peek into the future:

> Father Ron Lewinski mentioned the need to revisit the "Tomorrow's Parish" project, which St. Mary's engaged in last year. He would propose a plan involving a broad and more extensive base of parishioners looking at the parish values and where it sees itself moving in the future. He suggested that revisiting the project could be a means of parish renewal.[2]

During Easter, worshipers learned more about Lewinski. They observed his special respect for the Triduum (Thursday, Friday, and Saturday during Holy Week). He introduced parishioners to new rituals. At least one conversion resulted from the experience.

Considering the parish's uncertainty, he published a promise that must have been difficult to commit to. "I assured the Council, as I wish to reassure the whole parish, that our present church will be preserved. It will not be razed. I promise."[3]

Did he think they'd expand the old church? Or build a new one next to it? Some recognized Lewinski's tendency to have a bigger vision and suspected what it meant but they didn't know how to achieve it. Neither did Lewinski. He had a vision they didn't yet have, and faith they all should have had.

A month later, Lewinski used his column in the April 28th bulletin to explain his thinking. It consumed two pages and was a bold declaration.

> Last week I introduced the makings of a plan for the future. **Vision 2000** is a working draft that is designed to help St. Mary's address the rapid growth of the parish. Vision 2000 does not provide the answers. It is a part of a process that helps us to arrive at the answers together. The plan envisions a *four-year* process so that we can allow sufficient time for our thinking to evolve even as we monitor changing needs and demographics. St. Mary's Pastoral Council accepted vision 2000 as a working draft at its April 9 meeting and will take responsibility now for defining and implementing the plan. In brief outline form, this is how the draft of **Vision 2000** looks:
>
> **Preparatory phase**: collecting data, land surveys, demographic studies. Reviewing Archdiocesan policies and procedures. Dialogue with township and county officials and Archdiocesan authorities. Revisit *Tomorrow's Parish* results and develop a plan for spiritual renewal at St. Mary's. Town Hall meetings for the parish to keep lines of communication open.
>
> **Phase 1/September-November, 1996**: A five-session retreat-like process for the whole parish that calls the community to reflect upon its history, its values, its traditions and seeks to ask what we want to be and what God is calling us to be as a Catholic community in the 21st century.
>
> **Phase 2/December 1996-February 1997**: In light of what we will have learned in Phase 1 we will then ask what kind of leadership does the parish need? What pastoral services need to be in place? What resources will we need? What kind of facilities will we need? What accommodations do we need to make before we arrive at our goal? What kind of stewardship education will we need? During this phase, the parish will have opportunities to meet in small groups and open forums so that communication and dialogue continues.
>
> **Phase 3/March-May 1997**: If the community is ready at this point, a building and education committee will be established to begin working on more concrete plans for any needed facilities. (Remember that the current church building will remain intact.) A capital fund drive committee would need to be established to educate the parish about the needed funds. Refinement of the plans and designs continues.

Phase 4/June 1997-May 2000: Serious efforts take place to raise the needed capital the success of the fundraising will determine what can be erected. Continuing education of the community will continue and ongoing refinement of any construction plans. Continued development of parish programs and pastoral services.

Spring 2000: Dedication of the new facilities.

Phase 5/September-December 2000: After years of planning for growth, what will St. Mary's commit itself to in the future? How will we address the ongoing pastoral care of the community? What will we as a parish see as our mission in the world?

All of the above is a *draft*. It needs to be refined. The dates are hypothetical at this point. But a plan is being presented to help us get a sense of how we move to the future. Good things don't happen overnight. There has to be a step-by-step process in place whereby we can carefully make choices that we will be happy with. I know that there are some who question why we have to do any of this. The answer is very simple: if we do not plan now, we may be very sorry in the future to be forced into a position where we have no choices, no freedom to determine the shape of our community.

The process takes long because we need everyone's input. I have no predetermined idea of what lies ahead. But I accept responsibility for this community that Cardinal Bernardin has entrusted to my pastoral care. And that responsibility means that I exercise a leadership that is faithful to the vision of the gospel and the teaching of the Church and faithful as well to the community I serve. I am very concerned that as the parish grows we will be able to offer good pastoral care. The building is not the whole issue. With more than 850 households, I cannot pretend to be able to be everywhere and do everything. My responsibility demands that I do my best with staff in place who can assist me in pastoring the community and enabling parishioners to exercise their ministry within and beyond the parish. In this light, I hope to appoint a full-time music/liturgy director for the parish.... A full-time person will work in the school preparing children for the liturgy, teaching music, etc. The musician/liturgy staff person will oversee all our liturgical ministers, establish a choir, train cantors, serve as organist, plan the parish's worship services, etc. I am placing the highest priority on this position because we need to make the liturgy the source and summit of our life together at St. Mary's. If we are not anchored in the mystery of the Eucharist, we will lose our focus, fail to find our solidarity in Christ, and ultimately lose our sense of direction. Thus, we need to put our efforts and resources into worship that is inspiring, that nurtures the soul, that holds us together.

I also hope to add a full-time secretary for the parish and assistant to the staff. As activity increases in the office and as we move into our planning for the future, it will be important for us to make sure that there is follow-through in whatever we are doing. An administrative assistant will free the staff of minor administrative details so that staff can be more available to parishioners.

Sometime in the future, we may also include a lay Pastoral Associate on staff. People are asking for a number of pastoral programs. We will need help to coordinate these programs and to train informed leaders to lead them. Many have said that the gift of St. Mary's is its small size, and its close-knit network of relationships. If that gift is to continue, we will need to work at it so that even as we grow, we can maintain a sense of caring for one another. The assistance of a Pastoral Associate can help us reach that goal.

All of this may still sound a bit overwhelming or confusing to some. This report may raise more questions than it resolves. But it is the **beginning** of the planning process and what I hope will be good communication. Another approach would have been for me to quietly plan for the future, and after privately refining the plan, announce what has been decided. I am choosing instead to bring everyone into the thinking and dreaming process. I believe that's the best way to go, and the way in which I hope everyone will feel a part of the whole. In the meantime, let us continue to pray for the Holy Spirit's guidance and for spirit of unity and pride in the community of St. Mary - Fremont Center.[4]

Less than six months earlier, parishioners and the former pastor thought the greatest challenge was preparing for Christmas services. Many with the fortitude to finish reading Lewinski's epistle must have concluded they did not understand the man and his thoughts. Or he was crazy. For those who preferred the status quo, this was clearly not a plan to maintain it. The new pastor had a perspective they disagreed with. Prior to his appointment, the conflict between parishioners advocating for change and those seeking to maintain the status quo had churned into visibility. It put the Archdiocese on alert and put a focus on the parish. Lewinski's appointment was a strategic decision.

The people of St. Mary's parish weren't accustomed to visionary leadership from their pastor. In retrospect, many would realize he understood much more than they gave him credit for when he arrived. While still a high-level perspective, his remarks contained details suggesting experienced insight rather than wishful thinking.[5] Lewinski was a servant leader, as described by Robert Greenleaf. "The servant leader is serving *first*. It begins with a natural feeling that one wants to serve *first*. Then conscious choice brings one to aspire to lead. That person is sharply different from the one whose *leader first*... By clearly stating and restating the goal, the leader gives certainty of purpose to others who may have difficulty in achieving it for themselves. The word *goal* is used in the special sense of the overarching purpose, the big theme, the visionary concept... Not much happens without a dream. And for something great to happen, there must be a great dream."[6]

Over two decades earlier, before his ordination, Lewinski committed to being the best priest he could be. Asked now what he thought was the most difficult part of being a priest, he responded, "Preaching: preaching demands the preacher have a thorough understanding of the scriptures, knows the congregation he preaches to, and is able to make an effective bridge between the biblical word and the lives of people. ... The purpose of the homily is to break open the word of God in such a way that the word evokes a response..."[7]

In mid-May, Lewinski struggled to find a suitable home. He determined the existing rectory would better serve as a parish office. The Parish Council decided to rent space for Lewinski and one or two guests due to future uncertainty. This arrangement may have seemed strange to some parishioners. He explained, "While this kind of living arrangement for diocesan clergy may seem novel to us, it is quite common, especially in other parts of the country. I want to assure you that whatever we find for housing, it will not diminish my availability or accessibility."[8]

Lewinski received a letter from the Archdiocesan Director of Finance summarizing the parish's situation: "Thank you for the opportunity to visit with you and learn of the new life you are bringing to St. Mary's." The message conveyed thanks and an observation about the unstated change in pastoral attitude at the parish.

It continued, "… it certainly is a unique opportunity to see a parish completely rebuilt." For parishioners comfortable with the status quo, that would be a shocking statement to hear within a few months of getting a new pastor. "The growth of your community will be significant as the various housing developments progress." This recognized the undeniable trend in the area's population growth.

The letter stated: "The 'challenges' that currently exist in the parish regarding the facilities are as follows:

1. "The parish is landlocked with inadequate space for future building expansion.
2. "The church is inadequate to meet the growing community needs.
3. "The school has a waiting list and is in need of further expansion as the community grows."

Lewinski realized a solution for just one of these would not be easy. Many pastors in his situation would most likely select one and focus on it. As for the school, the pastor before him had already added classrooms and a gym, but the area's population continued to increase. Lewinski thought he might have a temporary answer to the second 'challenge.'

But the first—being landlocked—was the most significant concern.

The letter offered solutions. First was the acquisition of property to the east of the campus. This was land owned by the family of William (Bill) Wirtz, the Chicago Blackhawks team owner. The second was the acquisition of land on the west side of the campus. This farmland was owned by one of the founding families of the parish. The third option was to reacquire land to the north leased to a third party by the Archdiocese, but the earliest it could happen would be in 2005. The parish couldn't wait another decade.

Importantly, the letter hinted at the project's potential financial support from the Archdiocese. It closed with a prophetic comment: "I look at this as a unique opportunity to participate in the rebirth of the parish."

Still, Lewinski must have recognized the enormous challenge he had undertaken. How to proceed?[9]

Lewinski pondered options early in 1996. He prepared a message to share with his parishioners. It was an essay about this time in the parish's history, but couldn't yet be shared. The ideas it conveyed depended on a decision to start public action beyond whatever private discussions had occurred. The number of registered households had reached 890. The school enrollment was 209, compared to 89 six years prior.

On June 8, 1996, Lewinski and parish leadership met with Archdiocesan representatives and agreed it was time to build a new church and pastoral offices.[10]

Lewinski, however, had not been idly awaiting a decision. He had prepared. By mid-June, he was ready to share his observations with his parishioners. They scheduled a Town Hall in the school gym on June 12th. In the recent addition, the gym was commonly called "Diantha Hall" in honor of a former parishioner.

The intent was to foster good communication, engage parishioners, and get better acquainted. If someone wanted to attend but needed transportation, they should call the office for help. Even though he recognized they all could not fit in the gym, he invited everyone to attend.

Meanwhile, Lewinski continued to get more acquainted. He greeted people after services, attended parish meetings, visited their homes, participated in parish events, and got familiar with the surroundings. He announced ten dates and times for neighborhood pastoral visits with up to ten people attending. He explained that with 900 households in the parish, he couldn't visit every home, but small gatherings would work well.

All he needed were some people willing to host. "It's nothing formal, just a chance to visit and talk. There are a few things I'd like to ask, and I imagine you may have some questions or comments you'd like to share. By the way, I hope there might be some teens or college-age parishioners who might host one of these gatherings too."[11] Lewinski sincerely appreciated the parish's youth as well as the adults. His invitation was not a hollow effort to appease younger parishioners. He wanted to get to know people, and he wanted people to get to know him.

Lewinski arrived with a mandate to elevate the faith community's spiritual life and engage it with the modern world. It would take time, but he couldn't wait for everyone to awaken to the new day.

Lewinski had some important announcements at the end of June. Brother Michael, who had been helping with the transition from Fr. Keusal's term, was leaving for a teaching position. The parish also bid farewell to Ms. Jeanelle Elkins as Director of Music, though she would remain a substitute organist.

Lewinski had been looking for a Director of Religious Education (DRE). The program's genesis at St. Mary's was credited to the school's principal, Sr. Mary Paul, during the mid-eighties. When Sue Matousek, a convert to Catholicism, registered in 1988, she volunteered as a catechist. Fr. Keusal asked her to take charge of the program, including one hundred children. She ran it from her house once a week because no space was assigned at the parish. Meanwhile, Sue worked full-time at Fremont Center School, down the road from the church. A year later, Brother Michael arrived at the parish and took charge. He provided additional direction while Sue resumed being a catechist.

When Lewinski arrived, Matousek continued to support the REP (Religious Education Program) after her day at Fremont School. She faithfully did until Lewinski could offer her full-time work. She accepted the DRE position beginning July 1st.

Appointing a DRE wasn't only a response to a growing enrollment but a missionary effort to help increase participation. The General Catechetical Directory regards the title "Religious Education Program" as misleading and states, "According to the set of pastoral guidelines, catechesis is an aspect of the pastoral ministry of the Church. Though the Directory would never deny that catechesis is educational, it chooses to view it within the framework of ministry as one of the forms of the Church's ministry of the word. Other forms are missionary preaching or evangelization, liturgical proclamation, and the systematic investigation of the tradition called theology."[12]

Lewinski also hired James (Jim) Scavone as Director of Music and Liturgy. Lewinski hired Scavone to revitalize the music and parish choir. Scavone understood music associated with rites like the Rite of Christian Initiation of Adults (RCIA). He had worked in Church music for six years after earning a Bachelor of Music. He had been a member of the Music Staff for the Archdiocese, a group of liturgical ministers for the Office of Divine Worship (ODW) music program. He was also an instructor for the diocesan Cantor School before coming to St. Mary's.

Lewinski worked to enhance staff, liturgy (Jim Scavone), religious education (Sue Matousek) and the pastoral environment (Sr. Gael Gensler). Criticisms about the music, liturgy, lay participation, and religious education were heard, leading to change. Parishioners realized that this pastor was different. He not only loosened the reins, he shared them while harnessing a larger team. Many appreciated it, but those who felt threatened by it, or became uncomfortable about it, continued their criticism with the hope it would divert providential action.

Lewinski was doing what good leaders do: surrounding himself with capable and effective people. The contingent of parishioners wanting to maintain the status quo had to admit that change was occurring. Their concern advanced to the next level: how soon would it end?

---

[1] Sunday bulletin, January 14, 1996, p. 3.

[2] Sunday bulletin, March 10, 1996, p. 4.

[3] Sunday bulletin, April 7, 1996, p. 4.

[4] Sunday bulletin, April 28, 1996, pp. 3-4.

[5] After reading this story, I suggest the reader return to these comments by Lewinski. You may see them from a different perspective.

[6] Greenleaf, pp. 13-16.

[7] Sunday bulletin, May 12, 1996, p. 4.

[8] Sunday bulletin, May 19, 1996, p. 4.

[9] John Gorman, rector at the seminary in 1972, offered this timeless comment fifty years later: "Well, the idea is that you would have to start with some kind of vision, a vision that you can communicate to other people and have them work together towards that. You can't just have a vision if you're not going to do anything with it. The leader has to have a vision and has to have the ability to attract and support people as they live out the vision." —Gorman, John. Personal conversation, May 13, 2022.

[10] Meeting attendees included members of the parish staff, Pastoral Council, Finance Council, and School Board. Also Archdiocesan leadership and Vicariate I consultants: Bishop Gerald Kicanas (Episcopal Vicar), Rev. Farrell Kane (Dean), Rev. Peter Bowman (Vicar for Administration), Rev. David Baldwin and Mr. Chuck Holland (Office for Research and Planning), Ms. Jane O'Brien & Ms. Rachel Kuhn (Development Office), Ms. Jean Noble (Office of Catholic Education), Ms. Mary Hall (Vicariate Admin Consultant). Also Fremont Township leadership: Mrs. Kathy Pannhausen and Mr. Pete Tekampe.

The school was celebrating its 100th anniversary and was almost at capacity. Lewinski noted that the parish is growing rapidly and *must* plan for the future, both from facility and manpower perspectives. They noted, "it is a myth that the parish has a good deal of land." Lewinski said "this is a time of grace, not just a call for bricks and mortar. The parish must approach this growth remembering its values and traditions."

The following demographics were shared: 518 households from 60060 (Mundelein): 58%; 165 households from 60040 (Grayslake); 17%; 85 households from 60047 (Hawthorne Woods): 10%; 42 households from 60084 (Wauconda): 5%; 20 households from 60048 (Libertyville): 2% 9 households from 60061 (Vernon Hills): 1%; 61 households from others communities: 7%.

Fr. Baldwin confirmed a population increase since 1995. Br. Michael said Religious Education enrollment for 1996 is nearly twice that of 1995. It was noted that regardless of "parish boundaries," all parishes in the area were growing. Bishop Kicanas said that no new parishes would be established in the area. The average Sunday collection for the prior 12 months was $6,571 (vs. weekly expense budget of $8,260.) Only one-third of registered households are Sunday envelope users. The parish was encouraged to "dream no small dreams." Lewinski closed the meeting by thanking everyone, saying "This is the work of the Spirit. The Lord is calling us to something." —Parish Archives, *Parish Leadership Meeting* minutes for June 8, 1996.

[11] Sunday bulletin, June 9, 1996, p. 5.

[12] Warren, p. 9.

SHARING VISION

1996 - Second Half

In his July 28th bulletin column, Lewinski reflected on the neighborhood pastoral visits he'd been conducting with the help of hosting families.

> In the last few weeks, I visited with parishioners in seven neighborhood gatherings. I've enjoyed every one of these sessions. Each one has been unique. People ask me what I'm hearing. I've heard longtime parishioners share stories and fond memories of earlier years at St. Mary. I've heard parishioners talk about the journey that led them to Fremont Center. Some have raised questions or voiced their opinions about parking, the school, air conditioning the church, handicap access, the Mass schedule, reaching out to teens. Others raise questions about why only one-third of the parishioners regularly use their offertory envelopes. And everybody asks questions related to the growth in our area and its implications for expansion at St. Mary. Some are fearful of the future, others are excited about it.
>
> I am always eager to remind people that expansion means more than buildings. We need to talk about expanding our vision of what the church is all about. How will we carry on the mission of Christ into the next millennium? What kind of ministries and services do we need? A quick-fix solution is not the answer. Like our ancestors who dreamed and planned to establish what we now enjoy at St. Mary, we need to plan for the next 100 years.
>
> There are as many different opinions about things as there are parishioners. I'm glad parishioners get to hear what I'm hearing. Our listening and our sharing of ideas will bond us together as the community of St. Mary. I'm learning a great deal from these conversations. I feel I will have a better sense of the parish.
>
> There are 13 more gatherings scheduled. I plan to add additional dates. We will keep these get-togethers going as long as there are parishioners who wish to gather.[1]

Lewinski was explicit about the importance of building Church—the people—as much as needing a new church building. He was also walking the talk mentioned in his first column when he wrote, "I want to establish, right from the beginning, my firm belief in good communication." He didn't mean friendly chats over coffee or a drink at dinner. He valued those opportunities but sought more. He didn't just want a chance to tell people what *he* thought or what *they* should think. Lewinski wanted to

know what they thought. He sought a connection crossing the threshold from the casual into the causal. He valued heart-to-heart, soul-to-soul consonance. It didn't matter whether they agreed or disagreed with him. He expected both and could value disagreement as much as agreement.

He sought to hear from those who disagreed, just as Pope John XXIII had during the Second Vatican Council. This is a characteristic of Servant Leadership. "To become a *natural* servant is through a long, arduous discipline of learning to listen, a discipline sufficiently sustained that the automatic response to any problem is to listen first....true listening builds strength in other people.... The leader needs to have *a sense for the unknowable* and be able *to foresee the unforeseeable*. Leaders know some things and foresee some things which those they are presuming to lead do not know or foresee as clearly."[2]

On August 4th, the parish held its annual Pork and Corn Roast. Lewinski praised the efforts of the scores of people it took to produce the event. "The nature of a festival is to go beyond what is ordinary. A festival is an extravagant outpouring of time, energy, and resources to produce a sense of celebration that lifts us up beyond our daily routine.... In this high-tech, quick-paced, impersonal, and imitation-substitute world, we need festivals like the Pork and Corn Roast to keep in touch with the human spirit and with what is natural, beautiful and good.... the community building, the celebration of life, good food and friendship, the ground upon which we build a Christian community and can hear more clearly the wisdom and teaching of Jesus."[3]

Personally, Lewinski disliked carnivals. The Pork and Corn Roast wasn't a carnival, but it was a close cousin. He realized his feelings about such an event didn't matter and shouldn't tarnish others' enjoyment of it. His pastoral approach projected a hopeful regard for an event thousands looked forward to enjoying each year.

PADS (Public Action to Deliver Shelter) was a ministry some at the parish had long wanted. Lewinski devoted his August 18th column to promoting it. They launched it in 1996. Seventeen people were trained as Ministers of Care, and they hosted an average of 25 guests each Wednesday night in the church basement. St. Mary's was one of several Christian parishes participating in the well-organized program. Parishioners Sue and Deacon Bob Poletto promoted the ministry (and would lead it for several years). Lewinski's column solicited volunteers needed to work the "soup kitchen" and manage the night shift and morning cleanup. "Please open your hearts to this program," wrote

Lewinski. "Pray for success. And pray that all God's children may someday have a clean and safe place to lay their head at night."[4]

Another ministry, The Society of St. Vincent de Paul, was seeing its income exceed expenses. Thus they were able to contribute to St. James, a sharing parish. Lewinski encouraged still more additional outreach programs by asking, "What is Mission?"

Other ministries were forming. Love INC would soon be established, and Respect Life had become active. In July, parishioners David and Jean Bailey made a presentation to the Pastoral Council about a "Peace and Social Justice Ministry." They recommended an approach and the Council asked them to pursue it. Before Lewinski's arrival, growth in ministries was minimal, if it occurred at all. Parishioners could see that change was happening, and it wasn't limited to outreach. They scheduled a parish retreat at nearby Marytown for October 24th and 25th.

On September 16th, former pastor Fr. James Morrissey composed a typewritten letter from his residence at Maryhaven Inc. in Glenview, Illinois. He had visited his former parish during the Pork and Corn Roast on August 4th. His letter read:

> Dear Ron, I was happy to have the opportunity to meet you and to see the new look of the home where I spent 16 happy years. It's interesting to know that it is beginning a new life to meet the needs of a wonderful old parish which is having a second spring. When I came, there were approximately 300 families and now I see it has to number about 900! You mentioned the need for a new roof, but I can see that beautiful little church which everybody loves also means a larger partner to accommodate so many who have lived there for years and so many more who have been added to the family as well as those who are to come so the little old church needs help. The little old school needs help also as so many who want their children to have a Catholic education. When Cardinal Cody appointed me to St. Mary's he indicated that perhaps the nuns would only be there a few years. Your Eminence was wrong and fortunately the nuns are still there. St. Mary's has a great past and very interesting and exciting future. It means a lot to those who are pioneer families and it promises much to those who have arrived in later years, and those who are to come. I read the bulletin each week and am impressed with the spirit and enthusiasm it displays. God bless all your efforts as a family which shows such great promise.[5]

When Morrissey attended August's Roast, Lewinski had informed him about what was happening at the parish Morrissey had left in 1983. The letter affirmed the history and great potential of the faith community. Morrissey acknowledged the exploding population. He supported planning a new church and school. His letter was an encouraging testimonial.

The September 15th bulletin included a reminder of the important Town Hall scheduled for the 19th. Lewinski planned to present his "Vision for the Future." He had also identified a motto: "Grateful for the Past...Hopeful for the Future." In his column, he wrote, "The personal participation of parishioners in the life of the parish makes a parish more alive and effective. Each Town Hall meeting provides ample time for dialogue and listening. Good communication builds trust, which opens the door to understanding, which motivates participation and ownership."[6]

Not everyone could attend the Town Hall meetings. Usually, only a minority did. Often it was the *same* minority. Lewinski was mindful of the need for his message to reach *every* parishioner. They designed the meeting handout describing his Vision to be folded, addressed, and mailed. They sent it to every registered household. It informed parishioners they were on the brink of a significant change. Lewinski's essay represented his wish for inclusiveness. "Inviting" and "including" were characteristics he would continually exhibit during the six-year project. The resistance encountered from sharing his vision would be an ongoing challenge.

There were minor differences between the two versions, revealing Lewinski's thoughtfulness in this initial critical communication. There was a callout box on the first page of the **meeting** version of the handout. It rephrased Lewinski's message in the essay's body. It stated the parish is well-liked and has much potential. It admitted change is uncomfortable, but it must occur soon for them to avoid the consequences of inaction. It expressed the thoughts of Lewinski, the Archdiocese's beliefs, and the feelings of many parishioners.

> *While the growth and change may be inconvenient and even frustrating because of the implications it places on us, how can we not look at our growth as a gift from God? Believers and seekers come to St. Mary's because they find this parish to be a wellspring of faith, mutual support, inspiration and guidance. All of these growing pains challenge us as a community of faith to respond appropriately and without delay. If we fail to do so, we will find ourselves trapped and unprepared to deal with the future.*

This content changed in the **mailed** version. Lewinski wanted to connect with people who hadn't attended the Town Hall. Many had indirectly heard about things changing. This group included individuals trying to avoid change, for which they saw no need. Above all, he wanted to know it was *his* message parishioners received. He didn't need people hearing a second-hand version of what their friend *thought* they heard. His handwritten message was simple:

> Dear parishioners,
>   In an effort to keep you well informed, I'd like to share these notes from a recent parish Town Hall Meeting. I hope you find this helpful in keeping in touch with the spirit and activity of the parish.
>
>   In the Lord,
>   Fr. Ron Lewinski

There was another difference between the meeting and the mailed version. They replaced a picture of the parish school on the back page with an "invitation." Lewinski wanted to ensure people knew he was encouraging them to participate in upcoming events. He wanted them to know their importance to the effort's success. They needed to understand the Town Hall was not a one-time event. This vision essay wasn't merely a writing exercise. He sincerely wanted people to share the work of creating the future with him. Success depended on it.

TOWN HALL MEETING
November 21, 1996
7:00 p.m. Diantha Hall
Please join us for the next Parish Town Hall Meeting on Thursday, November 21, 1996, at 7:00 p.m. as we share our progress in planning for the future. **You** are an important part of that future. Your input and dialogue are valuable to the whole parish planning process.

The Diantha Hall school gymnasium was the sole large-capacity location for meetings. They would repurpose it within a year to meet the parish's growing worship needs. Lewinski's words included delegating responsibility and soliciting parishioners' ideas. Lewinski was addressing everyone and targeting those in the parish with a different perspective who could help inform others. He sought to reach those who could impede the parish's progress due to their hesitant or negative approach. He was not casually inviting people just to attend, but to be truly "present." Lewinski didn't want mere "input": what they "thought." He wanted "dialogue": a conversation.

And he not only *wanted* their participation, but he valued it.

This was a significant change from the earlier pastor. So different that some would regard it as hogwash, but enough others would find it inspirational.

In a later article, Lewinski reflected on the Town Halls:

> After presenting my vision for the parish that includes some future building, parishioners responded with what I understood to be a mandate to "proceed." I was deeply moved after the evening meeting when one parishioner stepped forward with a very significant gift to begin our building fund. The need to expand…stems from the fact that we are growing as a parish. Since January, we have welcomed over 200 new families. We now number 950 households. We are not only increasing in numbers but in our understanding of what it means to be disciples of Jesus, to live out our baptismal vows, to be Church.
>
> Our growth is a gift and a challenge from God. People come to St. Mary because they get a good feeling about the community. They like the family-like atmosphere. Our liturgy is prayerful and dignified. Our school is excellent. Our beautiful rural environment is a draw. We take pride in our history. We are committed to maintaining all these values as we continue to grow.
>
> The whole process will take a few years. Every step along the way, we want parishioner input. I would like everyone at St. Mary to take ownership for this project so that as we dream and plan for the future, our plans will truly reflect who we are and the mission to which we are committed.
>
> By this time, you should know me well enough to trust how highly I value consultation and open communication. I don't want anyone to feel left out or uninformed or to feel like they are not important to the life and full membership of the parish. Whether you have been here all your life or recently registered, you are a valued member of the parish family. I'm counting on your personal participation to make this project for the future a true family affair— the parish family of St. Mary working together with a vision for the future.
>
> You are wonderful people, St. Mary Parish! I love you and I am proud to be your pastor.[7]

The people and expertise needed for this effort were being identified. Reality was taking hold. A stated Vision helped transform the vague concept of "expanding the parish" into more concrete, actionable steps. Each question answered raised half a dozen more. With each small step forward, they experienced a sense of satisfaction and a growing fear of the unknown.

Minutes from a meeting on September 25th included the regular array of topics and comments. The summary notes held a revealing comment: "Father Ron placed himself with everyone else: a little scared."

Lewinski was not, of course, going to convey a posture of fear to parishioners. Still, throughout the project, he admitted to occasional skepticism. He possessed an underlying expectation that nothing is impossible with God. He believed it, even when there seemed almost no basis for it.

On September 26th, he invited parish staff and leadership to a meeting on October 17th with their consulting architect, Randy Fielding from Fielding & Associates. In the memo, he wrote:

> As we continue to look to the future, it is important that everyone has an opportunity to express their sense of what the parish needs might be and what direction we might move in. The future of St. Mary belongs to us all. This is our time to dream, to share ideas, to think not just about tomorrow but fifty to a hundred years from now. This will certainly not be the last time we will do some brainstorming. There will be many stages along the way in the planning process. I hope you will see this process as a positive move toward the future and that you will feel an integral part of the plan.[8]

In the bulletin on October 20th, Lewinski reprinted Morrissey's letter written on September 16. He noted Morrissey had been a priest for over fifty-eight years. The bulletin also stated former pastor Eugene Keusal was assigned to St. Edna's parish in nearby Arlington Heights after a sabbatical.

On October 21st, the Director of Finance for the Chicago Archdiocese wrote a brief letter to Lewinski. It confirmed the ongoing discussions concerning the acquisition of property. It then set expectations: "Once this phase is completed, I believe we can then move forward with the next phase, that is, the formal parish long-range plan for facilities, and then on to parish consultation, fundraising, construction, and hopefully a successful dedication of a new parish facility."[9] This didn't tell Lewinski anything he didn't know, but it confirmed the Archdiocese was an experienced partner in this undertaking.

Lewinski had assembled half a dozen parishioners as a preliminary "project management" team called a Core Team. When he received the latest letter from the Director of Finance, he had further reason for hope. On October 24th, he told the Core Team that one parishioner had pledged $1 million in five annual installments. He reminded the group that getting more land was the current top priority. Lewinski was scheduled to meet with the east (Wirtz) and west properties (Wagner) owners. He opined that the team should gather what parishioners see as "needs" and what they "value" to share it with the planners.

During the meeting, they discussed a plan for the Town Hall scheduled on November 21st. What questions should parishioners be asked (what do you want, how aware are you of options like daycare, etc.)? They proposed a parishioner survey to identify needs, desires, expertise, and talent for engaging parishioners.

Fielding & Associates delivered an *"Existing Campus Facilities Report"* in November.[10] The "Executive Summary" blurb on the first page stated, "This report discusses accessibility, life safety, mechanical, plumbing, electrical and structural conditions of the existing campus buildings. The information was gathered through visual observations and interviews conducted in October." The report reviewed the church, school, parish center (office), Gabriel House, and the "Community of St. Mary Site."

About the church, the report recommended an entirely new facility. The old building needed an automatic sprinkler system installed. They recommended putting in ventilation and air conditioning systems. They suggested replacing outdated electrical components and installing energy-efficient lighting. Except for the mention of a new building, these suggestions did not address the problem of limited seating.

Recommendations for the school, also an old structure, included removing the original building except for the recent addition of a gym, a kitchen, and a cafeteria. They would build new classrooms and provide growth by adding a second classroom for each grade level.

The comments about the Parish Center (the old rectory) noted the two-story building with original farmhouse bathrooms was not ADA-compliant. As in the other facilities, an elevator, and remodeled bathrooms, could overcome those problems.

The former convent (Gabriel House) shared the same accessibility issues. However, the report allowed only minor changes were needed if the building continued to serve as a residence.[11]

The page about the "Site" stated what was becoming clear to Lewinski and the Planning Commission: "The present site (approximately 16.9 acres), incorporated worship, Catholic and religious education, parish center, cemetery/memorial plots, and dairy farming. It straddles Erhart Road and is between Route 60 and Fremont Center Road. Accommodating anticipated growth of parish facilities will overbuild the site."[12] In short, the existing site was inadequate and had no future.

Six months had passed after Lewinski received the letter from the Archdiocese listing the parish's three primary challenges. Since then, he had shared a vision, formed a commission to manage the project, and begun efforts to pinpoint the parish's needs and values.

The factual and realistic report by Fielding & Associates confirmed Lewinski's observation. Its final resolution stated: "Acquisition of land to accommodate new facilities is required."

The Pastoral Council approved the formation of a Planning Commission (formally named the Planning and Development Commission). Their project was beyond what Lewinski and the Pastoral Council could expect to manage. The Planning Commission would form subcommittees to oversee specific aspects of the work. Its charter stated in part:

> The St. Mary Planning Commission oversees the immediate and long-range planning for the parish with particular concern for the expansion of facilities needed to accommodate the parish's various services, ministries, and the education and training that is an integral part of the process.
> They will expect members to engage in home study and subcommittee work beyond the formal Commission meetings.
> VISION 2000 is the umbrella under which the entire Planning Commission rests. It includes the education and spiritual formation of all parishioners who will be invited to participate in a discernment process to plan any expansion in ministries or facilities.[13]

In other words, this is no small, short-term project; it will require many people in a coordinated effort; we expect volunteers to do what needs to be done, not just attend formal meetings; parishioners will be engaged to help. Parishioner gatherings will provide an understanding of what we're doing, but a 'mandatory' educational process will enhance people's understanding of *why* we're doing it.

Lewinski was simply setting expectations.

The Planning Commission included a Core Team, Consultant support (from both inside and outside the parish), subcommittee support, and parishioner support. A member of the Planning Commission would chair each subcommittee.

A "Planned Offering Program" was a topic in Lewinski's column on November 10th. It was an approach to achieving a regular cash flow and increasing weekly financial contributions.

> While we have managed to operate in the black, our parish needs have grown and require a new approach to the budget. Staffing and maintenance expenses demand that we create a realistic budget. As the parish grows and activities and services increase, we need to operate on a sound financial base that allows us to move forward....

> In a few weeks we hope to be able to use the old convent for additional meeting space. The number of groups needing a room to meet has increased and we're finding meeting space to be at a premium. With a little cleaning up, we hope to have a meeting room in the old convent ready to accommodate approximately 25 people. Just another sign that we're outgrowing our current facilities.
>
> Let us continue to remember our beloved archbishop as he reaches the last days of his earthly sojourn.[14]

Lewinski was referring to the man who had assigned him as pastor at St. Mary's that year. Cardinal Joseph Bernardin succumbed to pancreatic cancer before year's end.

In November, the Archdiocese contracted with Fielding & Associates for the "St. Mary Project."[15] A registered structural engineer from Wheaton, Illinois, produced a "Soils Report."[16] It detailed the results of aerial analysis and soil borings on twenty acres of land between the cemetery and Fremont Center Road. After several pages of explanation describing topography, vegetation, photo-tone, stereo-pairs, glacial till clays, silty clay, strata, topsoil, and water levels, a reader could conclude the site was suitable for construction.[17]

In the November 24th Sunday bulletin, Lewinski recalled Bernardin.

> We remember him celebrating Mass in Grant Park, visiting us at our Pork and Corn Roast, and hearing him defend life, promoting justice and peace, pleading for common Ground. I will always hold dear the ten years I worked closely with Cardinal Bernardin as the Director of the liturgy office. He was always approachable, supportive and collaborative and reasonable in his expectations. He took a very personal interest in my becoming a pastor and was delighted to appoint me to St. Mary's.... He was a model shepherd, a faithful disciple and an effective leader.[18]

Lewinski began 1996 with many questions and a long "to-do" list. During the year, he formulated and wrote a Vision paper, established a Planning Commission, formed liaisons with the Archdiocese, and attended meet-and-greet events at parishioners' homes.

He ended the year having identified individuals with particular skills needed for the project. Those professions and skills included architecture, design, real estate legal counsel, communications, land development, engineering, carpentry, school planning, capital campaigning, landscape architecture, zoning, plumbing, construction, and construction management. Several skills existed within the parish. Future project management decisions would determine how many parishioners would be engaged and how.

It was a hopeful situation. He had received a pledge of $1 million and a sizable check to open a building fund.[19] The Sunday bulletin listed a dozen people as "Parish Staff"— double from twelve months prior.

Those who were resisting change realized these assignments were an expanding force to be dealt with, but they weren't giving up.

Lewinski had accomplished much during his first year as pastor.

It was only the beginning.

---

[1] Sunday bulletin, July 28, 1996, p. 3.

[2] Greenleaf, pp. 17-22.

[3] Sunday bulletin, August 4, 1996, p. 4.

[4] Sunday bulletin, August 18, 1996, p. 4.

[5] Parish Archives. Letter from James Morrissey to Ronald Lewinski, September 16, 1996.

[6] Sunday bulletin, September 16, 1996, p. 4. Lewinski knew that public forums had the benefit of enabling individual voices to be heard. Critics, therefore, could speak up. Their impact, however, would be lessened in a large Town Hall gathering compared to a small group meeting. A larger group has the advantage of hearing more diverse opinions while self-moderating the extremes.

[7] Sunday bulletin, September 29, 1996, p. 4.

[8] Parish Archives. Memo from Lewinski, September 26, 1996.

[9] Parish Archives. Letter from Director of Finance to Lewinski, October 21, 1996.

[10] Parish Archives. *Existing Campus Facilities Report,* November, 1996.

[11] In July of 1997, the upper floor of Gabriel House—the former convent—became the residence of Sr. Gael Gensler, new Pastoral Associate. The lower level remained as meeting space and a kitchen.

[12] Parish Archives. *Existing Campus Facilities Report,* November, 1996.

[13] Parish Archives. *St. Mary Parish Planning Commission Charter.* p. 1.

[14] Sunday bulletin, Nov. 10, 1996, p. 4.

[15] Parish Archives. Letter from Facilities & Construction at the Archdiocese of Chicago to Fielding & Associates, November 12, 1996.

[16] Parish Archives. *Soils Report - Air Photo Interpretation Study,* November, 1996.

[17] In May, 1998, a similar report would be produced for land south of the area occupied by the existing campus. It was for Phase II of the plan, which included a new school.

[18] Sunday bulletin, Nov. 24, 1996, p. 5.

[19] One telling of the story about an initial donation has Lewinski coming close to money laundering. Lewinski shared his expansive vision during an early gathering. Afterwards, people were shaking his hand and commenting to him as they left. Someone gave Lewinski an envelope, commenting "Here's something to help you get started." Lewinski acknowledged him and stuffed the envelope in his lapel pocket as he continued saying goodbye. The following week he went to the cleaners and did a last-minute inspection of the pockets, whereupon he found the envelope. He returned to his car and opened it. It contained a check for a significant amount. His jaw dropped, and he realized that days had gone by since he'd been given the check, but he hadn't thanked the parishioner. Lewinski may have regarded it as the best trip he ever made to the cleaners in his life.

GETTING FOCUSED

1997 Begins

Lewinski ended his first year at the parish feeling both a sense of satisfaction and anxious curiosity. Although he didn't know what would happen, he believed in himself and his community. More importantly, he trusted in God's grace.

In his Sunday bulletin column on January 12th, he recalled the accomplishments of 1996. He expressed his expectations for 1997.

> It was one year ago this January that I came to St. Mary - Fremont Center to serve as pastor. The time has passed very quickly. So much has changed since I first arrived. To begin with, there are nearly 300 more families in the parish than there were last January. Ministries have expanded that now include Ministry of Care, PADS, a Catechumenate (Rite of Christian Initiation of Adults), Phoenix (for divorced and separated), New Beginnings (for those returning to the Church), the initial stages of the Welcoming Committee, and a reconstituted Pastoral Council and Finance Council. We've seen our liturgical music program develop, a new bulletin format, a parish pictorial directory (now at the printer), a Planned Offering Program that has raised our weekly income, a new Mass schedule. We have also seen the former rectory transformed into much-needed offices and the former convent, now called Gabriel House, transformed into a much-needed meeting space. We've seen new lights installed on the church's exterior, a new roof on the old school and church. Most significantly, we have established a Planning Commission, begun negotiations for additional land, and initial studies and consultation for expanding our facilities in the near future.
>
> I am amazed by all that we have been able to accomplish together this past year. I am grateful to everyone who has been so cooperative and so generous with their time, talent, and treasure. It has been a year of putting new systems in place and beginning to take seriously the implications of the growth in our area. It has been a year of getting to know you, and you getting to know me. I am humbled by it all and grateful to God and to Cardinal Bernardin for the privilege of being called to this pastorate. It has truly been a year of grace for me. I am sensitive to how disruptive the transition to a new pastor can be.
>
> So what lies ahead? With some systems in place and some resources to work with, it is time now to develop our lay leadership, to deepen our spirituality as a parish, to reach out to our children and families, and to pursue our look to the future that entails some significant building. To accomplish all this, we need everyone's personal participation. As a parish, we stand at a wonderful moment in history. I'd like every parishioner to be part of that

history in the making, to share in the life and mission of the parish. In my homily last weekend, I spoke about how important it is for us to anchor our lives as individuals, as families, and as a parish in the Lord. Not only must we acknowledge Jesus as Lord and Savior, we must allow him to rule and reign over our lives, including our parish community. If we do not follow the Lord's lead, his light, we may look like a successful corporation, but hardly the instrument of Christ himself. How important our communal prayer will be then, as we try to discern what it is that the Lord will be asking of us.

When Jesus was baptized by John in the Jordan, he showed us his solidarity with us. Sinless though he was, he was willing to identify with us sinners. As we look to the years ahead, we can take comfort in knowing that the Lord continues to be one with his Church, including that unique expression of the Church we call our spiritual home, St. Mary - Fremont Center.

I look forward to many more years as your pastor. Thank you for the blessings of this first year.[1]

The ball was rolling. He was reinforcing their awareness that a lot of change had occurred. For most parishioners, it was encouraging; for others, it felt threatening. Some felt that more change had occurred in the past year than in the previous twenty.

The Archdiocese sent Lewinski a document immediately after New Year's. It stated, "This agreement releases a small triangle of land across Erhart Road from St. Mary's church." That area included an old farmhouse and a barn housing cows. The original holders of the lease kept a significant amount of farmland north of Route 60. They probably had little interest in this property, separated from the rest of their real estate by a state highway, and even less concern for the cows living on it.

It was a potential strategic acquisition as part of the future campus. It remained uncertain—especially after the report by Fielding & Associates —how to use this triangle north of Erhart Road. It seemed more practical for the parish to acquire land on the south side next to the cemetery.

Soon, good news arrived from the Archdiocese. They authorized Lewinski to negotiate the purchase of twenty acres west of the graveyard. This field, and the triangular plot, were a crucial beginning.

If the expansion plan succeeded, the parish would face a new challenge: traffic flow and pedestrian safety. The primary concern was the school just off Erhart Road. The only entrance to its parking lot was within a hundred yards of where Erhart met Route 60 at an acute angle. The intersection was already dangerous. So Lewinski began a dialog with the County. It would not be a simple or brief discussion.

A County official sent Lewinski a letter in early March stating: "... Illinois Route 60 is under the jurisdiction of the Illinois Department of Transportation (IDOT), and Erhart Road is under the jurisdiction of the Fremont Township Highway Commissioner. The intersection itself is under the jurisdiction of the Illinois Department of Transportation. We wish you success in all your future planning efforts...." In other words, "Good luck solving this one." When multiple governing bodies are involved, things typically seem to move slower, if at all.

On the same day, William E. Peterson, state senator, sent the parish a letter expressing his thanks for being informed and his "interest, concern, and support for your suggestions." At least the word was getting out. Something was up at St. Mary's in Fremont Center.

One of the significant communication pieces in 1997 was the March publication of "Ministries, Committees, & Organizations" of St. Mary Parish. In his introductory comments, Lewinski reported the parish now comprises approximately 1,000 households. He was saying, if you haven't been paying attention, we've grown a lot just in the past year. He advocated the principles of Vatican II when he wrote::

> We encourage the personal participation of all parishioners because we believe that will make a stronger, more vibrant, and effective parish. We believe everyone's opinion matters and that everyone has something to offer the community. We believe in the importance of mature lay leadership for the future of the Church, even as we encourage and pray for vocations to the priesthood and religious.... Experience has shown that getting involved in parish life can lead to a deeper faith and a better appreciation for the Church.[2]

His message was inclusive. He said things weren't like before I arrived. You have something to offer. I believe your opinion matters.[3] As Vatican II said (30 years prior), it is the shared responsibility between clergy and laity to be part of parish life. Traditional roles shouldn't be the only active ones. Your participation will benefit us and you. Being involved will help everyone better appreciate what we, as Church, can be and can do.

The twenty-one-page brochure began with a parish history. It identified the existing facilities[4] (including the barn), provided general information, described individual ministries and educational organizations, and concluded with the Prayer for St. Mary's. It was like a recruiting piece or an orientation guide used in public organizations.

Lewinski had commissioned another important publication: a Pictorial Directory. Parishioners Jeanne Rutledge and Terri Kennedy volunteered to produce it. The effort would become more challenging than expected.

The rural faith community began its project to create new worship and education facilities. In Chicago, an Archdiocesan task force and Arthur Andersen Consultants formed a work group for planning for Catholic schools. One of the first steps was interviewing parents of Catholic and non-Catholic children. The Most Reverend Raymond Goedert chaired the "Special Task Force on Catholic Schools." In April 1997, he informed Archdiocesan pastors about the effort. Whatever was learned might help inform the parish about its path forward.

Meanwhile, the Planning Commission developed a project timeline and updated it monthly. They identified milestones for each month. April had several important ones, including preparation of temporary worship space, getting a contract for additional land, and performing a parish census and survey. The coming months would include drafting a Masterplan; visiting other churches, schools, and parish facilities; identifying architects; and a Capital Campaign kickoff.

As he had done a quarter century earlier at his first pastoral assignment, Lewinski worked at getting to know people. He continued pastoral visits to neighborhoods. Parishioners hosted them in their homes. They allowed him to explain his vision for their community. It gave guests time to ask questions and resolve their confusion. Rumors were circulating about what this "new" pastor was like. The neighborhood visit was one of the best ways to find out.

A consulting engineering firm provided information in a letter about preferred methods to supply water and waste disposal facilities for existing and new campuses.[5] It said three things comprised the required water supply: (1) potable water for daily consumption, (2) fire protection (sprinklers), and (3) landscaping water supply. They allowed wells could provide for needs 1 and 3. "However," stated the letter, "the instantaneous high flow rate required to extinguish a fire cannot be met by a simple well." It also mentioned the negative effect of a parish hall with appropriate food preparation and dishwasher capabilities. "In view of these substantial septic system costs and the associated land use impact, we recommend that St. Mary's pursue cooperative efforts to extend sanitary sewers to the site."

Initially, the project had issues with traffic flow and expenses related to changing roadways. Now there was a concern about water and sewer. The growing potential costs were significant. On the other hand, their work benefited from the skills and experience of some parishioners. Their time and talent, and sometimes part of their treasure, were contributing to the effort. This saved the parish time as well as tens of thousands of dollars.

On May 12th, the parish conducted its first "walk-through" of the existing school, hosted by Gerilanne (Geril) Zern. The purpose was to escort groups through the facility and elicit comments. They sought feedback about many aspects, including classrooms; a Christian Life Center; an Art and Music Studio; a Library; a children's Chapel; a Computer Lab; the facility's entry and hospitality features; restrooms; teacher's lounge; corridors; conference room; gym; and storage. They collected over 200 remarks from the fifty-five attendees and shared them with Fielding & Associates for their planning.

In mid-May, parish representatives visited St. Irene in Warrenville, IL. This was one of several visits to other parishes as part of a "discovery" process.[6] Such research would continue throughout the year.

Despite progress, there were setbacks. A frustrating one was a delay in the Parish Directory that Lewinski had announced in January. The printer had lost the proofs. If they needed to retake all the portraits, parishioners would not be happy. Furthermore, the Pastoral Council and the Planning Commission wanted to establish a newsletter but required a staff.

On May 18th, Lewinski celebrated his 25th anniversary as a priest. Several dozen people attended the event. It was held at Lewinski's alma mater, Mundelein Seminary. Also, the Pastoral Council reported the Welcoming Committee had assembled packets and begun visiting new parishioners. A survey was sent to all registered households.

It was time to change the worship services. The church could only seat a little over 200 people per service. Lewinski had a solution, though he didn't consider it attractive: conducting Mass on the basketball court. The parish ordered over 400 folding metal chairs. The chairs, and a riser for the altar, were set up in the gymnasium. On June 6th, they inaugurated the school gym for weekend Masses. It seated twice as many as the church, thus providing immediate relief by reducing the number of Masses.

For the plan to succeed, rotating teams of parishioners were needed to set up over 400 folding chairs and a dais for the altar on Saturdays. A crew would disassemble them and return them to the storage shed the next day after Mass (except when school was not in session during the summer). One advantage was it allowed the parish to experiment with different seating arrangements. This could be useful when assessing what design might work best in the new church. Inevitably, someone forgot to schedule a crew, initiating a frantic last-minute effort to prepare the space in time for services. The Diantha Hall solution was regarded as "temporary." They didn't know it then, but "temporary" would mean setting up and tearing down the gym each weekend for five years.

An interim way to accommodate the school's growing enrollment was the use of mobile classrooms. They started a conversation about getting some.

Despite being far off, the parish distributed a questionnaire about a "Christian Life Center." Anticipating the needs now could avoid having to revisit later or change work already completed and paid for.

Correspondence continued while assessing the options for services like water, sewer, and roadways. On June 25th, the consulting firm alfred benesch & company reported.[7] The Village of Mundelein would not allow sanitary connections unless they annexed property to the town. Without contiguity to the non-existent village boundary, annexation was not possible. The Village of Mundelein budgeted no construction for sewer within the next three years. There were no ongoing developer negotiations toward a solution.[8]

They scheduled another mid-July walk-through like the one on May 12th. For a particular group of parishioners, it would become a reminder that change does not occur without challenge.

Attendees would witness their pastor "in action."

---

[1] Sunday bulletin, January 12, 1997, pp. 3-4. The Pastoral Council consisted of volunteers elected by the parishioners, and one appointee by the pastor. Rotating terms lasted three years and elections were held in Spring of each year. This provided stability for the advisory body. It operated according to by-laws that underwent periodic review. Despite an election process, Lewinski believed it should be a matter of discernment seeking strength from the combined gifts of the group rather than skills of any one individual.
In 1998 a revision (Article 3 Section 3) allowed for one teen member to serve a one-year term beginning July of that year—*PC Minutes June 8, 1998.*

[2] Parish Archives. *Ministries, Committees, & Organizations,* March 1, 1997, p 1.

[3] Lewinski was known to invite people to be on a committee even if they disagreed with him. That, in fact, was the reason he invited them. He wanted people's voices to be heard; and he wanted to hear what people had to say. He knew there wouldn't always be agreement. (Perhaps he also knew that one of the complaints about the prior pastor was that he was surrounded by "yes" men.) For whatever reasons, some people would decline his invitation even though friends, who knew Lewinski, urged them to accept it.

[4] Facilities named were the church, school, office, Gabriel House, Cemetery (though it isn't owned by the parish), and the barn.

[5] Parish Archives. Letter from "alfred benesch & company" to Andrew Pini, May 6, 1997. The firm does not capitalize their name.

[6] Anyone who has seen both churches will recognize a similarity in design characteristics although St. Mary's church was not modeled after St. Irene's.

[7] The firms does not capitalize their name.

[8] Parish Archives. *Record of Conversation,* June 25, 1997 between benesch & company and the Village of Mundelein.

ENLIGHTENING DARKNESS

July 1997

The priest was not wearing his Roman collar, but a trio had identified him as the pastor. They would shortly have his, and everyone's, attention.

It was one of those hot summer evenings when most people sought the comfort of a cool space. Yet, something motivated everyone sitting in the old church without air conditioning to endure the discomfort. At Fremont Center Township, west of nearby Mundelein, Illinois, July 16, 1997, had been a muggy day. For the two dozen attendees in this century-old building, the dialogue would soon warm up too.

The lower portions of the stained glass windows were wide open, expecting to benefit from the slight breeze pulsing across the vacant farmland from the west. Shadows of parish ancestor's gravestones cast by the setting sun crept toward the church a few yards distant. Inside, the lights were off to minimize further heat generation. The day's hot weather was causing an increase in the area's power usage. A blackout would occur before the end of this evening's gathering.

The occasion was a walk-through of the church, school, and parish office (the former rectory). The intent was to observe—and talk about—the current accommodations on the campus. It would stimulate thought about future possibilities. How much could new facilities be similar? To what extent should they be different? And what features should be considered that had been impractical, even impossible, to implement in the past?

The walk-through would inform attendees about characteristics to consider during the upcoming design phase. It offered an opportunity to solicit ideas *from* attendees. This involved physical components (e.g., baptismal font) and theological considerations for the building's art and decor.[1]

About a hundred people were divided into three groups. They would rotate through the church, school, and parish office. No buildings were air-conditioned. The sessions began at 7 p.m. Lewinski blended in with the two dozen folks in the pews facing him. He wore an off-white, short-sleeved dress shirt and light beige slacks for comfort. He likely wanted to "blend in," minimizing the distinction of himself as pastor as much as he sought comfort. He'd planned this gathering as an informational exchange, not an occasion for preaching. Grasping notes on two pages, he stood level with the occupied pews.

People of various ages, from their twenties through seventies, were seated in the front half of the church. They kept a comfortable distance between themselves. This improved their line of sight to Lewinski. They also derived meager benefits from small gaps of airspace between warm bodies. One rather Falstaffian woman was alone in a pew. A man sat with two women close on either side, behind everyone else. Neither Lewinski nor anyone in the pews had a book with them. Except this trio. That fact would soon be noticed and the reason understood.

The building was of a style typical of churches built before the mid-1900s. The rear double door led through a small foyer directly into the sanctuary. Parallel rows of wood pews framed a broad middle aisle. A narrow aisle on each side separated the pews from the outer walls. Carpeting covered the floor. They decorated the walls with stations of the cross hanging between the stained glass windows.

They positioned three white stone altars in the front at the traditional locations for churches like this one. Each side altar had a sacristy at its rear wall. The sacristies were used for workspace and robing before Mass or services.

The newest altar, a rectangular stone pedestal about two feet deep by six feet wide, was installed in front of the older main altar. It was part of post-Vatican II renovations. During Mass, the priest stood behind it, facing the congregation and reciting the Mass in the local dialect. Before Vatican II, the priest celebrated Mass in Latin, facing the main altar with his back to the congregation. Enclosed In the middle of the high altar was a gold tabernacle wherein they secured the Holy Eucharist. Church renovations after Vatican II often resulted in this arrangement of the tabernacle and altars.

Besides installing the new altar, they had removed the communion rail separating it from the pews during renovation. The rail appeared to separate the congregation from the altar area. Those unfamiliar with the communion rail may see it as a fence. Before Vatican II, the rail was the closest most people got to the altar.[2] In those days, parishioners knelt at the rail to receive communion. The priest, assisted by an altar server, would transit before the kneeling parishioners to distribute the consecrated "host" (wafer).

The baptismal font was near St. Joseph's altar on the right, and the ambo (pulpit) was next to St. Mary's altar on the left. The back of the church had a balcony reserved for the choir, organist, and overflow seating.

Lewinski began the session with an invocation, as was his practice at parish assemblies. He might have offered a different prayer had he known the gathering would soon become an animated exchange between himself and the trio seated behind everyone else. The other attendees were positioned—physically, symbolically, and perhaps theologically—between this trio and Lewinski.

Lewinski began talking about aspects of church design. He acknowledged the necessity for choir and musicians to be seen and heard by the congregation and make eye contact with the presider. He mentioned the need for good acoustics. "There's nothing worse than when they build a new church, and nobody can understand what they're hearing." Thus, he identified the need to involve acoustic engineers.

His next talking point was the reservation of the Eucharist, the consecrated bread. "Obviously, as Catholics, we have a high regard for the Blessed Sacrament, so we 'reserve' the Eucharist. And we reserve the Eucharist as the church teaches us. First, to distribute communion to the sick. Second, we reserve the Eucharist so people can have the opportunity for private prayer, devotion, and adoration. So the Blessed Sacrament needs to be in a place accessible to people. It needs to be a place that is reverent, beautiful, and inspiring."

As he spoke, Lewinski appeared relaxed and confident. He remained centered in front, casually stepping left or right as he referred to the outline he was holding.

"One church I visited, in Kansas City—a brand new place—is hard to describe. But one thing about that beautiful Eucharistic Chapel was that it had its own outside entrance so they could lock up the rest of the church. People can come in any time they want. They had one of those keypad security systems, so if you want to get in, you simply called for the access code."

He moved on to the next topic. "A daily Mass chapel: if you're building a church that seats 800, it becomes rather awkward when you only have twenty people for a daily Mass to have a sense of community as you're gathered around the table. So a Mass chapel has something of value. It can also be used for things like catechumenate dismissal or the children's Liturgy of the Word when they go to another space.

"A Reconciliation Chapel: you're familiar with our 'box' in the back of the church here." He motioned toward what looked like a shallow, oversized closet at the back of the church. Unlike most Catholic churches, this church did not have a confessional along the side aisle.[3] Long ago, someone had constructed a wooden confessional and placed it at the rear of the sanctuary.

"It's an important place," he stated. "I think the word 'chapel' is important. It is not just a 'room' or a 'space,' but it is where a sacrament is celebrated. A sacrament that comes from Christ Jesus in a very special way."

As he flipped to the next page, he mentioned additional topics. "A sacristy for the priest and other ministers to change clothes; but also a working sacristy, where all the worship preparation, cleaning, and everything else can happen." He was approaching the end of his outline. The gathering had been in progress for less than a quarter-hour. Time constraints were present, and the group still needed to tour the school and parish office.

"Just briefly, some of the last things here," offered Lewinski as he began his closing comments. "One thing I think has been disappointing about churches built in the last twenty years"—here he was referring primarily to churches built after Vatican II—"is they lack a great deal of good 'art' and beautiful pieces that can emotionally 'lift us up' and inspire us. Now we're seeing suitable pieces of religious art and devotional works of art placed appropriately in a church. Things that inspire, that are truly artistic, that truly move us. Here at St. Mary's, being a rural community, I think we value beautiful, natural, genuine, and authentic things—and we want to keep that tradition.

"Other things that could likewise be part of a new church building are a bride's room[4] and a crying room—not necessarily in that order." This evoked a chuckle from his audience. "Even a wake room. In many places around the diocese, it has become widespread for people to have a wake from five to seven at night and the funeral Mass at 7 p.m. or variations on that. One of the newer parishes I've seen has a room off the side of the church just for that purpose.

"It doesn't mean *we're* doing all these things. I just want you to know about things being done. And obviously, sound and lighting, air conditioning, and so on."

Lewinski mentioned rotating the group to allow the next group to come in. "We may have time for one or two questions."

An elderly lady, perhaps thinking about the parish's large population of mature people like herself, asked about handicap accessibility. The church had concrete steps rising to the entrance. There were also steps descending from ground level to the basement below. Without ramps, disabled individuals couldn't easily access the church or basement. Lewinski advised, "Accessibility does not refer just to the entrance. It also refers to the altar; they should have accessibility to the ambo, whatever. Handicap accessibility should be everywhere."

The next questions arose from the trio seated behind everyone on the St. Mary side. Despite eighteen months at the parish, Lewinski didn't recognize these people. Because they were toward the back, the other attendees were not aware of them. So when they began questioning, especially as they persisted with their comments, others turned to see who was speaking. The three may have been parishioners with whom no one else was familiar. Their presence did not manifest as innocent curiosity.

They wanted to challenge the pastor. The trio focused on a point confusing to Catholics after Vatican II. They may have expected to inject doubt about the remarks Lewinski had already made on the topic. They may have intended to weaken everyone's perception of his knowledge and understanding of the subject. If so, they made a significant miscalculation by choosing Lewinski—a priest known for his liturgical expertise—as a target for their questions.

A sandy-haired woman in her forties, with her hair up and wearing glasses, sat on the man's right. She raised her hand.

"Yes?" acknowledged Lewinski.

"I understand the altar needs to be beautiful, but you don't have the Blessed Sacrament on it.[5] Why don't you worship—" began the woman before the man interrupted. Her tone seemed genuinely curious, whereas the man's carried a strong hint of criticism. He continued her question as if his friend wasn't phrasing things the way he wanted. "Why do you bow to a stone table and not the body and blood, soul and divinity of Christ himself?"[6]

"Because the altar—" began Lewinski, but the man again interrupted.

"What about Christ in the Eucharist? That's what you're supposed to bow to."

"True," responded Lewinski, "*if* the Eucharist is present. We gather on Sunday not to adore the Blessed Sacrament's *presence*." Lewinski's casual manner became more animated, and instead of remaining in front of the pews, he positioned himself at the front of the middle aisle. "We gather first and foremost to *offer* the Eucharist actively."

"That happens every day," the man countered as if Lewinski's mention of "Sunday" would exclude the other days.

"It does," affirmed Lewinski. "We adore and worship the Lord present in Word and Eucharist. It loses focus for us if we have the tabernacle in static presence over here," pointing to his right, "and then we're gathered to offer this, actively, the Eucharist." He motioned as if setting a chalice on an imaginary altar in front of him.

"Wow," the man uttered in disbelief.

Lewinski concluded, "Our focus is going in two directions."

The lady now referred to a basis for her argument, "According to the Catechism, the two are inseparable."

"They *are* inseparable," agreed Lewinski. "There's no question."

"Then why would the tabernacle be off the altar?"

By this time, almost everyone had turned in their pews to see who was voicing these challenging questions. It seemed there were odors in the air they hadn't noticed before.

"Because we reserve the Blessed Sacrament for the sick and for private adoration," explained Lewinski.

"No, that's what it used to be at the beginning of the Church," she retorted.

"No, I'm sorry. I disagree with you. We reserve the Blessed Sacrament, first of all, for the sick. There's no question about it. I'll give you the documentation."[7] Lewinski paused momentarily before invoking another Church authority. "You can talk to the Holy Father." He was only half joking.

His remark evoked a rather condescending smile from the lady. She raised both hands, holding the book she'd brought above her head, exclaiming, "It's right here." The man echoed her, pointing toward the book to ensure Lewinski was aware of it. If this was meant to intimidate Lewinski, it didn't have the desired effect.

Lewinski recognized the text as the Catechism of the Catholic Church. "Well, that's one source we could argue." He'd soon reveal why.

"Okay," sighed the man despondently. He glanced at the book in the lady's lap, suggesting he was thinking, who is this man to disrespect my source which is part of the Church itself? He squirmed in his seat, now looking at Lewinski afresh. The man's expression suggested he realized this line of questioning was proving more of a challenge than he'd expected. The woman on the man's left said something too softly to be heard. Perhaps realizing her comments offered an opportunity for him to refresh himself, the man sat upright and took some deep breaths. The woman to his right was visibly frustrated, rubbing her eyes.

"I beg your pardon?" said Lewinski, not having heard the woman to the man's left.

"What's wrong with what's listed in the Catechism? We're supposed to believe the Catechism."

"That's not the *only* documentation," Lewinski explained." The Catechism does not talk about the *architecture* of the church.[8] It states very explicitly that the first obligation of a Christian is to gather at the altar of the Lord."

"The Offertory," proclaimed the man.

"Yes, indeed," Lewinski said.

"The Eucharist is reserved—" began the man.

"For private adoration and private prayer," interjected Lewinski, although his wording probably differed from what the man intended. Lewinski continued the line of reasoning. "So there needs to be a sacred space for that. Go to St. Peter's in Rome. It is a prime example. The tabernacle has never been in the center of St. Peter's.

"No, but it has in every church I've been in America," claimed the woman. There was a brief pause. This revealing comment supported Lewinski's suspicions about the trio's motivation. The Tabernacle was a central focus in Catholic churches across America built before Vatican II. But one outcome of the Second Vatican Council allowed locating the Tabernacle elsewhere in the church.

So claiming the center of the main altar is the *only* location for the Tabernacle suggests clinging to earlier traditions. Or limited experience regarding the variety of church architecture. What this trio might have found even more shocking is the knowledge that in the Church's early life, bread consecrated during worship might be taken home (provided it was kept in a place of respect and treated with reverence) because church Tabernacles didn't exist per se.

Lewinski responded, "Well, I know we will not resolve anything tonight."

We can't be certain what Lewinski was feeling, but we can imagine it was frustration. The walk-through was organized as a vehicle for informing parishioners. They were offered a chance to play a role in a crucial parish development. An unknown future was waiting to be imagined and then made real. Crossing the bridge of change leads to development and growth in individuals, families, and communities. Lewinski shared with the attendees some physical changes he'd witnessed at other parishes. He informed them about the variety of possibilities they could consider. He conveyed his confidence there might be no limitations that a genuine sense of purpose could not overcome.

Yet, here he was, responding to questions from people he didn't recognize and whose agenda he understood was manifesting as a distraction. He was reacting firmly but with respect. They persisted in restricting the discussion. They could overshadow all the other topics he'd raised: the Eucharistic reservation; a reconciliation room; a daily Mass chapel; the sacristy; artwork; a bride's room; air conditioning (certainly a factor this warm summer evening), and so on.

These topics were intended to enlighten people's concepts of church architecture. They identified differences between what existed now and what might *feasibly* exist in the future. They were meant to stimulate ideas and unveil possibilities. Lewinski's comments were offered to ignite a sense of purpose leading to action. Action that could accomplish things beyond imagination, even for Lewinski. The positive spirit and the potential he wanted to establish were being diluted. He believed there should be no argument about this issue. The trio's challenging questions were unproductive for this session's intent.

Whatever he was thinking, if there was any defensive aspect of his behavior thus far, it was swiftly reversed with an aggressive verbal response accompanied by animated body language.

Lewinski's statement prompted the first woman to speak up again. "The tabernacle being located on the altar is the most important thing."

"No, it's *not* the most important thing. I would challenge you that you are not giving due reverence to the Eucharist..." he firmly stated while pointing his notes, now rolled up resembling a baton, directly at the trio, "...to the actual *presence* of the Eucharist." He pointed the baton toward the altar. "That's what I would challenge you on."[9]

"I'm not sure you know what 'due reverence' is," stated the man as Lewinski was speaking. Lewinski continued, perhaps not having heard the comment but intent upon making his point. He stepped forward in the aisle, moving close to the trio. He used the baton to symbolically strike his challengers on the head as he spoke. He was like a teacher tapping a student as if to say, "How many times have I told you."

Up came the baton.

"If your focus is on the reserved Sacrament..." Tap.

"then I would challenge you as a baptized Christian..." Tap.

"what it means to stand..." Tap.

"at the table of the Lord and offer the Eucharist."[10] Again, he pointed the baton toward the altar.

Emphasizing his point, he continued, "I would challenge you on that. But, again, we're not going to resolve anything tonight, and we'll never resolve it for you because I know you're on this one track." This was a reminder that the gathering's purpose was informational, not aimed at making decisions. He was telling the trio, I know who you are, and I know what you're trying to do.

As the man attempted to continue, Lewinski waved his arms across his chest like a football referee signaling a failed attempt. He stated, "We're going to the next phase." He pointed toward the exit at the rear of the church. People arose from the pews as if they were spring-loaded. They exited, relieved this exchange was, at least for now, over. Lewinski ended the session in order to keep the evening's schedule.

It is unlikely Lewinski expected this encounter. However, he lived his childhood and teenage years in the pre-Vatican II Church. They had ordained him shortly after the Vatican II reforms. So he was quite aware of the differences between the pre- and post-Vatican II Church. He understood the teaching about the tabernacle's location. He had also experienced people's lingering resistance to the changes from Vatican II. He knew they did not always properly interpret the Council and its documents.

Even thirty years after Vatican II, this encounter was another example of why change on such a scale can span generations. Moses and Aaron had experienced it firsthand after exiting Egypt. Those forty years on the path to the Promised Land were necessary. They made the burdens of life in Egypt become distant memories, remembrances of life that needed to die, along with those who had lived with them. The passage of time enabled a new generation of believers to settle in an unfamiliar land and create a new beginning. They were unbridled by the constraints the Pharaohs had imposed on their ancestors.

Lewinski's encounter with the trio may have contributed to his thoughts several months later. In atypically strong language, he wrote, "I am discouraged and lose sight of the reign of God when I'm clobbered by the mean-spirited extreme right who act as self-commissioned church police dedicated to correcting at any cost what they perceive as error and setting the clock back on authentic renewal."[1]

This encounter was irritating but hardly enough to discourage Lewinski. He had already encountered resistance during the past year. There would be much more criticism and skepticism throughout the project. Sometimes the antagonism was enough to bring him to tears. During Vatican II, Pope John XXIII also experienced turmoil. He rarely interfered with it because he knew dialogue from different perspectives was a necessary part of the process. As Winston Churchill once wrote about disputes between British agencies regarding the accuracy of intelligence reports during World War II, "Let the argument rip healthily between the departments. This is a good way of finding out the truth."[12]

Lewinski sometimes tried to get people who didn't agree with him to work together. Some might call this tactic a form of "keep your friends close and enemies closer." Lewinski, however, was self-confident enough to seek the value derived from a relationship where a difference of opinion exists. He knew a team member who voices disagreement brings benefits. First, explaining their thinking can lead to alternative, perhaps better, ideas. Second, different reasoning can create healthy tension, motivating *everyone* to do better or work harder, regardless of perspective. Third, when the group finally reaches a decision, it becomes "ours," not just "yours" or "mine."

Those who witnessed the "confrontation" between Lewinski and the trio (one of his classmates would call such people "rabble-rousers") had seen some of Lewinski's characteristic strengths. First, he knew his stuff. He responded to them with near quotes from the same Catechism *they* were shoving toward *him*. He calmly told them why the Catechism wasn't a good source to support their argument. Second, he was nationally known as a liturgical expert, except perhaps by this trio. Third, he was receptive to different perspectives, but there came a point where he would stand his ground. Even high-ranking Church officials could testify to that. He often couched his disagreement with respect.

He didn't ignore this trio, put them down, call them out for what he thought they were,   or shout to emphasize his point. Instead, he challenged them while speaking with a firm and authoritative voice. In short, he set an example as a pastor, a parish member, and a leader.

✠

Once outside the church, the group gathered on the front sidewalk leading to the church's entrance. Dan Washburn, a longtime parishioner, facilitated this portion of the discussion. He was assisted by Geril Zern, who had joined the parish just a year prior, as the scribe. The intent was to start a conversation, encourage ideas, and collect notes. The comments were collected, combined, and refined. They became a list of attributes the parish would ask the architect to consider while designing new facilities. Thus, the parishioners sometimes unknowingly foretold some of the project's results.

Washburn began the dialog with a personal observation about an experience at a nearby parish that had just built a new church. "It is a beautiful building, but," he remarked, "it seems surrounded by a parking lot. Exiting the building, you see a lot of cars all around."

Someone in the group replied, "Well, we have the cows," referring to the barn—and cows— across Erhart Road from the church.

After the laughter, Washburn asked, "How about a gathering area? Is that important to people?"

Several responded, "Oh, yes!" Others suggested an indoor area for use during inclement weather, and an outside space would also be desirable. The church had no practical gathering area to socialize in after services, except the basement, which had no handicapped access.

A choir member observed, "You know, in the summer, when we all come out of the church, people will stay for a half-hour. We see it over at Diantha Hall. It has a nice outside gathering area. People are lingering more and talking to each other." Thus, even the temporary facilities provided by Diantha Hall became a sign of how people could use a larger worship space and the surrounding area. This was not the only peek into the future that services in the temporary worship space would provide.

Washburn identified something that resurfaced two years later in the parish design review. "I went to a huge church in Atlanta. They have five different exits. People are pouring out in five different directions. They don't have a common gathering area."

Someone else commented on another issue at the parish. Inadequate space for informational or sales tables after services caused an inconvenience. The limited sidewalk space in front of the church was at the mercy of the weather. At Diantha Hall, only a small portion of the hallway leading to the gym was usable without blocking traffic flow. They usually devoted it to selling retail discount coupons as part of the school's fundraising activities.[13] Another person noted having enough indoor space would allow for worry-free activities regardless of the weather. The group couldn't picture the new narthex, but it would provide ample space for many events.

A larger worship space would seat more people at one time, rather than multiple services in a smaller area. A larger gathering space would enable more time to socialize between services.

Washburn raised the next topic. "I'm looking at the statue of St. Mary over there in front of the church. Can you imagine whether a meditation garden or such would be useful? Any thoughts?" One attendee with construction experience cautioned a lot can be done with landscaping, but everything costs money. Someone else suggested space for a meditation garden might be reserved and completed as a budget permitted.

Washburn stated, "If you look at the lay of the land, the cemetery could be an asset: it cuts the campus in half The area between the new church and the cemetery will not be used. It is possible we could tie in a garden with that."

Now the experience of a school teacher informed the discussion. She said, "I think there is also a possibility we can use that kind of space with our religious education program outside. Also, our school program could benefit by bringing the children outside to appreciate the nature we have around here. Use a meditation garden for more than just Sunday events or adults walking through. Teaching our children from young on that it is important to appreciate God's creation. I know how much my eighth graders enjoy it when I bring them to the cemetery on All Souls Day to look at the gravestones. It is important to them—linking them with their ancestry. I have never seen the cemetery as a liability. I think the cemetery is one of the *greatest* assets we have. It is good to see how many of their family members they can find—the oldest, the youngest. I think the idea of tying the cemetery in with a meditation garden is just fabulous."

A choir member claimed, "It is also nice when you come a few minutes early for a meeting or service just to be quiet. It is nice to be somewhere in silence. Or just pop into the church in the middle of the day. It is so *quiet* and peaceful there. I would love to do the same thing on a night like this. Just drive up here and spend half an hour in a meditation garden where I know it will be quiet."

Washburn then raised the last topic. "The last issue to discuss is the meeting rooms and a basement. What do you envision, or are there any ideas about meeting spaces associated with the church?"

Someone mentioned, "There is no square footage cost to doing a basement." This implied the building cost would not be much more than a building without a basement. A parishioner with some construction experience expressed his disagreement. Another person observed it should be wheelchair accessible and satisfy commercial ordinances, thereby increasing the cost.

But what is a basement? One parishioner had difficulty using the different storage spaces to prepare for seasonal events. For her, a basement would be a single place to store things. She stated the current church basement is used for pancake breakfasts, PADS, meetings, and many functions. This offered limited storage space.

"I am looking at it differently from everyone else here," she claimed. "I want a basement, but basically for storage. Right now, we have things stored everywhere—in the barn, school attic, and Gabriel House. It should all be in one place. So we would want a basement, but it would be a 'true' basement."

There was some discussion about meeting space. They identified that they generally desired multiple rooms or a large room to subdivide using sliding walls. The lack of space prompted Washburn to express a need for more. "We are like nomads because we do not know where we are meeting; we're up there, we are at her house," motioning toward an attendee, "we are all over because we do not have meeting areas. A lot is going on in the parish, and there will be a lot more."

Then, the next group of people began exiting the church. Washburn announced the session's end and thanked everyone for their participation. They walked to the school's south side entrance to continue their facilities tour.

Jim Scavone, the Director of Music and Liturgy, was waiting for the group to arrive. The parish had completed this portion of the school during Fr. Keusal's term. It included two classrooms and a gymnasium for basketball and other indoor events. The kitchen, cafeteria, and storage room were on the gym's western side.

Beginning in June, Lewinski began conducting weekend Masses in the gym. This was a transitional tactic. The gym accommodated twice as many people as the church. To achieve that, it required set-up for services every Saturday afternoon, including chairs and an altar area. After the last service on Sunday, the gym was cleared for "normal" activities. People who preferred the church could still attend services there.

IMAGE #4

CROSS OUTSIDE DIANTHA HALL

A CROSS MARKED THE LOCATION OF TEMPORARY WORSHIP SPACE
USED BY THE PARISH WHILE THE NEW CHURCH WAS BEING BUILT.
(PHOTO CIRCA 1998)

Scavone began by explaining why the group was beginning here instead of inside. "One thing to start thinking about is the actual entryway into the church itself. It's more than a door. It is the entrance for the people of God into God's Church. We got a lot of positive comments from people about the landscaping we did out here at the entrance to Diantha Hall when we started worshiping over here."

They had erected a wooden cross near the entrance to the south side of the building. It identified the location as the worship space. On the wall next to the entry was a plaque reading "Diantha Hall—Parish Worship Center." The parish had named the area in honor of a former parishioner, Diantha Hoffman.

"What we need to do," continued Scavone, "is build on that and come up with a way to make the future entryway obvious. So people know what we're about when they enter the church. How do we enter God's house?"

Scavone invited them to follow him into the gym (worship space). A power outage had occurred. The little remaining light of the hot summer day entered through the windows on the west side of the gym. Scavone took a position at the podium, facing the group sitting between him and the windows. A burning candle stood next to him, functioning as a light source and also fostering a contemplative mood. And adding a bit more heat.

He observed one benefit of using Diantha Hall for Masses was the pedestal baptismal font just inside the door to the gym they were sitting in. Though it couldn't be used for immersion, its placement helped people become accustomed to a single font at the entry. A common characteristic of churches like the old church at St. Mary's was individual receptacles of Holy Water installed inside each side of the main entrance. It allowed for access to holy water but failed to promote its symbolism.

Next, he observed use of Diantha Hall allowed the parish to experiment with different seating arrangements. Metal folding chairs provided seating. Their arrangement could be changed to find what worked best. He suggested, "We might spend two or three months in one arrangement."

The teacher who had expressed appreciation for the cemetery now commented on Diantha Hall's open seating arrangement. "I think a perfect example is when we had confirmation here last year. It was so inspiring when the bishop could come down and stand in front of each confirmand. Sitting right next to them was their sponsor and the rest of the family. He went to each candidate, as opposed to the candidate walking up to him. It made for an absolutely meaningful experience. I don't think those people will ever forget that confirmation."

Scavone cautioned against merely observing worship space when visiting *o*ther churches. He encouraged them to attend services there because "actually *worshipping* in the space makes it take on a whole different experience."

"Music is integral to liturgy," he observed. "So much so that the church says we don't sing *at* the liturgy, we sing *the* liturgy. There's an important distinction there. We must pay attention to where we place our musicians and what instruments we have. Most churches these days have moved musicians out of the choir loft. The choir and musicians are part of the assembly."

Next, Scavone turned his attention to other kinds of spaces in the church. Lewinski had already mentioned a Eucharistic Chapel and a Reconciliation Chapel. He'd mentioned having a place for a wake. Scavone proposed, "Wouldn't it be nice to have a chapel for a wake where you feel comfortable, where you're at home—unlike renting a room in a funeral home?"

Scavone concluded by expressing his regret the evening conditions would not allow them to visit one more area. "The other site we were supposed to walk through tonight would have been the parish office to discuss what we need in office space. I wish we could have because if you could see my office, you would see it has become a storage space for banners, vases, candles, crosses, and anything else. We need to think about sacristy space, where the priests vest and where the servers vest. And where we store things: our music library, our environment that we only use at certain times throughout the year like Christmas." He chuckled as he observed, "Right now, for any item, there might be nine places where it could be." People became frustrated when they needed to search multiple locations to find something because no one could recall the last place they had stored it.

The campus tours on that warm July evening were a critical activity. They enabled two-way communication by having the facilitator share some thoughts while soliciting values and ideas from the participants. The experience began to expand the thinking of those attending. They were given the opportunity to contribute to the parish's future. The sun had set during their time together, but a new light emerged in their imagination.

The gathering concluded by candlelight. Attendees were so curious or concerned about the topics that they remained despite the heat and darkness. They didn't have to *see*. They learned just by *listening*.

The blackout was ironic in how it reflected the purpose of these gatherings: to dialogue and avoid having people in the dark.

---

[1] Finley, p. 28: "The early Christian practice of adult baptism by immersion gave graphic symbolic expression to this sharing in the death and resurrection of Christ. The writings of the Fathers speak of the waters of Baptism as both a womb and a tomb. The one baptized goes down into the water as Christ went down into the earth in death. The coming up out of the water is Christ rising in glory, victorious over death."

[2] The communion rail originated as a fence. In some early churches, the altar was in the center of the building, and a short fence enclosed it to ensure space for the bishop to celebrate Mass by keeping the congregation from getting too close. Over time, especially as the altar relocated to the front of churches in America, the "fence" was retained to separate the altar space from the congregation. Vatican II changes affected both how communion was dispensed (by allowing lay Eucharistic Ministers a privilege previously reserved for the ordained) as well as how it was received (the recipient being allowed to stand as an alternative to kneeling). Thus the celebrant, deacon, and Eucharistic Ministers dispensing communion now stand stationary as a queue of recipients approach, rather than the celebrant dispensing communion by moving along the communion rail at which knelt the faithful waiting to partake.

[3] Architect Dirk Lohan's firm designed the new church at St. Mary. He is not Catholic, but he is familiar with cathedrals in southern Germany where he was raised. During a conversation with the author he fondly recalled how, as a youngster, he used to play in a church near "those boxes the priest sits in"—the Beichstuhl. There were six "Confessor's Chairs" in that church, Salemer Munster in Salem, Germany.

[4] Two months later, Lewinski would comment in his column about the issue of marriages in the old church. "Because we have such a beautiful, unique church, many engaged couples would like to celebrate their wedding at St. Mary. They offer to register in the parish and promise to support the parish. ... The issue here is not money, but what it means for us as Catholics to be committed and responsible. ... We are not a drive-through service station. On the other hand, as a parish we have a responsibility to evangelize." The Parish Council discussed this issue at length without reaching a conclusion. In typical Lewinski fashion, he redirected the issue to the parishioners. "The Council did not resolve this pastoral dilemma. What would you suggest?" —Sunday bulletin, September 14, 1997, p. 3.

[5] In the Catholic church, the tabernacle is the place where the Eucharist—the consecrated host—is reserved, or "kept," under lock. The Eucharist (AKA "Blessed Sacrament") is bread which has been consecrated by an ordained minister and is subsequently regarded as the Body of Jesus Christ. Some Christian denominations also celebrate the Eucharist; but only Lutherans and Episcopalians—according to Fr. Thomas E. Legere ("Real Presence")—approach the Catholic understanding of the Eucharist. He writes "The group that actually comes the closest to having a feel for what Catholics think about the Eucharist is the Native Americans. For them, the use of

something in a ceremony gives it more than just a new meaning and a new value. It gives it a new identify. When something has been used in a sacred way, it can never be returned to ordinary use. The Native American will burn or bury the object since its very essence has been changed by the way it has been used." When a priest, or an ordained clergyman, performs consecration during the celebration of Mass, he repeats the words of Christ at the Last Supper, proclaiming of the bread "this is My body"; and of the wine, "this is my blood." Thus Catholics believe that Christ is really present in the consecrated bread and wine. In Christian religions, only Catholics hold that Christ's presence is permanent after consecration—as opposed to ceasing when the ceremony is finished. Thus they keep the consecrated bread in a tabernacle. (Any consecrated wine remaining after distribution of communion is always consumed by the celebrant or the Eucharistic Ministers who distributed it.)

The understanding that only a priest or other ordained clergy—as descendants in the line of Peter —can perform consecration is also similar to beliefs held by Native Americans. (—Wikipedia) "According to Black Elk of the Oglala Lakota, the first woman chosen to care for the sacred bundle was Red Day Woman, and all women subsequently chosen to care for the sacred bundle are regarded as holy people." --Brown, J.E. (1989) *The Sacred Pipe: Black Elk's Account of the Oglala Sioux.* University of Oklahoma Press, 1989, p. 18.

[6] The speaker's phrasing derives from the Catechism of the Catholic Church, paragraph 1374: In the most blessed sacrament of the Eucharist 'the body and blood, together with the soul and divinity, of our Lord Jesus Christ and, therefore, *the whole Christ is truly, really, and substantially contained.'*

[7] Here Lewinski was nearly quoting, ad hoc, the Catechism's definition of "Tabernacle": "The receptacle in the church in which the consecrated Eucharist is reserved for Communion for the sick and dying. Reservation of the Eucharist in the tabernacle lends itself to private devotional visits and adoration of our Lord in the Blessed Sacrament by the faithful." The documentation that Lewinski was referring to is the Catechism, paragraphs 1183 and 1379.

[8] The Catechism explains the basis of fundamental Catholic *beliefs,* not church *architecture.* A document, issued shortly before the dedication of the new church at St. Mary, does speak to the art and architecture of worship space. That document is "Built of Living Stones" by the National Conference of Catholic Bishops/USCCB. Lewinski often cited that document.

[9] Writing after Vatican II, C.J. McNaspy, S.J., observed: "There are liturgists who prefer the Blessed Sacrament chapel for theological reasons. Put simply, it seems psychologically more sound to keep the mystery of the sacrifice-banquet visually distinct from that of reservation, since people may become confused and find it hard to concentrate on the given action. The Mass is the worship of the Father by the Son, in Whom we are incorporated and with Whom we share in worship. The Blessed Sacrament is the worship of Christ our Lord by us." —McNaspy, p. 138. This is the point Lewinski was making.

[10] For those who knew Lewinski, his mention of "baptism" was no insignificant reference to the foundation for the concepts he was advocating. Lewinski had been passionate about the importance of baptism ever since his youth. His passion had earned him the nickname "Ron the Baptist," a play on "John the Baptist." Each year, besides his birthday, he celebrated the date of his own baptism. "John" was also his middle name.

[11] Lewinski, Ron. *The Reign of God,* Association of Catholic Priests, May, 1998.

[12] Roberts, Andrew. *Churchill,* p. 620.

[13] This particular program, called Market Day, included the additional challenge of needing to use the gym on Saturday mornings as a distribution center for the orders that had been placed; but needing to end that activity prior to setting up seating for the worship services that would begin late Saturday afternoon.

STAYING FOCUSED

1997 Ends

The walk-through of July 16th captured dozens of parishioner comments. They had invited the parishioners to (1) share their ideas; (2) hear about liturgical guidelines from Vatican II; and (3) dream of "a worship space that expresses who we are as a Catholic community, gathered together around the altar of God's word and sacrament."

The attendees might identify current facilities' shortcomings and envision future possibilities. Being the brainstorming phase, all ideas deserved consideration. Some don't pan out, but they trigger others that do. It was an unusual time of grace for a parish to experience. Parishes sometimes need to renovate, expand, or rebuild. Typically, it occurs on an existing property or by acquiring more. St. Mary's might gain enough land to build a new campus while using the existing one.

Lewinski had created an outline to guide his comments during the walk-through in July. Titled "A House for the Church"—meaning a building (house) where people (Church) worshipped—it reflected his "style." Most pastors have a way to remind themselves what they want to speak about. But Lewinski's summary reveals more. His source references: Mt 18:20, "General Instruction on the Roman Missal," "Constitution on the Sacred Liturgy," and "Environment and Art in Catholic Worship." He shared his thinking, but it wasn't all his. He didn't promote his own desires or just his ideas. Lewinski drew from scripture and Church documents. He knew if they built a church, it would not be to create the biggest and best of something. Their church would express the concepts of Vatican II.

The parish survey mailed in Spring had reached a 61% response rate by mid-July. It provided information important to planning and executing fundraising activities.

The week after the walk-through, the Archdiocesan Director of Finance sent a memo to Lewinski with a suggestion.

> It is my recommendation that the Wagner property [west of the campus] be acquired by the Archdiocese rather than the parish.... At the appropriate time, the property would be transferred to the parish along with the debt incurred on it.... During the interim, while the Archdiocese owns the land and

it has not yet been given to the parish, the land could continue to be farmed by the local parishioner.[1]

This sounded encouraging. Acquiring the Wirtz property east of the campus didn't look promising. Purchasing land north of Route 60 would divide the campus. Westward development was the best option. Without more property, they couldn't expand. Lewinski must have perceived the Archdiocesan memo as a nudge from heaven.

Discussions began. On August 25th, Lewinski expressed his thanks:

> Thank you for your help in securing the 20 acres on behalf of St. Mary - Fremont Center Parish…. We are all relieved that this most important component of our future has been secured.[2]

The Archdiocese confirmed that pursuit of the Wirtz property had ended lacking a response.[3] Now they were free to think about using the twenty-acre parcel. All they needed was a way to pay for it. But another issue remained. A 700-foot-long strip of someone else's land was between the cemetery and the twenty acres. It was an inconvenient separation demanding resolution.

The time came for evaluations. The Pastoral Council conducted a self-evaluation called "A Year in Review." Lewinski himself would undergo an appraisal by Bishop Kicanas, including input from the Pastoral Council. The Council also scheduled the evenings of August 11th and 19th for off-campus formation meetings. Also, in August, the parish purchased and installed two mobile classrooms west of the school to accommodate increasing enrollment.

By September, a Consultant Listing contact form identified fifty resources. These included parishioners, Archdiocesan officials, trades, engineers, and architects. The list would be dynamic.

With land issues almost settled, the path was clearer. Then, on September 8, 1997, another surprise came. Fielding & Associates announced a merger with Newman Architecture. Chuck Newman would assume Randy Fielding's responsibilities for the project. Newman Architecture that would produce the Masterplan.

One of the most crucial decisions Lewinski made arose from a mutual need. The Planning Commission and its subcommittees focused on building-related concerns. Lewinski believed that expanding the Church mattered too. He knew his strength was not "people work." He had identified people within the parish who could work on the building. He needed someone to engage the "people."

He hired a Pastoral Associate admirably suited to the task. Sr. Gael Gensler joined the staff on July 14th.[4] Having been raised a couple of hours to the west, she was familiar with rural Illinois. In retrospect, her arrival appeared to be another bit of providence at work.

> I was working in Wichita, Kansas, and my community[5] wanted me to go back to the Midwest to do formation work. They agreed I could continue to do ministry as well because, at that point, they had no one in formation. So I contacted Father Ron to see if he knew of any parishes in the area that needed that. He said, "Yes, I do, right here." So that is literally how it happened. It was that simple. I was looking for a job, and he was looking for a pastoral associate. I started in 1997. I was there for six years. My job was to help bridge the old and the new.[6]

Gensler did wonderful work. She engaged people for events, encouraged them to organize ministries, met with visitors interested in registering, etc. She is soft-spoken, intelligent, easy to relate to, and has a sense of humor. She bridged the generations at the parish and compensated for Lewinski's admitted shortcomings in interpersonal relations. Her influence helped St. Mary's grow as it did. As a former Pastoral Council member later acknowledged about Lewinski, "His strength was his team. Jim Scavone and Sr. Gael were great individuals whose strengths were Ron's weaknesses."

One of the project's first major steps that became visible to parishioners occurred next. On September 10th, the Catholic Bishop of Chicago (a corporation) entered into an agreement with the architectural firm Fielding & Associates on behalf of St. Mary Parish. They described the undertaking as:

> Development of a Masterplan for St. Mary's Parish, Fremont Center, Illinois. The project includes a survey of the campus, verification of the parish's needs, exploration of alternative site concepts, and preliminary renderings of the campus. Also included are cost estimates, a summary report, and presentations to the parish.[7]

Lewinski, always mindful of the need to educate, shared an article with leadership on September 11th. His cover memo to "Taking the Parish to the People" by Thomas P. Sweetser stated:

> I'd like to share the enclosed article for your reading. I think the author makes a few good points that may merit some discussion on our part. As we dream and plan and assess where we are as a parish, these kinds of thought-provoking pieces may help us clarify our own thinking and maybe even give us a few good ideas. While we certainly want to get some things done as committees and staff, we also need to massage our imaginations, fuel our

idealism, and deepen our convictions. Indeed, it is only out of the latter that the best things get done.

I hope to pass along other pieces to you from time to time. I would be very pleased if you could find time to read them. Who knows what kind of conversations might emerge.[8]

This showed typical Lewinski behavior. Reading was one of his passions. He remained alert for resources to help himself or others with whatever task they were undertaking.[9]

He wanted to fuel the fire of creative thinking. He regarded the transition period between the old and the new as the best time to dream about the impossible. Finding the promised land had been a 40-year journey. Lewinski didn't have that kind of time. He suggested reading the article. He sought to ignite ideas and discussion because dialogue is fertile ground for healthy growth.

The piece discusses making the parish more relevant to the modern world. Shifting focus from "in here" to "out there." Those who didn't see a need for more ministries wondered what he meant.

Lewinski and the Pastoral Council had what he termed a "lively discussion" about what to communicate. They discussed the importance of being Church at the millennium's end. Some parishioners were in denial of the population growth. Another group wanted more planning specifics. Indifference towards *any* expansion worried others.

Lewinski wrote in his September 14th bulletin column that he'd speak at all the Masses on November 9th. The topic was an update on planning for the future. He admitted he "would accept the challenge of speaking at all the Masses" though he himself had raised the issue during a Council meeting. "I can communicate where we are as a parish and where I feel the Lord is calling us. However, I'd also like to say that communication is a two-way street. When I hear people complain that they don't know anything about this or that, I can't understand why they don't ask. We must be mutually responsible for communications. Parishioners need to read the bulletin, speak to staff, to Council members, to the Planning Commission.... Well, you get the idea."[10]

They had also decided to move their Council meeting location from a cramped room in Gabriel House to the school's library. This would allow parishioners— always invited to attend the open meeting— more room, although few parishioners ever attended.

On September 19th, Randy Fielding met with the school faculty and staff. He intended to identify "needs" the planning architects should consider during the design phase. More space was an obvious one.

The group articulated fifty items on their list of "needs." They assembled nine ideas for future planning. The[11] parish also collected parishioner comments at Town Halls held that day. The community surfaced fifty items categorized as "fears, issues, and concerns."[12] They identified half a dozen challenges:

1. How do we gain parish support for the building project?
2. Channels of communication: how would parishioners be engaged?
3. How do we get people active in ministries to maintain parish intimacy?
4. How do we encourage/maintain youth involvement for future viability?
5. How do we get everyone to participate financially?
6. What sort of fundraisers would we need to have?

The Planning Commission established subcommittees to better manage the project. All groups consisted of parishioners, usually with appropriate skills or experience.

Ken Behm, a founding family descendant, chaired the Land, Water, and Sewer Committee.[13] He identified their responsibilities as (1) overseeing regulatory and zoning requirements; (2) obtaining zoning approval and permits; (3) performing many land studies and surveys (topographic, soil tests, etc.); (4) providing real estate legal advice.[14]

One early task was investigating the potential of connecting the new campus to public water and sewer. It could substantially reduce the project's cost. They began discussions with nearby townships.

Another was the Capital Campaign Committee (CC). Dan Washburn and Ann Steffenhagen cochaired it.[15] Ann was Ken Behm's sister. The CC began studying professional literature and talking with parishes that had done the same thing. They worked with the Development Office of the Archdiocese. They established a building fund account.

The parish needed a Masterplan before fundraising. The Masterplan would be publicized so everyone could understand the goal. They estimated it would be the Autumn of 1998 before asking all the parishioners for their support. By then, they also needed a solid financial foundation via pledges and contributions from "major donors."

Lewinski repeatedly said the project wasn't just about constructing new facilities. It embraced building a community of worshipers. Thus, they formed an Education and Spirituality Committee (ES). The committee sought answers to many questions. What does the Church say about where to position the altar and baptismal font? How does the seating arrangement affect services and the participants? How do we become more knowledgeable? How can we design a facility to meet our needs and understand the 'why' behind the design and decoration?

The laity did not commonly understand these things. The committee solicited parishioner membership while seeking a liturgical consultant.

They formed a Public Relations and Communications Committee to keep parishioners informed about the project's progress. Lewinski was the designated chairperson.[16] Their charter included information exchange through "educational, motivational, inspirational, and interactive means of communication vehicles." To support this, the committee identified forty-five items categorized as "communication channels," "activities," and "forms of communication."[17] They planned to produce a quarterly newsletter called *The Bell*. They named it in honor of the 1867 steeple bell housed in a copula in front of the church. Sr. Gensler provided editorial oversight. They scheduled the first issue for early 1998. That was the start of the next quarter and the second anniversary of Lewinski's arrival. They also decided to create a parish website. At the time, only about two dozen parishes in the Archdiocese had one.[18]

By the end of September, the Planning Commission had clarified its subcommittees, membership, and roles and responsibilities. In a memo to all committee members, Lewinski explained why.

> Now that we have purchased the land we needed, made a number of major building repairs, completed work on Diantha Hall as a Worship site and set up our mobile classrooms, we can begin to concentrate more intensely on the bigger picture for the future. This requires us to review and revise our organizational plan.[19]

The revised subcommittees:

1. Capital Campaign, 5 members
2. Masterplan Layout, 7 members
3. Public Relations and Communication, 5 members
4. Land, Water and Septic, 7 members
5. Spirituality and Education, 1 member

Ironically, the committee with just one member had the most extended list of tasks, while the Capital Campaign group was more focused: on sharing news and raising money.

On October 2nd, Lewinski issued a memo emphasizing the committees' importance. He asked each committee to meet and accomplish four goals:

- Develop a strategic plan
- Create a charter of member roles and responsibilities
- Communicate the above to the Planning Commission during a meeting on October 21st
- Ensure the Spirituality educates new subcommittee members

This last point reminded them about an education requirement for all Commission and subcommittee members. To kick-start things, he included a list of forty-three parishioners. In the census/survey, they had expressed their interest in participating.

Leadership had struck the match; the kindling was afire; now they just needed more fuel.

Meanwhile, the Pastoral Council strengthened the parish's organizational structure. They initiated an effort to write a Mission Statement that would be a basis for guiding future action. To ensure a two-way communication channel, it was decided that two Council members would be part of every Committee that the Council oversaw. Communication and unity are vital during a transition period.

In October, Lewinski conducted three sessions on "Understanding the Liturgy: a Rediscovery of Catholic Worship." As a recognized expert on Liturgy, the parish couldn't have asked for a better presenter. He spoke about "A Road Map for Praying the Liturgy," "Reading Signs & Symbols, Singing the Song, and Keeping the Silence," and "Making the Eucharist the Heart of our Prayer Life."

In October came a report from the parish's Spring survey. Some takeaways were:[20]

- 57% were ages 31-60, and 31% were 61 and older.
- 7% were converts to Catholicism; 5% were non-Catholics.
- Length at the parish was equally divided between less than three years, three to nine years, and over nine years.
- 46% had college degrees, and 21% had postgraduate work.
- The highest valued things were a sense of community, Liturgy, the rural aspect, and hospitality (in that order).
- Attitudes toward the parish's future were split: 38% enthusiastic, 42% move ahead, 15% frightful, 4% indifferent, and 1% had no plans.
- The focus on the future was 47% living the gospel, 37% communal worship, 8% Mass, 4% religious education, and 4% mission outreach.

In early December, Lewinski dedicated his bulletin column to some questions he had received.

What is most difficult about your role as a pastor? The most difficult challenge is balancing pastoral duties with administrative duties and leaving enough time to think, plan and pray so that I can do the first two things well. At the moment, I'm spending more time than I care to on administrative responsibilities, which leaves me less time to be in personal contact with parishioners. Finding time for rest and recreation is a real challenge.

What is the most frustrating part of being a pastor? Dealing with small-mindedness and negativism is difficult. I am frustrated and disappointed when I sense people fail to see the bigger picture, and get all wound up on a small issue. I am also frustrated that we are unable to reach a significant percentage of people in a meaningful way with the joy of the gospel and the richness of our Catholic tradition.

What do you find encouraging in the parish? The growth and development of parish leadership is beautiful to see. I'm inspired when I see someone get excited about their faith and the parish, and begin to do something about it. I'm humbled by the people who give so much of their time and energies for the good of the parish, or reach out in charity beyond the parish. I am awed by the sacrifices parents make for their children, and the care that spouses show for their infirm mate or another loved one. I am also encouraged by the quality of our liturgical prayer. When people sing and participate fully in liturgy, my own faith gets a boost, and I feel more animated as preacher and presenter.

I have my down days when the volume of expectations and the number of problems accelerate the stress. But I'm no fool. St. Mary is a wonderful parish. We have a lot going for us. It wouldn't hurt for us to all step back once in a while and see the whole picture. No, we are not perfect and there is so much more that we could do in response to Jesus's invitation to be his Church. Who we are and what we have as the church of St. Mary is unique and precious. Let us remind one another of the blessings we enjoy.[21]

By mid-December, Lewinski had received some recommendations for architectural firms. He wanted a firm that understood the parish's needs and the Liturgical guidelines he would represent. He had no reason to *think* such a partnership wasn't possible, but he didn't yet *know* it was. Choosing an architect would be a crucial decision from design and financial perspectives. He was feeling the same sense of anxiety as he'd had before they settled the land acquisition. He might as well adapt.

Now, several parishioners had noticed Lewinski's frequent absence. Was he on vacation *again*? He felt people deserved an explanation, which his December 14th column provided:

While St. Mary - Fremont Center is a very busy place and the hub around which most of us live out our Catholic faith, there are other things happening in the larger Church which affect us and to which we are connected. As a priest of the Archdiocese, one of my responsibilities is to be the link between the parish and the larger Church. What that often means is attending several meetings or serving on diocesan committees and boards, as well as keeping up with documentation and correspondence that comes to my desk.

One of the connecting links to our communion with the parishes in our region is the Deanery meetings I attend each month....

Last week, I was involved in another significant link to the Archdiocese. The Archdiocese has been studying our Catholic school system to see what needs to be done to provide a Catholic education for those who desire it and what it will take to fund our schools....

> Last week, I found myself at yet another Archdiocesan-sponsored gathering which was designed for pastors and parish finance councils. Although I wasn't looking for more work, I was appointed to the deanery ministry commission, which plans workshops and training programs for lay ministers and parish leadership....
>
> There are other links as well that I could share. There are issues of clergy shortages, liturgical renewal, new efforts in evangelization, preaching, etc., which are the subject of many of the meetings, committees, etc. I try to be that link **to** you and **for** you to the larger Church to which we belong.
>
> Hopefully, this gives you some sense of what is involved in my role as your pastor.[22]

Those accustomed to less committed pastors doubtless found this a perplexing explanation. Many probably thought, "What's that got to do with me?" Lewinski once related that some parishioners had asked why they had been invited to the Town Hall meetings. Most long-time parishioners were not used to being expected anywhere except Mass on Sundays. For Lewinski, the question was, "Is the Gospel being lived?"

Parishioners also were not used to a priest being involved with activities beyond their small community. His humility prevented him from saying officials saw gifts in him to benefit the larger Church. His schedule rarely included downtime. Unlike some pastors, he didn't wear Bermuda shorts and a golf shirt under his robes to go to the links after Mass.

The Communications Committee proposed to the Parish Council establishing a parish website. The ability to browse the web exploded in the mid-1990s. Only a couple dozen parishes out of over 300 in the Archdiocese had a website. The intent was to utilize this new form of communication to support the project. They were also doing conceptual work on a newsletter that could be produced quarterly and mailed to all parishioners to keep them informed.

They contracted a firm to survey the triangular plot of land across from the church and cemetery. Two days before Christmas, they submitted their report. They noted the "area has a limiting seasonally high water table at 13 to 22 inches below the surface. This would require either an at-grade or a mound-type septic system."[23] Lewinski had already abandoned using the triangle between Erhart Road and Route 60 for construction. He didn't believe it would be big enough.

While the parish ended the year with a worthy list of achievements, still more tasks awaited.

[1] Parish Archives. Memo from J. Benware to Ron Lewinski, July 21, 1997.

[2] Parish Archives. Letter from Lewinski to J. Benware, August 25, 1997.

[3] Parish Archives. Letter from J. Benware to Lewinski, September 3, 1997.

[4] Pastoral Council minutes, July 14, 1997.

[5] OSF is the third branch of the Franciscan Family formed by Catholic men and women who seek to observe the Gospel of Jesus by following the example of Francis of Assisi.

[6] Gensler, Gael. Personal conversation, June 16, 2019.

[7] Parish Archives. "Agreement Between Owner & Architect," September 10, 1997.

[8] Parish Archives. Memo from Lewinski to Pastoral Staff, Pastoral Council, Planning Commission, Sept. 11, 1997. The tone of this message is an understatement of his excitement about the material, and his eagerness for it to become a catalyst for further thinking and action. Phrases like "I'd like" and "I hope" can be read as "I'm compelled" and "I want." They are a consequence of Lewinski's true feelings being moderated by his humility and introversion.

[9] "He came [to my house] with what I would call a suitcase of books. If I wanted some information for work, he would look up something for me. Yes he liked to read." —Diane Ciesielski, Lewinski's sister. Personal conversation, July 21, 2019.

[10] Sunday bulletin, September 14, 1997, p. 4.

[11] Parish Archives. *Synthesized Notes from the Meeting with the Architect and School Faculty/Staff* (dated September 10 but probably was the 20th).

[12] Parish Archives. *Synthesized Notes from the Town Hall Meetings (AM and PM)*.

[13] Members of the LW&S Committee included Dan Boston, Terry Grom, Al Hertel, Bob Knowles, Vince Masse, and Stan Zagula. —*The Bell*, Vol. I, Issue 1, February 1998, p 8.

[14] Ibid.

[15] Besides Washburn and Steffenhagen, the CC included Ernie De Salvo, John Kroll, Tom Schofield, and David Titus. —*The Bell*, Vol. I, Issue 1, February 1998, p 9.

[16] Initial members were Lewinski, Todd Giles, Dave Kennebeck, Laura Kuderna, and John Riggio. —*The Bell*, Vol. I, Issue 1, February 1998, p 12.

[17] Personal Archives. "PR & Communications Proposal." 5 pages.

[18] The world wide web (www)—aka the Internet -- and web browsers for public use had become "available" just prior to Lewinski's arrival in 1996.

[19] Parish Archives. Memo from Lewinski to Planning Commission and subcommittee members, October 2, 1997.

[20] Parish Archives. *Report on St. Mary's Parish Survey* by Layman & Rice, October, 1997.

[21] Sunday bulletin, December 7, 1997, pp. 3-4.

[22] Sunday bulletin, December 14, 1997, p. 4.

[23] Parish Archives. Letter from John A. Raber and Associates to Lewinski, Dec. 23, 1997.

DAY 762

Winter 1998

Lewinski began his third pastoral year by sharing his thoughts. They weren't vague wishes but honest insights into his dreams for St. Mary's.

• At the top of my list, I hope we can see some noticeable progress on our Masterplan for the future. Along with that, I hope I can effectively communicate the need we have for expansion and appropriately educate the community toward an understanding of the whole project. I'd love to be able to announce by this time next year the date for groundbreaking and offer a sketch of what we envision for the future.

• In this next year, I would love to raise our Mass attendance from 40% of the parish to 50%. I continue to pray for a way that can attract others into a more participatory membership.

• I am resolved to foster a mission-minded parish. We can be proud of our sharing relationship with St. James. But I'd like to see us go one step further and adopt a parish in South America, the Caribbean, or Africa as a mission of St. Mary. I dream of seeing adults and college students spend some time working in the mission. Where I have seen parishes do this, the blessings that come back to the home parish are plentiful.

• I'd love to see the inside of our old church painted in the new year.

• I would like to do more for our children. In addition to strengthening our school and religious education program, I dream about ways in which we can challenge and excite our youth to a more active engagement in the life of the Church.

• I pray that in this next year, as a community, we can call forth at least one vocation to the priesthood or religious life. God has been good to St. Mary's in providing priests and sisters for over 100 years. I pray that someone may hear God's voice and respond.

• I am resolved in this new year to learn a little more about finances and fundraising. We have some major financial challenges that lie ahead of us. I hope and pray for the insight and wisdom, and panache it will take to run a capital campaign.

In addition to these dreams and resolutions, I also hope I get to know the names of more parishioners; to get better at preaching; to allot more time to develop my own spirituality and prayer life; to spend more time in pastoral care and less in the administration; and like the rest of humanity, to lose at least 15 pounds.

How about you? I'd like to hear about some of your hopes and dreams. Maybe I can share or comment on them in future articles.[1]

He wrote, "The Communications Committee of the Planning Commission is preparing its first edition of a parish newsletter that will keep our parishioners well-informed on the progress and development we are making toward our future expansion. Be sure to look for it. We want everyone to be well-informed."[2]

On February 8th, St. Mary's held its annual "Appreciation Dinner" in Diantha Hall. The event acknowledged the hard work of the many ministries and volunteers at the parish. These themed dinners included a period of entertainment after the meal. This evening's theme was Italian. Red, heart-shaped helium balloons proclaimed, *"You're the Greatest."* They floated amongst black and red balloons above each table. Red and white carnations mixed with baby's breath in tall glass stemware vases adorned black-and-white checkered tablecloths. Mike Matousek—son of parishioners Jon and Sue Matousek—and his band provided lively background music.

After the initial introductions and opening prayer, people filled their plates to enjoy a much-appreciated meal. The crowd packed the tables to capacity. The scent of spaghetti and spicy meatballs in marinara sauce joined the aroma of roast chicken wafting through the air. Crisp tossed salad and warm rolls complimented these entrees. Refreshments included cold water, soda, beer, or wine.

After consuming their meal, most attendees helped themselves to coffee and a creamy cannoli or slice of moist cake. People felt like they were at a friendly neighborhood restaurant. They enjoyed this dinner, conversation, and entertainment in the school's gymnasium.

Lewinski approached the podium as the guests explored their first or second dessert. The murmur of the crowd subsided.

"Before I introduce the program for this evening," he began, "I just want to take a serious moment to say how happy I really am to see all of you here tonight." Although he was reading from a prepared text, the audience sensed the sincerity behind his words. "This gathering is a beautiful mural of the talent and generosity that keeps St. Mary's going. I am truly grateful for all that you are, and all that you do. There are many days when I stand in awe of your willingness to lend a hand, to take responsibility—not only for programs and projects but in caring for one another, for reaching out to others in need and sharing the paschal mission of the parish.

"What scares me the most about being St. Mary's pastor is not all the challenges that lie ahead of us, including expanding our facilities, but really maintaining the greatness and unique spirit we already enjoy. There is so much good here that it scares me at times. Sometimes I ask myself how I can be so lucky. I am truly so grateful and so proud to be your pastor.

"You know, this is day 762," he noted with a smile and slight chuckle. "Who's counting? It was 762 days ago that I came to St. Mary's. When I see how quickly and beautifully we have grown, not just in size but in many ways that truly make us a vibrant community, I am truly humbled; but also very pleased. Thank you very specially for welcoming me and for responding so well to my invitation to share more broadly in the planning and the decision-making processes of the parish.

"I want to thank *you* for assuming so many new ministries and responsibilities; the challenge, really, of growing together. Yesterday, Vicariate One met with Archbishop George. At that gathering, Archbishop George charged us to take seriously Pope John Paul II's call to prepare for the celebration of the millennium. Pope John Paul sees the need for a new evangelization that rekindles the faith of good Catholics like yourself and stirs up the faith of those who have fallen away or grown cold, or maybe never experienced the joys of the gospel, or never had a real understanding of what Church is all about.

"As I thought about what our evangelization efforts at the parish might look like, I couldn't help but think that our best effort at evangelization is what we are already trying to do: to be a parish that values community life, to be a parish that values the ownership of the work of Jesus, to be a parish that celebrates the liturgy with reverence and with full, active, and conscious participation and enthusiasm.

"It is your love for the Church and your countless hours of volunteering, your participation on boards and committees, your sharing in the pastoral ministries—all of this makes for a parish that evangelizes by its very witness. And let me thank spouses too—spouses who often have to make sacrifices at home so that one or the other can give time to parish meetings and projects.

"As we continue to grow, I know some of you are concerned we might lose that close sense of community we enjoy so much at St. Mary's. But as we move more intently on our plans for the future, I believe it is a rare opportunity for us to rally around a common goal and vision.

"On March 10, we will present the first draft of our Masterplan for parish expansion. I want *everyone* to feel included in that process. Your interest, your enthusiasm, your ideas, and your recommendations will *make* this a successful project.

"This is a rare moment of grace when together we can plan for future generations, renew our faith and sink the roots of our community life still more deeply.

"Let me also take this occasion to beg your *forgiveness*, for I am sure there are many times when I have not given you the support and encouragement that you deserve. Believe me—there is no one more aware of your pastor's limitations than your pastor himself. I love to see all the activities at St. Mary's, but I also regret that I cannot be everywhere. And even when I am present, sometimes my mind is on overload, and my energies are drained.

"The hardest thing, it seems to me, about being a pastor is not the long hours or the tough decisions, or even all the prospects of the major building. The hardest thing is the regret I have that I cannot spend the time with every one of you that I would like to spend. In the humble recognition that I can't do all I would like to, no matter how much I try.

"Well, enough for all those serious thoughts. I want all of us here tonight to have a good time, so I won't go on and on, but" he paused for a few seconds of laughter, "I want you to know how much I truly appreciate you. This is an appreciation dinner, and I hope you sense, that you *know*, I appreciate you and love you very much. I hope we can also come to appreciate one another's gifts.

"I had the occasion a few Sundays ago to be present in the pew, incognito, on a Sunday in a Catholic parish in Florida. It was awful," he groaned, shaking his head and grinning. Sensing the sincerity behind his words and perhaps relating to a prior personal experience of their own, the diners acknowledged his comment with laughter. "I couldn't wait to get out of there.

"Absence does make the heart grow fonder. I wouldn't want to be in any other parish. You are the best. You are the greatest—that's what the balloons say, and it is true. That is what we celebrate here tonight.

"One thing that makes a good family and a good healthy community is a good sense of *humor*. You know, we can get all stressed about so many things in the universal Church and so many things around here that don't always go right. But that has been going on for 2000 years. What makes us think that we're going to put it all together in our generation?

"You know Pope John XXIII had a great sense of humor, worth our imitating. He was asked once, 'Holy Father, how many people work in the Vatican?' He answered, 'About half of them.'" Again, appreciative laughter. "Well, it is in that same spirit of good humor, learning to laugh at ourselves, that I hand over tonight's program. Thank you."

Lewinski had acknowledged their efforts, humbled himself, and admitted that challenging times still awaited them. Lewinski addressed his remarks to everyone in the parish. He'd express his gratitude at other events, but not with the same effect as tonight. He shared faith in the parishioners, hope for success, and love for his flock. People realized he was speaking from his heart. A standing ovation, whistles, and cheers returned the sincerity and depth of Lewinski's expression of appreciation.

The evening's entertainment was a skit featuring a special appearance by Monsignor Guiseppe Baccio Gallupe. It was a character Lewinski had long ago adapted for himself. He may have been inspired by the popularity of Fr. Guido Sarducci on the television show "Saturday Night Live." Lewinski's Monsignor was an emissary from Rome, visiting the parish to advise parishioners on what they could and could not include in their planning.

Lewinski's performance was most entertaining. His appearance in a black cassock and biretta, Italian accent, and straight-faced delivery of lines from behind tinted sunglasses invoked bouts of laughter. An example of one item on the Vatican's "forbidden" list, besides an Olympic swimming pool (Lewinski loved to swim), was a drive-through confessional. The idea seemed ridiculous because of the intimate nature of Reconciliation. They could not have conceived that twenty-two years later, during the Covid-19 pandemic, drive-by confessions would become a widespread practice.[3]

After the event, with the tables and chairs cleared from the basketball court, someone collected the remaining balloons, tied them together, and handed them to Lewinski. He immediately saw the opportunity for humor presented by a zeppelin of balloons floating above his head. Expressing his characteristic wide grin, he grabbed the person next to him to anchor himself as he mimicked the collection lifting him away.

At the end of day 762, Lewinski likely had a more restful sleep than normal.

---

[1] Sunday bulletin, January 11, 1998, pp. 3-4.
[2] Sunday bulletin, January 18, 1998, p. 4.
[3] https://www.catholicsun.org/2020/05/04/coronavirus-confessions/. See also other articles and various YouTube videos.

TAKING THE TEMPERATURE

Winter 1998

The first issue of *The Bell* newsletter appeared in February 1998. Three months prior, the Communications Committee came up with the idea of a quarterly publication. It was not simply a two-sided tri-fold with a few updates. The pages were standard letter size, and issues ranged from eight to sixteen long.

It included articles, pictures, and schematics. They had much news to share in the first issue's twelve pages. They spoke about Vision, the Masterplan, and introduced the subcommittees of the Planning Commission. They shared results from the parishioner survey, noting 1,100 households; a school enrollment of 216; REP enrollment of 271; church seating capacity of 220, and Diantha Hall seating capacity of 445.

The Bell had a column by Lewinski called "Around the Table." The title reflected his respect for traditional forms of communication, especially in rural communities. During the parish's history, families discussed and decided many things at family dinner tables. In his introductory column, he wrote:

> While our goal is to build something that is truly beautiful and appropriate for our use, our ultimate goal is to form a vibrant and hospitable faith community. Through dialog, shared information, good communication, and the personal participation of every parishioner, we can continue to strengthen that sense of community we value at St. Mary.[1]

"Around the Table" was Lewinski's opportunity to communicate to parishioners. A column called "Views from the Pews" enabled parishioners to share their thoughts:[2]

> "Change is always tough, but it is a sign of life, not death. We have a chance to do something great for the future. I've lived here for 35 years. If I didn't give my heart and soul to this project, I'd only be cutting off God's grace and the mysterious plan he has for us."
>
> "When I think about the future of St. Mary, it is both exciting and scary at the same time. It's going to be an adventure with ups and downs, but I'm hopeful."

One comment recalled a complaint from prior years about not having enough engagement with the younger generation. "St. Mary's is heading in a good direction because we are getting more people involved, including teens—and that's good." The remark came from a parishioner starting his first year at nearby Carmel High School.

The issue included a bulleted list of accomplishments through the prior year. It concluded with a FAQ page. One question was, "Will parishioners have any input?" The response:

> Parishioners have had input to this project from the very beginning. The Planning Commission has held Town Hall meetings and walk-throughs to hear the needs of the people. We will continue to hold open forums at each stage of the process where parishioners can ask questions, offer recommendations, and share their perspectives on our planning.[3]

Thus, there had been the opportunity to participate from the beginning. Before Lewinski's arrival, many parishioners had grown accustomed to their voices being ignored. Now, they began to realize their voice was heard. They could actively be part of what was happening. It was a new experience for them.

Over the decades, the church basement had been a blessing for this farming parish. Shortly before the Great Depression, forty years after they had built this church, parishioners wanted more social space. Their need motivated them to use jacks to raise the entire building. They manually dug out a hole for a foundation. Then they formed walls and a floor of concrete. They lowered the building onto it and finished the basement's interior. The renovation was a significant moment in the parish's history. Building new facilities and expanding the campus dwarfed the work of adding that basement.

On the evening of February 9, 1998, twenty-some parishioners met in the basement with Lewinski and an Archdiocesan representative. She was an experienced consultant who helped parishes expand their church or school. Here she faced something atypical and more extensive.

Many people besides those at this meeting were concerned about financing the building project. The consultant's reserved demeanor betrayed a dichotomy between the parish's stated goal and reality. Her words conveyed support and confidence, but her body language and facial expressions implied less certainty. Similarly, those who knew Lewinski—dressed casually in a pullover sweater—gathered from his demeanor a sense of discomfort and uncertainty about the evening's discussion topic.

A few attendees understood the hurdles ahead. Others weren't even aware of current difficulties within the parish. There was a diversity of experiences present. There were members of founding families, school teachers, parents, and the trades. They were not merely curious. They wanted this project to succeed. They hoped to learn how they could help make it happen.

The representative introduced herself. She observed that parishes like theirs usually expect money from regular weekly contributions. This was common throughout the diocese. The inference was it would be the same at St. Mary's. "I'm sure you can do this," she asserted. "It may be a bit of a stretch in your head, but you can do this." She added, "It's a matter of your willingness and determination."

The parish published the weekly contribution amount in the bulletin. Only a third of registered parishioners participated. The average personal weekly donation was less than what a couple spent on dinner at popular local restaurants. Doing the math, anyone could realize that increased collections alone could not fund the project.

As if reading their minds, the representative stated, "Of all the statistics on religious giving, Catholics are the lowest." She explained, "The part which is not as well known is that Catholics don't give as much because they're not *asked*. We do not ask Catholics with the same regularity as other denominations ask."

She said that first, they would solicit specific "targets." Those who might pledge a particular—and often higher—amount. This would occur before a parish-wide appeal. She explained, "Before the Capital Campaign begins for the parish—meaning all registered parishioners—we somehow try to draw key contributors together. We ask them to make significant contributions, something over and above what we will ask from everyone else. These people are not strangers to the parish; they are parishioners today. They are people who are already giving to the parish regularly through the offertory collection."

Attendees sensed some hope when she identified other forms of fundraising. Over time, they would benefit from these. They included weekly collections, silent benefactors, pledges, benefits from estates, company matching, alum donations, etc. The attendees realized there would be several ways of raising money. They understood why she'd said "success" would be a matter of their will and determination.

Then she voiced what many suspected. "There is a gap, though, between what I believe *can* be raised from the people in the pews and what you *need* to raise. So the gap is something we have to fill through major gifts and some arrangements with the diocese. All parishes do it. My experience is these conversations between the parish and the finance department at the diocese are ongoing." As if to stress her point, she repeated, "They are always ongoing." If her words were intended to provide hope and encouragement, it was overshadowed by her bearing and quiet conversational tone that lacked the energy-building enthusiasm the topic warranted.

She named two more monetary sources. They often helped meet any shortage. The first was "major gifts"—money donated toward functional or ornamental items, like pews. The second was sourcing from the Archdiocese, such as a loan or funds-matching.

Lewinski, leaning back in his chair next to her, had been silent. His facial expressions and body language revealed more than he had verbally about his sentiments. The Archdiocese had sent him to St. Mary's two years before to move it into the future. He was accountable to those who had placed him in this position. Lewinski had shared a vision with the parish within months of his arrival. He knew it would be challenging. He was also responsible for the parishioners, those to whom he was a shepherd. So there was pressure from both directions. He wasn't promoting just incremental construction that typically occurred. He was leading an effort for something much larger. It was as significant as building the church in 1889.

Besides the external forces, Lewinski faced internal conflicts. He disliked soliciting donations. Visioning the future and imagining possibilities, while not easy, were less challenging for him. Determining how to finance the dream, and taking ownership of his role in doing that, was not in his comfort zone. The purpose of tonight's meeting was to introduce the challenge to a cross-section of parishioners and to extract their ideas and advice. His demeanor revealed Lewinski's discomfort. Those who knew him well enough could sense it. If someone were to identify low points during the project, this certainly qualified as one.

When he spoke, he acknowledged the parish's challenge and how he regarded it differed from similar situations. "The difficulty in doing a Masterplan for here," he noted somberly. "It's not like some parishes that would simply need to put an addition on the school or some such thing. We're almost starting over again." He was cautioning people that this undertaking would be significantly different and more difficult.

"So now we're stuck trying to figure out what comes first. In some ways, I don't know myself what the answer is." They rarely heard such a frank admission from their pastoral leader. Lewinski had come to the parish with a lot of experience, but no one ever has all the answers.

"It's a chicken and egg kind of thing," he continued. Do we plan first and then try to get the money, or do we see how much money we can get so we know how far we can go? I think part of what will happen during the presentation of the Masterplan and getting feedback from the folks we will be 'feeling the temperature,' and it will be like a dance during the next several months—going back and forth. What happens in some parishes over time is, for example, they will build something like a gym, thinking someday they'll build a 'real church'; but it never happens. I would hate to find ourselves in that position, where we say we will build a 'phase' and never end up doing what we needed to do."

Three phases comprised the tentative twenty-year "plan" they had outlined. The first included a new church, parish center, rectory, and preparatory work for later stages. A new school was in the second phase. The third would convert the old school into an intergenerational center.

It was an ambitious idea with a cost soon to be estimated at $21 million. They allocated $11 million, including contingency, for the first phase. Most everyone believed this little country parish would be lucky to raise even a third of the estimated cost for Phase I.

Someone asked how long parishioners might need to pledge payments. They were told most people prefer paying "installments" rather than a lump sum in three-year periods or shorter. If St. Mary's still needed more money, they could conduct another fundraising campaign. Meanwhile, there will have been parishioner turnover.

She advised the initial funding plan—usually as a brochure—should describe the full vision. It should contain everything the parish wants to accomplish, even if in phases. This enables everyone to understand the intent. But the Capital Campaign focuses on only the first phase.

Lewinski expressed the challenge of predicting things over the coming years. The population in the area was booming, so new parishioners would bring additional funding. The more reluctant may be drawn to it after seeing what's happening.

The representative identified differences she'd seen elsewhere. "Some parishes don't charge tuition for the children to attend elementary school. They use the operating income of the parish to pay the tuition." That had not been, and would not be, the case at St. Mary's. She remarked, "There is also—not so far from here—a parish which doesn't have to hold capital campaigns. People there feel called to a greater sense of generosity."

She again mentioned how other denominations could raise large amounts of money. "I think Catholics are going to have to learn from other's experiences and success and adapt some for ourselves. It's not solely the pastor's responsibility."

The mention of school tuition invoked discussion of this controversial topic. Many families had children in the school. The parish installed two "mobile classroom" trailers in response to growing enrollment. Most parish families had no children school-age. Attitudes ranged from "the school is not my responsibility" to "as part of the parish, the school is my responsibility."

Most people did not realize how much money was needed beyond tuition. It required an additional $100,000 per year to sustain the school. They brought in just ten percent of this from Sunday collections intended explicitly for the school. Much of the money needed to operate the school came from various fundraisers conducted throughout the year. The annual "Pork and Corn Roast" was the foremost among these.

During this meeting, Lewinski expressed concern. "The majority of fundraisers are centered on school use. I still think that people's perception is we're getting 'all this money' from the fundraisers. But they're all such nickel and dime things that, in reality—when added up—it isn't that much. It was quite a revelation to see twenty-six discrete events occurring to raise money." It is easy to imagine both organizers and contributors tiring of twenty-six events in fifty-two weeks.

One parishioner noted, "I think that solicited contributions will be important. There are people who don't give regularly but who we can approach for a significant amount. Many of us probably know somebody like that. It takes much less effort to get a few large donations than several smaller ones."

"Exactly," the Archdiocesan representative replied. "I would see working with the parish down the road, with the Steering Committee, to do some kind of pyramid of gifts. You need a couple of gifts at one level, a couple of gifts at another level, etc. If you got a matching fund, you could raise almost a million, and that would be wonderful. That would be important for your current people to feel vested at that level."

She then touched on the importance of ongoing communication. "I think this newsletter you're launching," she advised, referring to *The Bell*, "will be key to that. As long as you keep talking about the project, keep communicating. That's the key. And each of you here also shares this with the people you represent, explaining this is the way we are moving. Each of you has to take ownership and begin to promote it, that it is a reality."

Lewinski injected some levity into the conversation. He shared an observation he'd made after arriving two years prior. "Well, at my very first parish council meeting, the hot issue was how we were going to get server's albs. We have certainly progressed to bigger issues."

After some chuckles, he resumed, "The issues have become bigger and broader all along. And they are good issues. We wouldn't have this issue if our community wasn't alive and well. We wouldn't be talking about a need for space and facilities and so forth if there was no need for them. I think we need to remind ourselves about that fact. You need to constantly remind me because it can be very overwhelming and draining." People who knew Lewinski were observing those effects during this meeting.

"It's not just a matter of getting a building up, and here's what it costs. We have people who have needs, we have people who are searching and who we need to serve, and we have a community that wants to pray, gather, and worship. What we want to generate is for the people, not just the bricks. We really need to be committed to that."

The Archdiocesan representative was there to advise and guide the parish. It was the attendee's responsibility to question and provide feedback. Lewinski's role was to keep everyone aligned with the objective. Many people—both volunteers and contracted—had already invested a lot of effort. But the future remained clouded. Like a good captain, he was guiding the ship toward its destination as best he could.

.The Archdiocesan representative suggested school alums are often another source of contributions. This led to a brief discussion about the cost of operating the school. A person familiar with those details revealed that they needed significantly more money beyond the tuition. It was usually raised through a series of small fundraisers. The exception was the annual Pork and Corn Roast. It contributed as much as $50,000. An attendee, realizing the school alone required a lot of financial support, commented, "I don't think people get this picture: that they are paying tuition, but we also must raise nearly twice that. They do not see it."

The discussion emphasized the need for more money. It highlighted the importance of communicating the school and parish's past, present, and future needs. The realization clarified the group's perception of the challenge they faced. Several awkward moments of silence occurred.

Lewinski moved toward closing the meeting. "The Planning Commission has talked about what we need to do next with some of these things. Are there any suggestions or advice at this point you want to pass along that we should talk about tomorrow regarding some of these things we have heard today?"

An even more awkward silence ensued. Lewinski sat motionless, in a thoughtful pose, awaiting a reply, but none came forth.

Fundraising for the project was falsely presumed to be a *new* challenge. It was a discouraging revelation that it was already difficult to keep the school operating each year.

Not getting a response, much less clarity, he probed differently. "Alright, let me take it one level deeper," he said animatedly with hands and arms moving, "in another area of the human psyche. From what you heard tonight, what are you feeling, what are you thinking, what's your temperature, what thoughts go through your mind and heart and gut? Nobody at this point has a clear indication of how we do this but in terms of a gut feeling about what lies ahead, where are you?" He leaned forward and smiled, inviting a comment.

A woman with school children responded. "I think communication is a major factor—so every time somebody turns around, there is information available. I'm a Pastoral Council member, and I've felt sometimes I'm not really in tune with what is going on. Obviously, we're working on that; but I can't imagine what the person in the pew only on Sundays is feeling or not understanding. For school families, we could tell the kids what is going on because a lot of it comes home through the kids." Lewinski made a note, as was his habit during meetings.

A mother with children in the school spoke up, saying, "There's got to be some way of choosing fundraisers and deciding how to raise the money. Obviously, we couldn't take the Pork and Corn Roast this year and put it all into the new church because the school would suffer. So how do we decide what fundraisers are conducted?"

Lewinski would seek to replace many small money-raising efforts with fewer bigger ones. One example was a future event in the narthex of the new church, sponsored by about three dozen people. It raised two-thirds as much as the annual Roast that required over 200 volunteers.

John Riggio, the Planning Commission chairperson, was present. He acknowledged the effort awaiting them. "More people are going to be needed for the Capital Campaign committee and the Communications Committee. It's going to be significant. That's something we need to focus on: how we're going to make this work."

One attendee proposed reviewing the parish survey they had recently conducted. "Most people said they see a need for change. What are these parishioners seeing?"

The Archdiocesan representative advised consulting with other parishes who had gone through a similar experience to gain a better understanding, including what obstacles to expect. She noted a parish in a western suburb of Chicago. "They're getting quite a loan from the diocese, despite the money they raised, about $1.5 million." Most people present couldn't yet put that in perspective. Lewinski had more insight than most, but he did not comment. The project cost at St. Mary's would be many times the amount just mentioned.

Lewinski advised, "First things first. We will announce the March 10 meeting in the bulletin this coming week. We have to work to get people there. It starts there. If we have a meeting that is a major, major, major beginning of a new phase of our life together, and we get only fifty people, we're losing right from the start. So we have to do whatever we can; we really need to make it clear to people that this is a key event."

He thanked everyone for their time and participation. The attendees gradually departed. Financing what they had was already a challenge. How realistic would it be to raise considerably more funds? The pastor, the Archdiocesan representative, and parish leaders, including the Finance Committee, didn't seem to know.

Where were the answers?

[1] *The Bell*, Vol. I, Issue 1, February 1998, p 3. Lewinski launched his first column with the statement "This first issue of *The Bell* marks a milestone in our move to the future." He also introduced "A Prayer for St. Mary" parish.

[2] Ibid., p. 5.

[3] Ibid., p 12.

A MASTERPLAN REVEALED

Winter 1998

Lewinski dedicated his March 8 column to an important last-minute reminder. It was about the upcoming Town Hall on the 10th to review the Masterplan. He reminded people it is a long-range, comprehensive vision for the future. It will continue to evolve. It is not a schematic design of buildings. The parish will build only what it can fund.

> I hope, above all, that we can approach the presentation of the Masterplan with a joyful and open spirit. We must look at this project as the work of faith. Why bother at all, except God is calling us to be a vibrant community of faith serving the needs of many people. We believe the Church can make a difference in people's lives and in our society. And so we need new facilities to gather the people, to train the leadership, to welcome the stranger, and comfort the broken. We need new facilities so we can educate and inform a new generation who can carry on the work St. Mary's began in 1864—a work our ancestors knew was the mission and ministry of Jesus.[1]

On March 10, 1998, they conducted a Town Hall in the school gym at 7:30 p.m. Terri Kennedy, Pastoral Council President, began by thanking everyone for attending. She stated this meeting would introduce the Masterplan jointly developed by Newman Architecture, the Planning Commission, and Lewinski.

She credited key parishioners who led in organizing, coordinating, and developing the plan they were reviewing. They were Ken Behm, Ann Steffenhagen, Dan Washburn, Jim Scavone, and Geril Zern. She noted that John Riggio, Chair of the Planning Commission, could not attend that evening. Referring to her notes on the podium, her next words invoked Lewinski's tone.

"This is a very exciting time for all of us at St. Mary's. It is important everyone is included in this project, from our oldest to our youngest members, from our newly registered parishioners to our founding family members. Seeing our Masterplan become a reality will not happen overnight; it will take many years to complete, but the support and cooperation of everyone will enable us to realize our dreams as a parish. Our work today will become a legacy for future generations of St. Mary at Fremont Center."

Kennedy announced that a printed copy of the Masterplan was available for each family present. She then introduced Lewinski to "lead us in prayer as we ask God to guide us, inspire us, and help us fulfill our mission as we embark on this effort. Thank you."

Lewinski, wearing his Roman collar, stepped up to the podium as everyone stood to pray. "Sisters and Brothers, St. Mary at Fremont Center is blessed with a rich history." Like many of the prayers he offered at the start of a meeting, this prayer was a personal request to God on behalf of himself and everyone present. He masterfully combined a historical narrative, a call to action, and deference to God's grace.

"Great and loving God, from generation to generation, you have blessed this community of faith, and by word and sacrament, you have held it together. We give you thanks for our ancestors who, with courage and determination, founded this parish and sacrificed so much of themselves so it might serve generations to come. We pray for this gathering of our parish community. May we respect the traditions you have entrusted to us. Dispel the fear and anxiety that might keep us from planning appropriately for the future. We pray that in keeping with the heritage and the Catholic tradition we have inherited that this community may remain a strong and vibrant temple of living stone.

"Here at this community, may the waters of baptism overwhelm the shame of sin. May your people live again through grace as your children. May we gather around your altar to celebrate the mysteries of our faith, to be fed at the table of Christ's word and body. Here may our prayers resound through heaven and earth as a plea for the world's salvation. Here may the poor find justice, peace, and freedom. And from here may the whole world, clothed in dignity as your children, enter with gladness your eternal city of peace where Christ reigns forever and ever, Amen."

The assembly took their seats as Lewinski began his comments.

"Well, let me add my words to Terri's welcome and thanks for being here today. It is a very important milestone in the life of our parish, a very wonderful and hopefully a very helpful meeting together. What we hope to do during our meeting tonight is to offer a picture of the larger Masterplan. As Terri mentioned, a Masterplan is something that, by definition, captures the dream of the parish. It is not something that is accomplished overnight but over many, many years. It is important that, when you want to plan well for the future, you look far down the road; otherwise, the decisions you make today may hinder what you want to do in the future.

"Our meeting today is only Part One of many, with information we want to pass on and share in the dialog we want to see take place. We will give you the opportunity after you have some time to think about the things you will see here tonight, to give some feedback, some input, and some recommendations. It is certainly my desire, and I know the desire of the entire Planning Commission, that we all—in whatever way we can—take ownership for this. With the diversity of gifts present in our community, by working together, we can produce something not only for this generation but for generations to come. Because we will present a great deal of information, we're going to save the questions for the end of the program.

"To get us started, we have with us tonight Mary Hall, who is our Vicariate[2] administrative consultant, working closely with Bishop Kicanas here in Vicariate One. They have been of great help to us already in our planning and other areas of Vicariate life as well. I have asked Mary to say a few words, so let's welcome her."

Mary Hall was an administrative consultant for the Vicariate office to which St. Mary's belonged. She brought valuable knowledge and experience from the business side of parish operations. Hall stated that a little over two years ago, she was part of a meeting with Lewinski and diocesan officials. They recognized St. Mary's needed to look at its long-term needs. In large organizations, this is analogous to Strategic Planning. Before Lewinski's arrival, long-range planning like this was not on the parish's radar.

She shared that St. Mary's and the Archdiocese would work together, and concluded, "I am thrilled to be here. I am ecstatic to see so many faces I have come to know. I almost feel as if I am a parishioner.[3] How lucky you *are* to have Father Ron as a leader and a visionary to take you into the future. So thank you for inviting me today."

Lewinski returned to the podium during the subsequent applause. He acknowledged another guest, Jane O'Brien from the Archdiocese. "It is the Development Office," he stated, "that will help us figure out how to pay for all of this."

He then introduced committee members Dan Washburn and Geril Zern. They started with a quiz designed to highlight some relevant statistics. Questions and answers included:

Question: What are the current seating capacities of the church and the school gym (used for weekend services)? Answer: 220 and 445, respectively.

Question: What is the total enrollment in the parish's REP for 1997-1998? Answer: 487 (216 in school, 271 not enrolled at the school).

Question: In the recent parish survey, what percentage of parishioners felt there was a need to expand facilities? Answer: 89%.

Question: Based on a study at Fremont School,[4] what is the number of homes proposed to be built in the next six years? Answer: 600 to 900.

Question: What was the percentage increase in baptisms at St. Mary's from 1996 to 1997? Answer: 57%.

Question: How many people have so far contributed to the development of the Masterplan? Answer: over fifty.

They clearly intended these and other questions to remind attendees about two things. First, what they should already know. Second, what they should talk about with their fellow parishioners.

People were being reminded the need to expand was not a subjective opinion from the pastor and a small flock of followers. Reasons for change existed even before Lewinski had arrived. It was time to address them.

Washburn and Zern continued. Zern stated the Planning Commission's core team began during the prior year with six individuals. It now included more than twenty, with another two dozen helping when needed.

Following that, Washburn observed the Commission had grown to five committees. He summarized each committee's purpose.

Zern and Washburn then elaborated on many milestones that had already occurred and spoke to the characteristics of a Masterplan. Their presentation served a dual purpose. First, it communicated to listeners that "this whole thing" wasn't just "Lewinski's idea." Rather, it was based on objective data recognized and supported by the Archdiocese and a high percentage of worshippers. Second, it showed fellow parishioners were engaged and committed to the effort.

Washburn stated their plan included "a theological vision driving the entire project. This separates a Masterplan here at St. Mary's from a business Masterplan. A theological vision guides all decisions." He concluded, "To address this, I'll ask Father Ron to come up." Lewinski then returned to the podium.

"Thanks, Dan and Geril." It was Lewinski's turn to comment from his perspective. "As mentioned, the spiritual vision, or theological vision, is something that drives the whole project. It's not some kind of 'additional perspective,' but really, it is the heartbeat of the whole process. A theological vision, spiritual vision, gives shape and form and meaning—a purpose, really—to a Masterplan.

"We are, after all, not a corporation seeking to increase our profit. Rather, we are a people of faith trying to respond to, and fulfill, Christ's invitation to us to be his disciples. And so our Masterplan then rests on the foundation of our spiritual vision. It 'embodies' our spiritual vision. There are several aspects of spiritual vision I would like to address.

"The first one is to say we believe our planning for the future is an act of faith, a response to God's movement among us. So our Masterplan is not just a consequence of demographic studies. It is a response made in faith to what we believe God is calling us to be and to do. Think about what happened to Mary. The angel Gabriel came to her and said Mary, you are to be the mother of the Lord. Her first reaction was, 'I don't know what you're talking about. How can this be?'. She doesn't understand. Scripture says she was confused. And yet she could say, with faith, thy will be done: I will be part of this plan of God's. It seems to me, as we approach this major project, it may serve us well to reflect upon the very name of who we are: St. Mary of the Annunciation.

"The second pillar of the spiritual vision is we believe we are the Church, a community of faith, rooted in baptism, called to be the Living Stone that forms Christ's Body. Our first interest is not putting up brick-and-mortar but rather to form ourselves truly as the Church that God wants us to be. We *are* the Church, and what we hope to do is build a *house* for the Church. Every time we register a new parishioner, we ask them what they see in us as a parish. They say there is something special here about that sense of community.

"Being a community doesn't mean we are all 'friends' with each other. It does mean we share something together that is very profound: our common baptism, our respect for life, our belief in justice and peace and human dignity, our rootedness in the gospel and in the sacramental life of the Church, our belief in the Father and the Son and the Holy Spirit. Those are the values that make us who we are.

"A third dimension to the spiritual vision is we believe Liturgy is the heart of our Christian community. What gives us shape as a community? Where do we find our identity and our solidarity? What really links us together? By our common prayer and our rituals, we are *formed* as a Catholic people. The liturgical and the sacramental experiences bond us together and lead us even deeper into the heart of God. I don't have to convince you because, on the parish survey, we asked what it was about parish life you value the most. By far, the top answer was the liturgy.

"A question remains for us as we move through the Masterplan. How can we build facilities that allow for beautiful, dignified, prayerful, communal celebration of liturgy? What would it be like to build a space that fits the idea of liturgical renewal in the documents of Vatican II?

"The fourth dimension of the spiritual vision is we have to remind ourselves we believe that we have a mission to carry on the ministry of Jesus and transform the world into the Kingdom of God. This time of planning and development is a wonderful season of grace. It is time for us to ask ourselves what it means to be parish anyway. Why are we here? What is parish all about?

"These things are important so that every one of us can present that spiritual vision to those who are not here tonight. It is your responsibility to pass on that word and help others to see, as you see, the bigger picture we're getting a better sense of day by day.

"What I'd like to do at this point is to ask Ken Behm and Chuck Newman to come forward and give us a description of how all this fits together with a Masterplan."

Behm stepped up to the podium and noted that serving on the Planning Commission was an honor. He briefly reviewed some slides of the existing grounds. They showed proposed locations of major new pieces of the plan, such as the church, school, and rectory. The design architect had prepared a variety of site plans showing how the land could be used differently. Behm then invited Chuck Newman to the podium.

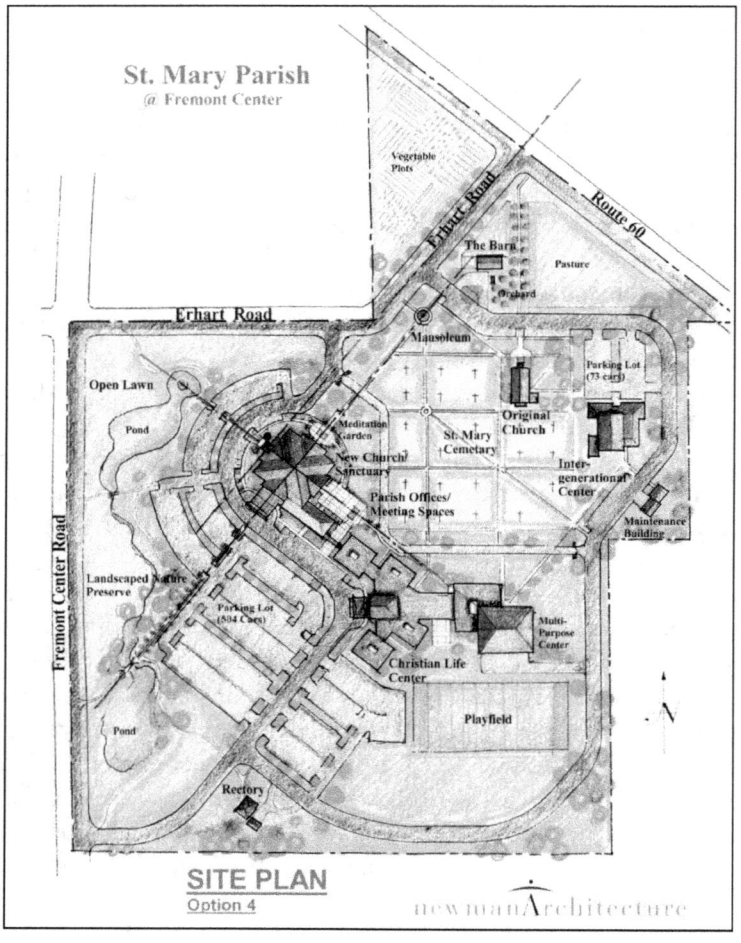

IMAGE #5

EARLY SITE PLAN BY NEWMAN ARCHITECTURE

NEWMAN ARCHITECTURE (FORMERLY FIELDING & ASSOCIATES)
PRESENTED A FEW OPTIONS FOR SITE PLANS.

Chuck Newman of Newman Architecture made several comments, essentially re-stating items from the parish's wish list. He briefly reviewed spaces within the buildings for office, meeting rooms, choir, REP, school facilities, and the rectory. He opined that the Intergenerational Center's importance might increase as a crop of baby boomers like himself were approaching retirement.

Newman stated that he and his firm had already worked with several talented parishioners. "It is wonderful to have expertise readily available whenever you need it." He observed St. Mary's had a rare opportunity during these times of shrinking real estate.

"The reality is that as property develops, there will be less and less opportunity to address the vision that your parish has today. You have that opportunity, and what's wonderful is you have a vision. Now, we're going to show you several Site Plans we have put together over the last several months. We'll look at certain aspects of the site and where we think the parish wants to go in the future."

Newman took time to review the features of five different site options on display. He commented on other elements such as roadway and intersection modifications, the relationship between structures and their parking allotments, a new rectory, a Christian Life Center with a school, an Intergenerational Center, a community vegetable and flower garden, a meditation area, and so on.

In particular, he noted the buildings shown in the plans were viable locations, not what they would actually *look* like. The details would come later. He ended by noting they expected these options to change. Meanwhile, they provide "a vision of where the parish wants to go in the future."

Newman concluded, "You can ask, How are we going to get there? I think Father Ron wants to talk a little about that."

Lewinski came back to the podium. "As you can see, this is a complex picture. The vision is very broad. What we need to do is look at it in phases. I do not see these things in stone at this point. But as the commission continues to work on these things and listen to what people are saying. Also, *observing* what is going around the parish in terms of *immediate* needs, it seems we need to break things down into phases.

"We would propose that Phase 1 is a new church, which would include the offices, meeting spaces, and rectory. Of course, the infrastructure for the site is part of that entire piece. Phase 2 would be the Christian Life Center, including the classrooms and other purposes. Phase 3 is the Intergenerational Center, which has to be the last phase because we have no other place for the children until the new school is ready. So it follows a natural progression.

"What determines all of this is not just our ideas but the funding that would support the plan. Ultimately, we will do what we can *do*. We cannot undertake something we're not able to support financially. Depending on how the capital campaign goes, we will see what exactly we *can* do. But these are the phases, at least, that we are proposing.

"What we are asking of you in this open house is that you begin to think about this. We'll give you a handout. It will serve as a refresher of some things we talked about tonight, as well as an overall picture of the site plan. You'll be able to offer your recommendations and suggestions, comments and questions that might raise other issues."

Lewinski then asked Ann Steffenhagen, cochair with Dan Washburn of the Capital Campaign committee, to speak. Anne took the podium and began reading from the notes she had prepared. She admitted the project seems like a monumental task and will take years. She shared that parishioners had "already bought into the dream." So far, $1.1 million had been received in contributions. She thanked the initial contributors for their generosity and proclaimed the building fund "is now open for contributions." The audience chuckled at this direct form of solicitation.

Steffenhagen noted the plans need Archdiocesan approval. She mentioned this to assure everyone of oversight from the larger organization. Also, to negate rumors by some people that this was the pastor's "pet program." She stated the Archdiocese's requirements. They would need pledges for 90% of the total cost of the project prior to beginning construction. That was $9 million for this effort. "We must show the Archdiocese we will do our part," she affirmed.

In addition, the parish needed to maintain its regular weekly contributions. Thus, they would need to find new ways to raise funds. Methods such as donations, stocks, estates, wills, grants, major benefactors, matching gifts, and other financial strategies. She concluded, "We are grateful for our past, and we are committed to our future."

During the subsequent applause, Lewinski introduced Jane O'Brien from the Archdiocesan Development Office. During her brief comments, she stated it was her job to work "on projects exactly like this." She concluded, "We are very optimistic and will help you find reasonable and realistic goals for yourselves."

Next on the program was Jim Scavone, Director of Music and Liturgy. He had been one of the first people Lewinski hired for the new staff. His role was to build and support the music-related aspects of Liturgy and Worship. He chaired the Education and Spirituality Committee. Scavone would lead the effort to educate and inform parishioners about things to consider while conceptualizing and planning the new church. He provided some context for his committee's purpose.

"Over the next few weeks, the Planning Commission will begin interviewing and selecting design architects. They will select a liturgical consultant who has several functions during the building process. He or she helps the community articulate their liturgical and spiritual needs to the architect. They facilitate an education process that not only educates the parish about liturgical needs but helps initiate a journey of spiritual formation. In other words, how do we attain that spiritual vision Father Ron spoke about? The consultant also advises the committee on the most effective design for liturgical objects, such as the altar and the ambo, and it helps critique, from a liturgical standpoint, the architectural design.

"The education process is probably the most important step. It is a very crucial step in answering what comes next. Whatever we build must reflect who we are as a community. What is our shared tradition? What are our beliefs about social justice, marriage and family, human dignity, and respect for life? What is an appropriate worship environment? The formation program helps us to answer these questions and brings us to a common belief about ourselves, our community, and our facilities.

"One thing that is really important to point out is the process brings us to consensus. Through formation, we come to certain beliefs together as a community. We determine what those beliefs mean for us as a parish and how they affect the facilities to be built.

"We are asking each of you to take home the Masterplan. Study it. Pray over it. Then come to one of the open houses and give us your reaction. What do you like about the plan, what do you dislike, and how would you improve the plan? We also have tonight an 'Introduction to the Masterplan.' It is a fourteen-page guide for the entire process.

"Further pieces of education for the parish include the Planning and Development newsletter, *The Bell*—hopefully, you have all received the first edition; Town Hall meetings such as this one; bulletin articles; and pastoral visits are all vehicles for communication. Both the staff here at St. Mary's and the Planning Commission recognize *their* responsibility to communicate with the parish.[5]

"However, we also recognize *your* responsibility to keep informed, to read the newsletter and the bulletins, to attend meetings and pastoral visits, and to ask questions as necessary. We really feel the communication process has to be a two-way street.

"The formation process is an educational program for those who wish to serve on the Planning Commission. While any section in this level is open to the entire parish, those who want to serve in some capacity on the Commission must participate in these sessions. We all need to work from a common framework.

"How do you get involved? There are several ways. First, most importantly, we ask each of you, in your individual prayers and in our prayers as a community, to pray over this whole process we are entering together. Second, we need to educate those who are not here tonight. Take home the Masterplan. Study it. Talk to someone you know who could not attend tonight's meeting. Encourage your friends and neighbors to read the newsletter and the bulletin. Also, let us know what kind of information would be helpful so we can share that with you. It is important that each parishioner recognizes their responsibility for participating in this endeavor. Thank you."

Scavone's comments received appreciating applause. He had nicely described what to expect regarding his committee's work, the importance of two-way communication, and everyone's participation.

Lewinski returned to the podium, sensing the mood. He expressed what most people presumably felt by this point in the meeting.

"I realize that, in some ways, this is a lot of information all at one time. It is why we are holding those open house sessions this coming Sunday and another one in April. It will give you a little time to think about and digest some of this material. There may be some questions you want to ask now to help you prepare."

He then asked Sr. Gael Gensler, Pastoral Associate, to moderate a question-and-answer (Q&A) period. She, with help from parishioners, was doing work essential for the growth and health of the parish. This included the formation and support of various ministries. Her contribution to St. Mary's expansion was crucial and would have a lasting impact.

Gensler positioned herself front and center and asked for questions. One question was about the timeline for the project. Lewinski responded, "The timeline depends a great deal upon the capital campaign. We cannot get bulldozers out here until we have a real financial commitment. So the first milestone is that this coming Autumn, we will have a capital campaign up and running. In the meantime, we're doing some additional work, and we will try to reach some major donors. And then reach out to some additional parishioners. The response will determine what happens next. That's all I can really say at the moment."

Someone asked about the expected cost. Lewinski declared a faith community near Lake Michigan had recently completed a $5.3 million church. He added if a pastoral center—meeting rooms and offices—were included, the total would probably approach $8 million. But he allowed those to be ballpark estimates. They could make a more accurate estimate after further planning, dependent upon the capital campaign results.

Another inevitable question was about water and sewer service. St. Mary's was a mile or two outside supply areas from the surrounding communities. Behm responded that, given the growth in the area, they hoped utilities would be available by the time construction began.

Lewinski commented that he and Bishop Kicanas had visited the mayors of the local townships. They sought to learn more about governmental plans, but sometimes they already knew more than a mayor did. His point was that St. Mary's planning was not being done in isolation. It included communication with local municipalities.

Gensler concluded with her own comment. "This has been a wonderful evening—very enlightening with a lot of information. What it confirms for me is what a privilege and what a responsibility we have when we say 'we believe' when we recite the Creed. Our faith has to be lived, and we don't live it for ourselves. We always live it for the next generation. So it is indeed a privilege to be with you at this time in history. God brings us together for a reason. I want to thank the Planning Commission for their hard work that has brought us to this evening. It really comes down to all of us together: *are we willing to be the parish that built a future?*"

The honesty and feeling in her statements were apparent. They served to emphasize the significance of what this faith family was called to do.

Lewinski made his closing remarks. "Again, thank you for coming out on such a chilly night. I realize it's late. We'll conclude with a brief prayer, but I hope that above all, you can catch the spirit of this, you can get excited about it, you can begin to own some of this, and also you will pass on the word to others who are not here to help them understand what we are trying to do. It is a *grand* plan.

"But again, going back to the spiritual vision, why is it that this group of people is gathered here at St. Mary Parish at this time? Why is it God has called us to be here? If God didn't think we could handle this task, we probably wouldn't be here. Given the witness and wonderful faith and encouragement of the folks who came before us, all we can do is try our best. We will do what we can with God's help. Let's conclude with a prayer by standing and singing the last three verses."

The audience stood to sing Marty Haugen's "All Are Welcome." The 1994 composition quickly became the theme song of the project.

Lewinski ended with a final blessing, "May God continue to bless us. Go in peace."

Many attendees departed with more questions than when they'd arrived. When would the plans show what the buildings would look like? Who would choose their appearance, and how? And all these committees! Committee decisions can be dubious, we know. Perhaps most important, how would the parish raise the $9 million needed to begin construction? How long would that take? Anyone watching Sunday collection amounts posted in the weekly bulletin might calculate it at over fifteen years.

Uncertainty threatened to replace the initial curiosity and excitement of those who initially favored the project. Concern and anxiety were creeping in. One can have great faith in a vision. Several people can want something to happen. Many can pray hard for it. But isn't there an absolute limit to what is possible?

Even though the first issue of The Bell had been produced in February, they printed a special edition in March solely to report on this Town Hall.

The Pastoral Council, Lewinski, and Gensler had been working with parish leadership on a parish Mission Statement. On March 15th, the bulletin announced it. It was based on input from the previous summer's survey and comments gathered at weekend Masses:

> The Mission of St. Mary, Fremont Center, is to foster and develop a vibrant, hospitable faith community rooted in the Eucharist and the liturgical life of the Catholic Church. Through our active participation in the priesthood of the faithful, we are committed to responsible, compassionate living of the Gospel in our homes, work, and society.[6]

Anyone familiar with the work of Vatican II will recognize its tone reflected in this statement. Comparing the celebrant's and congregation's involvement in the liturgy provides insight into the glaring differences before and after the Council related to "active participation." Before Vatican II, thirty specific actions (e.g., procession, reading scripture, etc.) occurred from entrance to exit. They were all executed only by the priest (and/or altar servers). Following the Council, the priest is solely responsible for just three actions.[7]

Lewinski would probably respond to those who would prefer the Latin rituals of pre-Vatican II days, "If you don't *understand* [the language and] what is happening, how can you faithfully *participate*? And if you can't participate, why are you here?" Given his respect for the sacrament of Baptism, he knew that—as Vatican II promoted—it was the right *and* duty of the laity, the priesthood of the faithful, to actively participate.

The phrase "priesthood of the faithful" comes from Vatican II. "Let it be noted that *Lumen Gentium* is the first conciliar document in the Church's history to speak of the common priesthood of the faithful."[8] When Lewinski graduated from high school, Pope Paul VI spoke at a Mass in St. Peter's, honoring work by the laity. He acknowledged it would be through the common effort of all the baptized that the Council would bear fruit. The faithful, however, need reminders that their call to action does not end at the same time as Sunday service.

The new PR committee's work appeared as an article in the Chicago Tribune on March 24th. It featured photos, including one of the ever-present cows and the old church.

> The cows across the street from St. Mary - Fremont Center are a dead giveaway that this is not your typical Chicago Roman Catholic Archdiocesan parish.... Rapid growth and development in communities the parish serves has boosted church attendance well beyond capacity. Meanwhile, nearby farm pastures are being swallowed up by new housing.... Church officials hope that with the 30 acres the parish owns and more acres they hope to buy, a campus can be built that preserves the rural ambiance... One prized possession in Lewinski's office is a black-and-white photograph of a smiling [Cardinal] Bernardin wearing a cowboy hat and holding a porcelain pig during a visit to one of the parish's annual Pork and Corn Roast in the late 1980s.... "One of the values in this community is a love for the land," he said. "The great challenge we have is to try to maintain this beauty while at the same time welcoming new families. We believe we can do that."[9]

Lewinski reported to the Pastoral Council the following May that the article had led to donations from outside the parish.[10]

They scheduled a "Calendar Meeting" for May 4th. Lewinski expected all ministry leaders to attend. He was still wrestling with helping people understand a different concept: in addition to the pastor, parishioners share responsibility for a parish. This was difficult to grasp for those who could remember pre-Vatican (and even pre-Lewinski) days. Back then, it was the pastor who controlled parish authority and responsibility. Remnants of such restricted thinking survived in ministries where the ministry lead did most of the work rather than delegating it.

In organizational development terms, the Calendar Meeting (aka Leadership Meeting) sought to improve vision, mission, leadership, and communication. The talking points were:[11]

1. Focus on parish goals.
2. Understand the scope of planning and development for the future.
3. Identify each organization and ministry's goals.
4. Establish a parish meeting calendar and secure meeting spaces.
5. Strengthen bonds between groups.
6. Embed the parish mission statement into the ministries by asking, 'How do groups reflect parish mission?'

There was a recommendation that a short prayer service be part of each meeting.

Helping the laity become leaders was an ongoing challenge for everyone.

---

[1] Sunday bulletin, March 8, 1998, p. 4.

[2] A vicariate is a "territorial jurisdiction" under the responsibility of an episcopal vicar (hence *vicar*iate). The Chicago Archdiocese is comprised of six vicariates. At the time, Francis Cardinal George was the vicar of the combined vicariates comprising the Chicago Diocese.

[3] Hall and her husband belonged to a nearby parish, St. Paul, in Gurnee, IL.

[4] Fremont School is located along Fremont Center Road about one mile south of St. Mary's parish. It is halfway between the current campus and the site where the parish was originally established in 1864.

[5] A 12-page "Special Edition" of The Bell was produced for this meeting. Half the issue contained detailed allocations of square footage for the facility's spaces.

[6] Sunday bulletin, March 16, 1998, p. 6.

[7] McNaspy, pp. 91-93.

[8] Guarino, p. 76.

[9] Chicago Tribune, March 24, 1998, Section 2, pp. 1-2.

[10] Pastoral Council minutes, April 13, 1998.

[11] Ibid.

GETTING EDUCATED

Spring 1998

Lewinski had a particular custom when presiding at Mass. There is a point called "The Offertory." Visually, it is an action by the celebrant whereby the bread and wine are offered "in sacrifice" to God. Liturgically, it is the congregation, as faithful participants, together with the priest, who make the offering "from the many gifts You have given us."

During Mass, all celebrants recite the prayers and perform the actions as part of the liturgy. Lewinski did something more. It was not observable but was extremely meaningful and reflected the Offertory's intent. As he waited in front of the altar to receive the presentation of gifts—the bread and wine—brought forth by parishioners (sometimes children), he discreetly observed the people in the pews.

He had gotten to know many of them. It was one reason he treasured the neighborhood pastoral visits at parishioner's homes. He recognized who was present at Mass. He knew people's life situations. He included the people and their challenges in his Offertory prayers at the altar. It was not obvious, but for Lewinski, it was part of the essence.

The first point in his bulletin column echoed this silent practice.

> In the last two weeks since we presented our Masterplan for the future of St. Mary, I have thought a lot about our 1,100 households that make up the St. Mary parish family. I reviewed in my mind the people who attended the Town Hall meeting, those who stopped by after the Masses last weekend to offer their comments and suggestions, and the many faces I see from my unique vantage place behind the altar and pulpit. I took the time to go through the pictorial directory as well and then the full roster of registered parishioners. A couple of observations:
>
> 1. I was filled with the spirit of Thanksgiving for so many good people who I know love the parish and do all they can for the community. I felt a sense of awe for so many who I know have serious issues to contend with at home. Cancer. Unemployment. Financial crises. Divorce. A troubled child. I am inspired by many of these parishioners because of how they carry on with deep faith.
>
> 2. My review of the parish family tells me that we are not a homogeneous group. Although we don't have noticeable language or racial distinctions, our diversity is more subtle or hidden. We are poor, and we are affluent. We are young, and we are retired. We are liberal and conservative. We have good memories of Catholicism, and we have poor or minimal memories to count

on. This diversity is not a deficit but an asset for the parish. It means if we work together, we can come up with a lot more creative ideas and approaches to common problems.

3. As I reviewed all the names and faces of St. Mary, I felt overwhelmed. First of all, I felt the desire to want to know every one of the names we claim as part of our parish family. There isn't a Sunday that goes by when I don't find myself saying, "I wish I could get to know that person a little better." I am aware that a large number of the men and women in our parish family portrait are not well known, not really involved, and seldom heard from. Some of these good people may have moved here from another parish where they were very involved. Now at St. Mary's, they aren't sure how they can fit in or whether they are ready to jump in. There are some who I think are just shy and are afraid to step forward. And there are some who never really had the chance in their growing-up experience to get a closer look and feel for the Church, and they now live on the fringe.

As I thought about all of this, I began to think that this new beginning in the life of St. Mary's is a wonderful opportunity for many of you to move closer into the circle. This is a doorway of opportunity. We are all at the same point—a fresh start. As we open doors for greater participation in making plans for the future, I hope you can encourage a fellow parishioner to walk through that door. We can all begin by committing ourselves to reading the literature that will be made available and attending the education sessions. The most important thing is to welcome this new period of parish life with an open and positive attitude. Pray for this project. Invest yourself in this endeavor. See it as a way of being your legacy for the future.

We are a great parish. We are a unique community with an unusual challenge that lies before us. Let us walk together and pray together that God will accomplish the good work he has begun in us.[1]

Lewinski's mention of going through the pictorial directory is an example to others. We commonly use the directory as a way to identify other parishioners. It can be a vehicle for parish leadership as well. It is a form of MBWA (management by walking around). "One large membership church staff reviews together several pages from their church pictorial directory every week at the staff meeting to see if there is anyone that no one of them knows. If that is the case, they decide together who will learn more about those persons and how."[2]

He shared a subtle reminder of the faith community's steady growth. They now had 1,100 households.

A dialogue began about acquiring an additional 12.7 acres of land south of the existing campus. It would provide space for a new school—Phase II of the Masterplan. This parcel and the larger one already acquired were sizable. Still, the County required about 30% to be reserved as "open land."

The Masterplan exhibits were available after Mass on the weekends of March 15th and April 19th. They were "new" to those who didn't attend the Town Halls (or chose not to). This also gave people who had seen the illustrations another opportunity to revisit them and ask questions.

The second edition of *The Bell* was mailed on May 11th. It was sixteen pages packed with information. It headlined an article about Newman Architecture presenting the Masterplan at the Town Hall on March 10th. The issue spoke about a "Spiritual Vision"; identified pending milestones, reviewed a presentation about Estate Planning from an Archdiocesan representative, and included the regular subcommittee updates.[3]

In his "Around the Table" column, Lewinski wrote about the Masterplan's importance:

> Once people got to see the color drawings of the site plan, there was a good deal of excitement. With a little imagination, people could see the possibilities for the future.
> The negative comments I heard had more to do with people's vision or understanding of what the Church or parish is all about. If one's idea of a parish is something like a drive-through you can use on Sunday for Mass, go home and leave it at that, then, yes, this is an ambitious Masterplan that makes little sense.
> But if you broaden your understanding of parish to mean a place where you can find some hope and meaning for life through liturgy, Christian formation, and education and service to others, then the picture becomes a little clearer. If you begin to see the parish as a community where you can be supported in living gospel values, raise a Christian family, and find counsel or challenge when you need it, then you can understand why we need more than an altar and a few pews.
> If you look around the area and see the growth in the population, you will understand why we cannot just build for ourselves today.
> A parish is a hub where our Christian lives merge. A parish is a mission center that prepares new disciples for service in the world. A parish is a lighthouse that serves the wider community, calling people to a higher set of values. What we are planning for it is indeed an awesome challenge. But how could we settle for less?[4]

Next to Lewinski's column, a quotation from Archbishop Oscar Romero stated, "We are prophets of a future that is not our own."

The issue featured a 'guest editorial' by Fr. Britto Berchmans. During the previous Summer, he had conducted a six-week series of talks about Adult Spirituality. They were well-attended. Lewinski had invited Berchmans who was teaching about Communications at the Salesian Pontifical University, under Vatican jurisdiction. He was from India but earned degrees elsewhere.[5] Berchmans' presentations and humor were welcomed. Telling three jokes during his sermons was a trademark. His presence was another important element of the education and socialization at St. Mary's. His article had simple but effective suggestions for the parishioners: smile; meet people; share your time; share your talent; pray.

This issue of *The Bell* announced the parish's new website. St. Mary's was among Archdiocesan parishes pioneering the rapidly growing media. Yet, there was still a digital divide between those who did and didn't have internet access. The issue also revealed negotiations were in progress for an additional 12.7 acres of land.

In his May 3rd column, Lewinski shared a question often asked by converts: "Why do Catholics worship Mary?" He explained that Catholics **do not** worship Mary but honor her as the Mother of God and of the Church. Even on Marian feast days, he observed that Catholics remember Mary but always address their prayers to God. He also noted that the parish name was adopted just ten years after the proclamation of the dogma of the Immaculate Conception. He wrote, "Why our ancestors chose Mary as our patroness under the title of the Annunciation may never be fully known."[6]

The term "Annunciation" confused some because the parish's name, as they knew it, was "St. Mary - Fremont Center." Some people recognized that Lewinski knew something they didn't. He'd share it in due time.

Meanwhile, he and others were trying to resolve a more mundane mystery. Why did the church's heating system keep adding soot to the walls? It would need repair before the painting could begin.

On the morning of May 17th, they held a Ministry Fair. Parishioners could become better acquainted with the various activities. Lewinski's arrival at the parish became an enabler for the formation of ministries. His Pastoral Associate, Sr. Gael, was a primary catalyst. The number had grown to where they needed to erect a 30' x 60' canopy to provide shade for all the tables. (It was also used for a Confirmation service the previous day.) Attendees filled out over seventy-five cards to request more information or to express their interest in joining a ministry. The event was testimony to Lewinski's desire to develop a vibrant faith community, and it emphasized why the parish needed more space to conduct activities. Organizers noticed visitors taking information with them to share at their own parishes.[7]

One evening, Lewinski joined a Capital Campaign meeting in the church basement. Besides cochairs Ann Steffenhagen and Dan Washburn, a consultant from CCS Fundraising, and the Archdiocesan consultant were there.[8] The attendees, mostly couples, had volunteered to solicit pledges from their fellow parishioners.

Lewinski began with, "This meeting is significant because it's the turning point that marks in some ways the end of Phase One and the beginning of Phase Two.

"Phase One was doing some of the initial research, getting some data together, and preparing a Masterplan. It doesn't mean that there will not be changes, but we have something to work with.

"And now, this second stage is a very important one. That, of course, is how do we fund the dream. Before I talk about it, and what is in your folders, I would like to ask Dan Washburn and Ann Steffenhagen to say something. Dan and Ann served on the Planning Commission's core committee. I'd like to have them share briefly how we got here, what has brought us to this point."

Washburn valued the project due to attendee involvement in ministry or parish work mentioned during introductions. The facilities did not support the current efforts, much less future growth. He ended by stating, "We can do it. We *will* do it."

Steffenhagen then spoke. "Well, I have been here a long time. About two years ago, we had a leadership meeting for the parish with the Vicariate, and we were discussing our goals. I remember we were sitting in a semicircle down here, and the bishop talked about some families being here many, many years. He asked, 'Would anybody like to make a comment?' I timidly put up my hand and said, 'I guess I'm one of those families.' As I talked, tears came to my eyes because I hated to see change. I love this little church. But I knew it had to happen.

"I was asked a few months later to be on this Planning Commission, which I accepted. Seeing Father's enthusiasm, the other parishioner's enthusiasm, and meeting all the new families has been a privilege. It has been a wonderful experience. I am very grateful to be on this Capital Campaign committee. I know we have a big job, but with all the enthusiasm and help from everybody in this parish, we are going to accomplish it. Because we need to make space for all our new members, and we have to carry on and help the old parishioners too. Thank you."

Lewinski resumed. "Inside your folders is a color reproduction. It's fresh off the press. This is already a revision of the renderings people have seen based on the comments we received from people at the open houses. Let me say a bit about the second phase. It has been an exciting process to try to select an architect. Chuck Newman has been our Masterplan architect, and he is also a candidate for the design phase. It is such an important project, such a unique project: this is not something just any parish gets to do. We have an incredible opportunity here to create something fresh. We want to do our best.

"So we began by selecting twenty-five architectural firms. We sent a request for information (RFI), asking for their portfolio and their interest in our project. We reduced those twenty-five to fourteen. To those, we sent out a request for a proposal (RFP). They were to tell us how they would approach this project, who in their firm they would assign to this project, give us some sense of their fee structures, and all those kinds of things. Obviously, throughout this whole process, we're looking at other things they've done too. Now we have reduced those fourteen to seven. In the first week of June, our architectural selection committee is going to interview those seven architectural firms."

On May 20th, they conducted a well-attended informational session. It would help parishioners understand church design elements and their theological basis. Several people discovered what they thought they knew wasn't quite accurate. It helped attendees recognize what they had learned most of their lives wasn't "the way it's always been." Churches worldwide are different in unexpected ways. Most attendees probably arrived expecting to have their perceptions enhanced or validated. Perhaps many left even more uncertain about their new church.

Their journey was progressing. The road ahead hid a couple of unexpected turns.

---

[1] Sunday bulletin, March 22, 1998, pp. 3-4.
A key phrase in these comments is "if we work together." Some people, of course, hadn't accepted Lewinski's vision and never would. Lewinski realized this, but still experienced grief and took the rejection personally.

[2] Weems, p. 53.

[3] Soon Bishop Goedert wrote Lewinski a letter praising the newsletter. "I read both issues of *The Bell* from cover to cover. They are very well done and extremely informative. Please keep me on your mailing list." Lewinski shared the letter with his Communications team, writing "Not a bad compliment from the #2 man in the Archdiocese." —Letter from Goedert to Lewinski, August 3, 1999. The "#1 man," of course, was Cardinal George, who had already autographed a copy of the first issue of *The Bell*. Each issue displayed a banner on the first page that summarized work completed, work in progress, and work pending in the near future. Typically the back page listed accomplishments, thus providing continuity for the reader.

[4] *The Bell*, Vol I, Issue 2, May 1998, p. 3.

[5] Berchmans has a PhD in Communications from the University of Illinois, as well as degrees from other institutions: Associate Degree in Western Philosophy; Bachelor's and Master's in Physics; Bachelor's in Theology; Master's in Journalism; and a Master's in Systematic Theology.

[6] Sunday bulletin, May 3, 1998, p. 3.

[7] Pastoral Council minutes, June 6, 1998.

[8] In Spring of the prior year the parish had thought parishioners with finance experience could manage fundraising. Gradually, they realized more specialized help was needed and they contracted with CCS.

THE POWERHOUSE TEAM

July 1998

A notable change in direction occurred in the summer of 1998 when the parish selected an architectural firm.

Lewinski wanted to ensure an inclusive approach to choosing an architect. Architectural concepts were not entirely unfamiliar to him. He had seen various building styles while traveling across the U.S. and worldwide. But his vocational expertise was the Liturgy. He knew the rites and how they should be performed. To create an appropriate design, he needed an architect's insights into how his knowledge could be married to theirs. It should include both the space's functionality and its appearance. Artwork that would enhance, but not distract or overpower, a participant's experience during worship and other functions warranted consideration.

Once again, this small parish in the countryside of northeastern Illinois had someone with valuable skills and experience. He was Andrew Pini, Vice President for Corporate Real Estate and Development at Health Care Service Corporation. They were the parent company of Blue Cross Blue Shield. At Lewinski's invitation, he agreed to help.

They began by identifying candidate firms and sending a "Request For Information" (RFI). They sent twenty-five RFIs by April. After reviewing the responses, they disqualified eleven of them. The remaining fourteen received a "Request for Proposal" (RFP).

Pini introduced a selection process to the Architectural Review Team. This committee included Lewinski and parishioners with various professional backgrounds. Besides specific criteria, the process used a rating method for the final selection of an architectural firm.

They sent the remaining candidates a "Request For Interview" letter, requesting a response by May 11th.[1] The replies were reviewed. Then, the team scheduled the firms for hour-long interviews during the first week of June. The selection team planned an agenda for the meetings. It included three specific areas.

During the first, the candidate firm would introduce its leaders and primary consultants and their qualifications. They would then explain their firm's impression of the project: the vision, the mission and aspects such as creativity, listening/understanding/communicating, flexibility, cost management, and qualitative and innovative engineering. They would identify their "knowledge and familiarity with the site and local codes, local influence and conditions, access to building officials and those regulating agencies needed for our development."[2]

During the interview's second phase, the candidate firm would explain their overall design approach to the project vision.

The third and final phase would be for Questions and Answers.

They allotted about an hour for the interview process. The team developed an "Interview Score Card" for use by each member. It specified ratings of 1 through 10, where ten meant "superior." They would also note comments on their scorecard. They identified the following areas for scoring and commenting on the candidate firm:

- Displays understanding of the project (vision, scope, client demands as previously noted)
- Displays creativity regarding design response to meet vision solutions
- Displays logical decision-making process in reaching design solutions
- Display of team resources/knowledge/familiarity with local influences and conditions and regulatory agencies
- Apparent team resources: experience/quality/ technical ability/deliverability/ capability
- Display of communication skills to the client (good listener, promotes dialogue with the client, etc.)
- Apparent integrity of Team Leader and Team Members
- Preparation for Interview

Thus, the decision process embodied strength by:

- being consistent for all firms interviewed);
- identifying specific qualities and characteristics of each firm;
- providing a baseline for assessing individual firms' experience and capabilities;
- including the voice of every committee member rating based on objective observation rather than subjective opinion.

They identified questions similar to what someone might expect during a job interview:

- How do you see the civil engineer and the landscape architect working together?
- How would you describe a building that is inspirational and filled with meaning? What would you say would be necessary architecturally to achieve such a building?
- Have you worked with the Archdiocese? How aware are you of Archdiocesan policies and financial constraints?
- What ideas would you bring for addressing our water and sewer issues?
- What other projects have you committed to? Will you have time for us?
- Have you worked in Lake County in the last three years?
- How do you address the basic maintenance of the buildings you design?
- Why do you want to do this project? What enthuses you about the St. Mary project?

They scheduled interviews in two one-hour slots starting at 6:00 and 8:00 p.m. during the first weekdays of June 1998. Many team members had day jobs. Interviewing is exhausting for all parties.

The firms brought various trades, experience, backgrounds, and expertise. The selection committee believed they were all capable of the project. But the team sought to disqualify contenders as much as qualify them. A firm's responses to questions, the preparation for their presentation, the confidence displayed under scrutiny, and the other criteria became part of post-interview deliberations.

Some firms had experience elsewhere building churches; others did not. A few had experience with the Chicago Archdiocese, a project partner. All worked with landscaping professionals who understood the parish's desire to maintain the prairie atmosphere and agreed with it. All had relationships with civil engineers who recognized water and sewer considerations were among the most significant challenges. The need for wetlands and septic fields magnified land space requirements. Other shared concerns were traffic flow, control, and safety because the property was situated amidst state, county, and township roads.

Of course, they had different ideas about the number and distribution of buildings on the campus. Possible construction materials mentioned during the interviews included wood (timber and beams), glass, stone, brick, metal, plaster (drywall), and concrete.

The team judged the companies on these topics through scorecard ratings. The subjective aspects were more challenging to assess. It was one of these that, in Lewinski's mind at least, tipped the scales in favor of one firm. That was Lohan Associates, at which Dirk Lohan was a principal.

One of Lohan's buildings under construction was the Blue Cross and Blue Shield of Illinois headquarters in Chicago. The architect was Jim Goetsch. Pini mentioned St. Mary's project to Goetsch. Lohan learned of it and was intrigued. He had designed various types of buildings, but not a church. Perhaps recalling the enchantment he'd known as a child playing in a European cathedral, he wanted to design a church for St. Mary's.

Lohan offered his firm's response to the RFP for Architectural and Engineering services in a letter dated April 24, 1998. It was addressed to Pini and the Commission. In it, he commented on his enthusiasm for the opportunity. He acknowledged the challenge of creating an appropriate space in a rural setting:

> I want to convey my personal interest in being the architect for your church project. I feel a sense of emotional confluence with the words of Father Lewinski when he writes of the importance of nature and the potential to achieve something special that will be a legacy for future generations. I believe that in the hierarchy of building types, the religious structure occupies

the highest rank because its functions transcend the merely utilitarian. Not only does it shelter and protect, but it should also nourish and elevate the spirit as well.... I am also intrigued by the challenge to preserve the rural spirit of your land.... In my own personal life... I have developed a great appreciation for the rural atmosphere and the issues involved in preserving it.[3]

As Lohan remembers it, he and Lewinski "hit it off pretty well." Lohan recalled twenty years later, "I liked him, and I think we got along very well with each other."[4] Regardless, they were still accountable to others within their realms of the project.

As Lewinski noted, all the architects they interviewed could design a building. What he sensed from Lohan was something different. Lewinski expected Lohan's approach to result in something that *should* be included to meet liturgical guidelines. Given his own knowledge of church architecture and Liturgy, Lewinski expected to influence the design from that perspective.[5]

The selection of Lohan's firm naturally triggered concern about the supposed powerhouse cost. A special reception at the Ivanhoe Country Club on August 14, 1998, somewhat lessened those fears for a select group. John Riggio, Planning Commission chair, observed: "All the architects looked at the land we have here. Every one of them wanted to do this. They find very few projects have this much land to work with and already have the right input. They're excited about it, to where they were decreasing their rates to win the bid. So we're excited about that."[6]

Still, many suffered some angst. How might a small country parish like St. Mary's afford such a world-renowned firm? Lohan's grandfather was Ludwig Mies van der Rohe (commonly "Mies"). He pioneered modernistic architecture along with Frank Lloyd Wright and a handful of others.[7] After coming to America in 1962, Lohan studied under his grandfather at the Illinois Institute of Technology. Later, he worked under him. Upon Mies' death in 1969, Lohan continued the firm. It became Lohan Associates.[8]

The cost concerns arose from the knowledge that this project would require significant financial support. The number of families in the parish was increasing. Yet, no one knew how much this project would cost or how to finance it. The parish's most recent construction had been an addition to the school over a decade earlier.

St. Mary's, the Archdiocese, and perhaps the architects shared a question. Would this prairie land parish be able to fund a powerhouse project?

[1] Parish Archives: Letter of May 5, 1998. Material for this chapter was derived from "Planning Commission Design Architect Interviews Minutes." June 1, 2 and June 4, 1998.

[2] Ibid.

[3] SMOTA Archives: letter from Lohan Associates to Andrew Pini, April 24, 1998.

[4] Lohan, Dirk. Personal conversation, March 2, 2018.

[5] McNaspy, p. 151 writes: "… in the architect-pastor relationship … neither partner must dominate; each must be sufficiently instructed in the other's metier and respectful of the other's professional competence to make the partnership fruitful."

[6] The "right input" being referred to here was the list of values and expectations—preliminary but important information from the parish—about what the architects needed to use as guidelines and goals in their effort to satisfy the parish

[7] One of van der Rohe's designs is the Farnsworth House on Illinois prairieland west of Chicago. According to Wikipedia "The house has been described as sublime, a temple hovering between heaven and earth, a poem, a work of art." Many drawings of his grandfather's work were on Lohan's bedroom walls when he was a youth in Germany..

[8] Lohan later established his own reputation. In the late 1970s his firm was chosen from among a handful of architectural firms nationwide to design MacDonald's corporate headquarters on an 80-acre wooded site west of Chicago. Other Lohan projects in the Chicago area include the Oceanarium at the Shedd Aquarium; the addition to the Adler Planetarium; the Harold Washington Library Center; two buildings on the University of Illinois at Chicago campus; the Sanai Temple on Delaware Street; and other sites. Farther from the city are Rockwell International Graphic Systems Headquarters (Westmont, IL); Eli Lilly and Company Interiors (Indianapolis, IN); Devon House (Ada MI); TRW World Headquarters (Plano, TX); a faculty academic center at Pace University (New York); and Mies van der Rohe Glass Tower at Bahnhof Friedrichstrabe (Berlin Germany). All were completed or in progress at the time his firm was chosen by St. Mary's. Afterward, his firm also completed an addition to Soldier Field Stadium in Chicago.

THE STARS AND SANDS

Summer 1998

June brought options for solving the church's soot problem. One solution—air conditioning—would require the electricity provider to get more power to the building. They had just installed air conditioning in the school gymnasium. Doing the same in the old church was a doubtful value proposition.

Fr. Britto Berchmans returned from his teaching post in Rome to conduct more adult education sessions in July. Many wished he wasn't working so far away. St. Anne's parish in nearby Barrington would dedicate a new church a year-and-a-half later. No one could predict that, because of Lewinski's encouragement, Berchmans would become a diocesan priest and be assigned to St. Anne's.

Lewinski announced at a Pastoral Council meeting the disappointing news Mary Hall had resigned from her respected position. She had been helping St. Mary's with its planning as part of her work. She had been effective in her Archdiocesan role, but new responsibilities were waiting for her.

Lewinski continued his pastoral visits to households. Though an introvert at heart, he had a conviction for what he was undertaking—and asking his parishioners to undertake. This gave him the confidence he needed for these social occasions. Yet he often found them draining. Rational thinking cannot always overcome natural forces.

The parish had been receiving publicity in the local papers. Something was happening at what had until recently been a quiet country church. The news about St. Mary's challenge and its expansion plan was spreading. On July 14th, the NBC (National Broadcasting Company) affiliate in Chicago aired a 5 p.m. segment about education issues at Catholic schools. They interviewed Lewinski. The public spokesperson in him had no trouble presenting a confident and literate persona to the camera. "We aren't just asking people to put up walls and roofs; what we're really trying to do is provide a legacy for the future."

Lewinski was naturally introverted and shy, but he sometimes became animated. He was proud of what St. Mary's was achieving. In his bulletin column, he told parishioners they should be too. "It's opportunities like the Tuesday broadcast that are a reflection of how blessed we are as a parish." He wrote they would soon send invitations to special events "so that we can more personally share our dreams and keep everyone abreast of the progress we've made." He noted they had contracted the services of CCS Fundraising to conduct the capital campaign scheduled to begin in October. A few weeks later they would welcome the CCS representative, Matt Hoolehan. Lewinski ended his comments with a reminder of the opportunity awaiting them.

> I have admitted a number of times that our planning for the future is an awesome undertaking. But it is also an hour of grace. We have a rare opportunity that few Catholics ever have to plan so broadly for generations to come. While it is hard work and will require a great deal of sacrifice, it is also a privilege to have this opportunity to work together for something greater than ourselves. It is an act of faith. How could we not be a better people because of it all?[1]

On July 1, Mrs. Debbie Dedeo became the first layperson to be appointed School Principal. Until then, a nun—Sr. Mary Paul, at the time—had always ruled.

The Archdiocese gave its approval for the acquisition of the additional 12.7 acres.

The 24th annual Pork and Corn Roast was approaching. One result of the Public Relations Committee's work was an article in the Mundelein News titled "Sacred Ground."

> Major preparations are being made to welcome Cardinal Francis George to St. Mary - Fremont Center for his first visit to the church. "I think it is a great opportunity for our parish, for us, to get to know him, and for him to get to know our parish," said Steffenhagen, a lifelong parish member. That is exactly why George accepted the church's invitation, said Jim Dwyer, spokesman for the Archdiocese of Chicago. "We think it's a great honor," said Pat Buckley, who, as chairman of the Pork and Corn Roast this year, has the job of preparing food for more than usual. There are normally 2500 to 3000 people in attendance, but this year Buckley has added an additional 25% to this food supply to accommodate everyone.... The congregation has nearly doubled from 600 families in 1996 to 1100 families in 1998. The growth is a paradox, Buckley said. While everyone likes the church because it is small, it has gotten larger because everyone likes it, he said, growth has caused a problem as the church built in 1889 seats 220 people.... On any given Sunday around 2500 people attend Sunday services, he said, with that figure doubling during Easter and Christmas services.[2]

On July 29th, the Archdiocese wrote a letter to Lohan Associates. They accepted the firm's services based on their proposal and discussions.

The parish held its 24th annual Pork and Corn Roast on Sunday, August 9th.[3] The temperature approached ninety degrees, rising from seventy-two degrees six days earlier, becoming the month's second-hottest day. Vendors selling refreshments were elated. But not the men who spent uncomfortable hours roasting twenty hogs in charcoal grills overnight.

At mid-morning, nearly two hundred people gathered on folding chairs under the tent. Others were standing around the periphery, seeking even the smallest bit of shade from the scorching sun. The parish always held a Mass outside on the day of this event. Today's presider was the recently appointed Archbishop of Chicago, Francis Cardinal George.

Vested in green, he processed into the tent, following lay ministers and the Knights of Columbus while the congregation sang the entrance hymn. Before beginning the service, he faced the assembly, many fanning themselves with event programs. The aroma of roast pork was in the air.

"I am happy to be with you on this wonderful Sunday in August," he asserted. "It is a little hot, a little humid, as it should be—not in a church, but in a tent. A gathering place which tells me that you *need* something more permanent than this so that all of you can come together to worship the Lord as His people." The congregation responded with laughter. Lewinski, also vested, exhibited a broad grin. "That's how we come together this morning at St. Mary's."

He then began celebrating the liturgy.

After completing the gospel reading, Cardinal George remained at the podium to deliver his sermon. He mentioned the challenges faced by the congregation. He recalled for them other people who had faithfully responded to God's call throughout history.

"I'm very sorry," he began, "for all those who are in the sun. And if I were a little *more* sorry, I would shorten the sermon; but I'm not *that* sorry." He paused during the laughter. "However, it's not too cool in these vestments either, so we'll suffer together.[4]

"Father Ron was kind enough to send me a little bit of the history of your parish. I read that the first patron of this community was St. John the Baptist, and then the name changed to St. Mary of the Annunciation, and now St. Mary at Fremont Center. It occurred to me that it might be good to think for a moment about the Blessed Virgin Mary *at* the Annunciation. Can you imagine that when she got the message from God's messenger that she was to be the instrument of God fulfilling all the promises made first to Abraham and Sarah, and all their descendants, her own people, that she could also foresee you and me, and that there would be at some point here, in northern Illinois, a church in her honor? Of course, she didn't. How could she?

"But what she *did* see is what we can see in faith. She saw God's will for *her* and how God's will for her bound her and all her ancestors in faith to all those who believed in promises that were about to be fulfilled. Because she had experienced the love of God and that the angel found her at prayer, she knew that she could trust God, and she said 'yes.' What she saw was enough. She saw the beginning—she saw, in a sense, all of it in that beginning. She didn't have to see—she couldn't see—all the details: the unfolding of God's plan so that even here, in a land she'd never heard of and didn't know existed, among people that she could never possibly know, she will be called 'blessed' because she consented to God's way.

"In the Letter to the Hebrews, we have a whole list of people who we call ancestors in the faith, beginning with Abraham, whom we call 'Father in Faith' and who the Jewish people remind us is the first one who listened to God. There are many people in scripture who have *heard* God. Adam and Eve heard God, but they didn't listen. They disobeyed. They didn't accept his will. Abraham was the first who listened to God. Because of that, he is our Father in faith, we who are grafted onto the tree of Judah into God's new people. He and his wife, Sarah, listened; and they both trusted that God would fulfill the promises to be made. That somehow, through the centuries, there would be a people who would be as numerous as the stars in the sky and the sands of the seashore.

"We are part of that number. Abraham listened, and he trusted even when the son that was born to him—when he was very old and his wife just as old—God told him that Isaac had to be sacrificed. We think with horror: how could he have listened to God? But, in fact, he probably wasn't very surprised. Abraham was a polytheist before he was converted to the true God. Among all the gods, there were many who were malevolent and some who demanded human sacrifice. So the idea that a god would demand that a child be offered probably didn't surprise him. What did surprise him was that at the exact moment of sacrifice, God intervened to save Isaac, his only son, so that his nation could begin.

"And in that sense, Abraham, who is our Father in faith, becomes a figure of God our Father, who sent His only Son, so that we could be saved through his death. But, if his death were all, then there would be no salvation. The Father saved his Son by having him rise from the dead, raising him from the tomb. So that, in his life, in Christ, each of us may know the love of God forever and ever.

"This story of faith, of people who trust because they know the love of God—even without the details, even without the future—is the story of the people who started this parish. They were pioneers, not just in settling the land, but pioneers in their faith. They couldn't have foreseen what the things they did would soon become. That, indeed, those who came after them in this household of faith would be far more numerous than the farming families that began this parish.

"They didn't have to know all the details. They believed in the same God we believe in. Their faith is the faith of Abraham and our faith as well. The faith is the Catholic faith proclaimed for 2,000 years, built upon the faith of Abraham. But we express it in different ways.

"You need another church, you need more buildings, because—thank God—your faith community is growing. I was born when Cardinal Mundelein was still the Archbishop of Chicago, shortly before he died. Never in my wildest dreams did I ever imagine that I would be Mundelein's successor as Archbishop of Chicago. He was kind of a mythical figure as I lived my childhood under Cardinal Stritch. Never imagining that here is where God's will would place me. Yet, in faith, I accept that—with some trepidation, with some wonder, still waking up sometimes thinking, 'What in heaven's name am I doing here?'" The crowd chuckled.

"My sister says sometimes, 'Do you imagine mom and dad would ever think that you would be the Archbishop of Chicago? What do they know?' The answer is, of course, that they who have gone before us in faith know what the Lord wants them to know, and that's enough. It's enough for them. It's enough for us. Because behind that always imperfect knowledge is trust in a God who loves us far more than we can imagine, a God to whom we must say 'yes' if we are to be men and women of faith.

"There is always, therefore, in this life of faith a kind of dialogue, isn't there, between control and surrender. Obviously, we have to control as much as we can in order to assure the future. So we get insurance, and we save money, and we make plans. How to plant crops. How to help our business to develop. How to educate our children. And how to create a new parish campus. We have to plan, and therefore, we have to control; but if control is all there is to life, if power is all there is, then we're not yet Abraham and Sarah's children. Nor do we have the faith of the Virgin Mary; or even of our parents and grandparents.

"There is, along with the dynamics of control, a whole rhythm of surrender, which is far more basic. Surrender always to God's will, to God's plan. Abraham and his wife Sarah surrendered so that new life could come from an impossible situation according to *human* plans. The same kind of surrender that Mary, at the Annunciation, said she would make so that God's will could be done by His hand. We surrender always to a Lord who has promised that he will come again and in ways that we can't know. So we can only wait for it.

"St. Augustine, who has the same faith as us, long ago said it was by design that Jesus concealed the last day from us so that we would always be on the lookout for him and his coming every day of our lives. That is how all those ancestors in the faith lived: always on the lookout for the fulfillment of God's promises—first and definitively in Jesus, but now, waiting still—as we are—for his coming again in glory.

"In the meantime, we work, we plan, we watch, we hope. In the end, there will be forever the love of God for us, and us for God and one another. That is what we're about. As you continue to plan so well—so marvelously well from the little that I know from the few details that I've been given. The Archbishop is the last one to get all the details, but that's okay." Again, some chuckles. "But you're doing it very well. You're fulfilling the dreams and hopes of the pioneers who started this parish. And more than that, the dreams and hopes of the Virgin Mary, of the saints, of Abraham and Sarah, of your fathers and grandfathers, your grandmothers, your mothers, your ancestors, my ancestors, in the faith.

"Because what we do is done in faith, we know that what is final is the love of God. Here, you are building a new expression of that love. Here, you are building a monument to the faith that tells us who God is and why we can trust him. He is the God of Abraham, Isaac and Jacob; the God of the Virgin Mary and all the saints; the God of your parents and grandparents; the God whom we know is the Father of our Lord, Jesus Christ—and therefore our Father—in heaven. This Christ, this Jesus, has died, truly; he has risen, truly; he will come again, truly. In the meantime, we watch, and we wait in faith. Amen."

After concluding the Mass, the Cardinal thanked Lewinski and the parishioners. He also recognized Fr. Morrissey, pastor from 1967 to 1983. And he acknowledged Fr. Britto Berchmans (the priest from Rome). Then he and Lewinski boarded a horse-drawn carriage for a trip through the field. They blessed the thirty-three acres of recently acquired land on which the parish would build new facilities.[5]

Shortly afterward, St. Mary's agreed to have the Office of Divine Worship (ODW) in Chicago act as liturgical consultants. Most Archdioceses across the country have similar functionality in their organizational structure. This was not an uncommon practice for parishes undergoing significant change. Most of ODW's work during the past few decades dealt with closing or merging parishes. This was especially the case in the city of Chicago, where churches were often not too distant from each other.

Thus, it was an encouraging assignment for the ODW to help Lewinski and his parish. The irony was because Lewinski himself had been Director of the ODW for a decade before coming to St. Mary's. It was how he had worked for the Archdiocese in the city. In fact, his ODW experience and other qualifications made him better prepared than many priests to take the St. Mary's pastorship at St. Mary's. His associates, both within and outside the Archdiocese, were aware of his background and that he had been assigned to St. Mary's. Effectively, his was an assignment to "walk the talk" and demonstrate what he had learned.[6] Lewinski had acted as a liturgical consultant during his time at ODW. But as a pastor, he could not accept the role at St. Mary's.

So, though he hadn't been a pastor, he had years of experience dealing with parishes undergoing significant change.

Things were moving closer to a legacy for the future.

---

[1] Sunday bulletin, April 19, 1998, p. 4.

[2] Mundelein News, August 7, 1996, pp. A1 & A3.

[3] Another "Special Edition" of the *The Bell* (just two pages) was produced as part of the parish's publicity and promotional efforts.

[4] A priest in the Archdiocese has told the story about starting his homily one time in an old church in Rome. It was a hot day and there was, typically, no air conditioning. Fully vested, and still learning Italian, he stood in front of a strange congregation as he was "feeling the heat." Seeking to empathize with the obviously warm and somewhat uncomfortable faces staring at him, he said "If you think you are warm, I am really warm in these vestments." The crowd responded with some looks of surprise and scattered chuckles. He thought they believed that he was joking, so he affirmed, in Italian, "No, really, if you think you are warm, I am even warmer." Again the same response, with a few more chuckles. He continued his homily and finished the Mass. Afterwards, someone asked him "Do you realize what you said at the start of your homily?" He responded with what he'd meant to say. "No" they replied; "you said 'If you think you are sexy, I am even sexier!'"

[5] Cardinal George would preside at the dedication Mass for the new church. It would also be one of the last places he would make a public appearance years later, just before his death. Until then, he would visit many parishes in the Archdiocese and across the country, including a church on the west coast. After returning to Chicago, he commented that a church out west had done a good job, but that St. Mary's had "gotten it right." This was a tribute to Lewinski's vision, leadership, and interpretation of the Liturgical guidelines promoted by Vatican II.

[6] As one associate put it, "He [Lewinski] was in community with other scholars—Paul Turner and others who were well-known national figures in liturgy. He was personal friends with them. This is one of the unique things: you have a lot of scholars about liturgy out there, but few of the scholars had actually had the opportunity to build a church. So he's one of the few who has actually put this all into practice, and theologians were watching it closely."

A SPECIAL INVITATION

August 1998

On Friday evening, August 14, 1998, the Planning Commission held a reception at the Ivanhoe Country Club. It was the end of the week following the Cardinal's blessing of the land during the Pork and Corn Roast. The clubhouse, golf course, and residential community are close to the land occupied by St. Mary parish. A spacious vaulted ceiling room with linen-covered standing-height tables welcomed about fifty invitees. Though not a black-tie event, attendees dressed appropriately for the occasion. Lewinski was wearing his Roman collar. They enjoyed refreshments, hors d'oeuvres, and casual conversation. They displayed images of the Masterplan by Newman Architecture on easels along the perimeter.

Tonight they intended to update invitees on the project's status. More importantly, to ask them to become early donors to the Capital Campaign. Anyone who observed the room would acknowledge that the individuals present were from the nucleus of those who regularly attended parish functions. An informed observer would recognize these folks could be relied upon to contribute their time, talent, or treasure to many parish activities. Most were parishioners the Archdiocesan representative had noted were donor candidates "are already in the parish." This evening was an invitation to invest in St. Mary's future.

After a half-hour of socializing, it was time to "get serious." With index cards in hand, Lewinski approached the standing microphone on the dais.

"I'd like to take a few minutes of your time to share with you a few things. The first thing I want to say—very, very sincerely and honestly—is 'Thank You.' Thank you for being here tonight, and thank you for your support and generosity to St. Mary's. I'm able every Sunday, of course, through the bulletin to say 'thank you' to folks for all they do, but you folks who are here tonight are special friends. It is because of you that St. Mary's is able to continue to do all that it does. I've been waiting for an opportunity like this to thank you—you who are the most generous, the most supportive, the most dedicated, and loyal. So, from the bottom of my heart, I really do thank you for all that you've done.

"I wanted this evening to be a time of real celebration for us. We've reached a turning point in the life of the parish—a good turning point. We celebrated that last Sunday with hogs, a horse and buggy, the Cardinal Archbishop, and all kinds of other good things. We're moving now into the future.

"Part of our evening here is to share with you some of the things that are coming. Because you have been so good to St. Mary's, I wanted to offer *you* the invitation first: to be included among those who will be partners in the future.

"I've asked John Riggio to review how we got to where we are. John, of course, has been our chair for the Planning Commission." Riggio came forward and briefly introduced himself before speaking. Then he continued, "I want to give you an update on some of the progress. The planning and development process started two years ago when the leadership of St. Mary met with the Archdiocese of Chicago. At that point, the Archdiocese said, 'We see what's happening here; we know what the future can bring; you need to spend some time to develop a Masterplan.' St. Mary's contracted with Fielding and Associates—who later became Newman Architecture after merging with another firm—and they developed our Masterplan, which we have displayed here tonight. The work was not done 'under the covers.' It was done with a lot of effort, and input, from a lot of you and a lot of others.

"We have several subcommittees working diligently to make sure that what is done here is developed for everybody. The Pastoral Council commissioned the Planning Commission. We went through a number of studies—including demographics. We worked with Fremont Center Township and the surrounding communities to determine what the growth projections will be.

"We acquired twenty additional acres west of our property and, most recently, an additional thirteen to the south, so with the fifteen we already had, that brings us up to forty-eight. There are not many parishes that can boast that they have forty-eight acres!

"We also held several walk-throughs of current facilities to get input from folks about what they liked and didn't like about them, but also about what they need in the future.

"We developed a communications team that has been doing an effective job of telling the parish at large about what's happening with Planning and Development. It is critical that everyone understands where we're going so that we can be sure we have their input.

"We have, as of late, contracted with Lohan Associates. This didn't happen by us just going out and selecting a firm. It started with twenty-five firms and a structured interview process. Lohan is world-class. You'll have an opportunity to meet with him, and I think you'll be very impressed—I know we were. It isn't just Lohan by himself, but the rest of the architects from the firm—a solid group.

"One thing was interesting as we went through the selection process. All the architects looked at the land that we have here. Every one of them wanted to do this. They find very few projects have this much land to work with and already have the right input: a list of values and needs from the client. They were excited about it to where they were decreasing their rates in order to win the bid. So we're pleased about that.

"One additional thing is that we're going to need fundraising. We're new to fundraising, so we've contracted with a fundraising consulting firm to help us. Dan will talk a little about that.

"But more importantly, I want to say that this task has been done slowly and methodically. We didn't want a 'ready-fire-aim.' We've interviewed a lot of other parishes that have gone through building and development. We've learned from their mistakes. We don't want to be in a position where we build something and then have to add on to it later. We'd rather take our time and do it right the first time.

"In closing, I want to say we have a great parish here, we've got a firm vision, and I believe we're moving in the right direction. Thank you very much." The group applauded and Lewinski returned to the microphone.

"We know we have a very special and unique place just by all the press we've gotten in the last month or so and even this past weekend. I got a call from a priest friend, and the telephone message said, 'I'm tired of seeing you on television and in the newspapers. Get a life.'" Lewinski laughed along with his guests.

"But it says a lot about what St. Mary's is all about. There's a certain pride that we can have in our place because it *is* different than any other place and we want to keep that distinctiveness. We're a unique community; a community that was formed during the Civil War years out of a group of farming people who sacrificed a great deal to provide what we have here today.

"We're unique, as John said, in that we have a spacious, beautiful site. We have a love for the land. That is something we heard in all the interviews and walk-throughs that we did: that people have a reverence for the land. We want to maintain that beautiful environment. We also have a very hospitable community. That grows out of the simple, honest, hard-working spirit that's been passed on from generation to generation and is passed on now to newcomers as well.

"Certainly, the thing that strikes us the most is that we are a growing community with a lot of growth yet to come, of course. And the growth is not just in the number of people but growth in services and ministries that are happening in the parish. And growth, as well, in the leadership of the parish. Our school and our Religious Education Program is growing.

The number of families, both young and old, who are joining the parish make it, again, a very special opportunity for us to ask the question: what do we need for the future?

"So, what is our dream? Our dream is certainly to maintain that wonderful community. We are, after all, as Church, about people—not just bricks and mortar. So we want to maintain that wonderful spirit of community and hospitality and to nurture it further. We also want the parish to be a light in the darkness, an oasis in a desert of a world that often enough searches for meaning and hope. I don't have to tell you that the 5 and 10 o'clock news rarely gives us too much hope. We as Church have an opportunity to say to the world there is something more. We have something we can believe in that will make us whole.

"As a good example of that, many of you know we had a funeral this week for a young girl, fourteen years old, killed in a car accident. Her family had only recently returned to the Church a year ago. One thing that her mother said to me as we sat in the emergency room at Condell Hospital shortly after her daughter had died was 'I'm going to thank God today.' 'What do you mean?' I asked. She said, 'How wonderful it is that God led us to this community at St. Mary's because where would we be now, to deal with this if it wasn't for the wonderful community at St. Mary's that will give us hope.'

"It *is* a wonderful commentary. That's what I mean by saying that the parish can be an oasis in the midst of a desert world: that we have something to give to folks. In order to do all that, of course, we need facilities. Most of you here are involved in all kinds of committees and ministries and so forth, so you know it isn't uncommon to compete for meeting space. We're bumping elbows all the time. In order to do what we need to do, to carry on the mission that's been entrusted to us by God, we need the space to do it in.

"I'm really excited about that possibility, and I hope you are, too. It's a rare opportunity that we have, as a Catholic people, to be able to plan for the future in a way much like our ancestors did almost one-hundred-and-fifty years ago at St. Mary's. This is *our* time. God is calling us to accept that mission not just for ourselves but for our children and the next generation and generations to come: so that the mission of Jesus may be continued and that the world we live in may have some hope.

"Our plan—you've looked at it before, and it's up here again for you to look at—is in three phases. The total plan is a bit ambitious, to be sure. The long-range plan is probably going to cost somewhere around $21 million. It is indeed an ambitious plan, but what we're trying to do is to plan ahead. Obviously, we will not be able to do everything at once, but if we don't plan now, we can make mistakes in how we use the land that could be very critical in the future.

"In the first phase, which we anticipate probably costing $10 million, we will include all the infrastructure that is needed. Remember, we don't have water or sewer, so that is a real headache for us. We also have to look at building a church—a church that is inspiring, beautiful—that really draws people here, where one can experience not only the community of God's faithful but experience the very awesome mystery of God. We believe we can do it, and we have a wonderful architect—world-class—to help us with that, and it's going to be very exciting to do.

"Part of that church structure will include—we hope—a bell tower where we can erect once again the original bell that sits outside of our church and let it ring again to call people to worship. We'll need meeting spaces for ministries, formation of leadership, organizations, and so forth.[1] We need office space not just to do parish business but for pastoral ministries that are so necessary in a parish: counseling, marriage preparation, and all of those kind of important ministerial functions.

"We also hope, in that first phase, to build a house for me to live in.[2] They had a trailer idea, but they're afraid I'd leave and not come back. I think I need something a little more permanent." The group's laughter acknowledged his humor. "So that's also part of the whole picture. In the second phase is the Christian Life Center. We're calling it the Christian Life Center because it's more than a school. It includes a school, but it also includes Religious Education Programs for children as well as programs for adults. We want it to be used by *everyone*, so we want to use a more inclusive name. There still will be a 'St. Mary school', but will be housed in the Christian Life Center. For the second phase, we estimate a cost of about $8 million.

"The third phase is the intergenerational center, which would turn the current school into a facility we can use for preschool and senior daycare. With the graying of our population and Saddlebrook[3] right on our doorstep, we feel we have a mission outward to that senior population. We want to be creative about how we approach that.

"Although I say that we do not include the Christian Life Center in the first phase, that's not really entirely accurate because the architect has to do design work and prep work for the Center in the first phase in anticipation of it. When do we get to it? As soon as possible, and obviously, so much depends on the capital campaign.

"To answer a question that many people have asked, no, we have not settled on an architectural style. We really are trying to keep ourselves open about that. But one requirement that we've made is that it has to blend into the environment and respect what is there already—the traditional buildings that are there.

"One reason that we chose Dirk Lohan as our architect was because we felt he fed back to us a real spirit, and a spirituality, about what a church ought to be that we didn't hear from any other architect. I've shared this story with a couple of you, but it's worth repeating.

"Dirk Lohan, who still has a strong German accent, said, 'One evening I came out at dusk, and I stood before your church, and I looked, and I said What do I see here? I see honesty, simplicity, hard-working people who love their families, and the church is important in their life. That's the kind of spirit I want to be sure we maintain.' He won us, I think, with that." The attendees responded with approving laughter.

"You know the others were quick to say, 'Well, you know, we can put up these kinds of beams at this kind of an angle, and it will look very nice on this landscape.' But Lohan spoke from the heart, and it seemed to us to be a good fit for who we are as a people.[4]

"I'd like Dan to come up and share with us briefly the question of how we will manage this whole thing."

Dan Washburn took his turn at the microphone. He and Ann Steffenhagen cochaired the Capital Campaign committee, responsible for fundraising. He admitted the task was daunting. He identified reasons for expansion. One was the obvious need for more space for meetings and activities. "We have more ministries now than ever before in the parish's history," he observed. "But we don't have the facilities to support it. As we get larger and our needs get greater, we will need facilities. So the biggest need we have right now is to expand."

A second reason was the bright and energetic Steering Committee members.

A third was parish leadership. "I look out and see people in the audience who are there every time we need something. It is your generosity and your time that makes this parish a success."

Last, he shared they had hired a specialist in raising funds for parishes like theirs. Washburn announced, "Starting Monday, they'll assign a staff member full-time. He will work in the office every day for three months and will guide us along the way."

Next, he aimed to expand their understanding of fundraising.

"Two questions have come to me during fundraising are (1) how much do we need to raise before we can break ground and (2) how much help is the Archdiocese going to give us? To answer the first, Archdiocesan guidelines call for 90% of the project to be budgeted and 60% collected. Now, that does not mean we need to get 90% of $21 million because we're working in phases. So, if we break it down, the first stage will be around $10 million.

"Now, if we can talk Father Ron out of the Olympic-size swimming pool, Jacuzzi, and other things, then we can cut that down a little." There was a brief burst of laughter, and eyes turned toward Lewinski. He simply grinned.

Washburn continued, "The guidelines say: pledge $9 million, collect $6 million. Again, these are *guidelines*. To date, we have raised $1.1 million. If we're looking at $10 million, we're already at 10%. That's a nice start, a very nice start!

"The second question concerns help from the Archdiocese. This project is already two years old. Throughout those two years, the Archdiocese has helped us with consulting and advisory services. Some we listen to, and some we don't. They've been with us, side by side. Another thing they've been helping us with is the purchase of land. The Archdiocese actually paid for land out of diocesan funds, allowing us to take our $1.1 million and invest it to earn interest. They will hold the land until we're ready.

"So, what's the next step? The next step is the parish-wide fundraising beginning in October. Between now and then, we have a lot of work to do in getting information out to parishioners. Before we even start with the wider campaign," he raised his hands to his chest as if praying, "we are going to be visiting each one of you. Why?

"Well, with fundraising, instead of the 80/20 rule, it is more like 70/30: 70% of the funds are contributed by 30% of the donors. And who are the 30%? The 30% has got to come from the leadership of the parish. Ladies and gentlemen, you are a part of it. In September, we will visit everyone. What we want to do is ramp up the fundraising so that when we go parish-wide, we'll have a fund started and momentum going.

"Now, what we ask of you is to prayerfully consider what sacrificial gifts you can give. We're not going to tell you how much to give; it has to come from your heart. But the scope and timing of this project really depend on it. Everyone here can help make this a success. The project is a good one, and the people here are very good people.

"We also need some help, some volunteers, to help conduct the campaign parish-wide. The intent is to visit every parishioner, not just people here or people coming to the 'next' meeting. We're going to visit every parishioner. So we need some volunteers to go out. We also encourage everyone here to spread the word. Maybe you know someone who hasn't gotten the word and who does not know the scope of the project. And we need help identifying potential donors.

"In the meantime, we will be publicizing the various naming and memorial opportunities and the various types of donations, whether it is a one-time cash donation, a trust, pledges, stocks, or children." Again, a response of laughter. "This vision *is* achievable. Together, with the guidance of the Holy Spirit, we can continue God's work. Thank You." The group applauded, and Lewinski returned to the microphone.

"When I'm overwhelmed by the extent of the plan, I always think of where we find ourselves: in Mundelein. I look at the enormous, world-class seminary that Cardinal Mundelein built 76 years ago at a very, very difficult time in the life of the nation. I like to think about and imagine what it was like when he went before his board of advisers to tell them what he was going to do during the war years: build this enormous university. He was a man of great vision and great dreams. We all know that's what it takes—dream, the vision, the enthusiasm—and we'll all do whatever we can. With God's help, we'll accomplish what we can.

"I invited you here tonight to thank you for *all* that you've done already. So often we talk about these pioneers in the past, the founders of the parish, and so forth. We look to the past about that. Well, tonight is a turning point; because tonight, I am inviting you to be part of a second generation of founders at St. Mary Fremont Center. I hope the vision excites you enough to want to do that."

He invited questions and comments. Roger Fisher, chair of the Major Gifts Committee, stepped up to the microphone. He exclaimed any successful organization needs a good Chief Executive Officer (CEO) and team to meet its objectives. He noted Lewinski was this team's CEO. The Archdiocese would want to use his skills elsewhere in the diocese. Thus he believed there was a narrow window for St. Mary's to benefit from Lewinski's talents. Lewinski would later joke about what Roger knew that he didn't. Fisher, as the parishioners would realize over time, was a firm supporter of Lewinski and an advocate of the project.

Then Lewinski introduced Ann Steffenhagen, cochair with Washburn.

"I'm a lifelong member of St. Mary parish. My ancestors were among the founding fathers of this parish, and so it is very special to me, although I know it is also very special to every one of you. I have been educated at St. Mary's; my children have gone to St. Mary's, and now my grandchildren are at St. Mary's. My parents attended, and I'm sure my great-grandparents were involved. So it is very special to me.

"We've presented our dream to you tonight, so I just want to ask each and every one of you to think about it because we want our parish to be open to everyone who wants to partake in our parish. We need a good school for the youth of the future. There are so many things happening in the world today and we want our youth to grow up to be responsible citizens and we need your help to do it. I just want to ask you to be helpful. So would you please do that? Thank You."

Lewinski thanked Roger Fisher, who lived in this community, for covering the cost of the evening's delights. He thanked everyone for attending and genially encouraged them to enjoy each other's company at Fisher's expense.

Lewinski hoped this group would become the "second generation of founders." He had given them more perspective. The "dream" of new facilities took a big step toward reality. The Masterplan gave them a sense of physical scope. If it were going to happen, it would be up to the parishioners to make it so. He had explained the reality that this would cost a lot of money. They were being asked to step up to the task. They may have left the event feeling like the parishioners who built the existing church had felt in the late 1800s. Those pioneers had built one larger than they needed but did it to provide for future generations.

Would the current parishioners be able to do likewise? Many believed so; but—like their forerunners—weren't sure how.

The parish had identified several "Needs" and "Values." They compiled these during the two-and-one-half years since Lewinski had become pastor. The list resulted from Town Halls, walk-throughs, after-Mass events, surveys, and conversations with parishioners. The Planning Commission, the Pastoral Council, and Lewinski had reviewed the items. They would give the list to the architects for consideration during the upcoming conceptual design phase.

Needs

- Must seat at least 1,100.
- At least four meeting rooms that can open to be one large room.
- The narthex should be able to serve multiple functions.
- Kitchen facilities near the narthex.
- One central processional route to get in and out of the church.
- Plaza or area outside suitable for blessing palms, Easter vigil, etc.
- A Chapel that is prominent, gives due reverence to the Eucharist.
- Day-long access to the Eucharistic Chapel.
- Central aisle leading to the altar.
- A church interior that doesn't look like a renovated old church.
- Handicap access.
- Easy access to outdoor garden and cemetery.
- A tower for the 1867 parish bell.
- Excellent sound system.
- Air conditioning.
- A sanctuary suitable for daily Mass or small group liturgy.

Values

- Must be reminiscent of our rural heritage.
- Humble/simple and clean.
- Open to the outdoors; use of natural light.
- Cost-efficient for ongoing maintenance.
- Sense of invitation and welcome.

- ○ Relates to the land, old church, and cemetery: a "Parish in the Park."
- ○ Uses beautiful, natural materials.
- ○ Authentic, original, noteworthy design.
- ○ Beautiful; something we will be proud of for generations.
- ○ Entrance should be obvious and convey warmth and hospitality.
- ○ Religious art should be integrated, not added later as an afterthought.
- ○ Must be designed within the norms of Vatican II to accommodate the ideals of liturgical reform.
- ○ Uses distinctive liturgical art to draw us into the mystery of God's presence among us.
- ○ The altar should be prominent and the focal point within the church.

How successful would they be in satisfying these needs and values?

---

[1] Seeking a suitable environment for Pastoral Council formation meetings, the parish used space at nearby Mundelein Seminary one evening and the Cardinal Stritch Retreat House on another during August.

[2] When Lewinski first arrived at the parish, he was living in what is now the Joseph and Mary Retreat Center close to the seminary and a few miles from the parish. Realizing the old rectory would need to be used for office space, he rented a condo about four miles from the parish. It was his home until the new rectory was built five years later.

[3] About half of the households in the parish were in the 35-55 age group; about 10% were 55-65; and 20% were over 65. Saddlebrook Farms is a 55+ retirement community about two miles from the parish.

[4] It is believed that Lohan was the only architect to visit the campus and walk the land.

A TEAM OF HORSES

September 1998

One month after the event at the Country Club, the Planning Commission hosted a special Open House on September 11, 1998. This was for a different audience, a broader group of parishioners. The Commission was working downward on the pyramid of prospective donors. The artist renderings for the Masterplan were displayed again. About a hundred people, most of them couples, attended.

Scattered throughout the space were blue and yellow helium balloons. A buffet table with various hors d'oeuvres was in the center of the room. They positioned a beverage table along a wall. A harpist created a relaxing musical ambiance. Twelve cocktail-height tables draped in black linen were scattered around the room. Atop each burned a tall decorative candle. This time, business casual was the expected norm. It was an atmosphere of subdued lighting, festive decorations, soothing melodies, and cold refreshments. This gathering occurred in the only suitable space on campus: the school gym.

As at the Country Club event, a brief period passed so guests could mingle and exchange reactions to the images on display. Some attendees didn't view them before the presentations started. Afterward, those people joined others to examine them more closely.

Lewinski approached the podium where he'd placed his notes. The agenda was the same as August's. It was the target audience that was different. Lewinski thanked everyone for coming, expressed his appreciation for their support, and introduced Riggio. Riggio summarized for this group what had transpired with the project. Lewinski returned to the podium to address this next tier of patrons.

"Throughout the phases that John has spoken about that led us up to this preliminary Masterplan, we've already had many, many people involved in this whole process. So it is not just a small committee. We added up the numbers the other day, which was well over one hundred. One thing that we have been blessed with, in a beautiful way, is the number of professional people that we have in the parish helping us. For instance, when we interviewed the architects, we were trained by a parishioner who does this kind of thing for a living.

"So we have approached all the steps along this process in a very professional way. Even the architects we interviewed were very much aware of that and were impressed by what we were doing." Lewinski had been speaking unscripted. Now, he referred to his notes on the podium.

"Tonight, we are gathering here as an evening of celebration. As John has said, we have completed part of that first planning process, and that is a reason for us to celebrate tonight: we have accomplished something.

"Now, some of us have expressed certainly a concern that, as we grow, we will lose that special character that is ours as a parish. It will change, yes. But as we work together, we can also hold on to the deeper values that are so important to us, those values of a community that believes together and is willing to work together in the name of the Lord. It is not really brick-and-mortar that we are so much interested in, but in trying to be the very best parish that we can be.[1]

"This is lofty and very ambitious, Lewinski, yes indeed." The crowd laughed at his verbal expression of what many of them were thinking.

"But if we, the parish of St. Mary, don't make a difference in the lives of our children and the lives of the larger community that we live in, what good would we be?

"To be this kind of Church to carry on the mission of Jesus means that we have to have a plan for the future. Now, most of you who have been active for a while have experienced one way or another the 'squeeze,' whether it has been in the pews or going to a meeting and discovering that another group is meeting there too. We simply don't have the room to do the mission that is entrusted to us.

"So, what's the plan? The plan, first, is to preserve our original church. It is a symbol and a sign of our roots and the heritage and the faith and the trust of those who came before us. Second, we also want to provide a new church, a church that respects this beautiful rural setting, a church that is inspiring and allows us to experience the awesome mystery of God in our celebration of the Liturgy.

"We also, of course, need office space so that we can continue our pastoral work. We need space so the ministries have a place to meet and be trained. We need space where the old and young can meet and learn and grow. And, of course, we want to preserve the rural environment, to have sacred space around us—a place to walk, a place to pray, a place where we can gather with friends and the outdoors. We also hope to put up a residence for the pastor and priests who will live here.

"How are we going to do that? We're going to do it the same way that our ancestors did; that's how. We're going to pray, we're going to do hard work, we're going to put our personal sacrifice into all of this, and we're going to trust in God's providence. That's how we're going to do it.

"Practically speaking, it is a big mountain to climb. Our entire vision, which will take many, many years to complete, has a big price tag: about $21 million."

This promptly elevated everyone's level of attention. Some lost their casual smile. No one gasped or groaned, at least not audibly. A few couples looked at each other as if to say, "Really?!" Some individuals altered their stance or stepped away from where they'd been standing. A few raised a drink to their mouth. It wasn't soda.

"The first phase of what we think is a priority for us to accomplish is $10 million. Again, it's an awesome challenge for us. We have, indeed, an enormous task ahead of us.

"And so it's going to take everyone's participation. But I know you can do it. I believe in you, St. Mary's. You are indeed a unique expression of God's Church. And you know something? Throughout this entire experience, I have a feeling that we're all going to grow together; that we're going to be a lot closer Church family. Because isn't it true in all of our families that when we work and struggle together that the community is really built up? With God's help, I know that will happen here as well. Yes, it's going to take sacrifice, but if we put our minds to it, we can, with God's help, build something that we can all be proud of. And most importantly, we can be part of a great legacy for generations to come.

"You know, and I know, we live in a society where people are in it for themselves—always concerned about themselves. We are different. We believe not only that what we are doing is not just something for us but something for those who are going to come after us. We know what our ancestors, the pioneers of St. Mary's, did for *us*. Now it's our turn.

"I'm counting on you to join me in this great adventure of faith. It's a rare opportunity when a community is called by God to build his Church. Now, I'll be honest with you; there are a lot of other parishes where my work would be a lot easier. But I'll also be honest with you in saying that there are few to none that I could ever love like I do St. Mary's. And there are few to none that offer you and I such a privileged power of grace to set a foundation for generations to come. I invite you to be a second generation of founders."

After Lewinski, Dan Washburn repeated the essence of his comments at the Country Club. He pointed out they had already obtained 10% of the funds for Phase I. The more frugal of those present might question spending money on this evening's treats instead of using it for the planned project. When Lewinski returned to the podium, he addressed those unexpressed thoughts. "I want to note that a parishioner covered the cost of our celebration here tonight. So there is no cost to the parish. Is there anybody from a committee who wants to say anything?"

In response, Roger Fisher again stepped up. A successful and humble business person, he chaired the Major Gifts Committee. They tasked it with soliciting larger-than-average contributions. Fisher was a longtime parishioner, and he'd gotten involved with the project for three reasons: (1) he loves the parish; (2) he sees tremendous growth; and (3) because the parish has a great 'CEO' (Lewinski) who can carry it off. Fisher explained he was in business development and believed Lewinski—a great priest—would be reassigned by the Archdiocese sooner than they'd like.

Fisher concluded his remarks by saying, "We need your help. I am the chairperson of the Major Gift Committee, so when I call on you, get ready. It will not be, as Dan Washburn said, just 'chump change.'[2] This is something you have to believe in. This is part of the future. In these times, when you hear so many sad things on TV, you should embrace this community. It is incredible. Please help me. Let's help ourselves." Then Fisher invited Ann Steffenhagen to the podium.

As before, Steffenhagen reflected on her farming family's history at the parish. She mentioned her family's education at the school. She noted the challenges ahead. She concluded, "We have the dream, this vision, and we cannot do it without your support. I want to use one analogy. My grandfather and father used to talk about a team of horses. When you have one horse on the team that would not pull, you could never pull the load; but if you had a good team of horses, they could pull and pull and get the job done. That's what we need at St. Mary's right now. Thank you." Steffenhagen's sincerity and earnestness received applause as Lewinski returned to the podium.

Lewinski closed by saying, "I hope that you'll stay around. This is a grand opportunity, so while we have everyone here, we might as well enjoy this party and everyone's company. The Committee people are wearing jumbo name tags, so if you have questions about any of the projects, stop any of us, and we will talk with you. Thanks again for being here tonight. Enjoy the evening, and let's look to the future."

"I have never run a capital campaign," Lewinski wrote in his "Around the Table Column" in the September issue of *The Bell*. "I find it very awkward and humbling to solicit funds." This was not a pastor pretending to be something he was not. Admitting inexperience is often seen as a weakness, especially by those who lack the strength to do it. Prior to this statement, he had written:

> We have talked, and we have listened. We have dreamed, and we have prayed. We have studied and surveyed. We have outlined a plan for the future. Now it is time to make the necessary sacrifices to achieve our goal. Far more than some kind of business venture, we have been entrusted with a mission from God. And so our sacrifices are an act of faith in response to God's call.

He noted his personal shortcomings about fundraising, then continued:

> My ministry is ordinarily to respond to your requests. Now I am called to make a request of you. I do not do so for myself but for St. Mary Parish and for the generations to come.
>
> The enormous challenge that lies ahead of us requires far more than a second collection. I'm inviting you to make an investment in the future of St. Mary's. To be a second-generation founder. Consider what you can do over the next 3 to 5 years to help us achieve our goal. Talk about this around the table as a family.
>
> I hope you will also invite others around your table and share with them your own convictions and your own enthusiasm for this project. As you prayerfully consider your own sacrifice, be an ambassador of good news and encourage others to take up the challenge of preparing St. Mary - Fremont Center for the future.[3]

This third issue reviewed Cardinal George's blessing of the new land during the Pork and Corn Roast. It touched on the "Celebration Gatherings" conducted in August and September with a new generation of founders. The center spread illustrated Lohan Associates' work at Pace University, Sanai Temple, Illinois Institute of Technology, McDonald's, and Frito-Lay. Each Planning Commission subcommittee made its report.

An essay, "At the Threshold of Opportunity," identified the parish's historic position. It mentioned the acquisition of thirty-three more acres of land. It noted how the current generation of parishioners was like the founders 130 years prior, tasked with building a new church. St. Mary's now had a three-phase Masterplan. Soon the Capital Campaign would begin. The essay closed, saying, "Together, through faith, determination, and sacrifice, we will demonstrate once again in the evolving life of St. Mary parish how it becomes possible to cross the threshold of opportunity."[4] In response to a Q&A question, "Why do we need a Masterplan?" they directed the reader to Luke 14.

After months of hard work, parishioners led by Jeanne Rutledge and Terri Kennedy finally relaxed. The Pictorial Directory had arrived. They swiftly distributed it.

Lewinski felt uncomfortable about what he was observing. During a Pastoral Council meeting in early September, he noted many parishioners appeared indifferent. Is it a wait-and-see attitude? He cautioned the process might seem slow. It is more time-consuming to rebuild a parish than construct a building addition. He acknowledged the "politics" of planning for the years ahead was making the task arduous. Educating everyone to look forward was a necessity.

Lewinski stressed the Council members needed to support their ministries. He encouraged a feeling of community, ownership, and stewardship promoted by the commissions. They needed to impart it to the parishioners. He asked Council members to focus on areas of concern and return with actionable ideas at the November meeting.[5]

St. Mary's was experiencing change on a scale rare in any parish's history. There were signs of change, but none reading *"The St. Mary Parish of the future will not be the St. Mary Parish of the past."*

---

[1] This phrasing is very reminiscent of Lewinski three decades earlier at the seminary. Speaking with his theology instructor, Sr. Agnes Cunningham, he said, "Sister, I have been convinced that God wants me to be a priest. If I had not been accepted at Mundelein, I would have known I was mistaken, but I *was* accepted. Sister. I want to be the best priest I can be for God." — Correspondence from Sr. Cunningham to the author in 2018.

[2] The pledge amounts sought by this Committee, which targeted selected parish households, ranged up to $1 million.

[3] *The Bell*, Vol. I, Issue 3, September, 1998, p. 3.

[4] Ibid., p. 6.

[5] Pastoral Council minutes, September 8, 1998.

NATURE AND THE SACRED

September 1998

Having selected Lohan Associates as the architectural firm, the project moved forward. The leadership team invited the firm to a meeting soon after hosting the next generation of founders. The balloons, appetizers, candles, and drinks were absent. Instead, long tables formed a U-shape in the middle of the basketball court. This gym would host many more meetings and Town Halls.

Tonight's attendees included Planning Commission and subcommittees members; parishioners with skills in various trades and occupations related to construction; representatives from Lohan Associates; and Lewinski and Dirk Lohan. A projection screen hung front and middle. A video projector was atop a small table in the center. Lohan had stacked several poster boards and a flip chart on a nearby pedestal. Participants sat along the outer perimeter of the tables so they could see each other.

Lewinski, dressed in business casual and a sports coat, opened the meeting at 7:00 p.m. "Good evening and welcome. Glad to see you all here tonight. We're beginning a new phase in our planning process tonight as we welcome Lohan Associates and many of you who are connected in different ways to this project. The purpose of this meeting is to get some idea of the 'state of the union' in the sense of where we are with everything, but also begin to look at what we need to do next.

"We'll go through some introductions," he stated. "But first, it would be wise if we took a moment to pray to ask for God's help and direction in our gathering here tonight."

Everyone stood as Lewinski began with the sign of the cross. "Sisters and Brothers, we continue with our mission to help build the Kingdom of God on earth. Tonight we mark a new phase in that mission as we enter more deeply into the work of providing facilities to house the Church of St. Mary at Fremont Center. Gathered here tonight, let us listen to the prayer from the Rite of Dedication of a Church[1] as we continue to plan for the future. May this prayer remain constantly in our hearts and minds as a reminder of what we strive to build." He recited the prayer to be used on the day of dedication.

Afterward, he continued to pray. "Almighty God, we gather tonight as we continue our work to plan for the future of the community. Inspire our words and inspire our hearts with this prayer of dedication. May we keep in our minds the community you would have us build. May your wisdom inspire our thoughts and lead us to work together to provide a house for this Church. We ask this through Christ, our Lord. Amen."

Everyone sat down. Lewinski resumed his comments.

"As we begin tonight, it is important to do some introductions. First, we want to welcome the team from Lohan Associates: Dirk Lohan, Al Novickas, and Jim Schubert will become well-known to us during the next couple of years as we continue to work very closely together to achieve our goals in this project. We've asked them to give us some sense of how they operate as a firm. Before we do, though, we'll go around the tables here and have each of you introduce yourself. Perhaps you can say a word about how you fit into this project—if you know." This was Lewinski's way of using humor to ease tension.

Although he had ended with a chuckle, the attendee's nervous laughter betrayed tension within the group. Each attendee gave a brief introduction, stating their name and role. At Lohan's turn, he smiled and exclaimed, "I'm Dirk Lohan. I'll try to find out how I fit in." Everyone joined him in laughter. Lewinski looked at him and said, "We'll turn it over to you now."

Lohan took his cue while sitting at the other end of the U from Lewinski, close to the flip chart. "I'm Dirk Lohan, Principal in charge of the project. We're an architectural firm in Chicago. I know several of you have met us and been involved in selecting us, and it's exciting to be here before you today to hear how we approach a project and have you talk to us about what you want this project to be." Here, Lohan glanced toward Lewinski as if to confirm he was correctly laying the groundwork according to what they had likely previously discussed.

"It's a dialogue that's important. My experience tells me that a *good* building, a building of *quality* and fulfillment of its mission, is one that derives from *collaboration*. It isn't something that the architect, alone, does in isolation. It is a *dialogue*, a process through which we have to move together." Another glance toward Lewinski helped underscore this point, at least between Lewinski and himself. "You will hear more about this process tonight as we talk about how we will work, what we will do for you, and what you will do for us."

Lohan continued by stating there were eighty people in his Chicago-based firm. "We are by no means experts in *church* architecture. We are generalists. We do all kinds of projects, from high-rise buildings to houses, from institutional buildings to hotels, etc." Next, he identified a well-known client: McDonald's Corporation in Oak Brook, Illinois, about forty miles due south of Mundelein. He explained it wasn't only the buildings at McDonald's that mattered. The whole complex—the environment—was important. He was approaching this project from the same perspective. The design for McDonald's campus followed an informal, interactive style —which he felt was that company's character. "People have said," he explained, "that the project has a Midwestern, almost prairie-style feel due to materials, colors, and very horizontal lines. It is not a 'high-rise' project."

He was informing his listeners while reinforcing their choice of his firm. "What's interesting about it is that they selected us from among five other architects nationwide. McDonald's had planned to do a complex in a largely residential town with upscale buildings and expensive homes. There was a lot of opposition to that by the community. They already had a whole design by somebody else. The town said no, you can't do that. McDonald's threatened to leave and go somewhere else—maybe to Mundelein." The group responded with laughter to his understated humor which was somewhat like Lewinski's.

Lohan continued, "At that point, they became more attentive to the character of the town, and they ultimately selected us. I remember the day when the CEO of McDonald's called me and said, 'I want you to do the project not because I like your design, but because I think you can work with us.'" He cast a reassuring glance toward Lewinski.

Then Lohan explained their approach. "I mention this to emphasize once again that it is so important to work together. We want to do what is the right thing, from your point of view, for you. Obviously, we have ideas and thoughts; once in a while, we may suggest some things to you, and you say yea or nay; that's the process."

He then identified another client, the Shedd Aquarium on Chicago's lakefront. As he spoke, he held up poster boards showing pictures and drawings of the projects. "We had never done anything like that either," he admitted. He was fairly certain they did not choose his firm because of his design expertise involving water.[2] Instead, they were chosen "for sensitivity in terms of the design, the approach, and the context of Chicago's lakefront and downtown." He then mentioned the expansion to the Adler Planetarium, which honored Daniel Burnham's Masterplan[3] of the Chicago lakefront.

"That brings me to our next point. One of our strong characteristics and beliefs is that we want to develop designs that grow out of the context—out of the local conditions and the regional quality of something. It is a very important consideration in our decision-making and our development of ideas."

Lohan highlighted a trait of these buildings. "In both projects on the lakefront, if you notice, the old buildings are silhouettes—as seen from the lake or the city. Our new addition is low so that the familiar character of the older building is maintained."

He identified other projects: a faculty center at Pace University in New York, a synagogue (Sanai Temple) in Chicago, and the Blue Cross Blue Shield building in Chicago. He explained that variety "…keeps you fresh, it keeps you young, it keeps you thinking, and is always a challenge. *Your* project is definitely a *challenge* for us because we cannot fall back on 'ready-made' things."

He next spoke to a quality Lewinski had identified as why Lohan's firm was more attractive: spirituality. He moved the display aside in preparation for using the slide projector. "For me, as an architect, there's a hierarchy of building types. I would rank a church at the top for the simple reason that the functional aspects of bringing people in and out are important but *secondary* to the spiritual nature of the architecture. It is the *quality* of the space that should be the overriding aspect of the design. The functional considerations are what relates to what: how many people will be accommodated, how wide the stairs are, etc. It is very *rational*. When you consider religious structures, there are other elements: the *spiritual* quality of space that you want to achieve.

"The issue is, how do you choose such sacred space? I jotted down a few important thoughts from my point of view on how we want to approach the project. The spiritual, sacred quality of space is important because it is an architectural framework within which communion with God is affected by the individual as well as by the congregation. It is that 'other' dimension that is important. Now, what creates sacred space? How do you create it? I came up with a few basic terms and aspects that we will be thinking about. That's what I want to share with you."

They turned off some of the overhead lights. Lohan projected a famous picture of Earth taken from space. He stated, "I put this picture up because our modern world is phenomenally complex. We are fed information at all times. It is important, however, to take a step back from life—and from the earth—to think about what we're here for, what we do, and why we seek a peace that goes beyond our routine of daily life." Lohan's phrasing could have come from one of Lewinski's homilies.

Then Lohan projected a series of pictures depicting various buildings worldwide. Each choice was an example of the qualities he felt expressed an aspect of sacred space.

The first was a meditation chapel atop a cliff near Portland, Oregon. "It is spectacular," stated Lohan. "It is a curving glass wall with some concrete. From the road, you come through a door, and then before you is this tremendous view of nature. The aspect that I'm talking about here is the relationship to nature. I think sacredness has a lot to do with nature, with natural things. I like to think that because you live out here, you like nature. A quality of nature is spiritual, there's no question about it. The relationship of a building to its surrounding nature is an important aspect, and it is particularly important in the design of a church. How we place it, where we place it, and how the view into it and out of it relates to the surrounding natural landscape has great importance." The view from the interior of the new narthex would honor this concept of viewing the campus' natural beauty.

The next picture was of a temple aside a pond and a Japanese garden in Kyoto, Japan. "If you visit Japan, you immediately see that man has captured the spiritual quality of nature. The relationship of their buildings and their traditional architecture with nature is phenomenal and moving. I chose this picture to underscore that in all religions, in all cultures, there is a need for worship and to worship in relation to nature. In early cultures, worshiping was done in natural settings, with trees, rocks, hills, mountain tops, and stone, etc."

Following these examples of exceptional architecture for spiritual and sacred spaces, Lohan surprised his audience by showing a picture of the current church at St. Mary's. He commented, "You have a wonderful little parish in the middle of rural northern Illinois landscape. That speaks strongly about the traditions of a farming community. It is relatively small. You've outgrown it. But the *quality* you have in this rural setting—great old trees, flat landscape, a church with a steeple—is a symbolic point visible from miles around. We would like somehow to preserve and enhance that quality. It's very nice to know that you've acquired a large piece of land where perhaps we can create that traditional rural setting that should remind you of the past and the traditions symbolized in the church as it is today."

Next appeared a picture of the interior of the predominantly glass Crystal Palace in Garden City, California. The burst of light from the image on the projection screen served to emphasize Lohan's next point. "This is simply to illustrate that to have a sacred space that moves people, that is emotional, you need to have some drama. Drama in the sense that the space has to be uplifting and breathtaking to some degree. It has nothing to do with size or physicality. It has to do with the 'feeling' of the space that you enter. People have said that the Crystal Palace is a breathtaking space when you enter.

"Another one, very different," he said while advancing to the next picture, "is this one." It showed a wood-beamed open chapel in the woods in Arkansas. "There is a strong relationship to nature that I would call "spiritual, sacred" because it is so different. It doesn't look like any normal, average, familiar building. That's a very important aspect. A church *shouldn't* look like any other building; it shouldn't look like a convention center or a hotel ballroom. *Nothing* like it." Lohan's remark was an acknowledgement that he understood one of Lewinski's main concerns about design.

Next followed a simple structure with a large man-made pool of water reflecting a white cross on the opposite side. The picture was taken from inside the worship space, looking out. "This is Japan," Lohan revealed. "To me, there is a symbolic quality, of course, in that cross. Again looking at nature, but with the water, there is also a contemplative quality. When you look at this picture and reflect on it, I believe it forces you, almost, to meditate."

An image of St. Procopius Abbey in Lisle, Illinois, was next. "What strikes me with this is the wonderful symphony of brick," commented Lohan. "Very simple, few materials, simple forms, well-detailed. That's the aspect that I want to emphasize. We want to do something that's well-crafted and that has a conviction about simplicity which is important in good architecture.[4] A famous architect from Chicago, Mies van der Rohe, was fond of saying, 'God is in the details.' Superior craftsmanship, then, is also important." When referring to Ludwig Mies van der Rohe, Lohan humbly did not mention that Mies—a contemporary of Frank Lloyd Wright—was his grandfather.[5]

Another photo was the interior of an abbey, showing a brick wall illuminated by natural light. "This picture illustrates one other point: the use of light. Light has always been the symbol of what you might call godliness and knowledge. The use of it, and the way it enters the space, has a lot to do with the quality of sacred space. It is important to consider that. It can establish a meditative quality that lets you forget your daily life and your chores, to listen to the Word and concentrate on your inner self." Later in the project, the wood-slatted "organ wall" behind the altar in the new church would become reminiscent of this image.

Lohan wrapped up this portion of his presentation. "We need to find a way to not isolate people from one another but to bring them together as an assembly, a congregation, a community of worshipers and believers. I hope that is an important aspect in your own mind as well. As we move forward, this is an important consideration." These words echo Lewinski's attitude toward design by honoring the concepts of Vatican II. Lewinski did not appear surprised at hearing anything Lohan had said. This presentation wasn't for Lewinski's benefit.

Lohan projected the last picture. "So, this is what we're beginning with. Your existing situation. We gave some thought to a modification, a second look at the Masterplan that has already been developed. We have some thoughts that we want to explain."

Lewinski interjected, "It might be helpful to talk about the steps involved in the project," as if he recalled a mental agenda.

Lohan agreed and introduced Jim Schubert, who would manage the project for Lohan Associates. Schubert displayed a high-level schedule showing completion of Phase I (the church and administration offices) extending three years into the future. He acknowledged it seemed a very long time, but it was "an ambitious schedule." The project had already been underway for two years.

He explained they would follow a design-bid-build process model. It would lead to the lowest cost for the highest quality. Throughout, there would be periodic reviews and approvals. They would incorporate any changes into the next phase. He suggested that between December and February, the parish should ensure it is on schedule; and determine how it will remain so.

"We are beginning, he continued, "in the design phase now, with the Master planning and conceptual design, which is a subset of the design phase. This is going to take a lot of dialogue... there's going to be dialogue during the entire course of this phase, and will continue after we complete the phase because it will set the framework for the project." They envisioned completing the current phase by Thanksgiving.

He set an expectation for the dialogue process of consensus building. Then the group could begin a systematic church and parish center design. They estimated three months for this. He stressed the need for communication and exchanging ideas and information throughout these phases. He noted the design and development phases would produce forty to fifty percent of the final construction documentation.

"The construction document completes that phase. You will have a set of documents that you can hand over to a contractor," he concluded. "The Masterplan and Conceptual Design phase will set the framework for all three phases of construction as you envision it now with the church, the school, and the intergenerational center."

At this point, Al Novickas asked Jim Scavone to discuss what the parish would do during the planning phase. Scavone's Education and Spirituality Committee felt a knowledgeable faith-based congregation could plan and communicate more effectively.

"Dirk and Jim," began Scavone, "talk a lot about community input. I believe we all recognize that we can't give that input until we go through some formation ourselves and come to a better understanding of what it really means to be Church and celebrate the Eucharist and all that implies." With these words, he was echoing Lewinski's point during the campus walk-through a year earlier. Lewinski had challenged a trio of questioners about their focus on the tabernacle's location and their reason for attending worship services.

Scavone continued, "Thinking about what we as a community are about is very much going to impact the ultimate design. For the Education

Committee, the bulk of our work comes before the schematic design stage next March. We have contracted with the Archdiocese, particularly David Phillipart, who will lead us through a formation process. It includes a variety of formats: retreats, workshops, and information sessions. Whoever wants to participate needs to go through formation. We all need to be speaking the same language and come to a common understanding when designing a church.

"In terms of time frame, we are starting shortly and working over the next six months or so into the design phase so the architects will clearly understand what we as a community would like to have." His comments reflected the expectation that the parishioners involved in the project would include many more people than those at this meeting.

Lohan's architectural philosophy arose from a core perspective of "context." A process of dialogue would develop greater clarity about church design. Lewinski's approach was a theological foundation for a faith community's development. It included building Church, a people of God. The interaction of these two approaches would produce a building and a congregation expressing the vision and mission of St. Mary parish.

Lewinski asked the architects to help the group understand the terminology being used.

Lohan responded. "'Master planning' and 'conceptual design' are considering all the spaces and relating them to each other, so we know where they will be one day: the entrance, the parking lots, the septic fields, the retention pond, all those things. Conceptual design, as part of that, is the broad-brush *concept* of the design, the general characteristics.

"Then, on the 'schematic design,' we will present a good image of what it will look like, what it is made of, and so on. We will do enough work in terms of elevations, plans, and sections and render a model that will allow you to see exactly what it will look like. I believe at that point, you will want to use the material for your fundraising because now you will have something that shows what you want to do. You will have an image that you can share with donors.

"Then comes what's called the 'design development' phase, enlarging the small-scale schematic design that doesn't have details. In design development, we look at all the major aspects of the building and development details. That gives the estimators and contractors something more realistic to work with. The emphasis is still on developing the design.

"The last phase is the contract document. This is when the design is finished; nothing changes. Then the emphasis is on making the drawings that the contractors need to erect the building and give you a final precise price quote. Does that help?"[6]

"Yes," replied Lewinski. Then, looking at Novickas, he guided the meeting forward, saying, "I think we should move into the next piece that will give us some idea of where we are."

Novickas rose and returned the poster board display to its position at the front. Then he placed on it a Site Plan that Lohan Associates had inherited from Newman Architecture. Everyone, of course, recognized the drawing that resembled a house missing half a roof.

What he was about to do would lead them in a different direction. Novickas stated they had already begun work. This included conversations with Lewinski and others and reviewing feedback from the Town Hall meeting. He was positioning himself to transition the group's expectations.

While the Site Plan developed by Newman Architecture met several specific requirements, he noted that it felt "a bit like a shopping mall." He questioned the building's rotated orientation; Erhart Road re-routing; multiple entryways and exits from the buildings; and a parking lot surrounding the church. He noted that multiple entry/exit doors negated the benefit of a single processional entrance.

"Based on a few discussions we've had with Father Ron, we have developed a very preliminary idea about how we might address some of those issues. There may be other issues," continued Novickas, "about the site plan, and today might be a good day to address those." While speaking, he moved Newman's site plan to another easel, revealing a new site plan that was visibly different.

Novickas explained, "Dirk mentioned we work with context. We started with one key idea: this is a rural site. The fundamental character of land development and disposition of property in northeastern Illinois is on an east-west, north-south grid system based on Thomas Jefferson's idea.[7]

"Another thing we considered was how components relate to each other. What happens when you congregate the facilities," he continued, motioning toward the earlier site plan, "is it becomes a megastructure instead of a church. So in this new plan, we have separated the church so it stands off as something special and different.

"We also believe it worthwhile to arrange the parking in a way that is relatively close without wrapping it around the building. We are proposing a building in a natural setting on three sides, so when you approach it, you see the building over nature, not over parking lots and cars. What we proposed here," he motioned at the area of land between the new church and the old, "we are calling our 'sacred zone,' encompassing the adjacent cemetery and existing church, as they are.

"We want some parking very close to the church for people who are disabled or have trouble walking. The main parking is located to the south.

What we propose here is to create what we call a pilgrimage path, where people walk from their cars down a fairly wide kind of garden path that is aligned in axis to the entrance to the church. So the experience becomes like walking through a park rather than a parking lot. Additionally, we propose the parking lot itself should be heavily landscaped with trees. You might recall the Chicago Botanical Gardens, which has a huge parking lot subdivided by islands with trees. It is a nice feeling—not like a shopping center parking lot.

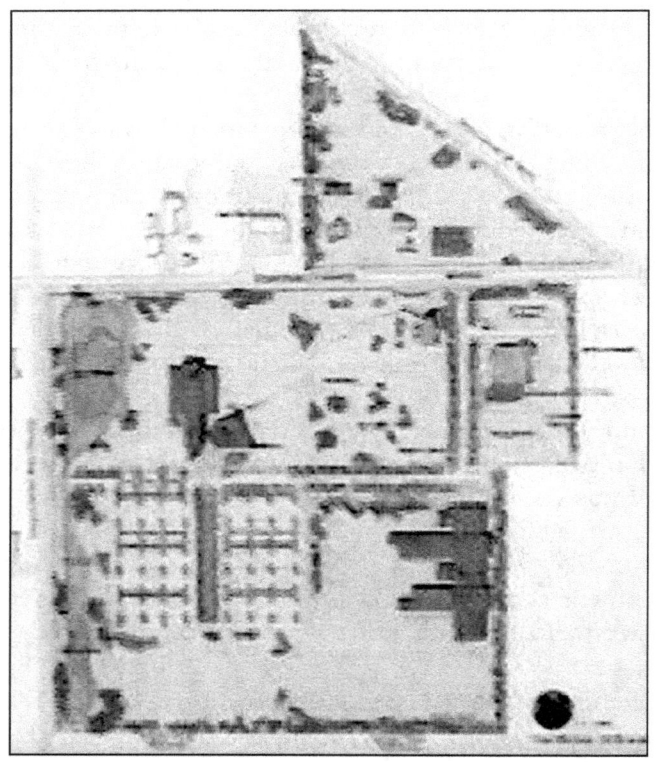

IMAGE #6

EARLY SITE PLAN BY LOHAN ASSOCIATES

THE ORIGINAL AXIS OF THE CHURCH WAS NORTH/SOUTH AS SHOWN HERE. SOON THE AXIS WAS CHANGED TO EAST/WEST, AND THE DESIGN OF THE BUILDING CHANGED TO ALIGN THE SANCTUARY, NARTHEX AND PASTORAL OFFICES UNDER A COMMON NAVE.

"I should also mention some traffic issues. Our traffic engineer has discovered Lake County is very stringent about providing access off a collective road. Fremont Center Road is a Lake County collective highway.

We're told it is most unlikely you can get access off that road because you have a feeder road, Erhart Road."

However, in keeping with the principle of honoring the past and keeping the rural quality, Novickas proposed an idea. "You have this beautiful old church. It would be very nice if when you came in, you saw that church and remembered that history. We are proposing this access point"—here he was pointing to a new road between the old church and the school—"as the main access point to the site so that you drive past the old church, come down toward the proposed school location and then approach the new church from the east."

Novickas returned to the concept of identifying buildings on the campus by locating them within a grid framework. "We did a little bubble diagram of your site up here." He pointed toward an upper portion of the drawing, with four colored squares and a triangle. "What this shows is that there are five different districts. One is this farm district in the triangle. A second preserves the existing church and school buildings. A third is a natural zone where the new church would be located. A fourth is a zone for parking. The fifth is a zone for the new school in the Southeast quadrant. We have taken a rural idea that finds a cluster of buildings separated by space here."

Some questions arose about the retention pond and the size of the parking lot. Lohan, knowing a proposal can become an expectation, intervened. "The important thing right now is to realize that this is a very preliminary approach to the problem. We had everyone coming in off of Fremont Center Road. Then we were told by our traffic consultant the county wouldn't permit that under any circumstances." His facial expressions showed his surprise and disappointment about the unexpected news. "So we were at a loss. What we are now proposing hadn't occurred to us because of the small scale of Erhart Road. But then, I am quite enamored by it, actually driving by the old church as part of a processional experience.

"The other thing I wanted to point out is that this new church would be visible over the pond, over the green space. It would be an icon along the highway. This is a wonderful, rich property. Like the old abbeys and cloisters that existed 100 years ago: they had a lot of land. You have quite a bit of land, which is very nice. So we can create this green zone which normally you have to squeeze much tighter. It is very nice. Another thing is the relationship to the cemetery. We have shown a footpath *through* the cemetery linking the two churches here."

Someone asked about the impact on Erhart Road. The earlier Site Plan showed it being redirected at a 90-degree approach to State Route 60. Lohan responded, "Well, we don't know to what extent this alteration of Erhart Road is possible. That involves the county as well. It is an expensive proposition to take a whole road out and build a new one. There's no question a right angle is better than the existing intersection."

Lewinski heard the discussion trending toward more specific concerns rather than generalities. As the facilitator, he needed to refocus the group. "This meeting's purpose is to show that there is another way to look at this whole thing. It isn't that we're settled on this site plan yet, either. Also, a purpose is to generate new questions, concerns, and issues so the architectural team can begin thinking about those issues now."

One attendee offered his perspective. "I think the whole concept of buying this land was to retain this rural setting. The idea of having the church surrounded by natural areas captures exactly what we told you we wanted. Whatever you do, don't change what you've done. I think you did a really good job."

To which Lohan responded, with an unspoken nod to his grandfather's principle 'less is more': "It is a simple plan; I think almost too simple. Simplicity is its strength. It's not fancy. It's as if that road has always been there."

Someone asked where the parish center would be located. Lewinski stated he didn't know, but "the value of separating the pastoral offices is it does preserve the church by itself." The attendees murmured in agreement.

The meeting continued with a discussion about a basement, the location and orientation of the future school building, and traffic flow for all facilities.

Lohan's earlier mention of having a design or model that parishioners could see had not gone unnoticed. The team needed such material to help people visualize what they were being asked to finance. Someone inquired about coordinating the architect's estimate and the planning for the capital campaign. A funds solicitation discussion included a reminder that the parish's mission was more important than the buildings. The ministries would benefit from having expanded facilities. However, donors would naturally focus on the tangible and visible benefits of their contribution. Novickas responded the process they were describing would produce the materials needed to address that concern.

Lewinski was eager to move forward. Yet, throughout the project, he tempered ambition with a measure of practicality. "In terms of a conceptual design and schematic design," he cautioned, "we want to have that as soon as possible, but we don't want to rush the process. We know it will aid the capital campaign—to have visuals—but we would be remiss if we race ahead simply to get something to show people. We're still talking about a three-year campaign."

He shared that some people were already responding with an "I'll wait and see" attitude. Lewinski observed if everyone responded like that, "we wouldn't have anything to look at." Being able to "see" a design could sway a contributor's decision.

Lewinski asked Lohan, "What do you folks need from us? What should we be looking at in the next month or two? What do you see us needing to do?"

"It would be very beneficial," Lohan responded, "if a committee was designated to interact with us on an ongoing basis. That doesn't mean other committees can't consult with us. But we will reach a point where we want to show something. Then a meeting can always be called—or even on a regularly scheduled basis—with the same people. Then there is a buildup of knowledge and understanding of the process. That would be very helpful to us."

Lewinski ended the session after some concluding comments. "Okay, I think we've exhausted our possibilities for tonight. I want to thank all of you for coming this evening. It may not feel like we accomplished a great deal," he rolled his hands in a 'traveling' motion. "What I wanted to do was first to have you meet the Lohan team. Second, for you to be present as we begin sorting out the pieces because it is like a puzzle in many ways."

He continued, directing his comments to Lohan. "This is an important meeting because this is where we're starting from. We'll get back to you. It is important to start together now, with all of us, as a 'new beginning' in a sense. And I want to thank all of you," nodding at Lohan's team. "It was really helpful to get a sense of who you folks are and to tease out a little further the vision we want to arrive at. We will meet again. Thank You."

Lewinski understood that while a lot of work remained, the meeting had been productive in several ways. It introduced Lohan Associates to more parishioners involved in the project. It allowed those people to meet and—importantly—assess Lohan and his team. Lohan showed visuals to trigger ideas and communicate perspectives he thought needed their consideration.

Most notably, Lohan's team had proposed changes to the Site Plan they'd inherited. They also explained their reasons for those changes. This was a significant redirection. It was a reminder that alternatives did indeed exist. Uncertainty is always part of the future

The group planned to reconvene on December 15th. First, fundraising needed some attention.

---

[1] http://blessedtrinitymissoula.org/wp-content/uploads/2015/04/Prayer-of-the-Dedication-of-a-Church-from-the-Rite-of-Dedication.pdf

[2] A part of the design for St. Mary's new church did involve water: an immersion baptismal font. With an internal measurement of about 5' x 7' and a depth of 18 inches, it contains about 400 gallons of water compared to the Oceanarium's 3 million, which is the world's largest indoor marine-mammal pavilion (source: britannica.com). During a subsequent Town Hall an elderly lady expressed concern about potential water leakage from the baptismal font. Lohan courteously replied that because he had designed the Oceanarium he was confident he could manage the baptismal font.

[3] Burnham (1846-1912) was an American architect who had a leading role in creating a Masterplan for development of Chicago as well as having been Director of Works for the 1893 World's Columbian Exposition (AKA World's Fair or "The White City") in Chicago. The Fair introduced several inventions and advances such as the Ferris Wheel (by American civil engineer George Washington Gale Ferris Jr., it accommodated over 2,160 people in 36 passenger cars of up to 60 people each), Juicy Fruit gum, an electric kitchen (including automatic dishwasher) and Vienna Beef (the "Chicago Hot Dog").

[4] Lohan, probably unknowingly, identified an outcome from Vatican II. "The Council's praise of 'noble simplicity' certainly rings a bell that most contemporary artists and architects find sympathetic." —McNaspy, p. 71.

[5] "'God is in the details' reveals the absolute nature of Mies's architecture, which displays such clarity that our perception of his buildings is elevated to an almost spiritual experience. There is also a strong hint that working out details requires great application—something akin to religious fervor." —Jim Eyre at https://wilkinsoneyre.com/thinking/god-is-in-the-details. Another quote attributed to Mies is "Less is more."

[6] During the meeting Lohan responded to more specific questions about the contracting process. He noted that his firm had not yet signed a contract with the Archdiocese. His comments pointed toward a difference in methodology between what his firm was accustomed to and how the Archdiocese approached projects like this. Effectively, he said the Archdiocesan approach might result in higher costs—or at least less accurate estimates—than the approach used by his firm: "The traditional way is the architect together with the designer provide an estimate at their own expense. That's the normal way. When we are asked to do that, we hire a cost estimator—who we pay—because they are professionals who do nothing but that; we don't. That's number one. Now many clients become distrustful of architect's cost estimates—our estimates, even though somebody else does them—simply because sometimes the market conditions change. So when you finally get to bid, there might be a problem. You get a price and it isn't what the architect's estimators said it would be. Sometimes the Archdiocese likes to hire—and it isn't clear whether it is a the Archdiocese's expense or our expense—what's called a pre-design estimate from a contractor simply because the perception is they know the market better than anyone else. Now we're getting to territory where we do not fully agree because contractors are very good at estimating from completed drawings and, in our experience, they are very bad at estimating from incomplete drawings. In the early stages of a project these very incomplete drawings, they are design drawings, they're not yet bidding drawings. So the guy who knows how to count doors or the number of bricks in the wall doesn't know how to count anything from a simple line drawing. Therein lies a problem and we need to discuss that and negotiate that with the Archdiocese so we can both be satisfied."

[7] The reader may find content at https://www.amusingplanet.com/2018/06/the-jefferson-grid.html interesting and entertaining. In short, the country's third President proposed an idea which was adopted in 1785—only 80 years prior to when St. Mary parish was established. It utilized grids to define property boundaries rather than using natural features, such as rivers, which had been used by the British. This had the advantage of scaling to large territories; but also allowed the government to plot and sell land to investors without them actually visiting the site.

FINDING FUNDING

October 1998

In early October, the Planning Commission organized a meeting in the church basement of about fifty parishioners. These people, most of them couples, had volunteered to solicit pledges from targeted households. Matt Hoolehan, the representative from CCS, identified himself. He welcomed everyone and then invited Lewinski to open the session. Lewinski did so, reciting the "Parish Prayer" he had introduced eight months earlier.

"Lord God," he began, "you founded your Church on the faith of the apostles and prophets with Christ Jesus as the capstone. Bless our efforts as we plan for the future of St. Mary's Parish. Fill us with the Spirit of wisdom and understanding so that we may know your will and carry it out in faith, hope, and love. By our prayer, work, and sacrifice, may we further the mission of your Son, our Lord Jesus Christ, who lives and reigns with you and the Holy Spirit, One God, forever and ever. Amen."

Lewinski said he could not stay for the entire meeting. He wanted to share some observations. Among the documentation given to the attendees was a Masterplan. It described aspects of the project and the concepts under consideration.

"First, we're really getting into the reality of this whole thing at this point. We are making the visits and making phone calls, and we're going to report on some of those in a little while. My first impression is that, even though we have talked about this for two years and written about it and everything else, it is not until people actually get that phone call that they respond, 'What do you mean?' It is not surprising in some sense that you catch them off guard. It's always that way when information is given: it seems to be for someone else other than me. But when you make that call, they know it is for *them*, and sometimes they don't know quite how to react. I have a sense that what will happen is that as word gets around, people will be more prepared for it.

"I just wanted to share a few thoughts on the Masterplan because I know people may ask you some questions. You may have some yourself. This," he held up the Masterplan, "is our selling point. Behind the Masterplan is a vision, a vision for a community of faith living, working, and praying together."

He reminded them about the project's true purpose. "I've said it many times—and I hope you make it part of your own language—that the reason we're doing this is not to put up buildings, but we're doing this to continue the mission of the Lord."

His next comment reflected the future. "This parish needs to be an oasis of hope and meaning in what is, in many ways, a troubled world. We, as a community, are not unlike a lighthouse. Our beacon says we have different values and can offer another way. Where are people going to get that?" Lewinski's image of a beacon, like that of a lighthouse, suggested he was already pondering a concept. That concept would eventually become the new church's steeple. It would be lit from the interior and be visible for miles from the surrounding roads and countryside.

He offered clarification of his remarks described in the Masterplan. "Now, in order for us to be those people and to work together and to pull ourselves together through education and prayer and formation and other activities, we need a place to do it. And *that's* the purpose of building. We do not intend the buildings to be monuments unto ourselves. They are necessary tools for us to carry on the mission. So, we have to communicate that. Some people may say, 'Well, I don't need any of those things.' I think what we are confronting in our society today is not just a religious problem, but a problem of people not knowing how to be community together. Unfortunately, we live in a society that is very individualistic, very private, and that thinks, 'if I don't get anything out of this, or if it's not for me, then why should I do anything.'"

He next commented on a prevailing attitude about the parish's mission before he had arrived. He now called on parishioners to consider not just themselves, their family circle, and the community inside the parish. He wanted them to envision something more, something without boundaries. It reflected one of his lifelong characteristics: a worldview.

"We're also doing some evangelization. We're trying to encourage people to look at their faith differently. I forgot to bring with me an article in the current issue of *Faith and Forum*, an architectural magazine. On the front cover is a picture of a new church in Rome, the Archdiocese of Rome. Some people don't think of Rome as a diocese, but it is. They were planning to build fifty new churches in the new millennium," he said, somewhat cynically. "They have now realized that this might be a *little* ambitious, so they have focused on twelve." This invoked some laughter.

"The interesting thing is the church's design: it is very, very modern. It is very creative, and it is by an American architect named Richard Meier. He is a world-famous architect. He is Jewish and has never built a church before. But the Vatican, who is sponsoring this whole thing, wanted to get the very best. Here's the catch: in their mission statement, they have said, 'Our purpose for building these churches is all part of one goal for evangelization in the year 2000.' Even the way they built the church, the way it looks, the way it attracts people, and the signs that it gives to the community are evangelization tools.

"I thought that was interesting, coming right from the top—the 'headquarters.' I think the message is for ourselves as well. Not only are the buildings that we're putting together something to house who we are, but even the buildings themselves will hopefully be an actual sign and a beacon to others—a piece in this entire process of evangelization."

The topic of this meeting was financing the project. Some people might view this effort simply as asking parishioners to contribute more. Lewinski's remarks were a reality check. He wanted to expand their vision *beyond* their faith community. He was redirecting their focus from local funding to broader evangelization. He bluntly challenged some people's attitude of 'we do not need to do anything more.' A parish doesn't exist for the parishioners alone; it exists for the world.

Lewinski often expressed his belief that a parish offers something not just *worth* sharing, but something that *must* be communicated beyond the community. His belief evoked memories of evangelist Billy Graham when he claimed, "I'm selling the greatest product in the world."[1] Lewinski repeated this in meetings throughout the project, changing the phrasing to "We're offering the greatest product in the world."

He'd stated his views on what he considered important about this funding effort. He continued by commenting on the logistical aspects.

"Yesterday, I met with the new Finance Director for the Archdiocese. I shared with him our concerns, and he's very interested—and supportive— of what we're doing. I strongly believe that if we were to meet our goal of $10 million, the diocese might very well support us at *this* stage and say go ahead, get a significant amount of capital." Lewinski didn't doubt they could raise a considerable amount, but how quickly? So he hoped the parish might start earlier than normal. He was speaking to the people who would determine the success of this initial effort.

He identified what would be required. "But we have to show a good effort so that we can move this along. In terms of what we're trying to do, people ask, 'Well, what kind of church is it going to be?' We don't know; we're still working on that. We would not want to choose an architect who said, 'I know just the church you guys want.' We need someone who will listen to what this community is about, someone who is sensitive to what the landscape is here, what the tradition is, and out of all of that, produce something that will fit our vision." His comments were not speculative. They had already decided to use Lohan Associates. However, the initial concepts still had not materialized as a schematic they could show to a parishioner being asked to pledge financial support.

Lewinski shared what was known by including it in the materials given to the attendees. The plans would, of course, change. He briefly touched on the highlights so he could respond to questions before leaving.

"The church obviously is a major piece. Within that structure, there will be the usual kinds of things that you will expect in a church, but also some meeting space as well, a hospitality room that we could use for brides, or wakes in the narthex—which is a kind of multipurpose area. Part of that Masterplan also includes some parish offices and meeting spaces, which we need very badly. The parish is growing, and we are trying to do more. We have almost peaked because we cannot bring on any other ministries or services: there is no room for them. So this effort is not only for what we have now but for the future as well."

He noted they had engaged a world-class architect, and the parish itself had many resources. "We need to convey to folks we are working with a great deal of professional expertise. We have great people working on this.

"Some people think, 'Well, if you want to build a church, just get those bulldozers over here and get started; what are you waiting for?' But there is a lot of necessary prep work. It is essential it is done and done *well*." A glance at his watch told him he'd been speaking longer than he'd planned. "Are there any questions you have about this plan?"

One attendee asked about the anticipated common questions. Why does this cost so much? Why such a big complex? Can't we scale it down —make it smaller and still functional? Does it need to be so fancy?

Lewinski understood that someone's reaction to the plan depended on many variables: their personal idea of what the parish was and should be, their familiarity with other churches and parishes, their perception of their own ability to subsidize this effort regardless of how much they did or didn't believe in the need. He commented the architects themselves were conscious of costs. "Mr. Lohan and his associates have been very good, being on the phone, hammering away asking whether we really need this, does that room have to be this size, and constantly scrutinizing us." He claimed one could go around the country and see comparable costs. He knew because he had done that himself shortly before arriving.

He said it was challenging to properly build for significantly less. The costs also included land acquisition and professional services. There were governmental requirements about parking space, water retention, and the size of the septic field. He cautioned that people might improperly compare it to residential construction.

"It is not a house that we're building. We must build something that will stand for one hundred years or more. The County will tell us how big things like the parking lot and septic field have to be. In terms of fancy, I don't think there's going to be anything that we would consider *extravagant*. On the other hand, when we find things that are beautiful, I think that's what the community wants. In terms of overall expense, I don't feel that it is an extravagant number."

Someone noted the area was experiencing so much growth that if the parish didn't plan adequately now, another expansion might be needed later. Lewinski responded, "Right, the most recent statistic was in the paper just about a week ago. By the year 2020, the county will have grown 47%.[2] And it will not be in Waukegan, the County seat. We're sitting on the empty acres, which will be part of that development."

He then commented on another thing: declining numbers of ordinations in the United States. The number of priests and nuns was decreasing. It was a different world than Lewinski had known as a child just five decades earlier. Nearly every family had a relative in or entering the priesthood back then.

His comments answered a frequent question about a seating capacity of 1,100. Lohan himself not only questioned it but challenged it. He stated, "The diocese has no intention of building another parish in our vicinity. The closest location to us that the diocese is looking at right now is on the Wisconsin border near Antioch.[3] And that's another reason for the church being larger. The day will come when there will only be one priest if that. So there will be fewer Masses in the future. That's why around the country, for a new church in a suburban metro area, there is a general rule of seating about 1,000 to 1,100 people.

"Those are good questions. The hardest thing that I'm hearing from people is that they are having difficulty thinking long-range. It is normal for everyone to think about tomorrow or their own lifetime, but we're talking about many years from now—even 100 years from now—not just the immediate future.

"There are cases in our own diocese where mistakes were made because of such shortsightedness. Once you 'do' shortsightedness, it becomes expensive trying to 'undo' it. It is really a mess. That's what we're keeping in mind." Once again, he was reminding them the vision for this project encompassed a time period that parishioners—especially long-established ones—were having difficulty grasping.

"As far as the capital campaign," he continued, "we know it is an incredible challenge, but we also feel that it is an opportunity for us to invest in the future. We expect people joining the parish will invest in that future as well. I can say, from firsthand experience, that even people who have *just* moved into the parish have been very generous. Those are the people who I have been most humble about asking, and yet they have been some of the most generous people of all.

"I was reflecting and praying about this. People keep talking about the ancestors here who built this place. I wasn't here when they did it, and I haven't been long. But I remember I had a very good experience growing up at Assumption Parish on the south side of Chicago. It was a wonderful parish. I *loved* the church. It was *home* to me. The school was a wonderful place. I have such warm memories. As I think about that, I don't know that I ever gave a penny to it as a kid. I just presumed it was there for *me*.

"But now, I'd really like to thank those people who provided that for me. I think I can now offer something to the next generation. As I say, when you go out there, remember that you're not just selling a project; you are evangelizing.

"I'll tell you one last story. During a visit that I recently made, the person was hard to read. But he called me back and said, 'You know you gave us this invitation, and we had to do some hard thinking about this as a family. We came up with two commitments.' I said, 'What do you mean?' He said, 'Well, we realized that we're not always here on Sunday. So, as a family, we sat around the kitchen table and decided that the first thing we have to do is make a commitment: from now on, we're going to make every effort to be here on Sunday. The second commitment is that we want to make a pledge as well.'

"That first piece," observed Lewinski, referring to the desire for more frequent worship, "is the more important one. Who knows: what you do may to plant that seed." This was also an indirect acknowledgment that in Catholic parishes, less than 50% of registered parishioners regularly attend Sunday services. Consequently, contributions from the pews are typically lower—on a percentage basis—than those of other Christian denominations. The project funding would depend upon the pledges now being solicited and current and future collections during worship.

Before departing, he commented on the Masterplan each attendee had been given. "It's a case statement but doesn't get specific with details. It is more a vision of what we're all about and some of the history and the theological basis for what we're doing as well. I encourage you to digest it." It was his way of saying the Masterplan was more than a handout for them to take with them. It was a homework assignment. He explained the reasoning behind the effort and provided an interpretation that would support their efforts to solicit pledges from a fellow parishioner.

This was the group's second session. They held the first a week prior. Despite his conflicting commitments, Lewinski's presence at this meeting showed the importance he placed on this phase of solicitations. The number of pledges they secured would indicate the campaign's potential for soliciting financial support from the parish. They could then approach a broader population. The intent now was to accumulate pledges totaling a significant amount. Success would increase the likelihood of obtaining a higher level of financial commitment in the next phase, and eventually from the Archdiocese.

Certainly, they were facing challenges. The ocean of change fluctuated between calm and stormy. Lewinski was no different from anyone else when dealing with whatever the conditions were. Except he had the added obligation, as a pastor, of tending to his flock. He sincerely cared for them. On October 11th, he wrote:

> I'm saddened when I hear attitudes that sound bitter, hopeless, and resentful. A senior citizen told me the other day that he accepts no responsibility for anything anymore because he's retired. He won't watch his grandchildren, he won't volunteer at the parish, he won't vote, and he listed several other things. Too bad. Surely retirement should mean freedom from some of the hard labor that kept us from pursuing other dreams. But does retirement mean no more responsibility?
>
> Another parishioner sounded like sour grapes when invited to get on board with our parish planning and development for the future. I've been here a long time. Grunt. I don't need a new church. Grunt. I want nothing to do with it. Grunt. Change is hard. Making a sacrifice is hard. But what does it mean to be the living Church of Christ? Shouldn't we be happy and grateful to see the parish alive in so many ways? I don't know about you, but I'm so grateful for the wonderful Catholic parish I grew up in that now I want to thank those who provided that experience for me by making a sacrifice for the next generation. I guess it's all a matter of attitude. As one elderly man told me, "Father, making a sacrifice for the new church is going to be hard. But I'm going to do it with trust in God because he's never failed to bless me fourfold when I made a sacrifice in the past."[4]

His writing reflects what he reiterated to the Parish Council during their October meeting. The Council must help the ministries accomplish their work. A sense of ownership, and stewardship, fostered by the Commissions, needs to flow through their ministries into the parish and beyond. Their Mission extends beyond the parish.

Small steps continued moving them forward. An Oktoberfest was held in Diantha Hall. Like pancake breakfasts and potluck dinners, it was one of several social events they hosted to counterbalance the work effort. More importantly, socializing helped people get acquainted, and it strengthened the sense of community important to a project of this scope. The Pastoral Council approved a request by the Society of St. Vincent de Paul to establish a drop box for clothing on campus. The church was being painted and the pews refinished. The capital campaign was progressing. Lewinski expressed satisfaction from working with Lohan Associates.

Early November found Lewinski continuing to explain the rationale for the $10 million cost of Phase I. Half was for the church. The rest was for preparatory work for all phases. He commented on the impact the project was having. "I realize there are many new parishioners who discovered that there is a major Capital Campaign only weeks after registering in the parish. I feel a bit shy about approaching new arrivals; on the other hand, approximately half the parish has been registered less than 2 1/2 years. I encourage new parishioners to look at this opportunity as a wonderful way to claim St. Mary's as their spiritual home."[5]

During the Pastoral Council meeting in November, it became evident there was still confusion about laypeople's roles and responsibilities. Lewinski had empowered the Pastoral Council and lay leadership long ago. They hadn't experienced the kind of expectations Lewinski brought with him three years earlier. It wasn't the "hands-off" attitude they had known, but more of an "it's in your hands now" delegation by the pastor.[6]

Emphasis on the importance of utilizing a parish calendar was increasing. One challenge was that the ministries were growing, but the meeting spaces were not. Lewinski had opened up the former rectory as office and meeting spaces. The old convent, now called Gabriel House, was also partially available. Otherwise, no "new" space was available, and there would not be unless they built additional facilities.

Thus, Lewinski directed all requests for meeting space to go through the parish office. There could be no guarantees of space availability solely because a ministry was accustomed to gathering at a certain time or place.

They gave name tags to Council and Planning Commission members. More meetings and Town Halls would occur. Parish representatives needed to be identifiable.

The Pastoral Council broke into groups during a special session on November 16th. They discussed questions related to the Vision that Lewinski had shared with parishioners.

1. How do you develop a community in a society that values independence?
2. What part of the vision moved you (what do you feel is the most important element of the vision, and why is it so important to you)?
3. What is missing from the vision? Do any elements need clarification?
4. Does the vision paint a clear and detailed picture of what we hope our parish will look like? Could you create a video presenting our vision based on the written document?
5. Are you "excited" by the vision? If so, why? If not, what will it take to make the vision exciting?[7]

Like any good pilot, Lewinski could not assume they were on course after a direction had been set toward a specified goal. Lengthy journeys require frequent navigation checks.

---

[1] Myra and Shelley, p. 314.

[2] This did not occur. A major factor was the 2008 economic downturn which could not have been foreseen when this meeting occurred. According to county demographic records, the housing unit increase between 2000 (two years after this meeting) and 2010 was 15% . Population growth had been constantly increasing in Lake County since 1980 until 2009 when it leveled off. It remained relatively unchanged until 2017 (the most recent population estimates at the time of this writing).

[3] Antioch is about 15 miles north of Fremont Center, close to the Wisconsin border.

[4] Sunday bulletin, October 11, 1998, p. 3.

[5] Sunday bulletin, November 1, 1998, p. 4.

[6] As quoted in Pastoral Council meeting minutes from May 10, 1999, regarding the noted absence of several ministry leaders from a parish leadership meeting. Lewinski said: "The ministry leaders need to know that they are leaders. Things are different now than they used to be. People are empowered to take ownership."

[7] Pastoral Council minutes, November 16, 1998. Collective answers included:

1. Open to opinions of others. Listening. Develop a sense of welcome. Challenge the assumption that independence is desirable in an open discussion. Informal gatherings. Be persistent. Follow-up. Invite others. Have parties.

2. Image of a lighthouse. Lay leadership. Family community. Build for the future.

3. What is missing from the vision. Do any elements need clarification?

4. For Lewinski, this question probably wasn't rhetorical. He may have submitted it as a way to ignite someone's creative force. Eventually, a video was in fact produced.

5. What the individual sees in their head excites them. Excited but mystified. Excited too strong. Intrigued.

NEVER LOOK DOWN

Winter 1998-1999

On December 15th at 3:30 p.m., the planning team reconvened in Diantha Hall. The outdoor temperature was an unexpectedly balmy fifty degrees. It would return to freezing right before Christmas. Lohan and company were thankful for Mother Nature's blessing today because they each had one- to two-hour commutes for these meetings.

After a brief prayer, Lewinski welcomed everyone and thanked them for sharing their time when the holiday was just over a week away. He explained, "It is important for us to keep on schedule as much as we can so we don't get behind on things."

Lewinski said the meeting's purpose was "to give you some sense of where we are compared to the last time we were together in September, where we're going, and what has happened in between. One thing that has become clear to me is we are always trying to hold values in check.

"And so, for instance, when we began the conceptual design in terms of values, we want enough room to accommodate many people, but a space that allows us to participate in the liturgy that the spirit of Vatican II has taught us we have a right to. We are not *spectators* at the liturgy; we are active *participants* in the liturgy. So how do you maintain those kinds of values? It's a genuine struggle when you're dealing with a large space."

Lewinski stated the team was visiting parishes in Northern Illinois. They had seen churches that had tried to satisfy a sense of participation. However, those "lost the other dimensions of a sense of awesomeness and reverence, so it looks like a Holiday Inn meeting room."

Throughout the project, Lewinski constantly returned to this point. It was, for him, perhaps the greatest challenge of design. How to create a space large enough to accommodate as many people as possible without losing a feeling of inclusiveness? He stated the best shape for the purpose was a square, not a traditional rectangle. It was the most economical.

Lewinski claimed they were no longer talking in the abstract; but now had a model, sketches, and photographs. He cautioned, "It is nowhere near a complete state of affairs, but they presented it to stimulate our thinking. Our intention is to listen to what both Al and Dirk have to say, give them some input and observations, ask some questions," Lewinski said. "We couldn't do what we're going to do here tonight with a group of 300 people: it would be mass chaos. Even with what you see here, we found things that were problematic the last time we met with Lohan's team. It is with different perspectives that we look at something. That's the value of this kind of collaborative confrontation we're having here today."

Lewinski wanted to ensure the design process reflected as many opinions as possible. He knew there was an opportunity for "chaos" even in a small group. He trusted it could be contained.

He turned the meeting over to Lohan. "I'd just like to echo what Father Ron mentioned. We are presenting tonight our first thoughts on how the architecture of this church might develop based on input we have so far from you, Father, and several others. But what is equally important is the research, the meetings, and the visits to other churches—*all* lead to the creation and development of such a building. We are challenged by this design. We are thinking and seeking with you to find the right answer.

"This search is, in a way," Lohan continued with a smile, "the best part of the entire project: coming to a solution to the various questions posed. We have taken just the first step, and we want to share that with you in order for you to react to it and encourage us. It is important because we want to do something meaningful for your entire parish community." Lohan's choice of words reflected his perspective that he and his client are "in it together." He was aiming for something more than the physicality of a building. Because this was a church, he wanted something that had both spiritual and physical value.

Lohan's conversations with Lewinski affirmed his attitude about design. Both agreed they were designing more than a structure. The design needed to possess meaning for the entire parish. It should also represent the community to the world beyond. Lohan turned it over to Novickas, who recapped takeaways from the September meeting.

"We have made some revisions." Novickas pointed to the site plan. "We've added a rectory." Here he pointed to an area in the 'triangle,' bounded by Route 60, Fremont Center Road, and Erhart Road.[1] "We've created a farm-like group of structures by the old barn on Erhart Road.

Novickas continued by reviewing the proposed school location. It was part of a later phase. They estimated a starting size of 60,000 square feet. The existing facility would remain in service until they finished the new building. Then the 'old school' could transform into an 'intergenerational center.' Comments arose about this, but Lohan intervened by saying, "We have not planned very seriously for the school site. Al didn't mention this, but this isn't a proposed design, per se. This is really only to illustrate a potential location and site plan." In other words, let's not spend effort on this now; it is part of a later phase.

Phase I included the church and rectory. Phases II and III are for the new school and intergenerational center. Planning for later phases was part of Phase I. They needed to anticipate facility locations and future infrastructure requirements.

A discussion about campus access ensued. Erhart Road and its relationship to Route 60 remained a thorny issue. Lohan stated, "The obvious solution is that Erhart Road would move so the intersection with Route 60 would be a 90° angle. And perhaps put a traffic light there. What we know so far is if you want to do this, then you pay for it. We think perhaps that might not be the highest priority for this project. It strains resources from other things."

Novickas next spoke about the parking lot and landscaping. He mentioned their landscape artist wasn't there because he was at an award dinner as a speaker and recipient. The landscape designer was Terry Harkness, a nationally recognized designer and a professor at the University of Illinois in Champaign, Illinois.[2] Novickas said their concept depicted in the site plan represented a row of farm-like trees along the property's southern border. The design intended to preserve the prairie atmosphere on the property.

Lohan interjected, "I think the most important thing at this point is as a group to hopefully agree on the basics of the site plan, which is a road and access that follows the rural tradition of this part of Illinois in that the roads are basically at right angles to each other and will minimize the landscape. You have the kind of church that is a beautiful building, you have the cemetery, and we're trying to build on that with a rural quality. It is what we saw when we first came into this area. That's what we're trying to preserve and enhance.

"I would like to now move," Lohan continued, "into some of the thinking about the design of the church proper and its function. There are two design aspects of this building that are essential issues that we need to deal with and that we need to solve. One, as always with any building design, is the functional aspect—the flow of people, the seating arrangement, the viewing angles to the altar—all of those are functional aspects that have to work and have to be resolved in such a way that they are satisfactory and can make the function of the service and the interaction of the congregation work."

Lohan then addressed something of special importance to Lewinski: spirituality. "The second aspect, which is an intangible one, is to find a solution which has a sacred/spiritual quality. Thinking about this is required on the part of everybody—including us, very much so. It is an aspect of architecture that is very hard to quantify. There are no formulas for it. It has to do with a certain feeling in the space.

"I would be the first one to admit that a little model like this," he pointed to the 20-inch-long wooden model on the table in front of him, "cannot give you a convincing aspect about the sacredness of the space or the spiritual quality we are creating. To some degree, you have to give us a little faith and trust. We start very small, but we are imagining the real space. When I look at this, I already see the volume of the sanctuary and so on. That will take a little imagination on your part, but we have made an effort to make the drawings large and the pictures larger so they are a little closer to reality and easier for you to imagine."

Lohan said he learned much about Judaism while recently designing a synagogue. His remarks suggested he was now learning about Catholicism and the Second Vatican Council. No doubt Lewinski was an influence.

"In studying examples of church design," continued Lohan, "particularly since Vatican II, I think there are designers and parishes which have had a difficult time making it work. There are probably two factors that play into this. One is that parishes are growing in size. You are a perfect example. There used to be a few hundred households, and now there are eleven or twelve hundred. The liturgy is the same, but bringing people closer—which is the essence of Vatican II—is not an easy task. Many churches very quickly assume a feeling of an auditorium or a convention center, and the feeling during the service becomes that.

"One way to solve the problem is to get away from the linear or rectilinear nave quality of a church, where you might feel you are sitting 'a mile away.' You don't know what's going on, and you can't see much because everything is very distant. Everyone here who has been in a large church has experienced that feeling.

"You have a small church where you have a couple of hundred people, so you feel close now. With a large number of people, it goes away. One solution is to wrap the seating around the altar—at *least* on three sides, even though there is an implication in Vatican II for a church in the round where the altar might be in the center and have parishioners all around it. In all the examples we have seen, there is not one church that is truly a church in the round. It does not seem to work, and I know Father Ron doesn't particularly like it. I understand that very well because it would mean some people are facing the priest's back. So we have found a seating arrangement I would like to think is a cross between the traditional and seating in the round."

Lohan moved to another overhead drawing and pointed to a square above a rectangle. The square was the sanctuary (church), and the rectangle was the narthex (lobby).

"We have designed a roof—a rectilinear space—that is one continuum, uniting everything under it. So we're placing the church, the daily chapel, the narthex, and various other functions under it. The sheltering roof is the central unifying architectural concept. We have made the traditional church nave, going out from the sacred space, a central theme. This space," he said while pointing to the narthex, "is for meeting and greeting and socializing after the service. It is a very important space. It is also a space where you go to the chapel. You have the duality of the large space for the weekend and the daily chapel at the opposite end.

"All the other functions which are more mundane, which are not as spiritual, are located in this odd-shaped building." Here, he identified the pastoral center containing offices, meeting rooms, and other spaces. It was separate from the sanctuary and narthex but connected near the southern entry to the narthex.

"Now, we are beginning a new millennium, and obviously, the imagery, the style, of what we are presenting is not traditional. I don't want to say it is avant-garde. It is based on traditional aspects of church design, such as the nave—a formal axis in the church, if you will. These are elements of church design that you are familiar with.

"We attempted to bring the linear aspect to this and not make it as if it were a big convention center type of arrangement. So I invite you to think of this as a design that is very contemporary and is based on fundamental church design yet incorporates traditional form and common elements. It is not postmodern architecture. We like to think of it as a contemporary solution to how a church should be designed in this day and age."

Lewinski interjected, asking Lohan to speak to heights contained within the design.

"Yes, very important," responded Lohan. "There are two heights. The main sanctuary space on the periphery is about thirty feet high. The gently curving roof of the nave is about forty-five feet at the peak in the center. We struggled, and invite your comments, with the basic form of the church." He was now positioned at an overhead drawing of the sanctuary, which illustrated the "gills" along the side walls and the interior seating arrangement. "What we have shown here is what we concluded was the better alternative.

"We felt very strongly about the importance for the space to allow daylight to enter from the outside. But from the inside, the view is not a window you look out of. The light from outside is conducted in such a way that it creates an illuminating wash on textured walls."

He pointed at the portions resembling gills. He explained, "These wavy elements have windows on the southern portion where the sunlight enters and washes the walls inside. Those sitting inside facing the altar are not looking out the windows. Another important element is the central curved roof that is elevated higher above the sanctuary. There is another series of windows to bring light in from above.

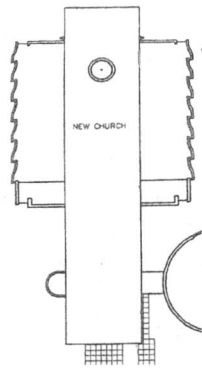

IMAGE #7

AN EARLY DESIGN BY LOHAN ASSOCIATES

THE NEW CHURCH (UPPER PORTION) AND NARTHEX
(LOWER PORTION) ARE ON A NORTH/SOUTH AXIS.
THE PASTORAL CENTER IS NOT FULLY SHOWN BUT
IS INDICATED BY THE ARC AT THE BOTTOM RIGHT.

"There is a third element that has a lot to do with light, which is the steeple. It is not a bell steeple, but in our mind is a metaphor recalling a traditional church and indicating this building as a church. However, it has a very specific function, and that is to bring daylight directly down through the cone shape onto the altar and highlight it.

"We achieve this in two ways. There could be glass in the steeple to bring light inside. We could separate the steeple from the roof with a ring of glass around it. Either way, the altar surface receives the light from above. Inside, you have a large cone, the 'base' element, over the altar. This designates a sacred space in the building. So the three sources of light are very strong elements in this whole concept."

Lewinski commented on the visits to other parishes the team had conducted over the past few months. "We saw a lot of churches had a tower, but when you entered, the inside didn't match the outside. So there may have been a beautiful dome over the church, but it is basically over nothing in particular when you are inside."

Lohan continued, "We often deal with the question of being truthful. That is, when there is a door shown in a design, it should be a door; where there is a window, it should be a window. This is something we believe in deeply—certainly, I do. The designation of where the altar *is* in a church should be where the altar should *be*. It should not mislead you. So that's what we're trying to do by positioning the outside steeple directly over the inside altar.

"One more aspect. The narthex is a very unusual space in this design, but its function is exactly what it should be. It isn't just a carpeted party room—it is a church-like space that is very vertical and high. A lot of glass surrounds it. When you enter that space, you have a fantastic view outside, down to the low-lying meadows, and in the other direction, up the hill to the old church. During the day, sunshine fills it. The concept is that when you go through the door from the narthex into the church, you are going from a very wide open space into an enclosed one. The light in the enclosed space has an indirect quality, a somewhat spiritual quality."

As he spoke, team members strove to understand the design concepts. Some notions were philosophical. Some were theological. Others were physical aspects regarding light and a sense of space. Lohan also referred to psychological and spiritual aspects driving the concept.

Novickas then spoke. "What we tried to do is apply a rural idea. It is a collection of farm buildings. Each individual building has a very specific function. All are clustered close together and organized around a central space. Thus the idea of this sheltered roof grew out of the rural tradition of how farm buildings are organized." Novickas identified the locations of administrative offices, meeting rooms, a hospitality room, a pantry, washrooms, coat rooms, closets, storage, and mechanical areas.

Pointing to the narthex, Novickas explained, "It is entirely fritted glass. Perhaps the narthex has wood slabs like you have in a rural structure to allow ventilation and a lot of light to enter. A sheltered roof overhangs the narthex by a few feet, and the columns are located outside the structure. The glass will soften the light. At the bottom of the narthex walls, however, is a ten-foot-high area of clear glass that could include sliding doors so that on a beautiful day, you could open them up, and the entire narthex becomes like an open pavilion.

"The next major space is the sanctuary space. Dirk mentioned that a key idea is to allow light to come through these glass "slits" between the serrated walls. We also propose a row of columns to create an ambulatory, a way to 'walk around' the sanctuary. The purpose of that," explained Novickas, "is that when you have a room with just a solid wall, the space becomes very static. We want to achieve a more dynamic kind of quality —to have a distinct sense of mystery.

"An issue that we have had a lot of discussions about is where to locate the Eucharistic Chapel. We are meeting again with Father Ron tomorrow. We're going to propose that the Eucharistic Chapel be on the north side of the altar. It is articulated on the outside of the building so that you can see it as you drive by. So access would be on either side of the altar.

"What you see in this rectangular area between the altar and the Eucharistic Chapel is the organ space. We've had some preliminary discussions, and the recommendation is to place the organ at that location. The choir is located over here on the side, close to the altar."

A team member challenged making the narthex and the sanctuary the same height. Lohan responded, "We like this very much because we think it has a church quality in its own right. It is a seamless continuum from the sanctuary going out of the church. I see it as a transitional space: you come from the outside, which is the open sky, into a very tall space and very open to the light. It will have a quality that prepares you to enter the sanctuary, a space which itself is more enclosing because both sides of the middle aisle have lower ceilings."

It did not go unnoticed that the design had a lot of glass. The topic repeatedly surfaced during meetings and Town Halls. Many didn't yet understand that the proposed material was not used in residential homes. Living in the northern Illinois prairie land—with its gusty winter winds and snow sometimes falling nearly parallel to the ground—reveals the effective insulating property (or lack thereof) of windows. So now a team member raised the question: how energy efficient was this glass?

Lohan responded confidently, "That's something we know about. We are known to do a lot of glass work. Glass technology today is such that you can have a range of glass, from traditional clear glass to shaded glass, that allows light penetration of less than ten percent. The same is true of energy because there are coatings in the glass. We are talking about fritting[3] or even louvers. We would design this in such a way that it is an energy-efficient space like any other part of the building so that it doesn't have to be unduly cooled in the summer or heated in the winter. The windows have to be insulated glass, obviously.

"The next thing we will do, if you let us, is to build these models bigger so you can 'feel' the space and see it. That's a long answer to your very practical question, but we know very well that there should not be any unusual penalty for having glass.

"You might look at buildings we have done. One is the Adler Planetarium, which we are just finishing up as an expansion project. Sixty thousand square feet, all under glass. The glass is highly shaded—it has a shading coefficient of over 90%: that's how much light is filtered out. Less than 10% of light comes in. You would think, 'It must be dark,' but there is plenty of light inside the space. *Lots* of light."

Lohan responded to a question about maintenance and replacement. "There are technical issues. We are definitely committed to designing something that is long-lasting. Which, of course, means it has to be well-constructed." The implication was that even the best design can become faulty over time, depending on the quality of construction. He added,

"The problem of maintenance is a problem of corrosion and so on; it is one for various materials that you need to maintain."

A brief review of the Sanctuary doors followed. The entry from the narthex into the sanctuary was separated by two large doors fifteen feet high. They were hanging barn doors that slid left and right, exposing the baptismal font. A similar set of doors separated the baptismal font from the inner sanctuary. Either set of doors could be open or closed depending on the event's needs.

Another point of confusion was the extent of visibility between the sanctuary and the Eucharistic Chapel. One attendee challenged, "How is that configuration making the Blessed Sacrament chapel prominent? That is what the code of Canon law requires. So how is this *prominent*?"

Lohan replied, "Let me ask you, where do you think we should put it?"

"I'm not sure," she replied. "I just have the idea that the tabernacle, or Blessed Sacrament, should be prominent when I come into a Catholic church. I shouldn't have to look around for it. That's Canon law."

Scavone chimed in. "I think some interpretation is needed about what the Church means by 'prominent.'"[4]

Another team member then shared her impressions. "When I first came in, I thought it looked very contemporary. But then, as I sat here, I thought about it, and it is almost like the shape of a barn. The more you study this, the more art form it presents."

Lohan responded, "The interesting thing is what you mentioned: with this version where we took the sanctuary underneath, the design becomes more traditional. Everybody has a perspective. Other people might think something else. That's why one has to examine this to get the right association. What we want to achieve is that everybody in the future will say this looks like a *church*, even though it is an 'unusual' church."

Lewinski then noted how to view the 3-D scale models. The 2-D drawings, showing building elevations from the side, were easily 'understood.' That is how people normally see buildings. The 3-D models presented an important difference: they could be viewed from any angle. But most often—because the models were on a tabletop—they were viewed from above. Lewinski injected, "Dirk, you made a very good point in one meeting about looking at these models as seeing them like from an airplane. But we will never see this building from that perspective. We really have to understand how to view it."

To which Lohan simply replied, "Yes, you never look down."[5]

Another team member shared his reaction to the design. "As I walked in, I thought, 'That is more contemporary than I expected.' As we discussed it, and as I understand the layout, I now think it is very wonderful. I think everyone came here with an open mind. We may have walked in and thought, 'That isn't exactly what I'm expecting, but I'm going to give it a chance.' I know I did that, and it has grown on me during the evening."

One woman remarked, "I like that the church is separate from the business portion. That's important. I like very much the way you are going to use light."

A different team member affirmed these remarks. "Some comments were made when we first came in and saw this. 'This doesn't quite match what I had in mind.' But I think that the explanation, the understanding, and the communication shed light on why we chose this and why we didn't choose something else, and why this serves this function and not that function. I would just like to say that there is still more research to do, and we would like to share more insights with you from the study and the research that we are doing in order to contribute to the further development of the concept."

Lohan acknowledged, "We actually *seek* that from you."

Several simultaneous conversations began among people seated close to each other. Suddenly, Lohan Associates were no longer "presenting." After a minute, someone announced, "We need to reconvene here as a group," and refocused the discussion.

The conversation continued with narthex functionality and where to locate utilitarian things like coat rooms, washrooms, etc. Lohan responded. "If I may, these questions are important, and there will be a lot of discussion among all of us; however, what we would like to get from you is hopefully a nod to go along this direction for further development, the principle of the idea, that's what we need because this office area can be arranged in a hundred ways while keeping the offices separate. Whether there is a chapel and where it is—we understand are practical things to think about.

"But I think what I hear is that this concept of a strong axial relationship from the entrance to the narthex to the sanctuary is a positive one. The separation of more mundane functions, like the offices and meeting rooms, is what you want." Several participants expressed agreement.

Someone asked Lewinski about the best seating arrangement. "Well, we can still play around," he replied, "with the angles of seating, but one thing that happens when you start to go more circular it becomes more theater-like. Second, in our tradition of processions and so forth, it is very hard to do that in a round shape."

He mentioned important occasions, particularly weddings, funerals, and holy times such as Lent. He addressed questions concerning devotional spaces and religious art.

Finally, they discussed the pipe organ, the tabernacle, and the altar. The design showed the organ pipes in a space between the altar and the tabernacle. But it was unclear, from a normal perspective, exactly what someone sitting in a pew would see. There was concern about how much of a distraction might exist if the pipes and tabernacle were visible behind the altar.

In answering, Lewinski once again used his knowledge and experience gained during his travels. It was something many other pastors might not have been able to do. "Think about the Eastern model.[6] The Holy of Holies is behind a screen. It is there in a typical Orthodox fashion. You know it is there. The sanctuary lamp tells you it is there. Your eyes are drawn there, but it doesn't mean that you have to actually see it."

Lewinski and Lohan then brought the discussion to a close. Lewinski began. "At this point, we're looking at the basic overall concept. The next thing we have to do is look at the details. We have to examine each one of those pieces. Now, the question is whether we should continue to develop in this basic direction."

Lohan said the discussion had been fruitful, and the work needed to progress. "We've heard a lot of suggestions and concerns, so in my mind, there is plenty to work on. We'll return another time. But we'd like to move forward; we'd like to move it along."

Lewinski responded in typical dry humor, "Alright, let's *move* on then."

Before Christmas, parishioners found the fourth issue of *The Bell* in their mailbox. The cover bore eye-catching illustrations by two children in the parish's school. When Lewinski invited everyone to participate, he didn't mean only the adults. So, the children in the parish were engaged in various ways.

The illustrations were black-and-white reproductions of crayon drawings (by "Marv" and "Lauren"). They showed how young brains and eyes saw the Masterplan. A column titled "Views from the SMALLER pews" shared responses from the Kindergarten children to specific questions:

Q. How many seats should be in the new church?
A. 101, 42, 250, 5, 448, 316, 1000, 602, 1200, 2 million
Q. What color should the new church be?
A. Among other answers was this, perhaps reflecting theological and farming themes: "White on the inside and red on the outside."
Q. What person should be a statue in the new church?
A. "God" outnumbered other responses. Interestingly, one response identified the original name of the parish: John the Baptist.
Q. What one thing should the new school have for your teacher to use that your current school doesn't have?
A. Hot tub; a restaurant; roller rink; a place where teachers can hang out; a rocking chair; nothing.

Q. What one thing should the new school have for you to use that your current school doesn't have?

A. Money; pop machine, roller coaster; horses; pool; bowling alley; Batman toys and Robin; nothing.

In October, the Building Fund had a balance of $1.1 million. By early December, $3.8 million had been pledged. It was a respectable amount but only a third of what the Archdiocese was waiting to see.

Lewinski's "Around the Table" summarized the current situation:

> A friend, an out-of-town priest, visited me when we were first in the process of securing additional land and beginning to draw up a Masterplan. He revisited the parish recently and, after looking around and reading back issues of *The Bell*, listed several things St. Mary's completed since his last visit: a growing number of lay ministries; a five-star pastoral staff; a beautifully articulated Masterplan; our own newsletter; the acquisition of additional land plus the blessing of the land by Cardinal George; the selection of Lohan Associates as our architects; studies on land, water, and sewer; the beginning of a capital campaign; and many parishioners involved in the planning process. He commented that all of these signs indicate a healthy parish on the move. "Ron," he said, "St. Mary's has really progressed a long way."
>
> Our plans for the future are indeed becoming a reality as we work closely with Lohan Associates, hear the enthusiasm of parishioners, see the generosity of parishioners during the capital campaign, and meet with county officials to secure permissions and permits. This is a great time to be part of St. Mary's. There's a feeling that the Holy Spirit is at work among us, preparing us not simply for some buildings but for a renewed sense of what it means to be Church together. For parishioners who have been active for years, it's an hour of grace to experience new horizons of faith and mission. For new parishioners or folks who haven't been very involved, this is a key moment to jump in and be counted as a close member of the parish family. For anyone who has felt disenfranchised in the past, it's a wonderful time to be welcomed home for a new beginning.
>
> My hope is that we not only see the growth and development of our Masterplan but that, individually and as a community, we might experience a growth in faith and a deepening of conviction to be the Church that God is calling us to be.[7]

The issue included the usual updates from the subcommittees and a Q&A section. It announced an "Adult and Children Photo Contest Season" that Winter. Prizes included $50 gift certificates to popular local restaurants, tickets for movies and video rentals, and discounts for services and merchandise at area merchants. All prizes were donated by sponsoring businesses. It was the first of more contests intended to ensure "the beauty and diversity of our parish campus are captured and preserved." There were two categories of winners: youth (up to eighth grade) and adults (ninth grade and older). The contest was another way to engage parishioners while providing material for the parish archives.

In December, Lewinski announced the Capital Campaign gears were engaged. During the next two months, all 1,100+ households in the parish would be asked for a monetary pledge amount. He shared with the Pastoral Council that one family had financed their offering by sacrificing a vacation. He suggested that early next year, there could be a new major fundraiser. It wouldn't conflict with August's Pork and Corn Roast, and it would help build the campaign fund. Indeed, the year 2000 saw the first occurrence of this new event.

Lewinski's motivation was reinforced by a discussion with Francis Cardinal George, Archbishop of Chicago. Lewinski shared with the Pastoral Council that Cardinal George was "very supportive" and suggested he was willing to do whatever is necessary to help because "Lake County needs St. Mary Parish." The Cardinal's support, along with that of the Archdiocese's new Finance Director, Tom Brennan, subsequently helped move the project along.

On Christmas morning, Pastor Emeritus James Morrissey died. Lewinski would honor some of Morrissey's achievements in the next Sunday bulletin. "Father Morrissey, with the help of parishioners, began the annual Pork and Corn Roast. He established a Parish Council, School Board, Finance Committee, and Liturgical Committee. Thank you, Father Jim, for being a faithful priest for fifty years and serving St. Mary's so generously."[8]

Morrissey had also begun the very needed school addition that was completed during Keusal's term in 1984. They had appointed Morrissey pastor at St. Mary's in 1967. It was shortly after Vatican II closed and five years before Lewinski was ordained. Until Lewinski's appointment, the parish had just two pastors—Morrissey and Keusal—after Vatican II. When Lewinski arrived, they would finally begin to experience some of the Second Vatican Council's zest.

Lewinski was nearing the end of his third year as pastor. He may have been too close to the forest to see the trees. His friend's observations emphasized the progress being made. He couldn't know it then, but they were barely halfway to the goal. There was still much more money needed. More concerning was an answer to the question: What will we build, and how will we decide?

Lewinski's lifelong understanding of Vatican II reforms, and his skill at guiding people along a prayerful path of discernment, would contribute to finding answers to those questions.

---

[1] At another meeting the same site plan was displayed with the rectory in a triangular area between Erhart Road at Rt. 60. While people were looking at the exhibits and having casual conversation, someone asked Lewinski "Where would *you* like the rectory to be – convenience wise?" He replied "Well, I don't think convenience is an issue. I don't expect to be running back and forth. I think its more an issue of being separate. The issue is trying to get away from the constant whirlwind of activity. People going back and forth in front of me. I'd almost rather be over here." He pointed to the Southwest corner of the campus, which is in fact where the rectory was finally constructed. "Some place" he remarked, "to get away from work." We can confidently conclude that he meant to get out of the 'office atmosphere', not to escape his responsibilities as pastor.

[2] In 2017 a book titled *Landscape Observatory: The Work of Terence Harkness*, was published (by Applied Research & Design Publishing) depicting Harkness' work. The publisher's blurb about the book said "The modernist history of landscape architecture is deeply marbled with veins of regional and phenomenological sensibility. Master designer Terence G. Harkness reflects this sensibility in every region he inhabits – whether the foothills of northern California, the high plains of North Dakota, or the lost prairies of east central Illinois." Harkness was a part of the "powerhouse team" from Lohan Associates at the time of this meeting.

[3] As a technology, fritted glass is said by archaeologists to go back as far as ancient Egypt, Mesopotamia, and other cultures. Of course, it appeared in a different form and for a different purpose. It became widely popular in architectural designs during the 20th century, especially after World War II, resulting in buildings with "lots of light"—as Lohan noted—inside, while helping to making them more visible to birds, thereby lowering bird deaths.

[4] Code of Canon Law (1983): "The tabernacle in which the blessed Eucharist is reserved should be sited in a distinguished place in the church or oratory, a place which is conspicuous, suitably adorned and conducive to prayer.—Canon 938.

The General Instruction of the Roman Missal: "In accordance with the structure of each church and legitimate local customs, the Most Blessed Sacrament should be reserved in a tabernacle in a part of the church that is truly noble, prominent, conspicuous, worthily decorated, and suitable for prayer."

Redemptionis Sacramentum (instruction from the Vatican in 2004): "The Most Holy Sacrament is to be reserved in a tabernacle in a part of the church that is noble, prominent, readily visible, and adorned in a dignified manner and furthermore 'suitable for prayer' by reason of the quietness of the location, the space available in front of the tabernacle, and also the supply of benches or seats and kneelers. (No. 130). —https://www.simplycatholic.com/where-should-the-tabernacle-be/.

[5] Two well-known exceptions, when viewed from the air, are Apple Park (California) and the Pentagon (Virginia).

[6] The Eastern Orthodox Christian church and the Hebrew Tradition—and others—reserve a special place for the Holy of Holies. In the Hebrew tradition, a Tabernacle is a room (in ancient times, a tent), not the enclosed 'cabinet' of Christian traditions. The purpose is similar: a place for sacred reservation.

[7] *The Bell*, Vol. I, Issue 4, December, 1998, p. 3.

[8] Sunday bulletin, January 3, 1999, p. 4.

THE THIRD WAVE

Winter 1999

The pyramid model was the parish's strategy for achieving financial support. Its tip is that part of the population that has the greatest capacity. The middle section is for the next tier with lesser wealth. Then comes everyone else. With guidance from CCS, they categorized parishioners into one of three tiers. Those at the top had been the first to be invited to become Lewinski's "second generation of founders."

The Major Gifts Committee (MGC), chaired by Roger Fisher, had specific "high value" targets at the pyramid's tip. The MGC offered a variety of "Memorials" in exchange for substantial pledges ranging from $10,000 to $1 million. This list of memorials was fifty items like pews, candlesticks, the kitchen, a piano, a baptismal font, and the entry road (Emmaus Drive) to the new campus.

The Capital Campaign Committee targeted the remaining parishioners. Ann Steffenhagen and Dan Washburn hosted a meeting on January 4, 1999. The Midwestern winter was fully present. Fortunately, freezing temperatures wouldn't return until the following Christmas. The event was well-attended by invitees despite the frigid weather.

The Major Gifts Committee had conducted solicitations of pledges from a select group of parishioners. The time had arrived to seek everyone else's support. This phase of fundraising often requires the most effort for the least return. All parishioners deserved to hear about the need and be offered an opportunity to participate.

Attendees were seated around tables numbered one through eight. Steffenhagen started the meeting. She introduced herself, Washburn, and Matt Hoolehan, the CCS consultant helping them. "I welcome all of you for coming here this evening, especially on this nasty, nasty night. I appreciate you all coming out." She addressed each table by number, asking for their cheers and applause. As she progressed from the first to the last table, the cheers got louder. Those at table eight stood and shouted their support.

She reviewed her background as a member of a founding family. This opportunity, she reminded them, was like the needs faced by those pioneers. It included school facilities, meeting space for more ministries, and a church with greater capacity. Steffenhagen concluded, "It's going to take a lot of sacrifice by every one of us. But I know—because I can see your spirit, your sacrifice just to come out this evening—that you're going to help us with this. That's what we need. Thank you very much. Father Ron will say a few words now."

Lewinski stepped to the podium during the ensuing applause.

"Welcome, and a happy new year to you all." He proclaimed. "It is great to see you all here; a cold night it is, but a hearty crew we are. As we begin our evening together, I'd like to invite us to take a moment to ask the Lord's blessing upon us and to ask Him to walk with us not only here tonight but throughout this campaign."

Lewinski led everyone as they recited the Parish Prayer.[1] He then resumed with, "Again, a hearty welcome to you. It is a great night for us at St. Mary's Parish to be gathered together. It marks a very important next phase for us in looking to our future."

Returning to the reason for tonight's meeting, he noted, "We are asking you to help us by making personal visits to your fellow parishioners. In the name of St. Mary's Parish, you can invite them to participate in what is a wonderful adventure into the future.[2] The importance of making a personal visit has already been emphasized to us by our campaign consultant. One thing we have already discovered by doing some visits is we're not just asking for a contribution. We are trying to create a sense of community within our parish and build upon that sense of community.

"We have found that what has happened is really an evangelization effort. We discovered people who have particular needs that we weren't aware of. Also, we're trying to correct some misinformation that's out there. It's kind of interesting: some stories that come back. I don't know where people come up with them, but it is very important that we're able to visit on a one-to-one basis so that we can all be on the same page as a parish. So I will ask you in the name of St. Mary's to make a visit, and I think you will find it to be a pretty rewarding experience."

As a result of the capital campaign, Lewinski discovered some surprising things. One of those came from someone who had solicited a parishioner and gotten a pledge from him. There was nothing particularly unusual about it, except the parishioner's name was Santa Claus. He had legalized the name because it reflected his appearance, including rectangular reading glasses and the seasonal role he played.[3] His picture, with the name 'Santa Claus', was in the Pastoral Directory.

"Also, I'd like to note that we are here because the parish is growing. In one sense, it becomes something of a burden because it is always difficult to face the challenge of growth. On the other hand, it is a *wonderful* time for us to be Church together. When we see the signs of growth and the many needs we have, those are healthy signs—signs of a healthy parish that is very much alive.

"We have a waiting list to get into school. Our Religious Education Program spans several nights and days to accommodate all the children. Sometimes we have to fight for a meeting room between this group or that group. We meet and celebrate Mass under basketball nets every Sunday. All these are signs of growth and are *healthy* signs.[4]

"We see the number of parishioners growing. This week is my third anniversary. When I got here three years ago, there were approximately 600 families; now, there are close to 1,200. So the parish has doubled in that time. The studies for this area of Lake County clearly show that there is more growth to come. That is what we have to prepare for.

"But our survey also shows that 77% of our parish is under 50. That is a remarkable figure to me. It means there are a lot of young folks, and that means that there is something coming in the years ahead we need to attend to. So those kinds of figures certainly are significant.

"The other thing that I wanted to say about the parish—besides the fact that the numbers are growing—is the whole concept of what the parish is. What we're trying to do is create a parish community that can serve the larger community in the next millennium in a way that truly responds to the gospel and considers the needs of people. Such has been the state of the Church from year one: wherever it has worked well, the community has responded to the changing needs of the larger community. It means that the parish itself changes too.

"So a lot of new ministries that have been created in the parish are signs of that evolving nature. The parish needs to be an oasis where people can find some nourishment, hope, some direction for the future."

He continued by noting that Lohan, the architect, had expressed a vision like theirs. "So we are very fortunate to have him, and I think he will lead us in a wonderful direction. Because he has already been working with us, he has taken the initial Masterplan that we had, and we've already made several alterations. Again, it's an evolving kind of plan. A little later, we'll show you so you can see some of those revisions."

He then mentioned how the Archdiocese would act as a lender, offering a much lower interest rate loan. He introduced Dan Washburn, who proudly stated that $4.1 million had been pledged, and received loud applause. "What's important," continued Washburn, "is to realize in that number is all those contributions came from parishioners. There has been no outside source of funds for the campaign—they are all fellow parishioners who have pledged an amount. Some 200 families have been contacted, and we have raised that much through their generosity.

"It is also important to note these people were approached by fellow parishioners, just like you. It is truly amazing that it has made no difference between old to new, both in age and length of membership here. Everyone has been equally generous. It has been an overwhelming privilege and a gratifying experience that has been taking place here. This brings us now to the current phase and what we expect from you."

He explained, "There's some pressure on your group to reach these people and pull them in before we go down to the Archdiocese to talk about financing. We don't want this campaign to drag on. We don't expect to keep you working on this; we promise that we want you to work for a limited amount of time."

The volunteers were grateful for Washburn's insight. They felt relieved to hear this would not be a prolonged effort.

"One more thing and this is fairly important. We ask that before you go out to call on people, you sit back and reflect on what you can do for the campaign and what *you* can pledge. So when you report next week for the first time, part of the total pledge amount will be your own. It is important when you ask other people to make a sacrificial gift; you can feel in your heart that you have already done your part. It just has a little more credibility to other people. When you haven't done so yourself, it's unfair to ask other people to contribute. So we ask you during the next week to reflect on what you can do."

The meeting resulted in another group prepared to approach their fellow parishioners. The goal to secure more pledges was an evangelical one. The contact between those soliciting and those being solicited led to discoveries of ministry opportunities. They identified parishioners with special needs. New and lasting friendships were formed between people. The campaign strengthened the community's social relationships while raising funds to support the project.

Lewinski used his column on January 24, 1999, to share an assessment.

> This month marks my third anniversary at St. Mary - Fremont Center. It feels like it has been much longer than that; so much has transpired over the last three years. I've seen St. Mary double in size. I've witnessed the growth of the lay leadership that has enabled the parish to serve so many more people. I am pleased to see our pastoral staff expand by reaching out and drawing in so many parishioners into the circle of ministry and greater parish participation. Our School and Religious Education Program has blossomed. PADS remains a bold witness to our concern for others. Our Sunday liturgies are prayerfully celebrated with a full and active participation of the assembly.
>
> The most noticeable thing that has occurred in the last three years is our planning for the future. Three years ago, we wondered if it was time to expand our facilities. Today we find ourselves with a Masterplan in hand and in the midst of a Capital Campaign. The positive responses we have received from the Capital Campaign are a clear sign of the vitality and "can-do spirit" of St. Mary.

Being the pastor of such a wonderful growing parish is both rewarding and challenging. I have grown these last three years. I have had to stretch my skills, and priestly know-how to meet an incredible number of situations. You have had a profound effect on my life. I am thankful to everyone for their dedication and generosity to the parish. I am also grateful for the love, support, and cooperation you have shown me as your pastor. You continue to form me as a priest and pastor. I tend to be a perfectionist and very conscious of all the needs. I am my own worst critic. I am aware of so many things that don't get done, people that don't get visited, preaching that misses the mark, names I can't remember, and needs and expectations that aren't met. I want to be everywhere, do everything, and do it well. I am humbled again and again as I come to terms with my own humanity and limits. You have been very kind to me. Like family, you have come to know my limits and have accepted me. That inspires me to work all the harder for you. Please note that there isn't a day that goes by when I don't think of your families, the individual needs that I've heard, and pain and struggles you have shared, and the marvelous witness of the sacrifices you make for others. My heart aches when I think of all those we aren't reaching or those who have given up on the Church even before they may have truly experienced what faith and community offer. When I stand at the altar with my hands extended in prayer, I hold you all in my embrace.

We've got a lot going on in the parish, and with God's help, we will continue to grow.

I now see the need to deepen our spiritual life as individuals and perish. I'd like to take us to a deeper level of prayer and catechesis, a more profound sense of living as a Christian community, a more committed sense of stewardship, and a more intense sense of mission. The approaching millennium presents a good opportunity to unleash the power of the Spirit. We are a blessed community. With God's help, we can continue to grow in solidarity as a parish. We can usher in the new millennium with a conviction that St. Mary Parish will make its mark on Lake County, ready to transform our society into the city of God.

Thanks for taking up the challenge of sharing this adventure of faith. I boast of you often. I am proud to be your pastor.[5]

A week later, he observed the Capital Campaign was making good progress (although privately, he shared it had not been easy)[6] and urged parishioners to continue in that spirit. "In a few weeks, I will meet with Archdiocesan authorities to establish a firm budget for our building project. I would like to take our best effort to demonstrate our community's will and potential so that the Archdiocese will feel secure in giving us the green light and offering us the financial help we will need."[7] It was Lewinski's way of gently nudging things forward. He knew support from the Archdiocese would depend upon how well the parish could show its ability to fund the project.

Though the Capital Campaign dwarfed everything else, it was not Lewinski's sole financial concern. He was working on the next annual budget (July 1999 - June 2000), and two concerns were maintenance costs and bringing on a business manager. The role's responsibilities were growing along with the project. The current staff member, Pastoral Assistant Deacon Bob Poletto, was there part-time. He was in the U.S. Air Force and subject to reassignment for months at any time. This effort needed someone's full-time attention.

As the year began, mission activities continued. Leadership training for Disciples in Mission began on January 28. Some eighth graders and REP students participated in a Martin Luther King celebration at another parish. The Liturgical Education Committee formation was continuing. Summer activities, including Intensive REP, Summer Kamp, and Vacation Bible School, were planned.

A Sunday bulletin cover announced "Commitment Sunday." It was followed by the project slogan and a brief reminder that now was the time to become a second-generation founder. A discerning parishioner may have noticed a subtle change. Instead of "Grateful for the Past...*Hopeful* for the Future," the slogan read "Grateful for the Past...*Committed* to the Future." The word "committed" had replaced "hopeful" when the project moved into the "put your money where your mouth is" phase.

The weekly donations were gradually edging upwards. "Commitment Sunday" was an intentional push for more funds. According to Lewinski, a week later, they received a "good response." The total amount pledged to date had reached $5 million.

Lewinski included an apology in his bulletin column. A Town Hall scheduled with Lohan Associates for February 28th was postponed. The explanation gave parishioners some insight into the actions occurring behind the scenes. "One difficulty we are struggling with is the site improvements on our new land. Recall that we need to invest in our own septic system as well. We also need retention ponds and special features that are expected in commercial building projects. To secure a permit for access off Fremont Center Road, we will be required to put in a turning lane. The county determines the number of parking spaces we must provide. These are a few issues that impinge on design and cost. We are working hard to find the most cost-effective way to address these issues so that we can keep the cost of the whole project in check."[8]

Lewinski attended a conference sponsored by the Common Ground Initiative. The topic was the liturgy. He proudly reported, "Most of the values and hoped-for qualities of liturgy could be identified at St. Mary." Then he shared a less encouraging observation about a movement that had begun a quarter century earlier. "The pace of change is often unnerving. Afraid of the chaos and tension, and impatience, we risk short-circuiting liturgical development by giving up too soon. No period of history has ever seen liturgical change happen as quickly as we have."[9]

Many ministries were engaged, including dozens of parishioners who had volunteered their time and skills. People working as teams such as these need to ensure time for celebration. Parish leadership hosted an annual Appreciation Dinner for that reason. They filled Diantha Hall with tables for the dinner guests and decorated them according to a theme. In 1999, the theme was a Luau.

Because Lewinski normally had little to do with planning the event, he became a target for the spotlight during whatever humorous skit they created. This year, he sat on the "throne" behind a table at center stage. With much fanfare, "natives"—men in grass skirts—crowned him "King Lewiniki." Then they brought him a platter on which rested a pig's "brain" ("for wisdom") encircled by many "eyeballs" ("for vision").

The "waiter" graciously cut off a small portion of the brain, gave King Lewiniki the fork, and encouraged him to consume it. Lewinski hesitated, then shut his nose while hastily swallowing the pink tidbit. Next, the waiter invited King Lewiniki to select a glossy eyeball. He did so with a slight grimace and received massive applause for consuming it whole. Lewinski's actions testified to his sense of humor and faith in his people.[10]

PIG'S "EYEBALLS"
INTENDED TO INDUCE "VISION" IN KING LEWINIKI BY INGESTION

During the Pastoral Council meeting in March, Lewinski updated the attendees on the slow progress regarding the site plan. The cost was rising. The county mechanism for the process was frustrating and contributed to the increase. Just the portion dealing with the land purchase, septic system, parking, permits and studies was about $3 million. The Capital Campaign amount had reached $5.3 million in pledges. Lewinski stated few parishes had raised so much in similar efforts.

He observed the gathering of lay leadership scheduled for May 3 is misnamed. It is not merely a "calendar-setting" meeting; it is the main Synod of the parish. Ministry heads and members need to regard it with due importance. If a ministry leader is disgruntled, then "they need to do something about it" to be a real leader.[11]

Easter of 1999 heralded good news. On April 4th, he wrote:

> On March 25, the Feast of the Annunciation, our parish feast day, I presented our Masterplan for the future to the Archdiocese of Chicago. I am delighted to announce that we have received formal approval to proceed with our plans. The formal meeting on March 25 followed several earlier meetings with Archdiocesan officials. They have carefully analyzed our plans in the past months from financial, pastoral, and construction perspectives. The board of Archdiocesan officials was very impressed with the good work we have accomplished and applauded the success we have had with our capital campaign. Bishop Goedert, Vicar General of the Archdiocese, who previously served as Episcopal Vicar for Lake County, knows firsthand about the history and needs of St. Mary. He offered his full support for our project, stating how important it is for St. Mary's future and the future of the Church in Lake County. As you might imagine, I left that meeting feeling very excited about our future. I truly believe that our Blessed Mother, Mary of the Annunciation, was interceding for us on our parish feast day and giving her approval.
>
> What this formal approval from the Archdiocese means is that our planning is right on track, and our vision for the future appropriately and responsibly addresses our needs. Our cost estimates for Phase I, which amounts to $10 million, are not out of line. We have permission to proceed with schematic designs when we feel our conceptual design is where we want it to be. Once a schematic design is prepared and construction costs defined, we will have to approach the Archdiocese again for approval before moving on to the next stage. We will be in constant communication with the Archdiocese as we continue fundraising while trying to keep our costs as low as possible so as not to incur a debt we could never repay. Although the Archdiocese ordinarily requires a parish to have 90% pledged and 67% cash on hand before permission is granted for building, they recognized our unique situation and have made an exception to the rule.
>
> In a few weeks, we hope to have some new conceptual designs from our architect, Lohan Associates. We have been delayed in this part of the process because our parish committees were not completely satisfied with the initial conceptual drawings. We are scrutinizing the architect's work to ensure it suits our spiritual vision, our pastoral and liturgical needs, our rural inclinations, and that the plans are cost-effective.
>
> With this good news, we should all feel encouraged about the progress we are making. Hopefully, this good news will ignite our enthusiasm for this project and give new impetus to our Capital Campaign. We have done very well, but there are still many who have not yet made their commitment to the future. Approximately 42% of the parish have made their pledge. Of the 154 new parish families this past year, 30% have made their pledge. Some parishioners are waiting for more information. Others must take care of previous financial commitments before making their pledge. Still others may

want to consider increasing their pledge. In a few weeks, we will appeal to those who have not yet been personally contacted. We need to pull together and do the best we can so that we do not make the mistake of paring down our plans to the point where we regret it years later.

As we reach this important milestone, I want to thank everyone who gave their time, talent, and treasure to this project. We are a very blessed community. I am grateful to everyone who has pitched in to help on the various committees. And to all who, in the spirit of good stewardship, have made a genuine sacrifice for the future of St. Mary, may God reward you for your generosity and your spirit of dedication.

Happy Easter![12]

The wheels of effort kept the project moving, even as it remained uncertain when the wheels of earth movers could begin turning. The fifth issue of *The Bell* arrived in April and explained the progress. It noted that, despite an eagerness to see something happening on thirty-three acres of new land, it was best to "move carefully and steadily forward.... We characterize ourselves as moving with intentionality; that is, purposeful and conscientious action."

This issue had comments from children in grades four through six:

Q. How many seats should be in the new church?
A. 6, 1510, 48, 900, 25, 113, 863, 2000, 56, 112, 50 pews per row in 3 rows.
Q. What color should the new church be?
A. Red & blue; periwinkle with gold outline; peach.
Q. What person should be a statue in the new church?
A. John the Baptist; God; The Holy Family; Elizabeth Ann Seton.
Q. Why do we need a new church?
A. The church we have now is too old to hardly even stand.

The old church wasn't in danger of collapsing, but in the eyes of a ten-year-old, perception is sometimes reality. One can sense a bit of parental influence in some answers.

Lewinski's "Around the Table" column was double its normal size. He repeated much of his April 4th bulletin column and included an analogy many in a farming community could relate to.

I hope that this milestone of obtaining Archdiocesan approval will stir up enthusiasm for this significant project. We need *everyone's* help. I know there are some who have been reluctant to pledge because they don't want to see St. Mary change. We all love the small country look at St. Mary. That's why we have to be realistic and plan wisely. If we stop or put forth only a halfhearted effort, our potential success will turn to failure. That would be akin to planting a crop but not tilling the ground and fertilizing the new growth. ...

It takes sacrifice. Sacrifice is what created the humble country parish we enjoy today, and sacrifice can be our way to create a lasting place of prayer, reflection, and worship for ourselves and others.[13]

The Q&A section addressed the problem of misinformation:

Q. I have heard all kinds of rumors about the new buildings; what's going up first and what isn't; when it is starting; and that the schoolrooms will be in the basement of the church! What is happening?

A. What is happening is what usually happens in the absence of facts, knowledge, and understanding: rumors begin. However innocent, what may have had a basis in fact, soon becomes fiction. That's why we have communication vehicles like *The Bell*, Town Hall meetings, the Sunday bulletin, etc. We suggest you use "official" channels of information (as you have done here) to clarify any misunderstandings. You are also welcome to speak with any representative of the Planning Commission and its subcommittees. Many questions still remain unanswered. It is human nature to speculate, but accepting as a "fact" everything one hears in the neighborhood is not the best way to get accurate information. Speak with someone who is active in the process. By the way, having school rooms in the church basement is not part of our plan—primarily because ordinances ban it for safety reasons.[14]

Amidst the work associated with financing, conceptual design, and other project-related activities, the number of ministries was growing. This was primarily the result of Sr. Gael Gensler's dedication. She encouraged parishioners willing to assume leadership roles that Lewinski's pastorship had enabled. The April 25th Sunday bulletin listed sixteen ministries under the Worship and Prayer Commission alone.[15] The Parish Outreach Commission identified five.[16]

One criticism of earlier parish leadership was that current world issues were rarely mentioned. That was not true of Lewinski's column on May 2, 1999, after the historic Columbine High School shooting on April 20 in Littleton, Colorado.

The choices we make shape our lives. If we react with anger and violence every time someone cuts us off the road or doesn't serve our table with the swiftness we would like, we give in to an evil that can grow and fester within us. If we begin to cheat our customers just a little bit, lie to our spouse just a little, or neglect our health too often, these wrongs can grow like cancer out of control. More than an abstract theological concept, sin is a real, destructive force that can destroy us. To pretend sin doesn't exist is foolish.

Pope John Paul II has called our culture a "culture of death." We abort our babies, execute criminals, neglect the elderly, kill people on computer screens for entertainment, waste our natural resources, allow our youth to legally build arsenals, and then wonder why there is such a lack of compassion in human respect for others and the environment. We cannot play with fire nor flirt with evil, yet alone cooperate with it, and expect to live unscathed. And where in all of this to our youth learn about the dignity and sacredness of human life? The absence of an awareness of the love of God in the lives of our youth and the moral demands that relationship imposes may well be at the root of behavior gone amok....[17]

Many worshipers honor the commandment to keep the Sabbath holy. But one can't be a Christian just on Sundays. Dark forces do not take a break; they are relentless. To believe otherwise would be self-deception.

Lewinski announced a significant change on May 9th.

> It's no secret that as the parish has grown and the amount of administrative tasks have mounted, the management of parish facilities, budget, and all other business matters have placed a heavy burden on our staff.... To address this concern, I am happy to announce the appointment of Ms. Mary Hall as our parish business manager/development director.... Mary has served on the Vicariate I administrative council and worked with St. Mary - Fremont Center for eight years in that position.... Her professional background encompasses banking, finance, operations management, real estate acquisition, and development.... Mary will be responsible for the day-to-day parish operation as well as working with parish leadership in the ongoing capital campaign and parish stewardship development.[18]

Hall's role broadened the business manager's responsibilities. Deacon Bob Poletto had worked as a part-time business manager going back to Keusal's pastorship. Keusal had encouraged him to become a Deacon. As an officer in the U.S. Air Force, Poletto had been assigned to a post in southern Illinois. Hall's arrival was timely and advantageous for the parish. She was familiar with the parish and its challenges. She benefited from not being a parishioner, thereby bringing more objectivity to the task. She belonged to a nearby parish that had also recently built a church. She would keep a hawkish eye on activities and be credited with helping ensure the project stayed within budget.

In May, their liturgical consultant gave a presentation about church architecture, as Scavone had promised the previous September. More eyes were opened as a result of this Town Hall.

On May 16th, another Ministry Fair was conducted. This time it was in Diantha Hall. The use of a large space continued to show how new facilities would benefit the ministries.

As part of the parish's outreach program, parishioner Peter Duffy became the "Social Service Coordinator." He'd seek to make connections between services with the county and those who had need of such services. Lewinski, continually emphasizing a broader perspective, shared with Duffy his personal expectations from the ministry.

On May 24th, they held in an ecumenical service for Kosovo refugees and victims of the Littleton tragedy. They were joined by the North Suburban Mennonite Church and Faith Lutheran Church, both nearby.

On the first weekend in June, Lewinski "happily" announced a Town Hall scheduled for June 17th. The intent was to present the proposed conceptual design for the new facilities. "We will explain how we arrived at the conceptual design and what it entails. Parishioners will be asked for feedback and recommendations."

The choice of which design to present had been challenging. The team had begun with three options. Only one design could be presented to the population at large. The decision would not come easily.

It would not have happened as it did if it hadn't been for Lewinski's leadership at a critical time.

---

[1] The prayer was introduced in The Bell with Issue #1. It appeared frequently in the Sunday bulletin and was often recited during the project.

[2] Lewinski was explicitly making an important distinction here with the phrasing "In the name of St. Mary's Parish." Avoiding the usage of a generic "we", or specifically his own name, the request would be perceived as coming from the faith community that the target was a member of. It was simply a way of expressing the truth while disarming critics who maintained this was "Lewinski's" project.

[3] 2000 Parish Directory, p. 5 (pictures) and p. 6 (alpha listing).

[4] Lewinski's remark mentioning the basketball nets derives from a comment he made to a parishioner saying he (Lewinski)—who had conducted Masses in a variety of places both inside and out—hated celebrating Mass in a space with basketball hoops.

[5] Sunday bulletin, January 24, 1999, pp. 3-4. Lewinski's phrasing "I hold you all in my embrace" is another reference to his Offertory practice mentioned earlier.

[6] Pastoral Council minutes, January 11, 1999.

[7] Sunday bulletin, January 31, 1999, p. 5.

[8] Sunday bulletin, March 7, 1999, p. 3.

[9] Sunday bulletin, March 14, 1999, pp. 3-4.

[10] The "pig's brain" was actually macaroni & white cheese molded to resemble a brain, with enough red food coloring to make it slightly pink. The "eyeballs" were globular vanilla pudding with a slice of olive as the pupil. Apparently everything looked "real" enough to fool Lewinski. When he later learned the material was actually more consumable than he'd thought, he retorted "Well, why didn't you tell me that *before* I had to swallow it!?" —Personal conversation with Lewinski, February, 1999.

[11] Pastoral Council minutes, March 8 and April 12, 1999.

[12] Sunday bulletin, April 4, 1999, pp. 3-4. A careful reader would catch the significance of the phrase "an exception to the rule." It implied the parish was being granted leniency by the Archdiocese regarding normal guidelines.

[13] Ibid., p. 3.

[14] Ibid., p. 7.

[15] Sunday bulletin, April 25, 1999, p. 4.

[16] Sunday bulletin, May 2, 1999, p. 6.

[17] Ibid., p. 3.

[18] Sunday bulletin, May 9, 1999, p. 4.

THE TEMPLE

Spring 1999

During a Pastoral Council meeting on May 10, Lewinski announced the delay of a scheduled Town Hall with Lohan's firm. He explained Lohan Associates didn't understand what they wanted.[1] For Lewinski, it suggested a problem with one or both teams. Perhaps it meant the parish didn't understand things themselves. Or they were failing to effectively communicate with Lohan's team.

It was another obstacle to overcome.

Lewinski convened a gathering on May 25, 1999, with a cross-section of parishioners and several committee members. The evening thunderstorms mirrored the occasional turbulence of the discussion in the school library. Outdoor temperatures were rising from the mid-fifties the day before toward the mid-eighties by the week's end. A few attending the meeting may have detected a slight rise in their own temperature. They sensed the historical responsibility they were facing.

The meeting's purpose was to choose a conceptual design for presentation to the parish. They had scheduled a Town Hall for June 17th, just three weeks away. Tonight's attendees were members from the Planning Commission; Pastoral Council representatives; chairs from the project committees; the school principal; parishioners from the trades; and, of course, Sr. Gensler and Lewinski.

Lohan provided options for them. His firm created them in response to what they heard from the parish. They were small-scale models (20" in length). The group could arrange three components differently. They were the church (sanctuary), the narthex, and the pastoral center (meeting rooms and offices). The differences were how the three components were positioned relative to each other. Each arrangement placed the narthex between the sanctuary and the pastoral center. The group referred to the three formations as "A," "B," and "C."

Lewinski had placed the model components on a circular table in the small library, aside the architect's floor plans for each alternative. The architects had changed the earlier north/south axis to an east/west orientation. The sanctuary was at the west end of the narthex, and the pastoral center at the east end. The main entrance was on the narthex's south side, which was parallel to and facing the parking lot.

The week prior, this group had already spent an evening discussing these options. A few moments passed as they gathered their recollections and formed thoughts to share tonight. After beginning with a prayer, Lewinski identified the models and began speaking.

"Last week, we already agreed having a lower roof on the pastoral center was more acceptable than having it be the same height as the church. So the roof in model A is the same height and size on the northern side as the southern side of these two structures."

Model A was "traditional" because its features were of a traditional church with a middle aisle bisecting the sanctuary. However, symmetry was the specific feature Lewinski disliked in this model. It reminded him of a large space lacking any significance.

Next, he held up model B. "Now, what makes this 'B' is the front wall of the sanctuary and pastoral offices are parallel to the parking lot, but the narthex is angled." He meant the narthex pivoted so it no longer bisected the two structures at each end. This would be less apparent in the pastoral center. But it was noticeable in the sanctuary because the altar, being slightly left of center, was no longer equidistant between the two side walls on the north and south.

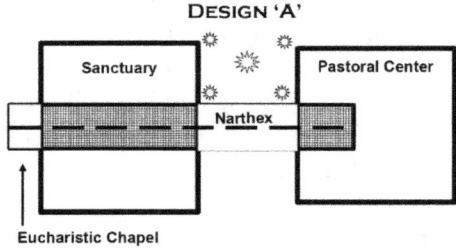

DESIGN 'A'

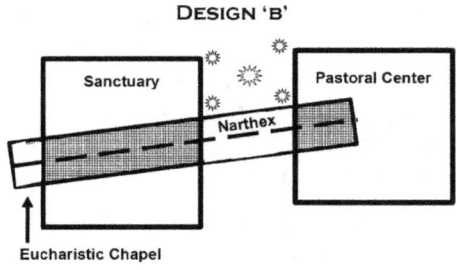

DESIGN 'B'

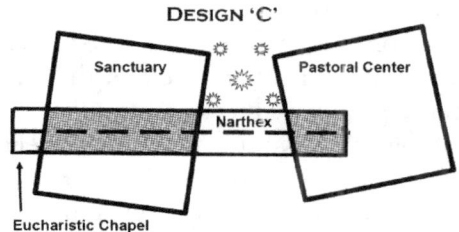

DESIGN 'C'

IMAGE #8 (SEE ALSO PREVIOUS PAGE)

MODELS A, B AND C

THREE POSSIBLE ARRANGEMENTS FOR THE SANCTUARY, NARTHEX, AND PASTORAL CENTER.

Lewinski continued speaking while Jim Scavone held up the third model. "And then there is 'C' where they kept the narthex parallel to the parking lot. The sanctuary and pastoral center are rotated off-center." This had the effect of forming a soft U formation when viewed from above. The result was a broader courtyard on the southern side and a more "enclosed" meditation garden space on the northern side.

"The dominant feature of A, B, *and* C," noted Lewinski, "is that the narthex itself holds the whole place together.

"One desire was to include the traditional look of a church which has commonly been a long nave. But we recognize that liturgically speaking, per Vatican II, to be in a long narrow church doesn't work for us. So the architect's genius was to take the nave and superimpose it upon the other buildings. When we discussed the liturgical dimensions of how to fit 1,100 people, we concluded the square would suit us best for that size. So, the nave—the long piece—becomes the anchor that ties everything together: church, narthex, and pastoral center.

"What happens in B and C is that you take the squares and rotate them slightly. It creates a different visual interest. If you look at model A, it seems very much like the traditional church: a high altar and two side altars. You don't get that impression from B or C. What is still valuable in B and C—which is the genius of how they did it—is you still have a central aisle leading to the altar. So you still have the traditional piece people are comfortable with—going directly to the altar—in all three. So it's not like you're going into the church crooked or you're going in at an angle. That defining feature of the nave keeps you aligned.

"Of course, the only difference comparing A to both B and C is the seating along the center aisle is different in B and C; but that's how it is now in Diantha Hall.

"The other thing Lohan talked about was that one goal was to create a sense of mystery in the church. Parishes have had difficulty with new churches because you have to seat 1,100 people and make a large room. Once you do, it feels, some people have said, like a Holiday Inn meeting room. So the whole idea of this high nave and the swivel is to get out of that sense of another huge square meeting room. If it were a small church seating only 250 people, you wouldn't get that feeling because of the intimacy of the walls being closer to you. The challenge was how do you create a sense of mystery, where you are enveloped in that space, and it takes you in different directions, other than just a big square box?"

One attendee, scrutinizing model C, spoke up. "I can visualize this, which is slightly disturbing—that angle. Today I tell people we are members of St. Mary's, and they immediately mention 'the little white church.' That is our symbol."[2]

Lewinski said, "That is a good point. It would be different if we were knocking it down." Another attendee acknowledged the value of retaining the old church even after building the new one. "I think it is a strong symbol that this is *still* who we are. What is more important: the building or what goes on inside the building?"

Someone recalled, "Last week, we were split between the choices." It prompted some discussion about individual personal preferences. One person said, "It requires a little meditating and thinking." Another replied, "It's taken a while for us." Perhaps no one wanted to admit that the group hadn't decided and nothing had changed.

Lewinski was making notes, as was his practice, in his thick daily organizer. They were questions or comments for later review. Now he offered his perspective on the struggle they were dealing with. Their decision was to choose between what some people regarded as traditional and what others considered modern.

"The fact is, church design is shifting. How do we move into the future? It is all in the eyes of the beholder. I consider this very conservative, frankly. I don't think this is modern at all." It was a surprising statement for those who thought Lewinski favored a traditional design.

"It takes time to get used to," he continued, "it really does, and it has to grow on you. If people totally revolt when we show this and say there's no way this can be our church, then that is something we will have to deal with. But the reaction I've gotten is they've been very open. I don't think we should sell people short.

"Over the weekend, I had people in my office of all ages. They saw the models side-by-side. Their first reaction was to favor one, but then the more they looked at the other, they came to accept that too."

The models resulted from a two-year-old process that sought to identify the needs and values of the parish. They collected these from all parishioners, including children. He reminded people, "You can't please everyone. We could build a model for a new cathedral, and they wouldn't like it, for whatever reason."

Lewinski expressed his thoughts regarding the upcoming Town Hall. "I'm hoping there will be some really good ideas—things that, for whatever reason, none of us have thought about. What often happens: someone on the periphery, who has not been part of it, will uncover something new. And we need to promote the traditional elements here: the Bell Tower, the steeple, the nave, a central aisle: those are solid foundational concepts."

A parishioner had picked up a model and studied it from a street perspective rather than a bird's-eye view, noting the roof line at the western end. She observed, "This is the same look as the old church." Lewinski, too, had observed that.

One person was new to the parish and presented a fresh perspective. She explained, "I'm a relative newcomer. Don't underestimate your community. Your community can be very warm and welcoming. I have experienced that. Your community is very workable if you give them half a chance. Be positive with them. Change can be good. You haven't taken away their past because you haven't taken away their church. They need to remember that the Church is *in* the building; the Church is *us*."

Lewinski replied, "Something like sixty percent of parishioners have been here less than I have, and I've only been here three years. It is important to remember people come from unique experiences. They haven't all been worshiping in an old church like ours. I think the mistake we make about any community is assumptions about their attitudes. We may find some say that this plan doesn't go far enough."

Someone stated that many people expected to attend the Town Hall would come from the nearby retirement neighborhood of Saddlebrook. The thinking was the older parish contingent, often grandparents, would likely have more traditional views.

Lewinski deflected the implication by sharing his recent experience. "Now, there's an example too. Over the wintertime, people from Saddlebrook who were traveling were coming back with pictures of different churches they are excited about, and they are far more radical than these models."

One of the attendees observed, "That speaks to their investment in the process: when they are on vacation, they are out taking pictures of churches. It speaks to how they have taken this change to heart."

Lewinski then shared something from an elderly parishioner. "I want to read something given to me yesterday after Mass. Mabel Bennett, from Saddlebrook, gave me a little note. She said, 'I did something last night. I got up about one o'clock in the morning because I just couldn't sleep, and all I could think about was St. Mary's. So I sat down to write.'

"So here," Lewinski said as he unfolded Mabel's note, "is what she sat down to write in the middle of the night. She calls it 'The Temple.'" He recited her composition.

> As I turn up the road
> I see the large expanse of nothing.
> "Nothing" I say, "Oh no!"
> There were corn fields there,
> Perhaps some cows,
> Maybe a deer or two.
> From the little church
> Where we prayed
> And now outgrew
> There can't be nothing.
> Soon the ground will break.
> The bricks will come and also the wood.
> Sturdy Oak for the floors.
> More for the desks and doors.
> The pathways will be made.
> The bells will be hung.
> So the chimes can be heard
> For you and for me.
> O Lord in heaven
> Your cross will be hung
> For all to see
> And your song will be sung.
> For miles they come
> Where once there was nothing –
> No, not nothing –
> This was meant to be.
> This will be your Temple.
> This is where you led your people.
> For one hundred years you waited.
> And now the time has come.
> We will build your temple.
> We will build your tabernacle.
> We will complete the work
> You set us to do.
> We are your people.
> We are your children.

"This was totally unsolicited," he continued. "People are thinking and praying. I think this poem is neither a conservative nor progressive view— it is a love for the church. This says something about who our people are —it is very beautiful and heartwarming."

Lewinski returned to plans for the Town Hall on June 17th. "I will speak at all the Masses to make a personal invitation and bring people up to date about where we are and encourage a good turnout. Each of us needs to talk to some folks, especially folks who would not ordinarily think about coming. This is an important, decisive moment. We would like them to be present.

"Also, I will raise the question about the rectory. The diocese has said to go ahead with financing it apart from the major project. The money we spend on the rectory will more than pay for itself. We can conceivably begin construction in late Fall. But my fear is hearing, 'All this is pretty good; we've got this entire project, and Father is building a house for himself, and we still don't have a church.' I want to ask whether going ahead with the rectory will be okay with everybody. I want to get that support."

When reconvening the meeting after a break, Lewinski gave them handouts.

"Okay, first, a little bit of a review. Our goal tonight is to leave with one choice so we can move toward a Town Hall meeting. I also have an announcement that I want us to look at. As I mentioned last week, we aren't on a 'shopping tour' just to see what's nice, what we like, and what we don't like. That has to be measured against what we said we valued and what we said we needed. Those kinds of things emerged in various ways through Town Hall meetings, conversations, and dialogues that have taken place over the last few years.

"So the white sheet I just handed out represents some of that. I don't know that we have to go through all of this, but it probably wouldn't hurt just as a reminder—a litany—for ourselves. It is a mixture of many things. Looking ahead, it will be essential for us to do something like this for the Town Hall meeting. So the people who haven't been a part of that process all along—or forgot there was a process—don't think this suddenly came out of nowhere. This has been rolling along for quite a while.

"What I'm going to ask you to do by the time we have a Town Hall meeting is review this and recall things. I just quickly listed these from memory, so I may have missed some major pieces. Here are some values." He then began reviewing the highlights on the handout, listing the "Values." He went through the list, briefly commenting on each item.

"So those are just *some* things we have talked about. I want you to add anything I have overlooked. I think you would agree this is important for the folks at the Town Hall meeting—to get a sense of why the architects did *this* as opposed to something else. The response is this is what we have given the architect. If you're going to hire an artist, you don't tell them what to paint, but you express what you hope to achieve. That's what we have tried to do with our needs and our values.

"Maybe it was good for us to struggle over the last few months. It helped us understand how taking these needs and values and putting them into form is not as easy as it sounds. It is almost like a riddle, trying to put those pieces together in brick and stone.

"I've written down a few things I've heard people say this evening. We want to make a list of our concerns to share with Lohan, irrespective of whether it is 'A' or 'B.' One is: could they move the church a little further north to save space for the future on the property's south end? The difficulty is it breaks up the grid pattern we also valued at one point. We can't move the whole road north because of the cemetery. But it is a question to ask the architect—whether this is the best land use for current and future needs.

"We also discussed getting an estimate for a basement with a walkout.

"There's also a question about the glass—especially facing south—how problematic is that to heat and air condition? Again, remember it is not just clear glass, and they said we could reduce what comes through there down to 20 or 30%. It is an issue that must be considered.

"Are there other questions or thoughts, looking at what we did last week and this week, that remain an issue?"

After a few minutes of discussion, Lewinski reminded everyone about the values they had collected. He noted designs attempting to meet those sometimes seemed to conflict. For example, viewing a rural landscape from the glass-enclosed narthex but having sufficient parking close enough for those who need it.

They looked at each model's advantages, including roof lines, alignment, sloping floors, curb appeal, and other features. They tended to over-talk and begin separate discussions. When the time was called for participants to cast their votes, there was no clear preference for any of the three alternatives. A second vote resulted in the same lack of consensus.

Lewinski spoke up. "I want to caution about using the word consensus —if consensus means coming up with the least common denominator, then I think that is a mistake. Then you get no really authentic design—it is all bandaged in some sense. Certainly, recommendations can be made because this is a conceptual design at this point. Still, we want to be careful of applying bandages because then the integrity of the building is lost. The other thing we should consider is that it is hard to make this kind of decision because we know the implications. They are long-term.

"We also have to ask ourselves what is it we are feeling, what is the fear inside of us as we try to decide, in terms of those implications. There has to be some risk. We have to encourage the community to do something they can be happy with and proud of, not just today but twenty, even fifty years from now. Like anything else, you do grow into it.

"Again, given all three models, an adjustment will be needed. The first part of that change is the reality that St. Mary's is not the same anymore.

There is no way to get around that. For the Town Hall meeting, we must be ready for anger and discomfort. There is the sobering reality that this is for real now.

"We had talked about this, but the reality is that there is now a new future for St. Mary's. That's the hardest thing: for our community to transition. I want to be sure people understand it is okay to have fears and that we make proper decisions. Even if we built a Gothic structure, it would still be difficult to get used to. It's going to be difficult. It's going to be a new home."

Like their previous meeting,   this one also ended inconclusively. Lewinski had repeatedly probed the group about their design preference. The discussion alternated between voting, questioning, and advocating some features over others. No model garnered a majority vote of those in favor, and Model C was identified as the one with the least attraction. He realized despite everyone's desire to reach a decision, they had not.

How would they ever decide what to propose to their fellow parishioners?

---

[1] Pastoral Council minutes, May 10, 1999.

[2] Cardinal Bernardin gave the homily at the 120th anniversary Mass at St. Mary in Fremont Center (1984). He began, "My Brothers and Sisters, parishioners and friends of St. Mary's Church. I want to tell you how happy and honored I am to be with you today to celebrate the 120th anniversary of your parish. Apart from the great and serious historical significance of this celebration, someone told me that this is the only church in the Archdiocese of Chicago where I would be able to see cows grazing while I celebrated Mass! It isn't often that I can have such a rural experience in my ministry as Archbishop, and I welcome it!"—*Bernardin's Homily at One Hundred and Twentieth Anniversary of St. Mary (Fremont Center)*, 8/5/1984, EXEC/C0500/132, Archdiocese of Chicago's Joseph Cardinal Bernardin Archives and Records Center.

SILENT VIEWING

Spring 1999

When Lewinski and the group reconvened a few days later, they were joined by parishioner Andy Pini. He had originally introduced Lewinski to Lohan Associates.

Anyone who had attended the two previous meetings must have recognized they were facing a challenge. There was a mutual desire to plan for the future. Of course, there were clear differences of opinion. The challenge was finding enough agreement despite the differences. If the discussion continued as before, their effort this evening would result in frustration and another failure.

Yet, a decision was required to keep on schedule. Having a new facility ready to occupy in a few years was the long-term goal. The most pressing short-term goal was sharing a concept with parishioners at a Town Hall in three weeks. The choice they were trying to make was just part of the preparations for that assembly of parishioners.

The group was back together to choose a design. They aimed to identify what best represented the values the parish had given to the architects. The previous session resulted in a lack of focus and unstructured discussion. Lewinski knew continuing that approach would lead nowhere. So, he prepared a process for this period of discernment. It would allow participants to reflect on their own perspectives, listen with an open mind to the views of others, and aid the group in identifying additional information for making a decision.

Lewinski opened with a greeting. "Well, thank you all for coming out this evening for our time together. We have tried to make some progress," he said with a nervous chuckle, "in the last several weeks, and hopefully, we're going to get someplace with that today.

"To make our time as productive as possible, we[1] have created a little process to follow. So the meeting has some order. I'll try to prepare us for that process. What we're doing this evening is of great importance. Certainly, for some time now, we have pondered with our community and in our committees what we value at St. Mary's. Faced with the awesome task of building a church and ancillary facilities, we must address how we can bring those values into the picture and move into the future."

Then he reviewed the values the community had given to the architects.

"Some values we have espoused have included a desire to be a close community—a hospitable and inclusive one. Our narthex will become a token of that.

"Also, an open and natural environment is more than just cosmetic, but a doorway to the sacred.

"Another is a conviction that we have a mission that moves us beyond our own doorstep.

"And a commitment to a long-range future as well.

"Along with those values is the belief that a church is not just a wrapper for the community but also a structure that can lift up the community beyond itself to encounter the very mystery of God.

"There's a value to relate our new construction to structures that are already a part of a rural heritage; not become enslaved to the past, but look creatively to the future.

"We discussed having a narthex and parish center capable of multiple uses.

"And finally, a campus that will be as functionally efficient as it will be aesthetically pleasing.

"Tonight, what we will try to do is attempt to select a conceptual design that embodies those values. And I'd like to say just a word about what selecting a conceptual design means.

"First, a conceptual design is a bare-bones broad sketch of a style and shape of architecture. It does not include details such as materials for walls or whatever. So, viewing the models, one has to creatively envision the difference that color, surface, and texture can make in a building. I suppose one way to look at it is this: if you were to take either building and renovate it with little problem, would it work for you? We can interchange a lot of those little pieces.

"If we can agree on a conceptual design tonight," said Lewinski hopefully, "then the architects can develop that design with more detail. They will move on to schematic designs, then lay out the rooms, the spatial relationships, and all that greater detail. We'll also announce a Town Hall meeting for June 17, which Lohan Associates will attend, and will present the conceptual design for the community to review. The architects will enhance what we see here tonight so that we offer the community an even more appealing presentation.

"Once we get the community's consensus that the conceptual design is acceptable, we'll proceed. It will allow us to get a whole new thrust for our PR and capital campaigns.

"What is tonight's process? We will unveil both concepts simultaneously, but we will ask you to maintain silence for the first ten minutes."

Of course, this group knew each other well enough to recognize that some outspoken individuals were prepared to express their preferences. So they regarded Lewinski's comment as a jest. Even Lewinski smiled broadly and chuckled because he knew how the group would react to his statement. But as he continued speaking, they realized he was serious.

"It is important to realize that we are not 'going shopping'—we are trying to see what the model represents. Imagine in our minds what that might be like as an actual building. If we don't take it to heart, we will lose the whole perspective of things. Reflecting silently will also keep us from being prejudiced by other people's remarks. Take ten minutes only to *look*. Ask yourself which of the two models, A or B, you prefer. Why is it appealing? Why would you choose one over the other? How does your chosen model embody the values we have articulated? Can you picture our community gathering for prayer in the new church? Ponder in silence the effect natural light will have in and around the space. After you've had a good look at both models, sit quietly for a while and imagine how we might use a structure like that.

"After ten minutes of silent viewing, we will go around the room and simply respond to two questions. When we do, it will not be a time for lobbying. Just state what was appealing to you, and if there was one thing you would want to alter, what would it be? We'll give everybody a chance to share their preference—not to dialogue yet—and then we will take a break and have some refreshments. When we get back together, I will point out a few particular details, and then we'll have full discussion to see if we can move toward some consensus.

"Just some final thoughts. First, I have been very pleased with what Lohan has presented. It has taken a while, a brief struggle almost like giving birth, but I know—at least for myself—that I have gotten where I can begin to picture some detail, imagine some landscaping, and so forth. And, of course, most importantly, how much of a difference the people themselves will make entering that building. Having gotten to this point, I want to thank Andy Pini. He has been a marvelous help to us—like an international negotiator."

To this, Pini retorted, "More like a referee." Many in the group laughed, but Pini's comment bore some truth. A participant from Lohan's firm recalled the project years later. He called one particular meeting between the parish and the architectural firm a "long horrible process."

Recognizing what Pini was referring to, Lewinski responded, "That too. Andy has been a good 'interpreter': we would say something, and

Andy would translate that to the architect and then translate it back to us. Because of that help, we have been able to reach this point."

Lewinski then recited a prayer. It was not "off-the-shelf." It genuinely reflected the meeting's intent and importance. Theirs was a historic decision affecting current and future generations of parishioners and people in the broader communities they serve.

"So I'd like to begin with a prayer first," Lewinski continued, "and then we will give you time in silence, as the music plays, to simply view both models. Let us pray."

Lewinski silently took several seconds to adjust mentally. Most participants likely expected to pray with sincerity and then resume discussions they were having during the previous meetings. They knew their effort so far had not resulted in progress, but no one had called a timeout. Lewinski was doing that now. They bowed their heads as he began his psalm-like invocation.

"For months now, oh Lord, we have planned and dreamed and tried to imagine what we can build that would be a worthy channel of your mysterious presence among us and beyond us, as well as being a home for our Church.

"To this church, families will bring their children to be baptized into Christ and so begin their Christian journey.

"To this church, your community will gather each Lord's day to remember your almighty deeds, share in the sacrifice of your Son, and so be fed on your Word and living bread for true discipleship.

"Here, lovers will come to seal the bond of their love in holy matrimony and so become a sign of Christ's love for his bride, the Church.

"Within these walls and on these grounds, young and old will find a place of peace, rest, and solitude where they can encounter God and discover their true selves.

"To this holy place shall we carry our beloved dead to commend them to you, oh God, in the sure and certain hope of the glorious resurrection.

"In this center, we, your people, will extend the care and forgiveness, hope and comfort that come from Christ.

"We will teach and guide here.

"We will sing and laugh here.

"We will call this our home because here we will find support and encouragement, challenge and inspiration, being shaped for life and for our mission.

"Tonight, as we review these plans, endow us with wisdom, and help us conceive what we might become in the future.

"Open our minds and let the breath of your Spirit free us of prejudice and fear.

"Help us work diligently together for the good of your Church, and bring to completion the good work that you have begun in us, through Christ our Lord. Amen."

When Lewinski finished praying, no one was prepared to return to the previous meeting's chaotic discussion. Instead, there was silence. Silence while they pondered the words he had recited. Silence as they recognized the gravity of their task. Their decision would literally stand as a visible testament to their work. Silence arising from each person's desire to avoid being the first to tarnish the sacredness of this process. Silence when realizing they bore a responsibility to each other and to the parish so someday they could recall this time with confidence, knowing they had done their best.

The silence transformed into choral hymns from the soft, reflective music Jim Scavone played from a compact disk. He unveiled the tall cloth-covered objects on two different tables. These were the models "A" and "B" discussed during the previous meeting. Lewinski had recalled his own observation during a meeting a few months prior in December when he stated the models should not be viewed from overhead. Lohan advised people to "never look down" at the models as a bird would from the sky. During a recent meeting, Lewinski noticed people "looking down" at models. Some, including Lewinski himself, had lifted them to eye level to get a more real-life view. So to prepare for tonight, he had elevated the models on boxes tall enough to provide a "street-level" view, as people would see them from the surrounding area.

Everyone stood and quietly circulated around the tables. On each table was also a large schematic showing where the model would be located on the property relative to other components like the new parking lot, retention ponds, cemetery, and the old church.

Lewinski's prayer was a reminder. They were not there to pick something they liked. His prayer reminded them of their responsibility to determine on behalf of the parish which alternative best represented the needs and values they had given to the architect. It was a litany of important events in parishioners' lives this facility would service. His was a request for God's grace to help each individual discern what God was asking of these people.

Together—the prayer, the music, and seeing the elevated models— these all had a transformative effect. Any anticipation of adopting a "business as usual" attitude or voicing a light-hearted comment faded. It was replaced by a sincere recognition of their joint task and their individual responsibility to achieve their goal.

When the viewing period ended, Lewinski retrieved his notes. "Our process is very simple at this point. We're going to ask the first of the two questions." They proceeded around the room at Lewinski's request, each person stating their preference and why. Some comments, interspersed with brief clarifying statements, were:

- *"B. I like the angles. It brings out long linear accessibility and adds character from different perspectives. It looks different from different directions."*
- *"I like A. I like the symmetry. I think it complements the current church structure."*
- *"I prefer B. I like the angles. I think it's very dramatic."*
- *"I like B. Same as the others. Also, it flows nicely with the landscape."* Lewinski commented, *"We will explain some consequences of doing the angles later."*
- *"B. The angle caught my attention; I thought that was unique and different."*
- *"A. It has simple country lines. I like the simplicity and country look to it."*
- *"A. I think it feels more rural. Maybe there could be a little bit more glass."*
- *"B. I like how the narthex opens up."*
- *"I like them both. I prefer A. It has the capability to be simpler and more accessible."*
- *"B. I like the roof line that would bring light in from the top."*
- *"B. Because of the angles and non-symmetric look."*
- *"A. Because of the symmetry. The angled lines on B give me an unsettled feeling."*
- *"B. I like the angles of the roof, but also the amount of light that comes through."*
- *"B. The Blessed Sacrament chapel on the back seems to be more impressive; I guess it's because of the unusual angle."*
- *"B. I think the angles create a lot of interest."*
- *"A. I think it is more conservative. I do like this country feeling more."*
- *"I choose A for the reasons the others have given, although when I hear the arguments for B, they are compelling."*

Understanding laughter greeted the last comment. Everyone saw features in both models they liked or disliked. Lewinski then summarized some highlights.

"Just for some clarification. First, I think that one positive feature is the entire plaza entry. You notice that putting the offices to the east and the church to the west creates a nice entry plaza that we could use to bless palms on Palm Sunday or some kind of gathering.[2]

"The bell tower in the plaza still needs to be designed. Hopefully, it will use the bell we have in front of the old church. Lohan's idea is to create a structure where you see the bell—it is not hidden but more open.

"In both models, the Eucharistic Chapel becomes a stellar feature. In either case, it becomes a great pillar of light. So if you are going down Fremont Center Road at night, it will be a light shining in the darkness, a light in the prairie. So it has some genuine positive features. The light from that space will also flood around the altar area.

"Another feature in both models is that as you enter from the courtyard into the narthex, you are still looking out to the land beyond. That could be landscaped with a meditation garden, and you could have some doors going out there, too.

"Both plans still envision the light coming down upon the altar from that steeple. I think light shining down on the altar is important.

"Both models also provide easy access to the meeting space. You can see that both plans immediately attached the meeting rooms to the narthex. You can seat 185 people at tables in the narthex, plus another 150 in those rooms, so you're talking about seating 300 people in that connected space. Also, we have saved a little by planning for just one kitchen, which would serve all purposes. It serves the narthex and the other rooms.

"The advantage of the angled nave, by shifting or turning the square, is that it creates some new interesting spaces within the worship space to allow more easily for shrines and other things. In the square piece and defined by the symmetry, it is harder to play with some of that. The square design also gives you a feeling like the old church with the altar in the center with the two side altars [which won't exist], whereas the angled model doesn't give that impression.

"The angled one also gives you better access to the Eucharistic Chapel because one side is wider than the other, and you can create a bigger doorway, a more unique entrance, to the Eucharistic Chapel.

"The disadvantage of the angled one is that it may cost us more to do," he declared with another nervous chuckle revealing some anxiety about the additional expense, "because the angled components would have to be specially made—maybe as much as 5% additional cost."

The conversation began. The first topic was the idea of a basement under the pastoral center. There were comments about the cost impact of a basement—estimated as at least $400,000. It would require an elevator and a fire prevention system, etc. Proponents of a basement stated they would be short-sighted not to examine the options for a basement. Someone suggested that if they eliminated the angled design, there might be a budget for a basement by saving the special costs Lewinski had mentioned. A good amount of time was spent on the basement.

Lewinski concluded, "We can price it out. We must be prepared to make sacrifices in other areas if we want a basement. I am absolutely certain that the diocese is waiting to see how well we do with the capital campaign. The price ceiling for Phase I is at $10 million, but if we don't increase pledges during the capital campaign, we may question whether we can ever reach that. The difficulty will be that the unpledged balance will cause our mortgage to be higher. But we can go back and price that out; we'll note that and take that issue back."

"So, how do we move this to the next phase," he asked, attempting to move the conversation onward. He leaned against a supporting pole with his notes on an adjacent bookshelf. As he spoke, he motioned toward them. His leaning stance implied a casual attitude. His arms folded across his chest, and his tone, suggested otherwise. "Besides the basement issue, what do we ask Lohan to do next? What do we have to do to prepare for the Town Hall meeting?"

Someone mentioned showing both designs at the Town Hall.

"No, I don't think we should do that," he replied. "You can see the difficulty *our* small group is having trying to sort this out. It would be even more difficult to show both designs to the parish. It would be chaos trying to figure that out." Lewinski knew it was not viable to offer more than one choice. Scavone responded, "I think we have to trust that we here are a good representation of the parish."

Someone recalled a statement Lewinski had made regarding the angles. Lewinski explained in a very animated manner—while holding up the drawing for people to see—the "genius" in the angled design. In each design, the nave remains a straight line toward the altar. So skewing the sanctuary helps avoid giving the assembly the sense that they are viewing a stage production. "The first thing the architect did was skew the sanctuary, not the narthex, to address the symmetry problem in that space," said Lewinski, noting the area to the left of the altar could seat a smaller number of attendees for a smaller service.

IMAGE #9

MARIAN SHRINE

THE WOOD CARVING BY AN ITALIAN ARTISAN IS SITUATED
AMONG THE PEWS TO THE RIGHT OF THE ALTAR.

Coming back to the general floor plan of the sanctuary, he pointed to a circle toward the north wall. "This little circle is a Marian shrine, so instead of putting Mary on a back wall someplace under an arch, we are bringing her right into our midst, like in the Acts of the Apostles with the disciples in prayer. There she is, along with us."

Lewinski asked, "Do we feel we're far enough along to announce a Town Hall for June 17th?"

Not receiving a response, Lewinski posited a decision. "Do we hear if, with modifications, we can all live with model A?" He looked around with a smile, awaiting an answer, and received a negative one.

"That's one 'no,'" he acknowledged.

Recognizing the group was struggling, Pini reminded them about some basics underlying their process. "Maybe getting a consensus on the *design* criteria is good. When I started getting involved with this decision effort two weeks ago, I just ran some design criteria by Father Ron and Jim Scavone. Those were: humble, rural, simple, beautiful (it makes a memorable impression on you), and functionally appropriate. I think if the parish is on track with the decision, then the rest becomes easy."

Lewinski then added, "It is always a delicate balance. What's happened in many places is they have ended up with a church that nobody wants."

Lewinski himself admitted ambivalence between the two models. "We feel rural now, but in twenty years, will some ask 'what is this?'" he posited. "Will it transcend time?" He recalled that Lohan—who was not Catholic—had observed—somewhat to Lewinski's surprise—that the nave is "a straight line, it still goes to the source of the food," pointing to the altar.

Given the parish's historic rural nature, someone speculated, "I'm going to think that the people will prefer the prairie look of A, the 'traditional' design." A retort came from someone else, himself a longtime parishioner whose family ties reached far back. "I don't know that you can say that because of the changing demographics."

Someone noted that both models are more contemporary than the old church. Lewinski observed that "the interior of 'A' is much like a Holiday Inn meeting room because it is a square space, whereas 'B' is less so. There is the bell tower and several other traditional features in 'B'."

"I consider myself a very conservative person," admitted a member of one of the founding families. "But to me, model B—the more 'modern' design—catches the essence. I didn't like the first rendition, but this really softens it up. To me, it adds character."

The conversation touched on estimated costs of other desirable features. One was rerouting Erhart Road and changes to Fremont Center Road (another $400,000). That, and the basement, could increase the cost by almost $1 million. As Lewinski had cautioned, something else would have to go if they desired those changes.

Lewinski raised topics he hoped to address at the Town Hall. One was the cost of a basement. The next was building the rectory before any other structures: he didn't want people to think he was putting himself first. A third topic was the parish's formal name—St. Mary of the Annunciation—instead of the common "St. Mary - Fremont Center." He joked, "It might be easier than trying to explain who 'St. Mary of Fremont' was." Parishioner Stan Zagula reminded them that the reference could be "St. Mary of the Annunciation—the Catholic community of Fremont Center," which was well-received.

They had exceeded the allotted time and agreed to meet the following week again for more review. Lewinski closed the session by saying, "Okay, thank you all for your time."

Thanks to Lewinski's process, the group made progress. Everyone recognized the importance of their decision. He'd defined the need in prayerful words about events everyone could relate to and recognize as important. The approach gave everyone time to prioritize their thinking before sharing their thoughts with others.

Lewinski had choices on this path. The fastest was to make the decision himself. As a leader, he knew that would be a mistake. As a pastor, he knew that was not the behavior of a proper shepherd.

So he did what he believed was right. He chose the harder path by involving parishioners in a mutual decision with a lasting impact on their parish.

---

[1] The "we" used here referred to Jim Scavone who, with Lewinski, devised an approach with the hope of elevating the value of the participant's contributions, respecting the variety of opinions, and improving the likelihood that a "model of choice" would result.

[2] An earlier plan had shown the church and narthex on a north-south axis, rather than the east-west adopted by the current model.

THE LOOK OF REVELATION

Summer and Fall 1999

In his June 13, 1999 bulletin column, Lewinski reminded parishioners about the important upcoming Town Hall four days away. He tried to prepare them for what to expect at the conceptual design's revelation.

> I hope that you will come to the Town Hall meeting with an open mind. I have heard from other pastors who have gone through the building project that when parishioners first see a conceptual design there is a variety of reactions. Part of that, I'm sure, is that we see at least some sense of what we will call our church in the future. Whether we realize it or not, we probably all have an image in our minds of what a church ought to look like. So when we see a conceptual design and it doesn't match what we were thinking about, it might at first catch us off guard. But that doesn't mean it is a poor design. You know what it is like when you move into a new home. You have to take some time to get used to it. It has to grow on you.
>
> In the last few years, you have seen my commitment to keeping our parish facilities beautiful and tasteful. Although it is still a gym, many were surprised by how beautiful we were able to make it ready for Mass. You have seen how we have redecorated our old beloved church, maintaining its beauty and distinctive character and charm. You have seen the careful attention given to our grounds. I promise to bring that same commitment of beauty and attention to detail to whatever we erect in the future. ...
>
> This is an exciting time for St. Mary. I urge you to get involved. I welcome your comments and suggestions. Above all, I want you to feel proud of your parish. We are engaged now in a momentous project that will mold us into a stronger community and have an effect upon generations to come. Please don't stand on the sidelines. It is a great time to jump into the center of parish life. It's a wonderful opportunity to discover a new sense of what it means to be a Catholic, a faithful disciple of Jesus, at the dawn of the new millennium.[1]

As usual, he was informing people and setting expectations. He was urging them to proudly be part of the change. He was preparing a way for his flock.

Finally, the time had arrived. The team's work over the past several months had, after much discernment, led to a selection. On June 17, 1999, they held the Town Hall. It was three years after the parish and the Archdiocese had decided to build new facilities.

This was the first time parishioners saw the conceptual design and met the architect. Previous meetings were between Lewinski's and Lohan's teams. A lot of discussion had already occurred. Tonight's meeting aimed to show what was being proposed and get people's reactions. Their comments would be used to improve the concept.

John Riggio introduced Lewinski. As customary, he began with a prayer. Jim Scavone introduced it with a melodic sequence of handbells. "Sisters and Brothers," prayed Lewinski, "the Lord has called us to a great task: to build a house of worship, a place where all are welcome and where the glory of God can resound. With song and sight, let us reflect upon this privileged moment in the history of St. Mary's Parish. Let our experience tonight, and all the work we do in the months ahead, and all the sacrifices we will make to accomplish our goal, renew us as God's holy people—a living temple of God."

Scavone led the assembly in singing "All Are Welcome." While they sang, a projector displayed images of various church architectural styles. Thus, the lyrics affirmed parishioners' unity while mentally preparing them for Lohan's comments. To aid their transitional thinking, the last picture showed the southern entrance to Diantha Hall. It was the space they were now occupying, the "temporary" location of weekend services. The image was a visual reminder of what was now and what was yet to come. At the song's conclusion, Lewinski returned to the podium to continue his prayer.

"Holy God, we praise your name. Lord of all, we bow before you. When more than 100 years ago, our ancestors founded this community of faith, they placed their trust in you, our loving and gracious God. They placed themselves under the mantle of St. Mary of the Annunciation to watch over them and to intercede for them. As we begin this new chapter in our sacred history, this same family of faith solemnly renews its trust in you that you might guide and direct us into the future. Free us from fear and anxiety, and fill us with joy as we accept the mission you have given us to build a church for generations to come. Make us your holy temple. Let your spirit dwell in us. May Christ be the foundation stone of all we do, and may our work please you. May Mary, who at the Annunciation trusted that nothing is impossible with God,[2] be our model and inspiration. We ask this through Christ our Lord. Amen."

Riggio continued with an overview of the agenda and presenters. He spoke about how the parish community had given the architects a set of criteria to guide their efforts. They gave everyone a handout. It listed the Needs and Values that Riggio just referenced. He announced Lohan and his associates would make about a forty-five-minute presentation. A half-hour for questions and answers would follow it. There were four specific questions on another handout. If attendees could not complete it there, they could return it with the Sunday collection.

Lewinski came to the podium and offered a riddle. "What is more powerful than God? The only good thing that we can say about the devil? The rich do not have it. The poor have plenty of it. And if you eat it, you'll die." While people sought an answer, he commented, "It is interesting, you know. They gave this riddle during a study. Seventy-five percent of children under twelve answered the question immediately." People laughed, many somewhat uncomfortably. "Of people with a college degree, only seventeen percent answered it." He paused to give people time to absorb this and conceive a response. "The answer is: 'Nothing.'

"Well," he continued, "if you think that riddle was tough, then look again at that sheet of values and needs. That was the riddle we gave to Lohan Associates. We asked them to build a church as beautiful as the one that we have and love; to build a church that can seat 1,100 people but that has an intimate feeling, and everyone can be close to the altar; build a church that blends in with our environment but also looks to the future; build us a grand, noteworthy church, but keep a modest budget. All of that is, in some sense, a riddle. The Needs and Values are the ingredients, of course, that will go into what we believe constitutes the kind of church that will best suit our community of St. Mary's.

"Despite the challenge, I believe Lohan Associates responded creatively to our values and needs. It is important that we keep reminding ourselves of those because we conceivably could come up with some plan that looks very, very beautiful but may not be usable and not really fit those values and needs. So it is a real challenge to include those into a space that works for us and is, in fact, beautiful and pleasing as well.

"I'm not going to take too much more time, just simply to say thank you to the many, many people who have brought us to this point. I am grateful not only for the ideas, the insights, and the honest and candid sharing of both fears and concerns but also for wonderful ideas and the many ways in which people have contributed their professional services. We have already saved thousands of dollars for the parish. We are blessed at St. Mary's. It is something we shouldn't take for granted. This is indeed a real privileged moment of grace.

"Last week, at our clergy convocation in St. Charles, over 600 priests gathered. As part of the introduction during the first evening, there was a video prepared by Paulist Publications on the diversity of the diocese. One place they featured in the film was St. Mary at Fremont Center. Of course, everybody has heard the news that we are in the process of building. Priest after priest came up and said what a wonderful opportunity it is for your community to go through this experience. How wonderful it is that you have this occasion when you can renew your faith through the very process of building. They also wished me well at the Tylenol counter."

He paused during the laughter. "But it was interesting to hear other people comment about what we are doing. Sometimes you know, when you are so close to something, you get caught up in it and don't realize what you're up to. It was good to hear so many people wishing our community well and really envying us of this opportunity. So without saying anything more, I'm going to hand over the program to Lohan Associates. Dirk, can I ask you to introduce your team here tonight and go from there. Dirk Lohan."

Lohan first established a protocol. "Good evening, and thank you for this opportunity. It is a very special occasion to share the work we have done and have me explain it to you and then ask questions.

"I should say that the project we've been engaged in for some time now has been a very rewarding one for me as an architect because it has been a learning experience. It has been one where I, and I think it is true of my colleagues, have been challenged again and again to search—to search for the *appropriate* solution and the *right* answer. I have with me two colleagues. Al Novickas, sitting here in front, who is the design architect in my office working on this project. Also, Scott Hagel, who has worked with Al on the drawings."

"The process and the search for the appropriate design solution have been based on two very overriding and important considerations. The first one is the search for a spiritual quality in the design or even a sacred one. To give the design—the context, the idea of the buildings—something that makes it more than an ordinary functional building of daily life such as an office building, or a restaurant, or store, or gas station. Something that lifts it and inspires the congregation to think about God in their lives on earth. The second aspect of the search was one to relate this design to your tradition, to this location, your history in this parish, and to find not only the design for a building that does that but also the site plan, the Masterplan if you will. Those are two things that I will be dwelling on."

Here the ceiling lights were turned off, and the first in a series of pictures was projected on the screen before the audience. "I'd like to talk for a few minutes about some thoughts that came to me as we developed this design in terms of imbuing it with the sacred spiritual quality. What are the elements of such a quality, the sacredness in a building? One way to do that is to look at historical and worldwide examples of churches and religious buildings which have that quality. Why do they have that quality was the question we asked ourselves."

Lohan showed slides from his first meeting with the parish leadership. Like before, he touched on design qualities like a sense of openness and the use of light. He spoke about the relationship to nature, simplicity, the symbolism of the spirit, humility, location, and a sense of the spectacular. He remarked on the beauty and calming influence of reflections in water, the materials used, and the placement of religious art.

Lohan continued, "Now, I would like to talk for a few minutes about the site and the property. We call this searching for a proper plan—the way the site is developed. Another word that we architects use is 'contextual' design, meaning to relate to an existing context. The context here is not only your old church but also your natural and traditional northern Illinois farmland aesthetics."

Lohan motioned to his team. "We come from the south—almost two-and-one-half hours coming here tonight. We love coming out here. That quality, the rolling gentle hills, different shades of green trees and grass, crops, and so on. It is beautiful for someone from the city. It induces peace and comfort. I have a hunch that is why most of you live here. But I think that you all know—and you are probably running scared—that one day you will look like Mundelein." The group received this with some laughter, though most people knew that the rapidly increasing population was changing the area's demographics. "You very wisely bought a fairly large piece of land. It will allow us to preserve some of that, even if further development occurs all around."

Lohan set some expectations by explaining that tonight is an overview of a concept. It is not a detailed description of things like materials and costs. He described the normal planning phases, from concept to completed drawings suitable for a contractor's use. Thus, the "circle of understanding" expanded from the core team to the people attending. What was important from Lewinski's and Lohan's perspectives was the parishioners were both informed and involved.

Lohan continued, noting the changes in church architecture from the linear—which distanced people from the altar—to a style that brought people closer to the altar. This honors the desires expressed during the Second Vatican Council. He stated they spent "time soul-searching and sketching of different options." They conceived an arrangement of the three components: the church proper, the narthex, and the parish offices. He projected a drawing of the conceptual design on the land in an east-west orientation. He did not dwell on it or go into more detail. He said the high nave's key feature was uniting the structures below it.

His next remarks accompanied a slide of suggested landscaping ideas projected on the screen. "One of the questions at this point is whether we can afford the expense of landscaping and beautification in the beginning. Because the budget is limited, you need to plan, and an idea for that is what you see here."

Next, the list of Values was projected. Lohan continued, "Your 'values and needs' were mentioned earlier. They are very much on our minds." He projected a slide showing space allocations for spaces within the buildings. This gave people an idea of how the functionality—derived from the values and needs—might be implemented as offices, meeting, and worship spaces. He explained 10,000 square feet were allocated for the parish center and about 20,000 for the church and narthex, totaling about 30,000 square feet. Of course, the 'values' in the list were not monetary.

Lohan next spoke to the most challenging aspect for the architectural and pastoral teams. "Some time ago, all of us—your building committee, Father Ron, our firm—were focused on a design like this," he explained, referring to what the project team knew as option 'A.' "It was absolutely straight—the two buildings were parallel to each other. The narthex was not angled but straight. In our discussions—and this was a difficult one because it went on for a long time—there was a feeling that it was very clean. But there was no artistic or creative challenge—no spark—in the design. Someone expressed a desire to add some asymmetry."

Lohan explained, "We then explored various ways of shifting and arranging the components. We came to this—what I now believe to be a much, much better solution—of an asymmetrical arrangement that slants the narthex slightly out of the rectilinear."

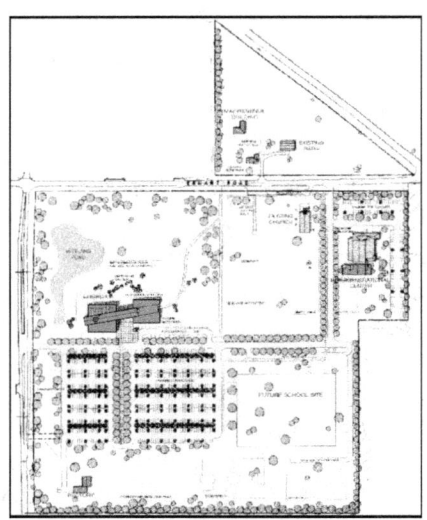

IMAGE #10

SITE PLAN BY LOHAN ASSOCIATES

THIS PLAN BY LOHAN ASSOCIATES REORIENTED THE CHURCH AND OFFICES FROM A NORTH/SOUTH TO AN EAST/WEST AXIS.

He was now referring to option 'B.' "It is a slightly disquieting, surprising element which makes it special and challenging for the visitor to understand. You are challenged to sort it out, and I think it is perhaps symbolic of a little more modern world to have this unusual challenge in this design."

Next, an artist's rendering from a Southwestern perspective was shown. It depicted exterior wood trim framing the glass walls.[3]

IMAGE #11

THE NEW CHURCH AT ST. MARY'S PARISH

THIS ARTIST RENDERING DEPICTS A DESIGN
INCORPORATING WOOD BEAMS ON THE EXTERIOR.
THE FINAL DESIGN USED STEEL BEAMS ON THE INTERIOR.

The steeple was easily identifiable. Lohan spoke about it being directly above the altar, with its base seeming to come through the roof. He said they intended the steeple to emit light.

The next drawing showed the glass narthex framed by wood. Lohan explained the wooden louvers, or slats, were a feature dependent upon costs. Another idea was to use fritted glass. It would reduce light infiltration and be more energy efficient.

He noted the drawings were conceptual ideas, not final selections. In the drawings, he illustrated the use of wood and glass for the narthex, metal roofing for the entire structure, and white-washed brick for the church and pastoral center.

He then shared a view of their attempt to design something with *rural* qualities. "I personally think this view has a presence and an image that very much says church. I'd like to say it isn't something you have seen before, although it is reminiscent of a barn and simple country buildings. Still, it has a somewhat contemporary expression by the way this narthex is angled, and as a result, the roof lines are slightly sloping.

"Very important, of course, but still very preliminary, is exactly how the bell tower and the entry door are designed. One thing we all know, and particularly your committee and Father have always requested, is that the entry door is prominent and unique. I totally agree. A doorway will tell you this is not a house but a special way to enter a sacred space."

Lohan showed images of other buildings, including some design concepts and materials he'd mentioned. Thus, attendees did not need to leave it to their imagination. The images were a concrete way to ensure they could see what he was talking about, aligning everyone's understanding.

He concluded by identifying an important exhibit. "Incidentally, on this table is a little model of the entire building you saw photographs of in the presentation. You are welcome at the end to look at it. It is still very small. As we develop further, I am sure we will build other models so you can look inside the building and not just the outside." Here Lohan unveiled the model, covered until now to prevent premature viewing.

When the applause receded, Riggio asked for questions. The first was about the Eucharistic Chapel. On the drawing, it protruded slightly from the main body of the church. Lohan responded, "Yes, the nave extends beyond the church and at the end is the Eucharistic Chapel, outside the church proper. How we treat the closure and openings is not yet defined. It will certainly offer the opportunity to reach the chapel on any day or evening from the outside. One needn't go through the church proper, which is a nice feature. A small chapel that you can visit."

Although the chapel's footprint is small by comparison (40' wide by 30' deep), its peak is the same as the much larger sanctuary because of the fifty-foot nave. Thus, it has a spacious feeling similar to cathedrals with which Lohan was familiar.

Some questions arose. What about traffic flow, access routes for entry and exit, parking space and location, heat loss from high ceilings, maintenance costs, the orientation of the buildings, identifying the main entrance, and the relationship to the existing church and cemetery? Having discussed these during prior meetings with the parish team, Lohan was prepared to respond with assurance.

One parishioner expressed a concern. "My question," stated the parishioner, "is about the infrastructure of the air conditioning and heating system. We went to a church recently that had a roof similar to what you showed. They had this ductwork for the air conditioning going along both sides of the church interior. It looked *horrible*. Please don't build that in as a 'feature.'" The crowd chuckled.

Lohan responded, "Well, I can only say that you don't know me; you don't know *us*. We would not do that. We couldn't sleep if we did."[4]

The laughter helped everyone be more at ease. Then a young adult arose. "My name is Sarah Kennedy. I would like to thank the board for your hard work. I really love the conceptual design and think this design would attract my generation to come to the church. Thank you." The young lady's comments received approving applause.

Lohan's reaction was light-hearted but sincere. "That was the best comment yet," he said, smiling.

An older parishioner contributed, "My generation agrees." More laughter and applause. The crowd was softening up.

"I am very pleased," offered Lohan, "to hear these comments, particularly from young people, because we see ourselves as contemporary people. We want to do something for the future and not the past only. Nostalgia is wonderful, and history is wonderful, but this is going to be around for the next hundred years. It needs to have a lifespan and timelessness and something unique that is done today. It is reminiscent; it recalls certain aspects of church architecture and the Illinois farm rural quality. We also want to give it a contemporary quality. That is important to us, so I appreciate the comment."

Another middle-aged parishioner spoke up. "I'm a longtime member of St. Mary's, and one beauty of St. Mary's is having the presence it does; that's why my husband and I came here: because of the presence. We had other choices than St. Mary's. I think you have managed to capture that. I want to say thank you." Again there was approving applause.

After the Q&A period, Lewinski briefly commented on things he'd heard. "One thing about the Eucharistic Chapel. It is a very distinctive space. When you are sitting in the church proper, you will know where the Eucharistic Chapel is by a solemn and noble entryway, by the lighting." He commented about doorways from the narthex to the outside meditation garden; using the narthex for funerals and other occasions; and, yes, there would be pews in the church.

He shared his perspective on the results of the process the building committee had been through. "It is sometimes complicated for the committee at this point. We have looked at these plans repeatedly in different ways. It has *grown* on us, but we realize for you to see it for the first time, it is hard to even know what questions to ask. Give it some time, and hopefully, it will grow on you.

"About those four questions on the handout. The first one is just an initial reaction on your part. We hope you can give us some initial impressions of what you saw tonight and how you feel about that.

"The second question is about the rectory. So you know, the diocese has encouraged us and suggested we look at building a rectory now—as a separate project with separate financing, but simply get it done.

"The third question is about recapturing—recovering, in a sense—some of our history. The official name of our parish is St. Mary of the Annunciation. We are entering this new chapter in the parish's life. We'd like to know whether it is okay to use that title in a more formal manner.

"And finally, we believe art and religious imagery are important. We want to include that in the church. We are thinking about this together with the architects, so it doesn't become a 'tack on,' not an afterthought, but the art is really worked right into the structure. The question is, what do people at St. Mary's have a devotion to? Apart from Mary, who is our patron—certainly Mary will have a place in the church and an image—who else do we want? So some feedback would be helpful as well.

"I want to also remind you the other piece that goes with all of this is the capital campaign. You are now being commissioned as ambassadors of explanation and clarification to help us with that. Once we have some better images of what we are trying to do, it may boost and inspire the pledges because people can *see* what we are trying to do. So what I'm saying is to pass the word.

"Finally, I just want to thank you for coming out tonight. It is an exciting time. It is scary in some ways because you look at these things on paper and wonder. Is this the way it is going to look? How are we going to do all this? But I think what we see is something very inspiring. It is not ordinary. It is something we can be proud of. We made a color reproduction of one view presented this evening. We have one for every family that is represented here tonight. I want to thank Lohan Associates for being with us tonight. I encourage you to walk around the model to look at it. Look at it from eye level because you're not a bird. That way, you'll be able to appreciate it better. Thanks again."

The crowd lingered, and people gathered around the model. They asked Lohan and his team questions. Many eyes were seeing it for the first time, igniting conversations between attendees throughout the room. When the existing church was built, it followed a traditional design characterizing most country churches in the Midwest and across the country. Lohan's design differed in that it represented a response to the values and needs the parish had given him.

The designs were also displayed after the services on June 26th and 27th for parishioners to examine further.

In July, the sixth issue of *The Bell* reported on Lohan's presentation.

> While the Town Hall was the first time that the Conceptual Design was publicly presented at a meeting, it is actually the result of an evolutionary process involving parish delegates (Pastor Ron Lewinski and the Planning Commission), the architectural firm, Archdiocesan representatives and county officials.[5]

The article recalled the design was based on the Needs and Values the parish had given the architect. It described how the steeple was positioned to direct light onto the altar. A photo of the old church was compared to a drawing of the Eucharistic Chapel at the end of the new church. The comparison showed the similarity in roof lines. An overhead schematic illustrated how the nave, sanctuary, and pastoral center were offset to intentionally foster a sense of mystery. Other features were highlighted and explained in the extensive article.

The "Views from the Pews" column included testimonials from the feedback. Lewinski must certainly have regarded them as reassuring:

> "This is no cookie-cutter church, thank God. Be Proud, St. Mary's!"
> "I came away from the meeting with a great deal of confidence in the architects."
> "I feel the design is excellent because it reminds me of a rural and old church but also moves us into the future."
> "I really like the design…this is the kind of church a person of my generation would want to celebrate Mass in." (Recent high school graduate.)
> "A spectacular representation of the 'Values'."
> "I like a traditional style, but if this encourages the younger set to attend Mass, so be it!"
> "The Planning Commission has done a wonderful job."[6]

Lewinski's "Around the Table" column occupied a full page. He emphasized the importance of different opinions and ideas when making a decision.

> Our Town Hall meeting on June 17 was an exciting moment in our parish history. On that night, Dirk Lohan, our architect, first shared with us as an assembly the architectural components of sacred space. He showed us numerous samples of architectural style, use of light, connections to nature, etc., that have an effect on church architecture. Mr. Lohan taught us how to see what we might otherwise overlook with only a cursory, unenlightened review.
>
> People often ask, "How are decisions made about the planning for our new church and offices?" The answer is that a final decision about any aspect of the project is arrived at only after a multi-layered process of study and consultation.
>
> What about parishioner input? I consider parishioner input very important and vital to the project. The needs, ideas, insights, values, desires, and tastes of the community all go into the mixing bowl. Requirements from the Archdiocese and the county, civil engineering data, architectural expertise, liturgical norms, etc. must be added to the mixing bowl before a workable concept evolves. Given all the details, decisions can then be made.
>
> I once heard a monk at the Trappist Abbey of Gethsemani preach about the role of the Abbott. He said the Abbott takes a triple vow concerning decision-making in the community. First, he noted, the Abbott must listen to every monk in the community, from youngest to oldest, from most experienced to least. Secondly, the Abbott must listen to the voice of the Holy Spirit, speaking to him in prayer. Finally, the Abbott must listen to his own heart as the voice of the community and the voice of the Spirit resounds

within him. Only then can he make a responsible decision. I think that describes well my approach to decision-making...

In summary, our goal is to achieve a decision we can all live with, even when it is not someone's first choice.... The rewards for a community that works hard together, respects one another, and remains open to all opinions are great beyond measure. May we work and pray together to achieve those rewards.[7]

An article spoke about the value of diversity during this time of transition. It named the skills and experiences benefiting the parish. These included an abbreviated list of Lewinski's qualifications prior to coming to the parish: Fr. Ron Lewinski—teacher and liturgical specialist; former assistant for Archdiocese on building and renovation of churches; nationally respected author. Qualifications of participating parishioners included Director of Facility Management for a $100 million project; CFO; Information Technology consultant; Chemical Engineer; Architectural design consultant; Sales and marketing management; Global standards management for Abbott Labs; Village trustee; Professional grant writer; Mechanical Engineer; and others.

Lewinski ensured the issue included Mabel Bennett's "The Temple," though it wasn't identified as a midnight inspiration.

The $5.6 million in pledges was acknowledged. They were over the hump but far from the $9 million they needed to satisfy the Archdiocesan requirements.

After three and one-half years, Lewinski was beginning to sense a return to some normalcy in his personal life. His habit had always been to work beyond the boundaries of whatever parish or organization he was part of at the time. In his July 4th column, he explained he'd soon be absent from the parish for a brief period. He wrote about missionary work, such as the annual missionary appeal they were currently conducting. Another was the pending missionary venture by parishioner and doctor Al Dietz, joining a medical team in Bolivia. Furthermore, Sr. Gael Gensler would be on a mission with forty teens from St. Mary's and other Christian parishes to Pennsylvania, constructing housing for the needy.[8]

The parish mission was an ongoing conversation. During a meeting on July 13, it touched on Youth Liturgy. The concept went beyond a religious service to encompass Catholic life external to such services, instructing children how to pray, and ensuring all ages are included in parish activities.

Lewinski's lifetime view of Christianity had always been beyond the local Church he was part of. His study of Vatican II had instilled in him a worldview. An elevated sense of mission was in the air, and Lewinski announced his own plans for a personal mission.

> I, too, have heard the call to mission and accepted an invitation to teach for a few weeks in Singapore and Malacca, Malaysia. The Church is a minority in Southeast Asia and does not have the resources with which we Americans are blessed to further the work of the gospel. Though I was hesitant to leave the parish for a few weeks, I feel an obligation to share some of what I can give to those who are in need. As a priest of the universal Catholic Church, I am ordained not just for St. Mary but for the mission of Christ wherever it might be....
>
> This break will allow me some time to reflect on where we are and where we need to go. I welcome the opportunity to retreat for a while to review my own pastoral priorities and commitments. Having been involved in missionary ventures like this before, I know that I will return home, having gained more than I will be able to give. And so St. Mary will, in the long run, profit from this mini-missionary experience....
>
> I hope you will keep me in your prayers. Perhaps these missionary efforts of a few might inspire the many to consider a similar call.[9]

The constant skeptics in the parish would regard this as another example of how this priest was again off on vacation—one they were probably paying for.[10]

This "explanation" of his pending absence is rich with Lewinski philosophy. He shared he "too" had heard the call, meaning there were others, and suggesting perhaps someone reading his words hadn't yet recognized the call being directed at them.

While reluctant to leave, he felt obligated to share his gifts and knowledge. Shouldn't that be the perspective of everyone who is part of the Church that St. Paul wrote about?

He reminded parishioners that as members of the local faith community, their outlook—indeed, their obligation—is to look beyond its boundaries, at God's world, as their mission.

He wrote that time away from the normal routine would help him, as it could the reader, get a better perspective of life.

He expected the results of such contemplation would, in turn, benefit those he touched. This wasn't a selfish effort to escape but a method of advancing himself and others.

He asked for prayers, not as a routine request, but knowing there was some danger in his plans. By saying Christians were a minority, he was understating the conditions. He knew the area he was going to was actively anti-Christian. He could not risk wearing his Roman collar. The prospect of the worst that could happen was far from the idyllic getaway skeptics might accuse him of pursuing.

Finally, he casually urged the reader to consider pursuing their own missionary work. He frequently used this "suggestion" technique of sowing seeds hoping something would take root and grow.

The Pork and Corn Roast that August celebrated its 25th anniversary. They acknowledged the achievement with a special booklet. The event continued to be a major attraction for the parish and a financial benefit for the school. But new avenues of fundraising were being explored that held promise of a good profit with much less manpower investment.

Though he was thousands of miles away on August 29th, the Sunday bulletin carried Lewinski's comments. He noted Catholics are only 4% of Singapore's population. He stated, "In the last few days, I have been asked to assist four parishes in their initial planning phase for building a new church..... It's a great privilege to assist in this planning. Little did I realize how our own parish planning process would give me the experience to help others."[11]
The Spirit is always at work.

When he returned from Singapore and Malaysia, he declared it was good to return home. Part of his story explained why.

> At times I felt a bit frustrated because the needs are so great and yet all I could do was plant a few seeds. Humbly, I had to trust that what I planted would be cultivated by others and watered by God.
> We take a lot for granted in the USA. I met a young priest in Malacca who was committed to ministering to an Aboriginal community some 40 km out of town. Father Charles was summoned to the police station and told not to return to the Aboriginal community. When he attempted to visit the native community again, he was stopped on the road by the military police who threatened his life. There are other stories like this that I could tell. But suffice it to say we are blessed in the USA to be free to practice our faith openly without repercussions. We must fervently pray for our fellow Christians in countries where choosing to be a disciple of Jesus comes at a great price. After a few weeks of listening to stories of life and death and tremendous sacrifices, one's perspective on life and Christian practices is deeply affected. Forgive me, if in my transition back, I appear to be impatient with minor issues or petty concerns.[12]

The following week, Lewinski announced the firm of Frederick Quinn Corporation had been selected as the general contractor. There was still much work remaining, especially land preparation.
Meanwhile, the old church's windows needed repair. It would be expensive, but if they waited any longer, it would get even more expensive. They began assessing options and seeking advice about what action to take.

Lewinski observed the parish enrollment had risen to 1,200 households. Three years prior, there were 850. All the better for attendance at the next Oktoberfest on October 22nd.

On October 31, 1999, in Augsburg, Germany, the Lutheran World Federation and the Roman Catholic Church signed a "Joint Declaration on the Doctrine of Justification." For the two Churches, it resolved a 500-year-old conflict. The World Methodist Council adopted the Declaration in 2006, and the World Communion of Reformed Churches (80 million members of Congregational, Presbyterian, Reformed, United, Uniting, and Waldensian Churches) adopted it in 2017.[13]

What did it mean for St. Mary's parish? In his Oct. 31, 1999, column Lewinski briefly explained the history behind the Declaration. He concluded:

> On this Sunday, Lutherans worldwide observe Reformation Sunday. And so, it is appropriate timing for the signing of this agreement. Let us continue to pray that the dialogue that has been in progress and has already achieved so much will continue to lead us to that full and complete unity that our Lord so deeply desired of his followers. Pastor Bruce Cole of Faith Lutheran Church in Mundelein and I would like to foster the spirit of ecumenism by offering a joint program together. While the dialogue between the Churches continues at a high level, we would like to do our part by encouraging your prayer and study.[14]

Lewinski pursued ecumenical unity by inviting Cole to facilitate an annual ministerial and staff leadership meeting at St. Mary's on April 8, 2000. Cole accepted and was well received by attendees.

In November, Lewinski reported on an information dialogue between seventy priests and Cardinal George. It concerned pastoral issues affecting parishes. He described one of them this way:

> The irony of parents sending their children to a Catholic school and not celebrating Mass on Sunday; the dissonance between an ethic of pro-life but favoring capital punishment; the demands parishioners make for various ministries, services, and facilities, but no accountability for responsible stewardship; frequent reception of Communion but rare use of the Sacrament of Reconciliation, etc.
>
> These pastoral issues have no easy resolution. Nor is the discussion of these issues intended to be any kind of indictment of the majority of Catholic parishioners who are trying their best to live their faith in the community of the Church. But from what I could hear from my brother priests, these are issues that weigh heavily on pastors at the turn of the century. Please pray for your priests and our Archbishop who shepherd the Church of Cook and Lake Counties.[15]

The Sunday after Thanksgiving, Lewinski acknowledged the parish's good fortune. He announced they had created a book…

> …which contains the names of all those individuals and families who have formalized their commitment and stewardship to St. Mary's.[16] It is important for us to acknowledge our donors. While it is a private matter what each is able to contribute, as members of a community, our Church family, we are also accountable to one another for the good of the whole. We need to express our gratitude for the sacrifices that are being made for the Church's life in the next century. When I decided what financial commitment I could personally make, I thought of the wonderful Catholic experience I enjoyed as a young boy at Assumption B.V.M. (Blessed Virgin Mary) parish on Chicago's far south side. I took the school and the church of my boyhood for granted, never thinking at the time who paid for those wonderful buildings. And I doubt that, as a young child, I ever contributed much to the parish. So now I feel it is my turn. In gratitude for what I received as a child, I feel obligated to provide a church for those who will come after me.[17]

Lewinski reflected on the many opportunities the holiday presented in his column on the Sunday before Christmas. He wrote, "Since Jesus came to teach us how to love, when you give a gift to someone this Christmas tell them how much their friendship means to you. Attach a handwritten note expressing your love and affection, your gratitude and appreciation for the one receiving the gift. (Yes, you guys, too. Men have a harder time doing this, but when it's done, it can be powerful.) The note will outlast the gift. The point of all this is that Christmas at the dawn of a new millennium is a special time of grace and Jubilee. So how can you make this millennium Christmas a Christ-filled event?"[18]

His advice is derived from personal experience. He frequently sent a handwritten note expressing his gratitude for a gift and his appreciation of the giver. Sometimes he simply responded to behavior he had observed or been the object of. He wanted people to know he appreciated it. This private recognition from a man who seemed to have enough to do besides writing notes endeared him to so many people worldwide.

December 25, 1999, was the last Sunday in December 1999, in the decade, in the 20th century, and in the second millennium. Lewinski wrote, "People of faith rejoice in the 2000th anniversary of God becoming incarnate. Y2K entrepreneurs, champagne merchants, and apocalyptic prophets will make the new millennium what they will. But for people of hope, Christmas at the dawn of the new millennium means undying love and eternal hope. It is time for people of faith to rally around the cause of our joy. As we celebrate this last Christmas of the century, I pray that you and your families will take the time to conjure blessings and give thanks for the gift of God's presence in Jesus Christ. As we prepare to greet a new millennium, may we all experience a resurgence of faith, hope, and love and rediscover how close God is to us in Jesus."[19]

The project's pace was slowing. The parish had identified solutions to the uncertainty felt three years earlier. This resulted in less news to report, so they delayed the next edition of *The Bell* until December. The seventh issue summarized work completed so far. Because they had produced a Conceptual Design, the focus was now on the details. A floor plan showed the layout of the two primary facilities the nave spanned: the Sanctuary (church) and the Pastoral Center. Basic floor plans highlighted the features and benefits of each.

An emphasis continued on the fundraising activities and events celebrating the progress so far. They announced a "Gala 2000" for the coming March. They offered prizes such as a 1929 fully restored Ford Model A, $10,000 cash, a Bed and Breakfast getaway weekend, a golf package, and more. As for most parish functions, the prizes were all donations from parishioners or friends of the parish.

The content took a moment away from reporting to acknowledge a dynamic of change. "The biggest challenge that we have as individuals and as a parish is to avoid being overwhelmed by the scope of the project. The transition to a larger parish is naturally taxing. The new faces in church each week are wonderful to see and are a reminder that growth requires some adjustment."[20]

Lewinski's "Around the Table" column reported money-saving steps necessary to stay within the budget. He reminded everyone that fundraising was still a priority, even with nearly $5.6 million pledged (60% of the estimated cost for Phase I).

> We have made enormous progress with our planning for the future since we first began our planning in the summer of 1996. We are now at the threshold of an important milestone for St. Mary Parish as we prepare to break ground in approximately 4 to 5 months.
>
> The process of value engineering and cost-cutting has been very difficult. It has meant we have had to delete or alter parts of the plans in order to reduce costs. In making these cuts, we have considered several factors: the safety and durability of the materials used; retaining the integrity of architectural design; and selecting materials that will be "maintenance-friendly." We have also put aside some things that conceivably can be added later and taken care of to ensure the church is recognizable as sacred space rather than a large "meeting hall," etc.
>
> Some examples of cuts we have reluctantly made include moving the access from Fremont Center Road to Erhart Road; opting for plaster interior walls rather than brick; excluding a basement; forestalling the Bell tower; using carpet rather than tile in a large portion of the narthex; eliminating some landscaping; and abbreviating the parking lot and the plaza area outside the

church. Other changes will not be so noticeable but require serious study and research to get the most from the dollar.

Still, it is very important that we do not streamline our plans to the point where we have no room for items such as religious art and musical instruments that will enhance our worship.… Religious art is not decoration; it is an essential dimension of sacred space that lifts us beyond the mundane to higher realms.…

Despite concerns about cost-cutting and fundraising, I want to reassure you that what we are about to build will be very beautiful as well as very functional. This includes not only the worship space in which we will gather as community in celebration, but meeting and administration space to support our work as Church. We are blessed with a world-class architect whose keen eye and commitment to our goals will help us erect a worthy and sacred space we can be proud of. I am putting my heart and soul into this project to be sure we do our very best. I have no doubt that people will come from far and wide to see and admire our new St. Mary Church and Pastoral Center.

After the holidays, we will plan another Town Hall meeting so we can bring you up-to-date on the design and plans. In the meantime, thank you for your continued support and faithful stewardship.[21]

The cost-cutting was not over. It would eventually result in removing one of Lewinski's most treasured elements: the grand doors to the sacred space of the Sanctuary. They experienced disappointment with the Christmas collection as well. It was $10,000 under budget.

Provided the parish, nation, and world survived the swiftly approaching Y2K problem (AKA the year 2000 problem, Y2K scare, millennium bug, Y2K bug, Y2K glitch, Y2K error). At least one believer expressed their faith at New Year's with a yard sign reading, "HE is Y we have 2K."

---

[1] Sunday bulletin, June 13, 1999, pp. 3-4.

[2] "Nothing is impossible with God" (Luke 1:37, the story of the Annunciation for which the parish was named) was Lewinski's theme throughout the project. It is also engraved on his marker in the cemetery at St. Mary's (see end of 'Afterword').

[3] Comments about the image from the critics of the project was that it reminded them of a corn crib between two pig pens. These critics apparently didn't recognize the irony in their comment. The parish had asked the architect to retain the rural nature of the surrounding farming community.

[4] The architects designed the ductwork similar to what the parishioner described, but it is contained within the ceiling of the ambulatories. The only evidence it exists are the narrow horizontal vents feeding the body of the sanctuary. The design is as decorative as it is functional. The ducts are so well hidden that twenty years later Lohan couldn't recall the design, and asked where they were. — Personal conversation, July 18, 2018.

[5] *The Bell*, Vol. I, Issue 6, July, 1999, p. 1.

[6] Ibid., p. 7.

[7] Ibid., p. 3.

[8] Afterwards, Gensler observed that these mission opportunities broadened the teens' awareness of what it means to be poor, and how poor people are treated.

[9] Sunday bulletin, July 4, 1999, pp. 3-4. As he often did, Lewinski ended his comments with a call to action.

[10] Lewinski, however, knew what the skeptics would think so he noted that his absence from August 11 through September 11 was at the combined expense of the Archdiocese of Singapore, the Diocese of Johor Bahru, and his own personal savings.

[11] Sunday bulletin, August 29, 1999, p. 3.

[12] Sunday bulletin, September 19, 1999, p. 3.

[13] https://en.wikipedia.org/wiki/Joint_Declaration_on_the_Doctrine_of_Justification

[14] Sunday bulletin, October 31, 1999, p. 4.

[15] Sunday bulletin, November 7, 1999, p. 4.

[16] It is the author's understanding that this book is retained in the Parish Office.

[17] Sunday bulletin, November 28, 1999, p. 3.

[18] Sunday bulletin, December 19, 1999, p. 3.

[19] Sunday bulletin, December 26, 1999, p. 2.

[20] *The Bell*, Vol. I, Issue 7, December, 1999, p. 6. Tucked into the next page was a photo and brief description of the group meeting described in the chapters "The Temple" and "Silent Viewing" of this book.

[21] Ibid., p. 3.

WALKING A TIGHTROPE

Winter 2000

The Town Hall Lewinski had announced in his December column arrived on February 17, 2000 at 7:00 p.m. It was a week after potluck dinner and two days after Lewinski's fifty-fourth birthday. The Planning Commission once again met with curious parishioners in Diantha Hall. Representatives from Lohan Associates brought a larger 3-D model for the attendees to examine.

John Riggio began the meeting by welcoming everyone. Despite the weather, he assured them the gathering would adhere to the two-hour schedule. The presenters were also anxious to depart as soon as possible. Midwesterners were recently re-sensitized to coarse conditions during a historic winter storm. Chicago received two feet of snow between January 2nd and 4th. It was followed by record low temperatures (under 20 degrees Fahrenheit below zero). The National Weather Service identified the blizzard as the second worst to hit Chicago in the 20th century. So most attendees came wearing a heavy winter coat or parka. They filled the chairs, eager to learn more and get back home.

After they overcame some technical difficulties, Riggio began. "Tonight, we want to stimulate your thinking. Also, we want to help you understand what we have accomplished and where we're going with the campaign toward building the new St. Mary's." He then introduced Ken Behm. Because they'd already lost part of the scheduled two hours, Behm quickly explained who would be speaking.

Present were representatives from the architectural firm Lohan Associates; a woman from the Land Design Collaborative (landscaping); the CEO and representatives from the contracting firm Frederick Quinn Corporation; the Director of Music and Liturgy at St. Mary's; the parish Business Manager; and, of course, Fr. Lewinski. Riggio returned to the podium and asked attendees to withhold questions until the end of each presentation. He stated all presenters would remain afterward for questions and comments. He then introduced Lewinski, who came to the podium.

"Maybe we could stand for our prayer," he suggested with a smile. "Before we do that, I would like to thank you for coming out this evening.

It is an exciting time, a wonderful time. Hopefully, you will see how things are coming about. We are pleased with St. Mary's, the committees, and how our architect and contractor have worked together so well to meet our needs and concerns. We are really pleased. It is getting to where we are seeing some things physically happening on campus, and indeed, it is a very exciting moment in our history. I think what is most exciting about all of this is the design itself and the quality of work we will see. A truly fitting facility in praise of God and our service to this community."

Everyone stood. Lewinski began, "My Sisters and Brothers, the community of St. Mary has been entrusted with the mission of living the gospel. Working together, we help build the Kingdom of God on earth. Tonight we mark a new phase in that mission as we enter more deeply into the work of building a house for God and a house for God's people. Gathered here tonight for this Town Hall meeting, let us listen to the prayer from the Rite of Dedication for a church. As we continue to plan for the future, may this prayer constantly remain in our hearts and minds as a reminder of the work we are called to accomplish. Let us pray."

Lewinski recited the same prayer as eighteen months earlier when introducing Lohan Associates to parish representatives. It would be heard again during the dedication two years later. He concluded, "We ask this through Christ our Lord. Amen. May the peace of the Lord be with you always. Let us share a sign of Christ's peace." Attendees shook hands with their neighbors and extended a wish for peace.

Riggio returned to the podium long enough to introduce Al Novickas, the design architect from Lohan Associates. Novickas efficiently reviewed the current status, including progress, since a meeting in November. He expressed the continuing emphasis on adhering to the parish's values. "First, the spiritual quality of the design. Second, somehow relating to the farming heritage, which is what is unique about this parish."

He stated it had been determined "because we are the first development happening in this area, we would have to pay a very substantial cost to improve the roadway." This referenced the county's requirement that the parish pay for changes to nearby roadways. They estimated the cost at about half a million dollars. This equated to about 5% of the plan's budget, which did not include those costs. He pointed to a location on the narthex's south side, where they designated a plaza outside the entrance.

"We made another change that you requested," continued Novickas, "A much closer automobile drop-off at the plaza, the front entrance to the church." He explained the concept was to "keep certain components of what you see in a rural environment." He showed the structure now on an east-west axis. The narthex remained between the sanctuary to the west and the pastoral center to the east. Thus, people in the narthex could easily see the outside meditation garden through the northern glass walls.

He then pointed out a more significant change. "You may recall an earlier rendering we showed last time. We have made some changes. The primary change is to the structural support on the outside. It was wood, and there were some concerns about maintenance. So we opted to move the structure inside the building. That alters the appearance a little, but it keeps the building's central character."

He then addressed the concepts of the steeple above the altar, the wall and space for organ pipes behind the altar, and the Eucharistic Chapel behind both. "Behind the steeple is a large wooden wall that separates the Eucharistic Chapel from the altar. It also hides where the organ pipes are located. So it is an acoustically transparent wall. It has slats to allow the organ music to come out. But the organ pipes themselves will not be a prominent feature. It won't detract focus from the altar itself."

He continued his narrative using his own words, but Lewinski's influence was discernible. Lewinski was speaking to his parishioners through Novickas. Hearing Lewinski's message from someone else improved its chance of being accepted. "You can also see above the altar here the large sheltered roof that we had designed. It recalls the nave quality of traditional churches. It still accommodates the Vatican II idea of a church in the round, where people can gather around the altar on all three sides.

"The other feature is the access to the Eucharistic Chapel. It is visible directly to the right of the altar. Beyond that area will be a stained glass window. When you enter the church, you will see the altar, and you will also see the stained glass that identifies the access point for the Eucharistic Chapel; it will become very prominent." The word 'prominent,' of course, connected directly to comments about Canon Law during earlier meetings between the parish and Lohan's team.

Novickas described how the steeple would appear to penetrate the roof and direct light toward the altar directly below it. Lewinski favored this design concept. However, they later identified structural challenges that made actual penetration and channeling outside light impractical.

Novickas stated the sanctuary's ceiling "will be a light-colored wood to bring some warmth to the space. There is also a baptismal font," he said while pointing to it, "located directly at the sanctuary's entrance. It has a rectangular design which defines the use of that space."[1]

Novickas showed an artist's rendering of the building from a northwest perspective. "What you see at the front here is the Eucharistic Chapel. We will illuminate it from the inside. It will be a special feature visible as you drive by in the evening." This invoked the 'beacon in the night' metaphor Lewinski often used concerning evangelization.

Novickas next spoke about the Eucharistic Chapel. "The distinguishing feature is the vertical character; it is relatively narrow and higher, which gives it an exceptional, we would like to say 'sacred,' quality." He finished by commenting on the various facilities in the Pastoral center, such as a kitchen, hospitality suite, meeting rooms, and office spaces.

Next, Charles Metzler from Frederick Quinn introduced himself and spoke about his firm's background and how they manage projects. He briefly stated his firm's qualifications. This was their 12th year of working with the Archdiocese and their 32nd project. Cardinal Bernardin had written them a letter of recommendation. "One of the beautiful parts of bringing in a contractor like us as early as you have is that we can work together. We can work with the architect, Father, the parish building committee, and with the alternate contractors to figure out what is the best for you for your dollars."

He was reassuring an audience undertaking the most expensive project in the parish's history. "We probably have talked to seventy-five alternates already to get to where we are now. There's still a long way to go."

He projected pictures of several buildings they had completed or were working on. A wide array of styles and materials were shown.

Next, he identified their approach to a project. Expense management was, of course, one of those items. "We will take the drawings completed so far and work on those with Lohan Associates and estimators in our office through value engineering. What does that mean? You are walking a tightrope between pleasing everybody, doing it at the right price, and still not sacrificing the building's quality.

"Working as a team, we can define everything we need to construct a building exactly the way you want. Of course, if you want to add 30,000 square feet, that would be a change order for us." The laughter from his listeners showed their acceptance. They didn't expect to make that kind of request, and they understood the impact if they did.

He stated there had already been several meetings, and once construction starts, there will be weekly status meetings. They needed several permits from various agencies before construction. He added, "We also like to pre-qualify the subcontractors. We want to ensure that the people working on the project are the people we want—and you want— that will deliver a good and safe job. When the invitations go to bid, we try to get three to five sub-bids from every trade. You might have someone in the parish, for example, in the excavation business, that you would want on the project. It is your decision, once you know what the numbers are, whether you want to select that alternative." Parishioner firms eventually did subcontract work on the project in different trades.

He showed an example of a field report: "Everything in the field is written up as a progress report that is reviewed during a subcontractor meeting. We hold an owner's meeting every week. The purpose is to communicate. There is nothing more important. We want everyone to know what is going on and have a record from day one to the end of everything that has happened on the project."

He had spoken about cost and time. Next came the third leg of the project management stool, quality. "Along with our own safety program, we use an independent firm that does frequent safety inspections. They come unannounced, so the project manager doesn't know when they are coming, which helps immensely with the insurance. The rating for our firm, based on about a $120 million work program, is '.81'—less than one percent—which is excellent for a contractor."

During his agenda portion, Metzler covered his major talking points. By sharing detailed information, he built the audience's confidence in his firm's abilities. When he asked for questions, there was only one. A parishioner expressed concern about the impact of dust (during the summer) and noise on parish events. The parishioner's daughter would be having a wedding. Metzler assured him it wouldn't be a problem.

Riggio returned to the podium and stated Lewinski would next discuss the rectory. Riggio jokingly assured the audience the team had eliminated the hot tub, sauna, and lap pool to save money.

Lewinski approached the podium during the laughter. He couldn't resist adding, "I'm glad they kept the indoor plumbing." Parishioners whose heritage was farming easily recognized this reference. Some could recall outhouses among family or friends as recently as the 1950s.

Lewinski was happy to report the team found a cost-effective solution. A local builder of residential developments would customize a floor plan suitable for a rectory. Lewinski explained what that meant, noting with his typical dry humor no one else there had probably ever lived in a rectory. They were planning two second-floor suites for the resident priests—one being himself. There would be a suite on the ground floor for occasional visiting clergy. He shared the Archdiocese had already signed the contract. After four years of commuting, Lewinski was looking forward to a residence on campus. He quipped, "As soon as tonight's snowfall melts, they will probably start construction."

Riggio gave a weather update by stating no snow had arrived yet. He then introduced Jim Schubert from Lohan Associates. As the Project Manager, Schubert would schedule and track the project's progress. He explained that the team had met county officials in July and August of the previous year. He claimed the offices in Waukegan "have been so cooperative and very professional. The staff up there is very talented. They've done a lot of work and cooperated with us in meeting with us so often. They have been holding our hands to be sure that when we submit for a permit, it will be rubber-stamped."

He then spoke about a somewhat thorny topic: the steeple's height. "The county has implied that we have one variance—a steeple higher than they allow under their current zoning ordinances. So we will submit, within the next week, a variance for the steeple. The county has been spending time with us on that as well. They gave us no reason to believe they would reject the steeple, so we're glad about that. We think the steeple will be a very important icon—a signal that this is, in fact, a church. If the steeple becomes a variance, that will not hold up the beginning of our site work. We plan to start on May 1st.

"We are scheduling all this," he continued, "working with Frederick Quinn to get the building enclosed before winter sets in. That's why we are pressing ahead with the schedule—July 14th is very critical for us. We don't see any problem in being able to meet that schedule. As I say, we will issue the first major package in two weeks. When that is all said and done, it will be November 17th of 2001, when you dedicate your new church.

"We're all very excited about that, and we're on schedule right now." This was the first time parishioners had heard a date for completion. They applauded in appreciation. Schubert and the other speakers had provided welcome information and specifics about what to expect.

When he asked for questions, Schubert received the inevitable one about whether there will be water and sewer service. "No, not at this point. I'm not sure if a developer has any plan to bring in services, particularly sanitary. I think that is coming from the north. But it is so far north that it would be cost-prohibitive for you to pay for it."

The next question was whether there would be a basement. Schubert's practical and concise response was, "There is no basement planned, no."

Returning to the subject of a steeple variance, a man asked, "I'm curious about possible objections to the height of the spire. How could it negatively influence anything, even air traffic? What reason do they give for controlling the height?"

Schubert explained. "First, in answer to your first question, it won't affect anything negatively. It won't cast any negative shadows. The actual height as we designed it is only about ten feet in relative height above the existing spire of your old church. That's because your existing church is on a higher elevation. So we don't think that it is going to be a detriment. The only reason they would reject it is because the current zoning ordinance limits the height of buildings."

Here, Novickas stepped forward to provide more insight. "They must draw a line somewhere, and in this case, the existing zoning ordinance allows you to construct a building sixty feet high. Ours is 110 feet, so we violate the limit. They write the building ordinances to limit the damage to an adjacent property because of shadows or looming presence. So they want to govern that. The zoning ordinance is primarily written for light and air quality reasons."

During a subsequent meeting between the team and county officials, they determined a variance wasn't required after all. It turned out the County had no specifications for steeples.[2]

Riggio next invited Jim Scavone, Director of Music and Liturgy, to provide an update about religious art and devotional spaces.

"One thing," began Scavone, "that you probably noticed as we were going through all the models and pictures is that there is no artwork in any of the images. The reason is that we are not yet at a point where any artwork has been designed. So we are not even in contact with artists. We are in the very early stages. One thing to keep in mind is that the building's design allows for adding more artwork that will be located throughout the campus. One of our values early on was that the artwork did not look like an add-on at some point. We want to provide architectural structures that make the artwork part of the building.

"This speaks to us about the importance of the artwork that we will use. There are a couple of things that we've committed to already in terms of what will be there. We just don't know what they will look like or who will do them. Obviously, a shrine to the Blessed Mother will be in the church space. And we are also committed to some representation of the Annunciation. We plan to do that as well. Also, a Holy Family shrine will probably be located in the meditation garden. Other than that, we've not committed to other shrines or artwork."

Next, he asked helpers to distribute prepared forms to the attendees. "Fill out the form," he instructed, "and leave it behind tonight. On the form are many possibilities for shrines throughout the building. We need to narrow down that selection. There is also space on the back for you to list any saints or other images that we have not included. We ask that if you list a particular saint, then tell us why it would be important they be represented in our community. We will then continue our search and determine what will be in our building.

"I would just like to speak briefly," he continued, "about some criteria we use to select artwork. We must remember that sacred art's purpose is not mere decoration. It should inspire us, lead us in prayer, and direct our thoughts to God. One criteria we will use is openness to various styles of art. We don't want to limit the art to one particular style." This was partly the influence of Lewinski. His vision of the art and design at St. Mary's went beyond the parish's, and even nation's, boundaries. His appreciation for art was influenced by Vatican II, personal travels, and knowing the Church was once the world's most important art patron.[3]

"One thing we try to keep in mind is timelessness: something that 100 years from now will still stand as a beautiful and inspiring depiction. We are open to different mediums: sculpture, painting, tapestry, reliefs, whatever. One thing that will probably be quite apparent when we open the church is that we will not yet have all the artwork we desire. Provided we allow for the space, it will show that the artwork was important enough to be planned for in advance."

Lewinski interjected a request that people prioritize their preferences and identify up to four selections.

"After the Marian shrine, we need to prioritize pieces essential to celebrating the liturgy—crucifix, liturgical appointments, that kind of thing. I would also like to talk real quickly about the commissioning process. We have just begun preparing letters. We will send them to artists and ask for their portfolios to narrow down that selection. Then the artist usually works with the community to develop the final product that we feel will represent our community well.

"The last thing is to talk real briefly about the organ. Al mentioned that during his presentation. As of now, all we have done is contract with an organ builder to work with Lohan to ensure we have adequate space for the organ. As we have learned, it is a lot trickier and has many more details than one would think. We are working with the organ builder to determine the design and cost before proceeding. We want to be sure that they provide the space so that when the time comes, there is no problem installing an organ system."

"How will the art and the organ be funded," asked a parishioner, knowing there could be some significant cost involved and wanting to avoid having that cost become part of future mortgage payments.

"We will fund the art that is a priority within the project cost," responded Scavone. "We will also have to look at our options for funding the organ and any additional artwork. I don't know if we have yet come up with any options."

Riggio returned as master of ceremonies and proposed everyone take a one-minute break, after which he invited the parish business manager, Mary Hall, to comment. So far, each speaker had delivered good news about the project's progress and prospects. "Good evening. I had to chuckle as I came up because someone said to me, 'The pressure is on.' There's no pressure. We are going to build a church, we will grow into it, and we will pay for it. We will build the best parish in Lake County." They responded with approving applause.

"I just want to let you know where we are today," she continued. "Five hundred and thirteen parishioner family units have pledged to the capital campaign. We currently have $3,675,000 on deposit for the building project. Budgets and other gifts total $5,743,000." Hall continued to comment on options for pledging and making payments. She reminded them the parish started accepting credit cards the previous September.

She welcomed anyone to contact her in the office if needed. She expressed her thanks "for allowing me to be part of your family."

Hall observed the historical importance of the upcoming groundbreaking ceremony and construction. "It is a memorable time in this day and age. Many of us don't have a chance even to see one church built. I have been through a couple of them. Some of you longtime parishioners have seen your parish grow and now will have a brand new church building to worship in. So please think about the privilege in that."

Riggio returned to the podium and brought some good news with his closing comments. "It is *still* not snowing. I want to thank each of you for taking the time tonight to come and join us. I want to thank the committees and subcommittees for making this happen and, more importantly, all our subject matter experts here tonight. You can have further conversations with each of them. Thank you."

Last, Lewinski expressed his thanks. He reminded parishioners to come forward to look at the updated model on display. He explained with a hint of childlike wonder, "It opens up like a doll house, and the roof comes off. You can see the pews and the people inside."

Many people were donning coats, eager to get home before whatever bad weather was coming. Several others remained to examine this larger model. They could imagine themselves in the building, and the sense of space it would embody.

People left encouraged by what they'd heard, especially the fundraising and this new model. The level of anticipation was increasing. It would be elevated still further during the upcoming groundbreaking ceremony. Then a foot would be put to the shovel, and the reality would strike home.

They were really going to build a church.

---

[1] The design characteristic Novickas was referring to was a rectangular shape of a tomb. Vatican II encouraged more thought be given to baptism and its significance. Being an expert on the Rite of Christian Initiation of Adults (RCIA), Lewinski would have been keenly aware of the opportunity to include an appropriate baptismal font in the new church. The chosen design had water flowing from a higher point into a larger rectangular pool. The higher portion would accommodate infant baptisms (and also served as the sole source of holy water upon entering the sanctuary). The lower pool, with about 18" of water in a rectangle measuring 8' long by 5' wide, would be used for all other baptisms. The tomb-shaped font signifies triumph over death. Especially for adult baptisms, the practice identifies the tomb with being joint heirs with Christ in his dying and rising (Romans 8:14-17, Romans 6:4-5, Ephesians 2:5-6).

[2] *We thought we had to get a special variance for the steeple. So we had a hearing at Fremont Township offices. We met there and brought the meeting to order. There were five county board members and there was one lady board member who was the chairperson. She said to the recording secretary, an elderly man, "Would you read the ordinance on church steeples." He sat there and didn't say a word. She repeated. "Would you read the ordinance on church steeples." She said it a third time. His face was getting red, and he said "Madam chairman, there is no ordinance on church steeples."* —Ken Behm, Aug. 13, 2018.

[3] Nadeau, *"The Vatican and Modern Art"*

GROUNDBREAKING

2000

The upcoming Lenten season offered more opportunities for parishioner education and participation. Father Robert Barron from Mundelein Seminary spoke at the Masses on March 11th and 12th about a three-day opportunity for parishioners to engage in a Lenten Mission beginning March 13th.[1]

The parish had the advantage of being only a few miles from Mundelein Seminary. They often hosted guest homilists. One of them, Fr. Pat O'Malley, became a favorite. He was a down-to-earth Irishman. He regaled events from childhood, hikes in the Colorado mountains, or whatever was happening with the major sports teams. He interwove scripture with real life in practical, entertaining, and educational ways.

The parish benefited from Lewinski's connection to the seminary, which gave him insights about the seminarians and newly ordained priests. Whenever the time came to find another assistant pastor, St. Mary's was the fortunate recipient of someone especially gifted.[2]

It was a sunny day when they gathered for the groundbreaking ceremony. But the westerly wind gusting at 30 mph across the farm fields swept away the warmth along with anything loose on the ground. The event had early press coverage with an article in the Daily Herald. It occurred two years after Cardinal George had visited the parish to bless the construction site.[3]

The ceremony began on March 25th at 4 p.m. in Diantha Hall. Bishop Kicanas presided at the well-attended Mass. Afterward, the assembly exited the temporary worship space and processed down the sidewalk past the cemetery and casually observant cows. They followed the gravel road leading south and then turned westward to enter the field.

Parishioners Tim and Mariann Mayer led the procession. They carried an 8' high wooden cross that Tim—a woodworker—had constructed. Besides bearing its weight, the couple needed to brace against the opposing wind. Workers had cleared a path into the field but it was still uneven ground. Behind them followed altar servers, deacons, priests Lewinski had invited, and whatever determined parishioners had decided to witness this historic event. They gathered around where the new altar would be situated. A choir member had brought a battery-operated megaphone. Otherwise, only people standing downwind could have heard what was being said. Lewinski and Kicanas had donned hardhats.

IMAGE #12

GROUNDBREAKING

THE PROCESSION WENT FROM DIANTHA HALL, PAST THE OLD
CHURCH, TO THE LOCATION WHERE THE NEW CHURCH'S ALTAR
WOULD BE POSITIONED (MARKED BY THE CROSS).

After everyone assembled, Lewinski welcomed the group. "We give thanks to God for the founders and benefactors who have come before us. As a sign of our gratitude, we are asking Fr. Franz-Peter Tebartz-van Elst from Muenster to offer a prayer of thanksgiving in German, the original language of this parish community."

When Fr. Franz-Peter finished, Bishop Kicanas remarked, "Father Franz speaks German quite well, doesn't he?" After the laughter subsided, a lector read from Ephesians (2:19). Kicanas continued by offering prayers of the faithful. "Let us pray. God of love, we praise your holy name. For you have made us your temple by baptism and inspired us to build on earth churches dedicated to your worship.

"Your house is a house of prayer. Your presence makes it a place of blessings. You give us grace upon grace to build the temple of your spirit, creating its beauty from the holiness of our lives.

"Your house of prayer is the promise of the Church in heaven. In your house, your love is always at work preparing the Church on earth for its heavenly glory as the sinless bride of Christ.

"Lord, bless the community of St. Mary's as we break ground for a new house of worship. Inspire us to become living stones, built as an edifice of spirit into a holy and royal priesthood. Bless all those, past and present, who, in the spirit of sacrifice, have worked and prayed and contributed to making this groundbreaking possible. From the generous gifts of this community and with the help of your Holy Spirit, may we build a noble and worthy temple to your glory. Bring to completion the good work you have begun in us as we look forward with joy to the day when we will celebrate your holy mysteries in a new church dedicated to your glory in honor of St. Mary of the Annunciation. We ask this through Christ Jesus, our Lord. Amen."

Lewinski turned toward the bishop. Both their robes were flailing in the wind. "Bishop Kicanas, as the representative of the Church and Lake County, I invite you now on behalf of our entire parish community to join us as we take that first dig for our new church."

Kicanas and Lewinski gripped the handles of gleaming chrome spades. With a firm shove, they pierced the surface of what for centuries had been farmland. Representatives of some founding families were next. Then some newer parishioners. Lastly, John Riggio (chair, Planning Commission), Al Novickas (Lohan Associates), and Charles Metzler (Frederick Quinn Corporation) turned over the soil.

It was reminiscent of when their founders built a church in 1889. In those times, President Cleveland signed a bill to admit the Dakotas, Montana, and Washington (42nd state) to the union; the Eiffel Tower opened at the World's Fair for 32 million visitors; George Eastman began selling film in rolls; the cross-continent Canadian Pacific Railway was completed; the Wall Street Journal started publication; Nintendo was founded; and Edison showed his first motion picture.

Now, one hundred and eleven years later, the parish broke ground for its newest church.

As the ceremony ended, parishioner and lector Jon Matousek invited everyone to put a spade to the ground. Several youngsters eagerly grabbed a shovel, while others needed coaxing from the elders. Parents proudly took pictures. It was their last gathering in a field soon to be transformed into new worship space. Despite a brisk and windy day, they felt a connection to the past. The pioneers' spirits seemed to be present, offering their prayers and support.

Photos of the event made the front page of Mundelein News on March 31st. One featured parishioners Tim and Mariann Mayer carrying the cross he'd handmade. Another showed Lewinski wearing a white helmet and preparing to plunge a shovel into the ground.

The following month, *The Bell* newsletter published a reflective article written by Fr. Franz-Peter:

The groundbreaking celebration for St. Mary Fremont Center was the first time in my life that I had the honor of being part of a groundbreaking celebration for a new church, and it probably will be the only time in my life that I will be involved in such a moving and touching event. Right now, we in Germany struggle much more with closing or clustering parishes than with the challenges of the increasing number of parishioners. So, Father Ron Lewinski's invitation to say a prayer in the German language for which we remember the fathers and mothers in faith who founded your parish in the nineteenth century was a great gift and an honor.

As Bishop Kicanas delivered his sermon, I became aware of the importance of having something to show what our Christian faith is about. This became obvious when the whole assembly was invited to join the procession to the chosen place for the groundbreaking. Passing the old church and the cemetery created many memories concerning those who once left their homes in Germany, ready to start a new life. At once, their energy and their lives became a very strong witness to me. Even the strong head-wind we had to struggle with while passing the field became a very powerful symbol on this very evening. When shaping our lives, our church, and our parish, we are bound to deal with rejection, questioning from others and from ourselves. But these definitely are the experiences which strengthen and make us faithful and confident in expecting a good future.

As I took part in this celebration, it was very moving to watch the procession coming down the cemetery hill. What I saw reminded me of the image of the Second Vatican Council's image proposed by the Church "being God's people on the way." Later, when old and young gathered around the cross and they said the prayers, a deeper meaning to what was happening emerged. Watching all ministries and generations of the Church involved in digging and shoveling spades of soil at his very place where soon the altar as the real center of this parish will rise, I was thinking and praying:

It is God who gives us (1) the energy for shaping our faith according to his mind for this new millennium; (2) the patience for waiting and expecting that new experiences will grow by His time; (3) the hope, to continue and fulfill what our mothers and fathers have already invested in this place throughout the past century and to take over their heritage to this and the next generations.

Therefore it was such a grateful moment to watch the kids among us being encouraged by their parents and grandparents to participate. For me, it was a real Emmaus experience seeing God's people on the way and personally having been invited to be part of it with them. Thank you to you all for this encouraging witness of your faith and energy. Be assured, I will tell the story plenty of times when I am back home in Germany. What I have to tell is more than an event. It is a real image of faith and Church![4]

In his Sunday bulletin column on March 26, Lewinski declared:

This is a great day for St. Mary - Fremont Center! After more than three years of planning and with a rich and faith-filled history behind us, we will break ground for the future. As Bishop Kicanas, who represents our link to the Archdiocese and the universal Church, and parish representatives with a shovel in hand dig into the earth, St. Mary Parish will begin a new chapter in its history. What we do in the field today is truly an act of faith. Our commitment to build a new church and the personal sacrifices that support this building are a sign of our belief that our Catholic faith is something we value very highly. We break ground today not only for ourselves but for generations to come. It's as if we stood on the rooftops and proclaimed to all the world: "We believe God has called us to carry on the mission of Jesus. We are grateful for all that the Church has been for us in our lives. Today we want to ensure that there will be a church that will welcome future generations.

A new parishioner told me the other day that he and his family chose to belong to St. Mary Parish because it was unfinished. I asked him what he meant by that. He said, "The parish is obviously still growing in the awareness of its mission and the development of its leadership. So we feel it's a good time to jump in. We don't have to feel like everything is so perfectly structured and in place that there isn't room for us to make our contribution. We want to grow with the parish." I thought to myself, I hope we can always say that St. Mary is unfinished. Because the mission of Jesus continues to move us in new directions, calling us to respond to new needs, to constantly develop our leadership, to deepen our prayer, our understanding, our spirituality. There should never come a time when we feel we are finished, for it would probably be the death of us.

As a parish grows, its spirit changes. It is inevitable. We cannot be afraid of that change. We can get nostalgic about the "good ol' days." We can wish that things were as simple as they were in years past. Those are honest emotions. Sometimes changes in parish life leave some people feeling left out because new faces have assumed leadership, accepted responsibility, contributed new ideas. Some may even feel some resentment as they remember a time when they were more active. New souls bring new spirit. We believe that the Church of God is what ultimately really matters, and not my personal attachment, for God shapes his Church as he wills.

As we begin building a new church, it is a moment of grace for us and an opportunity to renew our commitment to the ever-changing, ever-growing Church of Jesus Christ. May our doors never be closed to those who seek Christ. May we never think that we have finished our work. May this groundbreaking be our solemn act of trust in the Lord who calls us to build his Church out of living stones—our lives.

As we mark this historic turning point, let me express my gratitude to all who have given so much of themselves to the parish. It is a privilege to be your pastor. The challenges before us are immense, but they are also exciting. Even in the most frustrating moments of this building process, I truly believe that the Lord will enable us to accomplish what we need to do. That's why we can say that He is the cornerstone of His Church. Thank you for your enthusiasm, sacrifices and helping hands.[5]

Lewinski was continuing to unite and build community both locally and globally. He respected the heritage of the people he was shepherding while reminding them their mission included people and places beyond their small community. He invited a delegation of bishops from Germany to visit from April 7-9. Pastoral Council President Terri Kennedy, and her husband Vince, hosted an evening at their house so Council members could meet the bishops and have a brief cultural exchange.

In April, the eighth edition of *The Bell* displayed a front-page photo showing the crowd surrounding the wooden cross during March's ceremony.[6] The issue discussed the pending construction of the new rectory. It featured a guest essay by Deacon James Johnson Jr. Another article focused on honoring the parish's past and the Ceremonial Groundbreaking in words and pictures. Lastly, it described the successful black tie "Gala 2000" held on March 4th that netted $30,000.

A "Views from the Pews" recalled a parent's experience. "As I stood there watching the children wandering the field, I thought how impressive it was that the past generations farmed this land and built our current church here not only for themselves but for the little ones that today are my age, with little ones of their own. Someday these little ones will stand here with their little ones to worship the Lord and do His works."[7]

Regarding work, Lewinski reminded the Pastoral Council once again of the need to engage parishioners rather than having an "I'll get it done myself" attitude. He also identified a more serious issue of declining parishioner assistance resulting from receiving a "we don't need your help" response. That sentiment lingered from previous years and was even more unacceptable behavior in present circumstances.

During the same Council meeting, they decided to revisit past discussion topics prior to the upcoming formation meetings. The subjects included spirituality, stewardship, sense of mission, purpose beyond parish borders, and adjusting to life amidst the change occurring.

St. Mary's had been hosting "Hospitality Sunday" once a month after regular weekend services. It was another socializing event, using a refreshment and donuts as an attraction. Sr. Gensler noted that a "hospitality mentality" should not be limited to a weekend but cultivated among the entire parish. Furthermore, each event could be supplemented with an exhibit, demonstration, or some way of informing people about the parish's life. This aligned with Lewinski's ever-present awareness of the need to educate people regardless of the topic's perceived importance.

Late in April, the Mundelein Review's front page featured a photo of—what else—a cow with the old church in the distance. The article stated 500 people attended the Groundbreaking.

> "The parish has grown dramatically in the last four years," said Mary Hall, business manager for St. Mary parish. "The current pastor, Father Ron Lewinski, came here about four years ago. When he arrived, we had almost 600 families in the parish. We now have 1250." Linda Zucco moved to unincorporated Mundelein with her husband Jack and children four years ago and joined St. Mary Parish. Zucco said she is very excited by the growth of the parish and the new church. "We're building a house for God.".... Hall said the old church is an important part of the heritage of St. Mary's parish and will

continue to remain so long after the new church is built. "It is the fiber of this parish," she said. "It will always be here. It's a landmark."[8]

In June, Lewinski renewed the neighborhood pastoral visits he had conducted during his first summers at St. Mary's. He offered a dozen dates during the Summer for parishioners to host gatherings of eight to sixteen people. Many families had joined the parish since his earlier visits. They brought with them recent experiences from elsewhere. He believed those could benefit St. Mary's when discovered and shared.

The parish planned another pilgrimage, this time to the Holy Land. They held a meeting on June 22nd as part of the preparation. The trip was scheduled for September.

With the flurry of project planning receding, Lewinski provided an update.

> Many have been asking when we can expect to see some of the work begin on our new church. We are still completing the requirements for all the permits. It is a long and complicated process and involves several governmental agencies such as the Health Department, Zoning Office, and the Lake County Department of Transportation. We expect to receive the necessary permits very soon and then we will begin the work immediately. In the meantime, we have been busy getting estimates for various parts of the project and making budget cuts wherever we can to stay within the total budget approved by the Archdiocese. While it has been a painful process to eliminate some features that we won't be able to afford, we are doing our best to create a church that is well-designed and beautiful to behold. One of the things we are doing right now is researching the possibilities for religious artwork. The art pieces in a church are often the very thing that distinguishes a church from any other building and give it its distinctive character. We may not be able to do all we would like immediately, but we will plan for some pieces now and leave room for additions as funds become available. Before too long, we will be able to publish a list of some of the things that parishioners may consider donating.[9]

On July 9th, Lewinski's column announced Fr. Ken Kiepura's assignment as associate pastor. Ordained in 1969, he was an experienced priest. Most recently, he had been pastor of St. Mary Parish in Buffalo Grove—another parish related to the history of St. Mary at Fremont Center. Lewinski noted some discouraging statistics about the state of Catholic parishes and their staff ratio to parishioners. He emphasized how fortunate they were to welcome Kiepura.[10]

In his introductory note, Kiepura wrote, "I enjoy working with people and ministering to them. That for me, is the real joy of being a priest.... As you may know, priests have a voice in determining the parish to which they are assigned. The Archdiocese and Priests Personnel Board gave me a list of about 15 parishes that were looking for an associate pastor.

"I talked to several pastors, including Father Ron, about their parishes and what they were all about. I was drawn to St. Mary's by the life, faith, and vitality that seems to characterize your parish family. As I understand the parish, it is in the growth pattern not just in size and numbers but, more importantly, in faith and life. Being part of such a parish family is energizing and life-giving to me.

"I consider it a privilege to be with Father Ron, the staff and all of you. May God bless our time together with many good gifts."

Like Scavone, Matousek, Gensler, and Hall before him, Fr. Ken was promptly welcomed and appreciated. The parish was blessed to have gained such skilled leadership. It was a radical difference from when Lewinski had first arrived.

In July, the Pastoral Council confirmed the five topics to be included in the formation meeting with the School Board in October. They were spirituality, stewardship, adjusting our lives in light of the building project, a sense of mission, and support for marriage and family life.

The stained glass windows in the old church were finally getting cleaned and repaired. "Did you know," asked Lewinski in his column, "that the center section of the window above the altar should open? When the window has been cleaned and repaired, it will allow gentle breezes to flow through the church. Finally, within the next two weeks, the two transom windows in the choir loft should be reinstalled."

August was once again Pork and Corn Roast season. In his column on the weekend following the Roast, Lewinski wrote, "... it looks like this year's Pork and Corn Roast will beat all previous years' income. ... We have also received the good news that within a few days, we can begin excavation for the rectory and the church."

Lewinski shared his joy over the latest milestones at month's end.

> Very early last Monday morning, as the sun was enveloping the landscape, the heavy-duty construction equipment that dotted the hillside over the weekend fired up their engines and dug into the earth. The building of St. Mary's new church had begun. After more than four years of planning, the roar of the graders and massive tractors was like music to my ears. It's been a long and painstaking ordeal applying and waiting for permits. It's taken many hours of meetings with parishioner-based committees, architects and contractors, civil engineers, zoning boards, etc., to get to this point. But, at last, we've reached the stage where we can begin to see things taking shape on the

land. Thanks be to God. And thanks to all of you who, through your prayers, enthusiasm, support, and good stewardship, have brought us to this milestone.
...

Our REP program has grown tremendously over the last two years, with nearly 400 children in our School of Religious Education. St. Mary is grateful to our volunteer catechists and Sue Matousek, Director of Religious Education, for the dedicated and enthusiastic ministry they offer our children.[11]

A new school year began in September. The bulletin's "Welcome" column identified forty individuals/families new to the parish. Space for parish activities continued to be a challenge. They were grateful to see the land being prepared for new facilities.

"Sometimes," wrote Lewinski, "it feels like I'm juggling a number of balls at once, but frankly, I find that exciting. There's never a dull moment. The catch is trying to find enough private space to rest, pray and think so that there's enough energy to do all the above." This wasn't the only time Lewinski expressed such feelings. It was one reason he put so much importance on time for a spiritual retreat. He almost always visited Thomas Merton's former habitat, the Abbey at Gethsemani, for a retreat.

A week later, the bulletin reported the net profit from the Pork and Corn Roast was an astounding $82,000—three times more than normal. "Our thanks to Jim Anewalt, chair, and Ryan Hand, cochair, and all the committee people they coordinated to make the 26th annual Pork and Corn Roast a wonderful and memorable experience."

Meanwhile, Lewinski and others continued to promote the Capital Campaign. They said the intent of "the Capital Campaign is to anticipate the next three to five years and to figure out a personal plan of contributing on a regular basis. The expectation is not to ask parishioners for one large gift all at once. Budgeting a regular contribution into your finances over a longer period makes it a sizable gift that is more manageable. What can you put aside each week or each month?"

Lewinski and Gensler also kept nudging the Parish Council and its commissions along an established path of discussion. The topics were spirituality, stewardship, mission, adjusting for change, and family life. During October's meeting, the Council appointed chairs for each. Lewinski urged them to "keep the fires burning" by asking, "Does this still have value?", "Why, specifically?", "How do we define success?" and "How do we expand the conversation?" He recommended each chairperson invite two parishioners to the next Council meeting for further discussion. They also discussed some more enticing matters like the upcoming pancake breakfast and Oktoberfest.

In early November, Lewinski reported, "I'm so proud of our wonderful Capital Campaign volunteers. They have been making the rounds and meeting with parishioners to share information about St. Mary's future and to seek out new pledges. I'm happy to hear how more of the St. Mary family is getting into the spirit of what Christian stewardship is all about. Our colorful new Capital Campaign brochure is a knockout! We have parishioner Mark Styczen, a professional graphic artist, to thank for sharing his gift in designing the brochure."

Before Thanksgiving, Lewinski expressed excitement about "the construction progress on our new church, pastoral offices and rectory. We've been planning for years now, so the sight of roads being cut and walls going up boosts our enthusiasm. The rectory is most clearly visible now that the roof is in place, ready to be shingled. We anticipate occupancy for the rectory in February 2001."

Early in December, Lewinski announced Jim Scavone, Director of Music and Liturgy since 1996, would be departing to work on the east coast. Lewinski stated Scavone was the parish's first full-time Director of Music and Liturgy. "Not only did he get us singing, build up our wonderful adult and children's choirs, train cantors, establish a bell choir, and plan countless numbers of liturgies, he also taught us to love the liturgy and encouraged us to make the Church's Prayer our own." Lewinski promised to engage a committee of parishioners to conduct a national search for their next Director.

Two weeks before Christmas, Lewinski was pleased to announce a visit by a bishop from the Archdiocese. Lewinski observed the timing of the Holy Days was unusual. "This year's celebration of Christmas will come quickly after the Fourth Sunday of Advent. In fact, we will no sooner finish the Advent Sunday Mass on December 24th when a few hours later we will be celebrating Christmas Eve. We are very happy to announce that Bishop Raymond Goedert will be celebrating the 6:00 p.m. Mass in Diantha Hall on Christmas Eve. Bishop Goedert is the Vicar General of the Archdiocese and the former Vicar for our Vicariate. We welcome him to St. Mary's. His presence will give an added tone of festivity to our celebration of the Christmas Mystery." Goedert had, of course, been involved with the parish's expansion from the beginning. Now he would see the vision manifesting on the snow-covered campus.

On the threshold of Christmas, Lewinski wrote, "… this year's Advent has taught me humility, a poverty of spirit, a sense of incompleteness. I've come to think of it as God's reminder to me that no matter how much time or energy or planning I could muster up, I will always be incomplete. The good news is that the Lord is ready to fill our incompleteness with his loving presence. I may not feel prepared for Christmas, but the Lord is ready for me."

---

[1] Robert Barron, later Bishop, is the founder of the Catholic ministerial organization, *Word on Fire*, and was the host of a PBS documentary TV series called *Catholicism*. He served as rector at Mundelein Seminary from 2012-2015. He is informally called the "bishop of social media", with 3 million followers on Facebook and over 116 million views of his YouTube videos. *(Wikipedia, Nov. 2022.)*

[2] Lewinski in fact mentored several seminarians who excelled in their priestly work during subsequent years.

[3] Daily Herald, March 16, 2000, p. 1.

[4] *The Bell*, Vol. I, Issue 8, April 2000, p. 8.

[5] Sunday bulletin, March 26, 2000, pp. 3-4.

[6] *The Bell*, Vol. I, Issue 8, April, 2000, p. 1.

[7] Ibid., p. 10.

[8] Mundelein Review, April 27, 2000, pp. 1, 7, 16, and 17.

[9] Sunday bulletin, June 18, 2000, p. 3.

[10] "We should feel very blessed to receive another priest on staff. It's no surprise any longer that the number of priests we are ordaining these days is not keeping up with the increasing population and the death and retirement of priests. There are 19,000 parishes in the United States. The number of parishes without a resident pastor has risen to 2,334 nationwide. The current ratio of priests to Catholics is 1 to 1,257. Even with Fr. Ken the ratio at St. Mary will be about 1 to 2000 parishioners. The average number of Catholics per parish is approximately 3,100. We are above that average too." —Sunday bulletin, July 9, 2000, p. 3.

[11] Sunday bulletin, August 27, 2000, p. 3.

AN EXPLANATORY EXPLORATORY

2001

The Feast of the Epiphany in 2001 marked an important anniversary in both Lewinski's and the parish's lives. Construction would continue for another year, but monumental changes were becoming visible. The foundation of the new structure was in place, and the steel skeleton of the building would soon begin rising. Anyone who predicted this just five years earlier would have been considered not prophetic but psychologically "affected." Lewinski wrote:

> This week marks my fifth anniversary as pastor of St. Mary - Fremont Center. How quickly the time has passed. Looking back over the past five years, I'm amazed how much the parish has grown. Five years ago the Sunday bulletin contained 3 short pages of information, there were 4 people on staff, and the average Sunday collection was $5,900. There were 650 households in the parish and relatively few active lay ministries. Five years later we have over 1300 registered households, 7 pages of bulletin information, 7 people on pastoral staff, and an average weekly collection of approximately $11,000. The number of lay ministries and actively participating members has expanded greatly. The greatest sign of our growth is the building project now in progress that will give us a new house of worship and a welcome place for meetings and parish business.
>
> All of these signs of growth over the past five years do not tell the whole story. What I value the most are the number of relationships that have developed within the community. Parishioners continue to connect with one another at key moments in their lives, such as sickness and death, marriage and baptism. There's a growing sense of mission outward in the parish that is truly inspiring. I have seen a growing spiritual depth to parishioners' spirituality that is evident when they speak about their lives. Getting to know parishioners more and more with each passing year has been rewarding for me personally. It's been a privilege to enter into people's lives and to see the faith and convictions by which they daily live out their baptismal vocation. These relationships have had a profound influence on how I preach, for what I pray, and how I define my ministry.
>
> In the last couple of years I have been fairly consumed by the building project. At times, I have felt guilty about some of the things I'm not doing because I'm so involved with the planning and oversight of the building project. But I've come to understand that this is my call right now—to oversee the development of a new parish campus that can better serve our needs. I firmly believe that our environment has a subtle but very significant effect on how we view ourselves and our mission. A church has to be more than just

> functional. It needs to raise our spirits, draw us more deeply into the mystery
> of God, and hold us together as a community. Every detail makes a difference.
> Trying to build something that is truly beautiful allows us access to the Divine
> by a means that goes beyond words.
>
> As we prepare to occupy our new facilities a year from now, I am already
> reviewing in my head what comes next. I would like to see us use this coming
> year as a period of retreat, preparing us for the transition to our new facilities.
> It's a wonderful opportunity for us to deepen our convictions, broaden our
> sense of mission, and renew our understanding and commitment to liturgical
> prayer. As the parish continues to grow, it will be important that everyone feels
> connected in the coming year. I'd like to see more small groups bond together
> for prayer, support and service. I'd love to see more opportunities for personal
> spiritual direction and adult education. I long to see the diversity of our lay
> ministries continue to grow and move outward beyond our parish doorstep. I
> hope we will see more parishioners come to a deeper awareness of the spiritual
> significance of Christian stewardship.
>
> Reflecting on these past five years, I have so much for which to give
> thanks. There is no other place I'd rather be than at St. Mary - Fremont Center.
> You are a wonderful community, St. Mary! Thank you for your love and trust,
> your support and cooperation, your faithful witness. Let us hold fast to our
> faith and open our hearts to all that the good Lord still has in store for us.[1]

He shared credit for the parish's growth with staff and parishioners.
Yet, it would not have happened without his support and encouragement.

St. Mary's was now anticipating two annual winter events. An
upcoming "Parish Appreciation Dinner" on February 12th was the first.
The second, "Gala 2001: A New Space Odyssey" on March 24th, like the
same successful event in 2000, would net an additional $21,000.

In his January 28th column, Lewinski's words had a particularly
reflective and prophetic tone. He mentioned the increasing tendency of
numbers (Social Security Number, Personal Identification Number, voice
mail, etc.) to replace names. About to turn fifty-five, he wrote:

> I'm so old, that I can even remember a time when children and adults
> would say, 'please' and 'thank you' or 'I'm sorry.'
>
> No, I'm not sour on society, but I am saddened that we are losing a sense
> of awe and reverence for the sacredness of life within each of us. I recall
> visiting Singapore where the custom at Mass is to bow profoundly to another
> at the Rite of Peace. I asked my Chinese friend why they bowed. She said, "I
> bow to the presence of God that lives within you." Imagine what it would be
> like if every Christian had that attitude toward every human being! It wouldn't
> matter then whether the other was an unborn child, a terminal patient, a
> convicted criminal or another driver who cut you off on the road. For in every
> stage of human life, we would begin to see more than flesh and bones, but the
> very trace of God's presence revealed before us.
>
> Without basic courtesy, reverence, and respect for another human being as
> the precious handiwork of God, our behavior can go into a tailspin.

Uncontrolled anger turns into violence, violence is mistaken for justice, inconvenience excuses even the worst of sins, and egocentrism becomes the god we worship. The more our society becomes desensitized to the plight of the poor, the needs of the elderly and the fears of the defenseless members of our society, the more ripe the climate for abortion, euthanasia, and capital punishment. These become political issues and somehow lose their spiritual origin and inherent demands placed upon us by the Author of Life.[2]

The ninth issue of *The Bell* appeared in February. It included an article by Andy Pini. Like others applying their knowledge and experience to the task, he was influential behind the scenes. He listed his professional credentials. He testified to the value brought by the architect (Dirk Lohan) and general contractor (Frederick Quinn Corporation). He expressed his pride in being part of the parish's transformation.

The issue carried an article by Jim Richards, Project Manager for the general contractor. He first visited the site in January 2000. "Value Engineering" was their approach. He wrote, "We were quite lucky that several parishioners are local subcontractors and were able to offer competitive prices in many instances. We have been restricted in our awarding contracts by the policies of the Archdiocese, which require union contractors. We were pleased to award subcontracts to parishioners for landscaping, asphalt paving, and plumbing.... together with Father Ron, whose vision and imagination for the new St. Mary church keeps us all moving forward. You can be assured you have some very gifted and dedicated people behind the project...to create a truly beautiful and holy place you will enjoy for many years to come."

The issue brought disappointing news. They had the original bell—housed in a copula by the old church—inspected. It was determined to be in good condition and tuned to A-sharp. However, budgeting concerns eliminated the bell tower planned for outside the entrance. "Hopefully," read the article, "there may be a generous donor who would like to see the Bell tower erected, who might step forward with a special gift."

Another article discussed the nearly completed rectory. It explained why it was located away from the new building. "Situating the rectory apart from the church and the pastoral offices and meeting spaces provides a healthy separation from the daily pastoral work. Thus you will notice that the new rectory is located on the far Southwest end of the new campus."[3]

On February 18th, three days after his fifty-fifth birthday, Lewinski shared some of his joy at watching the construction. He noted the physical, symbolic, and theological reasoning behind things. His effort in planning sometimes came down to the square inch (such as the cross in the baptismal font) and hidden objects (relics of St. Maria Goretti and St.

Catherine of Siena in the altar and a stone behind the Cornerstone). Another hidden feature is a room-sized cavity below the pastoral center, filled with water for the fire extinguishing system.

Lewinski wrote in his article:

> Notice the windows of the church's north and south walls. They are different sizes and at different levels. There's nothing ordinary or predictable about them. The light of the sun will shine through these windows creating patterns of light that will change from one time of day to another, from one season to another, casting light and shadows on the interior that will be God's own decorating touch. How symbolic these windows will be of our own lives that receive the light and grace of Christ in so many different ways, shining through the windows or experiences of our lives, changing from season to season.
>
> How about the middle section that will be our narthex (gathering space)! Fifty feet high, glass on the north and south that opens us up to the world and lets the beauty of our land come in. Try to imagine all the different kinds of gatherings our community will enjoy in this space in the years to come.
>
> My favorite space already is the Eucharistic Chapel, the open section on the far western end of the building. Here we will reserve the Blessed Sacrament. Here we will come for private prayer and adoration. From the light that will shine from the chapel outward in every direction, passersby will come to know that this is the center, the heartbeat, the life-source of our community, the Holy Sacrament that holds us together as one family in the Lord.[4]

As Lent approached, Lewinski included a call to action in his column: "As I see it, this Lent marks the beginning of our transition into the new church. We can already see the outline of what will be a most impressive house of worship. Think of these next twelve months as a procession toward the new sanctuary. What must we do both as a community and as individuals to make our way to the house of the Lord?"[5]

He noted that spiritual reflection and growth opportunities were something to consider and act on. Prayer and action do not negate each other and are not substitutes for each other.

The first Sunday in March, Lewinski called the Gala 2001 "a grand success." After having awarded a noteworthy cash prize, the black-tie event raised $21,000. He had a reminder about an upcoming trip. "On Thursday, March 8th, twenty-one pilgrims from St. Mary's will begin a pilgrimage that will trace the journey of St. Paul to Greece and Turkey. I will lead the group as we visit Athens, Corinth, Ephesus, Rhodes, and other places that were part of St. Paul's missionary outreach."[6]

IMAGE #13

'HIDDEN' PLACES AT ST. MARY'S

RELICS IN THE ALTAR, A STONE BEHIND THE CORNERSTONE

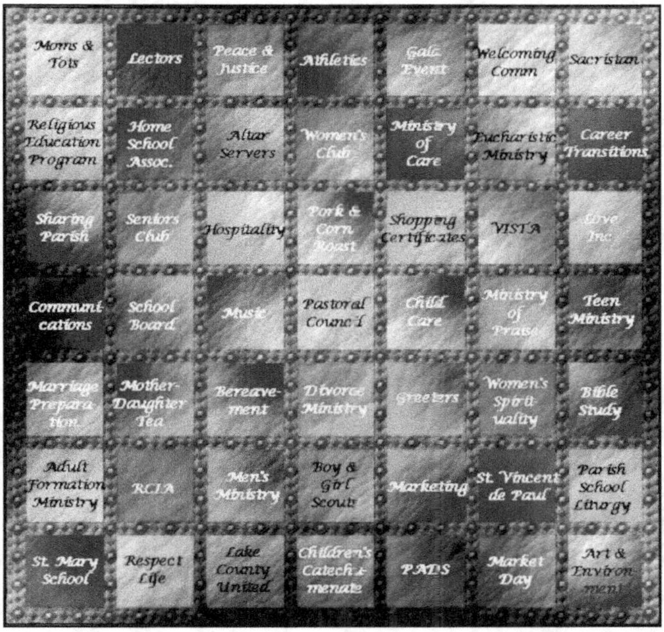

Moms & Tots	Lectors	Peace & Justice	Athletics	Gala Event	Welcoming Comm	Sacristan
Religious Education Program	Home School Assoc.	Altar Servers	Women's Club	Ministry of Care	Eucharistic Ministry	Career Transitions
Sharing Parish	Seniors Club	Hospitality	Pork & Corn Roast	Shopping Certificates	VISTA	Love Inc.
Communications	School Board	Music	Pastoral Council	Child Care	Ministry of Praise	Teen Ministry
Marriage Preparation	Mother-Daughter Tea	Bereavement	Divorce Ministry	Greeters	Women's Spirituality	Bible Study
Adult Formation Ministry	RCIA	Men's Ministry	Boy & Girl Scouts	Marketing	St Vincent de Paul	Parish School Liturgy
St. Mary School	Respect Life	Lake County United	Children's Catechumenate	PADS	Market Day	Art & Environment

IMAGE #14

MINISTRY QUILT

WHEN LEWINSKI ARRIVED IN 1996, THERE WERE
ONLY A HANDFUL OF MINISTRIES. BY 2002,
THEY HAD NOTABLY EXPANDED AS REPRESENTED
BY THIS 'MINISTRY QUILT'.

IMAGE #15

EUCHARISTIC CHAPEL

ARTIST DESIGN RENDERING BEFORE CONSTRUCTION.

IMAGE #16

EUCHARISTIC CHAPEL

PHOTOGRAPH OF THE FINISHED CHAPEL
THE PEAK (NOT VISIBLE) IS FIFTY FEET HIGH.

IMAGE #17

STAINED GLASS WINDOW

DESIGNED BY DIRK LOHAN, THE ARCHITECT,
THE WINDOW IS SITUATED TO THE RIGHT OF THE ALTAR
IN THE PASSAGEWAY TO THE EUCHARISTIC CHAPEL.

IMAGE #18

SANCTUARY

THE EUCHARISTIC CHAPEL IS BEHIND THE WOODEN SCREEN.
BLACK HORIZONTAL SLOTS ARE WHERE ORGAN PIPES WILL BE
VISIBLE AFTER THE ORGAN IS INSTALLED.

Those on the pilgrimage formed lifelong memories of places Paul had visited. There is no substitute for being where the apostles and early disciples had been. One physically senses the danger they encountered. This parish's evangelization faced challenges, but not as life-threatening as in Paul's day.

Lewinski knew "because parish can touch so many other relationships in people's lives, it can always be 'the community that supports other communities.' ... Parish has the power to change the way people see their family lives, their time at work, their neighborhoods and their friends. So it can be decisive."[7]

An Archdiocesan representative visited the parish before the pilgrimage group's departure. In his column, Lewinski wrote, "Ms. Sheila McLaughlin, who has been the Director of the Office for Divine Worship for the Archdiocese of Chicago, led us in a process that helped us to reflect upon and name our experiences of liturgy at St. Mary's. It was a great evening. There were many positive comments about our liturgy."[8] McLaughlin was the third Director in Chicago. The original was Fr. Dan Coughlin, who later became the first Catholic congressional chaplain in Washington. The second was Lewinski, who had the role for a decade before taking a sabbatical and coming to St. Mary Parish.[9]

On March 18, 2001, the bulletin deviated by featuring two pictures of the frame under construction. The following week, another picture featured the circular base to support the steeple on the roof's peak. They soon discovered the "donut" was eight feet off center. They designed the spire to be directly above the altar, based on Lohan's explanation of "truth in architecture" during a Town Hall. Because moving the altar's location would affect the entire floor plan, the steelworkers needed to correct their $60,000 mistake. Meanwhile, 80% of the masonry walls were complete, revealing more of what the building would actually look like.

On April Fool's Day, Lewinski was rejoicing. He and Fr. Kiepura now resided on campus. Lewinski and had been commuting a few miles between the parish and a rental. Moving in, he admitted, "has enabled me to feel like I'm finally coming home."

Lewinski noted that Fr. Keusal was named Pastor Emeritus of St. Mary on April 1st. He celebrated his 40th anniversary of ordination with friends and family before returning to Mt. Carmel parish in Oahu.

They had scheduled May 9th to celebrate the departure of Scavone as Director of Music and Liturgy. His replacement, Fred Vipond, would begin his ministry on the following weekend. Scavone developed the music and liturgy during the first years after Lewinski's arrival. Vipond continued to expand the ministry, applying his particular training and talent to a unique organ planned for the new church.[10]

Scavone published his farewell message in the May 13th bulletin. "It's hard to believe," he wrote, "that it's been five years since I made my first trip from Chicago to here. I can remember seeing the fields and the cows for the first time and thinking, 'Where am I driving to?'. The time has gone very quickly." Over time, other staff members departed. Each would recall their experience at St. Mary's as something special.

IMAGE #19

THE FIELD OF DREAMS

FARMLAND WEST OF THE OLD CHURCH AND CEMETERY
WHERE THE NEW CHURCH WOULD BE CONSTRUCTED.

Lewinski published an expanded column in the June 10th bulletin, discussing sacraments and rites. He wrote, "On Pentecost, we received two individuals into full communion. They had already been baptized in a Christian Church, and because we never re-baptize anyone, we invited them to make a solemn profession of faith and then confirmed them."

Preparing someone to join the Church is a matter of formation. It might take a few months or a few years. It depended on an individual's prior experience and the person themselves. Lewinski did not want people to simply "register" for a "school-year term" of instruction and orientation, culminating in Baptism and/or Confirmation at Easter. Instead, he advocated a process whereby a candidate could begin at any time and proceed at their own pace.

"We sometimes use shorthand in referring to this process," he wrote, "by calling it the RCIA [Rite of Christian Initiation of Adults]. This is not another program off the shelf of the religious market."[11] Although he explained much in his column, he humbly did not share his role in RCIA as one of its founding fathers.

By mid-June, the walls and roofing of the key features—the church, narthex, and pastoral office space—were easily recognizable. The outer appearance of the structure would not change much during the coming months. Critics, of course, did not miss the opportunity to complain that nothing was happening. Lewinski noted it was simply because they couldn't *see* the progress with HVAC, electrical and other infrastructure occurring on the inside.

Standing outside, Lewinski wore a light-colored short-sleeve shirt and gray slacks. With a clipboard of papers in hand, he could be mistaken for a supervisor, except no workers were present. Pastoral Council members stood before him. They'd assembled on the gravel road between the cemetery and the new campus. They gathered on the hill's crest near an old wooden bench overlooking the construction site. Lewinski often sat there, watching the work and contemplating the extraordinary effort—not just erecting a building—they had undertaken to expand this faith community.

His manner revealed his energy level. He was eager to help this group feel some accomplishment after their efforts over the past years. It was an opportunity to get feedback and solicit questions, the kind parishioners were likely to ask during an upcoming Town Hall. He was in good spirits. He was doing what he loved: helping people to understand something better, to see things differently. Their ideas were finally changing from tenuous dreams into visible reality. He hoped they would see before them what he'd been envisioning for so long. He wanted them to share his excitement, knowledge, and happiness.

The sun was high above when he launched into his comments. "Welcome to our work site. Our project began five years ago, in June of 1996. We gathered a lot of the leadership to look at where we should be going in the future. It was determined at that time that we should begin to consider what we would need to meet the community's growing needs. We have come a long way in those five years. You can see the progress we've already made. What we'll be seeing today is part of the first phase of our project for the future. It includes a new church, meeting rooms, pastoral offices, gathering space, and parking for almost 400 cars. In the distance, you can see that we've already finished the new rectory. That is one part of the project that is already completed. Thanks be to God." Lewinski was glad to live on campus after five years of commuting.

"We're going to be moving towards the work site, but I want to point out one important thing. We tried to weave together what we already have on our beautiful campus with what we are about to have. So even the church's design had to not compete with our very loved country church. Obviously, the size of the new church is overwhelming in some sense, but still, there will be a subtle blending of the features.

IMAGE #20

ST. MARY LANDSCAPE

THE ARCHITECT SUCCEEDED IN MAKING THE NEW CHURCH (IN THE DISTANCE TO THE RIGHT OF THE TREE) BLEND WELL WITH THE LOCAL TOWNSHIP COMMUNITY BUILDINGS IN THE FOREGROUND.

"Another thing is significant, I think. A value that was expressed again and again was the desire to respect the land. To make a connection between the land and the building itself. That's why we ended up with a lot of glass in this building. We wanted to bring the outside 'in.' We are blessed with this twenty-acre site. It allows us to seek that goal as best we can. Now let's go down to the site itself."

Lewinski pointed to three large areas clad in black insulating material. The offices were closest to them on the east end, the narthex in the middle, and the sanctuary at the west end. Standing at the site's southeast corner, he identified where Emmaus Drive, the main entry off Erhart Road, would enter the parking lot.

On the way toward that area's southern side, he pointed out a porta-potty for the workers. He suggested it was part of the plan for new washrooms. His typical dry humor evoked chuckles. He couldn't pass up the chance. He added, "We feel very confident that in the wintertime, we won't have the problem with the kids always wanting to use the bathroom during services." This, of course, elicited more laughter.

Moving north toward the building, he described the future paved plaza. "You can picture people gathering here preparing for a wedding celebration or afterward greeting the guests. We could conduct some of the smaller rites of the Church—the blessing of palms at Lent, perhaps—out here as well."

He stepped through what would be the exterior entrance. He identified the entry from the narthex to the sanctuary and held up a sketch depicting the ceremonial doors. Eleven feet high, they would form a grand entrance.

He commented on the expectations for the large space. There would be doors on the northern side leading to a meditation garden: a place to walk and pray, and where couples could have wedding pictures taken. The floor would be carpet rather than tile. They made the ceiling of special material to reduce noise. The narthex would be used for wakes, dinners, social events, and other gatherings. It would seem luxurious compared to the current facilities in the church basement. Further, it would accommodate overflow for services, especially Christmas and Easter.[12]

Next, he led the group back outside and to the structure's western end. He entered what would be the Eucharistic Chapel. An artist's rendering was on display. He highlighted features like the dramatic fifty-foot-high ceiling, the rising tabernacle wall, and treated glass at the ground level to provide privacy. He identified where a six-foot wide hinged wooden door would secure the space and separate it from the sanctuary. "I suspect this will become a favorite place for prayer," he claimed.[13]

He again seized the opportunity for humor. He explained entry from the exterior would be via a keypad lock "so parishioners in good standing will be able to enter." His sarcasm invoked a response: "Well," answered someone, "there went my number."

Lewinski had mentioned having keypad access three years earlier. That was well before an architect had even been selected.

He walked into the sanctuary, showing where the Mary shrine would be located amidst the congregation. Nearby, on a wall not yet constructed, he explained, would be the sanctuary lamp that would identify the location of the Eucharistic Chapel. Then he pointed to the high nave. This was an essential design feature. He stated, "How very different the interior here feels from what you see on the outside. It is not symmetrical, yet inside, you don't have the feeling of being off guard or twisted around. You can see that the right side is larger than the left side but is still well-proportioned. The nave cuts across—at an angle—from the Eucharistic Chapel, the church, the narthex, and into the pastoral center. It makes a theological statement about all these things going on in our life as a parish. We have private devotion in the Chapel. We have worship in the sanctuary. We have socializing in the gathering space. We have business in the offices. We have ministry formation in the meeting rooms. But it is all held together by this one piece, pulling everything together. And, from the other end, it all leads via common access to the altar. So you have a baptismal font in the back of the sanctuary, the altar, and the Eucharistic Chapel all on a clear axis."

IMAGE #21

THE NARTHEX

LOOKING WEST FROM THE PASTORAL CENTER, THE 11' DOORS TO THE SANCTUARY ARE AT THE FAR END. THE THREE DIMENSIONS OF THE NARTHEX ARE ABOUT THE SAME AS THE OLD CHURCH. IT FUNCTIONS AS OVERFLOW SPACE EVEN THOUGH THE SANCTUARY SEATS FOUR TIMES AS MANY PEOPLE AS THE OLD CHURCH. THE NAVE CROSSES INTO THE SANCTUARY, WHICH IS SEPARATED FROM THE NARTHEX BY GLASS ABOVE THE ENTRANCE.

Next, he pointed toward a large empty room-like space behind the altar, elevated with a sacristy below it. "The organ pipes will fill the cavity you see behind the altar. Now, in front of all of that will be a curved wooden screen so you won't see all the pipes. What is wonderful is we will have a beautiful space. It will not only be beautiful to look at, but with the sound, it will create a total experience. Sound and sight together. That is something we can really be proud of."[14]

He directed their attention toward the irregularly placed and differently sized windows in the north and south walls. Their irregularity is intentional. They should convey that the church is not simply a large meeting space but a special place where a diverse group gathers to worship.[15]

He explained the reasoning behind the spacious design. "The height is important. From ancient times, the proportions of a building have a lot to say about the sacredness of the building or its special character. When a building is high, you feel out of proportion or out of control. That is how we should feel in this space. Unlike a Holiday Inn ballroom, this is space around the Lord's table where we are on his turf, not ours. We should be humbled by the very proportions, and what we feel and what we experience in this space."

Having spent several minutes talking earnestly about the design features, Lewinski pivoted to some levity. He pointed to the location at the back of the sanctuary for a Reconciliation Chapel ("confessional"). He explained the space would accommodate both curtained and face-to-face confessions. A unique feature would be a trapdoor in the floor for a penitent whose sins couldn't be forgiven. His dry humor revealed he was genuinely enjoying his captive audience.

The characteristics of the baptismal font were next. Lewinski's comments gave insight into his involvement in certain design aspects, especially when the subject was as close to his heart as baptism. (Each year, he regularly celebrated his baptism date as well as his birthday.) "The font is suitable for immersion and pouring, as the Church expects of us these days. When you enter the church, one part of the font is higher so you can dip your hand to sign yourself. That part flows into the lower part of the font. The water is only about a foot-and-a-half deep, so no diving."

If one wasn't paying attention, his humor might easily be missed.[16]

Lewinski continued as if he had said nothing funny. "Living Seas are doing the purification system. It is an ultraviolet system that purifies the water, which is always cleaned and recycled. They'll make the font out of solid carnelian granite. It should be very impressive as you walk through these ceremonial doors. It is there to remind us when we enter where our life began. It represents the centerpiece of our lives. Our life begins in the waters of baptism. You can see it is on an axis to the altar itself."

IMAGE #22

ACCESS RAMP

A RAMP BEHIND THE ALTAR ENABLES ACCESS
TO THE ALTAR PLATFORM WITHOUT NEEDING TO
CLIMB THE STAIRS IN FRONT OF THE ALTAR.

He motioned toward the area left of the altar. It would be where the choir would face the congregation. They and the celebrant would have direct visual contact. This was another desirable feature he had listed during the walk-through in 1997. He pointed out an access ramp leading from the main floor up to the altar area to accommodate anyone disabled. The ambo (pulpit) was located where the ramp met the altar area.

Someone made a keen observation. "At one time, you told us the base of the steeple would be above the altar. Now it looks offset." He referred to where the beams formed a donut shape on the roof but not over the altar. Lewinski replied, "It has to be moved. They made a mistake. That's one reason for the construction delay. The roof would have been done by now, but it was the contractor's mistake, so they had to make the change. The circle for the steeple has to be moved eight feet east."

They returned outside, where Lewinski noted the cultured stone being placed around the base of the building. He identified the air gap between the exterior brick and the cinder block covered by styrofoam sheets. "The airspace behind the concrete block," he explained, "has an insulating effect."

Moving to the north side, he spoke about the meditation garden between the church and the pastoral center. "One reason for the building's orientation is to have this meditation garden here. As you look this way," he motioned eastward, "you see the old church and cemetery. The design weaves them together.

"For example, they could have done the pastoral center so that the wing is blocking this view; but they intentionally opened it up so you could see the older spaces." He was referring to an option in the conceptual models that few people had seen, known as 'Model C.' There had always been emphasis—by both Lohan and Lewinski—on maintaining a visual and physical connection between the old and new campuses.

Walking to the pastoral center's interior, Lewinski identified the area's rooms and features. Brides preparing for a wedding could use a general-purpose hospitality parlor, including a washroom. It could also be used for private meetings. An adjacent room was for choir practice and the music director's office. Next, a large meeting area could be subdivided into two or three smaller rooms.

Directing their attention to the opposite side of the hallway, Lewinski identified additional spaces. A unisex bathroom and changing room; men's and women's bathrooms; a kitchen/pantry; and a mechanical room. He concluded the tour by noting the offices would be on the south side of this section, with regularly sized and spaced windows—unlike the sanctuary.

Anyone at the 1997 walk-through would realize Lewinski's comments back then were predictions of what they were seeing now. He couldn't have known what things would actually look like. But he understood the reasoning behind ceremonies in liturgical space and the relationship between things.

Leading the tour informed him of what aspects people deserved to see and why. These tours were practice runs to influence his thinking while developing a docent guide with parishioner Ed Hendricks.

The tour members went home excited. They felt a renewed sense of anticipation. The narthex space alone was as large as the old church. How wonderful it would be when they could use it as a welcoming space before and after services. It could be a splendid area for luncheons or dinners and a grand formal place for holding a visitation service before a funeral. The meeting rooms would be a welcome alternative to the current often poorly lit and cramped spaces. The sanctuary would hold four times more people than the current one, reducing the number of weekend Masses. These and many other features they'd spent months working on were taking shape.

What had once seemed impossible was actually probable.

---

[1] Sunday bulletin, January 7, 2001, pp. 3-4. For an example of how Lewinski believed that every detail makes a difference, see Image #36).

[2] Sunday bulletin, January 28, 2001, p. 3.

[3] *The Bell*, Volume I, Issue 9, February 2001.

[4] Sunday bulletin, February 18, 2001, p. 3. Lewinski's speculation about the effect that light would have when it entered the sanctuary was prophetic. During the Vigil on the night before his burial in 2017, light from the setting sun came through the stained glass window next to the Eucharistic Chapel and eventually rose to illuminate Lewinski as he lay in a coffin before the altar.

[5] Sunday bulletin, February 25, 2001, p. 3.

[6] Sunday bulletin, March 4, 2001, p. 3.

[7] DeSiano & Boyack, p. 97,

[8] Sunday bulletin, March 11, 2001, p. 3.

[9] McLaughlin was succeeded by Todd Williamson, who proclaimed scripture during Lewinski's funeral service in 2017.

[10] Sunday bulletin April 1, 2001, pp. 3-4.

[11] Sunday bulletin, June 10, 2001, pp. 3-4.

[12] During a conversation on July 1, 2018, Lohan recalled that this "extended" use of the narthex space was Lewinski's idea.

[13] Lohan complimented Lewinski on the Eucharistic Chapel, saying, "The thing that I had not actually identified before in other churches was the Eucharistic Chapel. It was a brilliant idea of Ron's in my opinion." Personal conversation, May 11, 2018.

[14] Lohan reflected, "In the churches that I knew, the organ is usually on a balcony at the back, or right next to the altar, where all the pipes are exposed. I like organs, but not when they attract too much attention, away from the central feature. The idea at St. Mary's was to hide it but make it audible." —Personal conversation, July 18, 2018.

[15] They modeled the design after a chapel in France. During his seminary years, Lewinski had studied in Lyon, France.

[16] Regardless of the topic, Lewinski often would impart a brief, humorous comment. Sometimes it was heard by only one person. One parishioner shared, "I came to enjoy his sense of humor. He would say something so quietly that only *you* could hear. It was funny when you were the only one laughing because nobody else heard what he had said."

ISN'T THAT GREAT!?

Summer 2001

The Planning Commission hosted a Town Hall on June 20th, merely nine months before the new church's dedication. The organizers projected photos of construction in progress as people arrived. A parishioner narrated the picture captions for those who could not read them. A tapestry of Christ—the Alpha and Omega—hung on the wall aside the projection screen. Lewinski had extracted the tabernacle from its temporary storage and placed it on a table beneath the tapestry. A variety of easels held sketches of various site plans and elevations.

Lewinski welcomed the gathering of roughly one hundred and twenty people. "Thank you. We're going to begin with a prayer. First, I hope you've had an opportunity as you gathered here this evening to look at some things we have displayed. We'll talk more about that. There is so much as we grow and evolve. Certainly, we already have much to thank God for, and we look to the future while asking for God's help. We'll sing the first three verses of 'All Are Welcome' in your hymnal." Fred Vipond led the group from the upright piano. By now, the song had become so familiar that many could recite it without referring to the hymnal.

When they finished, Lewinski prayed. "Almighty God, out of living stones—your chosen people—you have built an eternal temple to your glory. With your divine guidance, we have begun constructing a church and pastoral center we will dedicate to your honor and glory. We thank all who have already given so much of their time, talent, and treasure so that your people may have a place to worship and gather in Christian Fellowship. We ask you to hold us together in lasting faith and to prepare our hearts for what lies ahead. In these months before our solemn dedication, increase the spiritual gifts you have given to your Church so that our parish community may continue to grow in forwardness and zeal for the mission you have entrusted to us.

"Lord Jesus, you built your house upon a rock. Strengthen your Church with solid and lasting faith; we pray.

"Lord Jesus, you are the master builder. Give success to the work of our hands as we build a new church to praise you; we pray.

"Lord Jesus, you are in the midst of those who gather in your name. May we always feel your abiding presence among us; we pray.

"Lord Jesus, you prepare a dwelling place in your Father's house for all who love you. Help the community of St. Mary of the Annunciation to grow in divine love; we pray.

"Lord Jesus, you never cast out anyone who comes to you. Open your Father's house to all those who have died, especially the deceased founders and benefactors of our parish; we pray.

"Together, let us pray as Jesus taught us." The assembly joined him in the Lord's Prayer.

"May God—who began his good work in us—continue to guide, protect, and defend us. May God bless the efforts being made to build for the future and deepen our trust in His providence over us." He closed by making the sign of the cross.

"I'll ask John Riggio to get us started."

Riggio said the project team wished they could take everyone on a personal walk around the construction site, but it wasn't practical. Instead, they showed a version of a video from Lewinski's tour a few days earlier, prepared by parishioner Ed Leuthner. After watching the edited 15-minute recording, the attendees expressed their appreciation with loud applause.

Riggio continued. "Isn't that great? Our work is coming along, and I hope you're as excited as we are. If you haven't been involved, now is the time. You can help make this time successful in several ways, which Father Ron will tell us about. There are sign-up sheets at the back.

"Father Ron has reminded us time and again that this project is not just about putting up a building, but about building community here and strengthening what we already have. Thank you for coming tonight. It shows you care, and we appreciate that. As you look around, you'll realize that several fellow parishioners are not here tonight. I encourage each of you to take a missionary step by communicating to them exactly what is happening. Bring others and get them involved. This will be something for everyone, not just those of us here tonight.

"I'm going to turn it over to Father Ron now. He will share with us the progress we have made and what lies ahead."

Lewinski stepped up to the podium. Using his typical dry humor, he mimicked late night TV commercials, "Nothing like a good home movie." Referring to the video they'd just watched, he continued, "And tonight for $19.95, you too can have…" After the laughter, his serious tone returned. "I hope we can take you in small groups through the building so you can get a sense of it yourself because when you are inside, it feels different. Could some people who were there tell us what it felt like to be inside?"

Some of the people who had accompanied Lewinski on the tour responded.

Ed Leuthner was first. "My feeling walking into the space is that it is just awesome. It is so different from what I expected, and I was so pleased."

Someone else observed, "It had a very comfortable feel. It is not finished. There is a lot to do, but I think this is a space we'll feel comfortable in."

"It was overwhelming," stated a parishioner. "It doesn't feel huge until you look up. There is so much space up there, not just in the narthex but in the other parts. It was overwhelming, even with nothing in it."

"I agree it was overwhelming," echoed someone else, "but when we stood where the last pew is going to be placed, it is very close to the altar. It reminds me of having Mass in the old church. It is still going to be small and personal."

Another person spoke up. "My impression was, quieting and focusing —two key words. It is something that draws you in and focuses your attention on why you are there. It elevates your spirit as part of this whole experience of God."

With no other comments forthcoming, Lewinski continued. "You know, it was five years ago, on June 8th, that our Parish leadership and Archdiocesan officials gathered in the basement of St. Mary's church— some of you were there—to ask a key question: are we ready to do some serious planning for the future? And the consensus then was, 'Yes, we need to build for the future.'

"And so began five years of planning, dreaming, research and study, consultation with parishioners, fundraising, purchasing land, negotiating with county and diocese, county hearings on steeples, and parish Town Hall meetings like this one tonight. Today, all one has to do is drive by the site to see how far we have come. We are a Church and a parish that is growing very wonderfully. We have a church going up designed by an internationally respected architect, Dirk Lohan, and under construction by Frederick Quinn Corporation, a general contractor with a lot of experience. We have come a long way.

"With the basic pieces now in place, and construction proceeding, it is a time for us to focus our time and our energy on preparing for the dedication of our new church. So we begin a whole new chapter, you might say. We hope the dedication will be in the springtime, in April.

"The dedication of a church is certainly one of the most significant moments of a parish's life. It is not just a celebration of a building but the people who built it. The dedication of a church is about a people who will worship in that holy space. It is a celebration of our consecration as God's people, a people with a mission from Jesus to transform the world. The dedication of a church calls for the *rededication* of the Church, God's people. As John and I have said repeatedly, this is about building a community of faith for generations to come. We need space to be a community. So we build.

"What I am proposing tonight as part of our planning is that we consider extending that dedication celebration throughout the year, making 2002 an entire year of Jubilee for St. Mary's. A year filled with several events that will help us mark this significant time in our history. There are several possibilities. We may want to do a parish mission or retreat together. We are planning a return to our roots in Germany— perhaps connect with a sister parish there from a place where many of our founding families came from. Also, parish concerts and various activities throughout the year.

"It is truly a time of grace. It is a time that we should not take for granted. As we move into the new church, we need to see ourselves as a new community in a new light. So I propose we begin a year of celebration in January 2002. We are going to need a lot of help to make that successful.

"On the tables in the back are various ways you can assist and help make all of this a fantastic year, a great time of celebration for us. The progress we have now reached calls for some immediate preparation for the dedication. A dedication is not something that just happens; it results from a great deal of time and effort.

"We have several needs. I encourage you to see how you can help. For instance, we want to put together a dedication commemorative book. We are going to need help with hospitality. We need to prepare a beautiful invitation to send. We want to train some docents who could give facility tours with explanations and the meaning behind why things are the way they are. We want to trace our roots back to Germany. We'd also like to do some special events. We'd like to do something every month of the year." Lewinski was crediting these activities to a group called "we." He desired to involve as many people as possible.

"I also want to say a few words tonight about our capital campaign and the funding for our project. Right from the beginning, we knew we would face an overwhelming mission because we were called to prepare for the future. So we knew that we would have to build not simply for our own needs today but for what we would need years from now. That, of course, placed a significant burden upon us. After several meetings with the Archdiocese, we concluded that, given all that we had to do, a $10 million budget was reasonable.

"The Archdiocese required us to add a 10% contingency to the project. Contingency, as you know, is money set in a budget you *hope* will not be used. In my optimism, I hoped we *wouldn't* need all that money and could use it someday for art and other things. However, the inevitable happens, so we've already used most of that contingency. It leaves me with a bit of a knot in my stomach because, like any good pastor, the last thing that I want to see is an enormous debt.

"Nevertheless, we have worked hard to ensure that we try to stay within budget as much as we can. We have had to let go of a few things we planned—such as the wood on the ceilings and a few other minor things. There is no frivolous spending of dollars. We are building a quality structure—a church that will stand the test of time and a church that will be a true spiritual home you can take pride in.

"There is nothing 'cookie cutter model' about this. Some very beautiful things are part of this entire building. The good news is that this little church on the prairie has done very *well* with the capital campaign. We have gone over the $6 million mark with pledges, and parishioners have been very generous and faithful in fulfilling their pledges. That is something not to take for granted.

"Let me say that I am genuinely grateful to all of you who have done so much already. Those of you here tonight are indeed the supporters. That's why you are here. We hope those who have already fulfilled their pledge might consider continuing to make voluntary payments to whatever extent they can. We also hope others who have not yet pledged will see the good things happening, the reality of what is going on, and will want to do their share. Again, you need to encourage folks in that regard. Special gifts are also always welcome. When each person does what they can, even if it is very little, it is then that great things happen.

"I would also like to say a word about the rectory. The work is complete, and we have the pastor back on campus for the first time in five and one-half years. Father Ken and I are certainly happy to have a new home. There is no doubt the new rectory will be an attraction for priests who may consider St. Mary's as an assignment in the future. When I arrived at St. Mary's five-and-one-half years ago, we turned what was the rectory into parish offices. Those of you who have stopped by the parish offices know how our staff has already outgrown that space.

"In the meantime, we were renting a condo in the area for my residence. So this new rectory is a welcome change. When we brought our plans for the new church to the Archdiocese, we were told to build a new rectory, too. They asked us to use the money we had been using for rent as a mortgage payment instead, plus some additional funds from our operating expenses. So, although the rectory is shown as part of Phase I, we managed the funding differently.

"We have been blessed with many wonderful trade skills that have helped us build the house, and I want to acknowledge that. On July 7,

Saturday, Father Ken and I are holding an open house so you can come and look for yourself.

"You know, despite the burdens that a project of our proportions places on a community and its pastor, we cannot lose sight of how far God has already brought us. Those who were present on June 8th, five years ago, in the church's basement, know that we wondered if we would ever really reach this point. We are here. In these five years, we have worked miracles, and the story continues.

"I'm hoping that we can arrange for you, perhaps on Saturday mornings, to take a small group of people at a time through the structure so you can see for yourself how marvelously God has already blessed us.

"There is one other thing that I want to say. When we build a church like this, it is not just for ourselves. We are charged with evangelization to spread the word.

"Again, thank you for your support and cooperation and your generosity. Mary Hall now will give us more about those details."

The audience applauded as their business manager stepped forward. She briefly reviewed the project that had begun in June 1996. Then she answered a question on everyone's mind. "To date, we have received over $6.1 million in pledge commitments. We have received $2.4 million in pledge payments and an additional $132,000 in interest on that money." Then, following Lewinski's lead, she quipped, "Remember, you can make payments on your Visa or MasterCard. Call me at the office."

Hall described various aspects of the project's finances. One was roadwork required by the County at the intersection of Fremont Center and Erhart Roads. She acknowledged people at the Archdiocesan offices who had been helping the parish. Hall ended her comments with an appeal to anyone who hadn't yet made a financial commitment.

When Lewinski returned to the podium, he introduced Jim Richards. "Jim works in the trailer at Fremont Center Road and keeps a good eye on all that is going on day in and day out. He is going to share with us what we can expect to see on a month-by-month basis." The trailer Lewinski referred to was the on-site "construction office." The project team conducted regular status meetings and managed the project from there.

"Thank you, Father Ron," said Richards. "I would like to say first what a pleasure it has been to work with Father Ron and Mary Hall at St. Mary Parish. We look forward to Tuesdays."

He began a month-by-month review of what milestones to expect, beginning with the immediate future and moving into the Autumn. He reported they would repave Erhart Road and the parking lot in September. "Hopefully, on October 1st, the steeple will arrive. We haven't decided if we will set it with a huge crane or have a helicopter put it in place, but I'm sure we will have quite an audience on hand—whether we want them or not." The crowd responded with laughter because they knew it was true.

"Father Ron promised to be up there to tighten down the first bolts." Howls of laughter broke out as attendees imagined Lewinski in a hard hat and, holding a large wrench, struggling to secure the fifty-foot structure. "I don't know if he was serious when he said that."

Schubert finished describing what to expect during the first months of 2002 before saying, "In April, we will polish the doorknobs and turn over the key." The group's applause acknowledged the planning, his confidence in it, and people's enthusiasm. He concluded: "You will have something to be very proud of. Thank you."

Lewinski returned to the podium. "Don't hesitate to call us. No question is too silly or dumb. We want you to understand what is going on and how it is all put together.

He continued, "There is some *more* good news to report—a wonderful surprise that Fred will tell us about." He left the podium, paused, and returned to it realizing some people hadn't yet met Scavone's replacement. "By the way," he chuckled, "this is Fred Vipond, our new liturgy and music director." Smiles and some friendly laughter greeted Vipond.

He had recently joined the parish. He had a degree in music and training as an organist. Vipond had Bachelor's and Master's degrees from the University of Michigan. He had been Director of Music at three Chicago Archdiocese parishes and Director of Marketing at World Library Publications in Illinois.

Vipond came forward. "Thank you, Father. And thank you," he addressed the audience, "once again. I say it every time: you all are so kind to come to me after Mass. The welcome I have received is the most genuine and affirming I have ever received at any parish. I am thirty-eight years old; I have been doing this since I was twelve, so I have worked in several parishes. It is a joy to be here with you. The *other* joy—that Jim Scavone was able to give to me as he was leaving—was, 'By the way, did I tell you some good news?'

"After I heard it, I had to pick myself up off the floor. It is the dream of any trained organist.

"Quite often, when parishes build—we've all heard the story: we'll build the gym and the school, and eventually, we will build a church. How many parishes never quite get around to building the church! Even if the church is built, there is not always enough left over to take care of things like air conditioning or stained glass windows. Very *low* on the list, often, is a musical instrument worthy of the liturgy. I am happy to tell you this is *not* the case at St. Mary's. "If you recall, an enormous chamber is above and behind the altar. That's where a magnificent new pipe organ of 52 ranks will be installed in about two years. A rank of pipes is like an entire row of little soldiers. For every key on the keyboard, there is a corresponding rank. We will have 52 of those ranks, which puts our instrument in the **large** pipe organ category, which for an organist is a fantastic thing to say.

"There are not many more details to share, except the major one: Roger and Jacqueline Fisher have given 100%. They have donated the entire cost of the organ." The assembly greeted this news with prolonged applause, prompting Roger and Jacqueline to stand and humbly acknowledge it with smiles.

Lewinski returned to the podium for his final "pitch" and closing comments. "The last thing, as you look at the different displays, you can be very proud about the fine pieces we will put into the church. The money that we have placed into the church, the priority where we have placed it, are locations in the church that cannot be changed in the future. So we have put the money into areas where it really counts.

"But, over the years, we hope we will continue to embellish upon that space. Something we hope we can look to in the future, and perhaps yourself or some friends or some ingenious way to do this, is a bell tower. We have a wonderful bell from the original church of St. Mary's, the very first church.[1] We'd like to put it back into a bell tower. We have a design for a tower, but we don't have a budget for one. So, again, there are some memorial opportunities—some of these are larger opportunities—but there are others that you might want to take advantage of.

"Finally, again, thank you for coming this evening. It is important to keep the enthusiasm going. Spread the word. I hope you'll take an opportunity this evening to look around again, ask questions, and consider signing up for the many activities we want to do this coming year. It is an exciting time, a wonderful time, and a once-in-a-lifetime kind of opportunity. We can thank God for this opportunity. We will be a stronger and more vibrant community. You are wonderful people. We all can be proud of all that God has already done for St. Mary's and that, with God's help, we can yet accomplish. So thank you, and good night."

The attendees left feeling encouraged and excited. They saw, if only briefly and indirectly, the construction progress in the video. They heard the praise of fellow parishioners who had physically toured the construction site with Lewinski. They learned from Mary Hall, the Business Manager, that a significant milestone of $6 million was achieved. St. Mary's organ would be one of Lake County's best, if not the best, church organs. And they had Fred Vipond, the new Director of Music, with the skill to play it. Planning was underway to celebrate their achievements every month throughout the coming year. And their priests were finally resident on campus in a new rectory. Any of these is a reason to celebrate. If someone left the Town Hall without recognizing the blessings in the parish, what was needed to open their souls to the work of the Spirit?

In September, the tenth issue of *The Bell* featured an article titled "A Spire to New Heights." Its focus was on the steeple scheduled for installation in January. The spire was the last major structural component, but it was more than a conical steel assembly. It would become the shining light of an oasis, a symbol visible from the surrounding countryside. The article explored how the concepts of "spiral," "conspire," and "inspire" related to the importance of the spire, the church building, and the Church body.

The issue discussed the Eucharistic Chapel, the building's prominent western feature. Seeing the space, anyone who had been at the confrontational walk-through in July, 1997, might recognize what Lewinski was imagining, though at the time he didn't know what the completed Chapel would look like. Lohan later credited Lewinski for coming up with the concept, calling it a "brilliant" idea.

The construction costs and the capital campaign were also explained.

Another article discussed the significance of placing the baptismal font near the sanctuary's entry, aligned with the altar. Regarding its tomb-like shape, the piece explained:

> The rites of baptism, the first of the sacraments of initiation, requires a prominent place for the celebration. Initiation into the Church is entrance into a eucharistic community united in Jesus Christ... Water is the key symbol of baptism and the focal point of the font. In this water, believers die to sin and are reborn to new life in Christ... The font is a symbol of both tomb and womb; its power is the power of the triumphant cross; and baptism sets the Christian on the path to the life that will never end, the 'eighth' day of eternity where Christ's reign of peace and justice is celebrated.[2]

They devoted the center spread to acknowledging the various construction supervisors and managers who had supervised the building's construction. Some were parishioners. Al Hertel and his crew worked on plumbing. Peter Sonza-Novera's landscapers awaited the final grading of the property.

Lewinski's "Around the Table" column was half the size it had sometimes been. There was still work to do and money to raise, but he could relax his grip on those reins. He repeated the invitation he'd extended during the Town Hall for people to become involved in the Dedication Jubilee events.

Lewinski's column on July 1st recalled, "We had a wonderful Town Hall Meeting on June 20th. Parishioners had the opportunity to review the progress we have made on building the new church and parish offices. With several materials on display at various stations around Diantha Hall, it looked like a trade show at a convention. The 'show and tell' approach helped everyone to get a sense of things to come. I'm appreciative of all the hands that went into preparing the evening. I left the meeting thinking to myself, *Yes, ministry today does require some high-tech skills to get the message across.* If you missed the meeting, you can view a collage of pictures that tell the story of our progress by checking out our website. The next issue of *The Bell* will be sent out soon."[3]

On July 7th, Lewinski and Kiepura held an open house at the rectory. Afterward, Lewinski recalled, "A steady flow of parishioners walked through the house that day. All the remarks I heard were positive. One remark, which I thought said it all, came from a man who, after touring the home, pulled me aside and said, 'Father, I can't wait to tell my friends what a wonderful rectory we have for our priests. It makes me so proud to be a St. Mary parishioner.' It's words of pride like that which I am confident will also be said about the new church in the coming months. A big thanks to all who came to grace our new home with your visit."[4]

Lewinski's ideas about Jubilee events weren't simply justifications for "parties" or excuses for gathering. He recognized the upheaval caused by construction and the surge of new parishioners. It was altering the social dynamics of what had been a quiet and unchanging community just half a decade earlier. He knew from his pastoral visits, the Town Halls, and surveys, that parishioners were concerned about losing the sense of hospitality and friendly community they felt. By offering distinct events, the attendees would recognize their treasured feeling of "community" was not disappearing. The parish benefited from the variety of backgrounds and experiences the newcomers brought with them. Rather than being a death toll, the transition invoked new life.

Later in August, Lewinski happily reported about some of the art for the church. He had received pictures from northern Italy of the Madonna sculpture in progress, which he shared with Council members. He was determined to populate the space, where the concrete floor had just been poured, with the work of artisans. He wasn't satisfied with merely getting something that "looked" nice or was the least expensive.

> Last Monday, one of our statues arrived from St. Ulrich, Italy. The Infant of Prague is a beautiful wood-carved figure in natural nut wood tones. The interior finishes, the artwork, and altar appointments are a main focus for me and the committees these days. One of the most exciting projects I've set in motion is contact with Zukuzenzele Weaving Center in South Africa. The

Zukuzenzele Weaving Center is sponsored by a local South African diocese that has trained native women in the fine art of hand-weaving tapestries. The Zukuzenzele Center is working on three large tapestries that will hang over the doors at the baptismal front. The three tapestries depict the three epiphanies: The Visit of the Magi, The Wedding Feast at Cana, and the Baptism of Jesus. Each tapestry will be 10 feet long and 6 feet wide, woven in true folk art style in multiple colors from woolen spindles. What is wonderful about the project is that it will give us something beautiful that will remind us of the universal Church. Our contracting with the native weaving center will also ensure an income for women in a very poor village.[5]

Subsequently, the tapestries would sometimes evoke comments because Christ is depicted as a black man. Lewinski's mention of the "universal Church" was a gentle reminder about the comprehensive scope of the word 'catholic.'

One of the three tapestries would become a source of temporary disappointment for Lewinski. It was delayed in customs and unavailable for the dedication.

During August's Pastoral Council meeting, the group realized there would be five vacancies to be populated. Four members were reaching the end of their term, and one was resigning. They resolved a way to manage it. Lewinski reported that the profit from August's Pork and Corn Roast approached the previous year's success. The chair for this year's event agreed to prepare for next year's Roast on the condition they would mentor someone to be the next chair. Although it would continue for several more years, cracks were emerging in the quarter-century-old tradition.

The good news about the Roast's profit was offset by the World Trade Center tragedy on September 11. Lewinski's column cautioned against developing a resentment toward Muslims:

Vatican II acknowledged that Muslims "are related in various ways to the People of God." The Church has acknowledged that Muslims "profess the faith of Abraham" and, along with Catholics, "adore the one and merciful God." The Council urged both sides to forget the past and to "strive sincerely for mutual understanding," making "common cause for safeguarding and fostering social justice, moral values, peace and freedom."

The extremism, hatred and hostility we see in Islamic terrorists do not really represent the mainstream of Islamic belief and practice.[6]

October 11th was the first feast day of the newly beatified Pope John XXIII. Elected at age 77, they regarded him as a "placeholder pope." He astonished the world by convening the Second Vatican Council. The pontiff opened it but would not live to see it close. The Pope, and the

Council, imprinted Lewinski's early life with new perspectives. Lewinski shared thoughts from John XXIII's book, *An Invitation of Hope*.

> In the daily life of my office, I sometimes hear opinions which disturb me. They are expressed by people who, zealous though they be, lack prudence and judgment in their evaluation of human events. They can see nothing but calamity and disaster in the present state of the world. Over and over again, they say that this modern age of ours, in comparison with past ages, is disintegrating. I feel that I must disagree with these prophets of doom who are always forecasting even worse disasters, as though the end of the world were at hand.... may God keep us from so exaggerating that we come to believe that the heavens have closed over our heads, that darkness has fallen over all the world, and that there is nothing left for us to do but weep as we plod along. Instead, we must take courage. God has made people and nations curable![7]

The Pope's message seems as relevant a half-century later as when published in 1967. At that time, Lewinski was entering the seminary.

Early November brought news from Bishop Kicanas. After six years as auxiliary bishop, he was leaving to become Coadjutor Bishop of Tucson, Arizona. Kicanas had presided over several functions at St. Mary's, most recently the Groundbreaking Ceremony in March 2000. The parish, and Lewinski, would miss his influence.

Meanwhile, the parking lot and Emmaus Drive entryway had been paved, and external brickwork was underway. They were trying to complete as much outside work as possible before winter.

By November's Pastoral Council meeting, the five topics they had been concentrating on had expanded into two dozen areas of discussion. Common ideas among them included communication; taking ownership; methods of providing physical, spiritual and psychological support; and scripture study and reflection.

On December 9th, Lewinski reported in his column the History Committee had made progress. "After much research, we have pinpointed an area between Strasbourg, France and Nuremberg, Germany, where many of our parish ancestors claimed their roots. Now, in celebration of the Dedication of our new church, we are planning a European Pilgrimage which will take us to the cities and villages and countryside where our parish ancestors once lived. In Hausen, Germany, we will be greeted by local residents and establish a 'sister Parish' relationship. We will thank God for the faith and courage that led our ancestors to found St. Mary - Fremont Center. Our Pilgrimage will depart on October 1, 2002, and return to Chicago on October 12. Brochures will be available at the parish office. What a nice Christmas present this would make."

Lewinski's Christmas column summarized their steps so far.

> A Blessed Christmas to you and your loved ones! ...
>
> It's a great Christmas for us at St. Mary's this year because we have so much for which to give thanks. We are blessed with a congregation of 1400 households who make St. Mary a hospitable, faith-filled community. We can boast of a vibrant lay leadership found in a diversity of ministries, special services and educational and faith-building programs that serve a wide geographic area. We have a super pastoral staff that stands ready to serve and facilitate countless activities. We thank God for an excellent Catholic School and Religious Education Program. We are pleased to offer shelter for the homeless every Wednesday night, to participate in Habitat for Humanity and reach out in various ways to the needy. Most of all, this year we give thanks for the construction of our new church and pastoral center that is nearing completion.
>
> The decision to build was made five years ago. Since then, we've undergone an intensive planning process and fundraising effort. We knew we had to build for the future. Since we began, the size of the parish has grown from 600 families in 1996 to more than 1400 today.
>
> The challenge was to build a church that could seat at least 900 people with an architectural design that would blend in with the rest of the campus. We eventually chose a design that is reminiscent of buildings in our rural heritage, with lines that follow the outline of our old church. Parishioners asked that the new church might relate to the land and its beautiful landscape. The use of glass accomplishes this by bringing the outside in. The plans for walking paths and outdoor shrines also recognize the outdoors as sacred space. The hospitable people of St. Mary wanted an ample space to gather before and after Mass with one entry so that everyone could meet each other. The beautiful and elegant narthex in the center of the building accommodates this value. There's an element of surprise built into the design. When you walk into the church through the 11-foot-high ceremonial doors, a sweeping sanctuary soars upward to a height of fifty feet. The beautiful use of granite, different woods and tile create an environment that is prayerful, dignified and uplifting. The splendid, noble Eucharistic Chapel, that you can see on the far west end, will be used to reserve the Blessed Sacrament and will without a doubt become one of the most well-loved prayer spaces in the parish. You can anticipate the raising of the 50-foot-high steeple in January and a solemn dedication in the Spring.
>
> Yes, we are blessed indeed! The new building is a witness to the vitality of our community that is grateful for the past and committed to the future.... I hope you can see in this time of growth and transition, a fresh invitation to become an ever more intimate partner in the life and mission of St. Mary Parish. As proud as we are of what we are building, our greatest asset is the community itself.[8]

They were close to achieving what had been only a vague dream a few years earlier.

[1] The original church from 1864 was located a few miles south along Fremont Center Road, close to where it joined Rt. 176. Afterwards, a new church—the existing church when Lewinski came to the parish—was built in 1889. It took five years for them to move the graves, one by one, to the new location.

[2] *The Bell*, Vol. I, Issue 10, September, 2001, p. 10.

[3] Sunday bulletin, July 1, 2001, p. 4.

[4] Sunday bulletin, July 15, 2001, p. 3.

[5] Sunday bulletin, August 26, 2001, p. 3.

[6] Sunday bulletin, September 23, 2001, p. 3. See Images #38 and 39.

[7] Sunday bulletin, October 14, 2001, p. 3.

[8] Sunday bulletin, December 24, 2001, p. 3.

CROSS BLESSING

Winter 2002

In early 2002, the cross for the steeple arrived. Members of the Men of St. Joseph carefully unpacked it. It was made of two heavy cylindrical steel crossbeams. Together, they carried it to the foot of the altar shortly before the blessing ceremony on January 6, 2002. Six years had passed since Lewinski arrived at the parish. Tonight they honored this cross. It would be a crowning symbol of what he and the parish had achieved during his first term as pastor.

Lewinski wore gold-colored vestments while officiating at the special occasion. The service bore Lewinski's unmistakable imprint, beginning with a prayer.[1] "We gather tonight much like friends might gather around a campfire to tell their favorite stories and share their personal memories. At this important juncture in the life of our parish, it is good for us to remember our past, to remember what we are all about, and to be reminded about what our faith calls us to be. Listen to the excerpts that follow much as you'd listen to a loved one sharing their heart."

Choir member Jim Robinson announced from the loft, "From a letter written by Father James Morrissey, pastor of St. Mary's from 1967 through 1983, to Lewinski in 1996.[2] Father Morrissey died on Christmas Day in 1998." Robinson read:

> I was happy to have the opportunity to see the new look of the parish where I spent sixteen happy years. It is interesting to know that the parish is beginning a new life to meet the needs of a wonderful old parish that is having a second spring. I can see that the beautiful little church which everybody loves also needs a larger partner to accommodate so many who have lived there for years and so many more who have been added to the family. St. Mary's has a great past and a very interesting and exciting future. It means a lot to those who are pioneer families, and it promises much to those who have arrived in later years and those who are yet to come. God bless all your efforts as a family which show such great promise.

After his reading and each of the subsequent readings, the choir chanted a chorus, and the assembly sang the refrain.

Mary Ann Przytula, a schoolteacher, read from the *Dogmatic Constitution on the Church* from the Second Vatican Council:

> Gathered together in the people of God and established in the one body of Christ under one head, the laity are called as living members to apply to the building up of the Church and its continental sanctification all the powers which they have received from the goodness of the Creator and from the grace of the Redeemer.
>
> The apostolate of the laity is a sharing in the Church's saving mission. Through Baptism and Confirmation, all are appointed to this apostolate by the Lord himself. Moreover, by the Sacraments, and especially by the sacred Eucharist, that love of God and humanity which is the soul of the entire apostolate, is communicated and nourished.
>
> The laity, however, are given this special vocation: to make the Church present and fruitful in those places and circumstances where it is only through them that it can become the salt of the earth. Thus, all lay people, through the gifts which they have received, are at once the witnesses and the living instruments of the mission of the Church itself according to the measure of Christ's gift.

Next, lector Jon Matousek—who a decade hence would lead a dozen parishes through the Parish Transformation process that resulted from Lewinski's work—read from the Church's rite for blessing a new cross:

> Of all the sacred images, the figure of the precious, life–giving cross of Christ is pre-eminent because it is the symbol of the Paschal mystery. The cross is the image most cherished by the Christian people and the most ancient; it represents Christ's suffering and victory, and at the same time, as the Fathers of the Church have taught, it points to his second coming.
>
> The cross is the sign under which people gather whenever they come to church, and in the homes of the baptized, it holds a place of honor. When the times and local conditions permit, the faithful erect a cross in a public place as an attestation of their faith and a reminder of the love with which God has loved us.

Art teacher Kris Crotty read from a recently published document, *Built of Living Stones, guidelines for art and architecture* by the National Conference of Catholic Bishops:

> What makes a church different from any other building is not its form or shape but rather how it facilitates for a particular community of believers a regular unfolding of the Christian mystery, the eternal divine plan for humanity as revealed in the person of Jesus Christ. Eucharistic assemblies, housed in church buildings, have Jesus Christ at their center. He is the Word spoken by divine mystery, the beloved Son of the Father, the head of the community of believers, and the prophet who challenges and inspires them to live for God and neighbor. Every church built for the people of God unfolds his presence.

Another choir member, Liz Knuth, recited a passage about an earlier pastor—himself a pivotal pastor in his time. "Listen now to the words of Cardinal Stritch":

> Fr. Bernard Laukemper was pastor of St. Mary - Fremont Center from 1927 to 1932. He preached and celebrated Mass in the church. He was an enthusiastic and strong leader who initiated a number of changes at the parish and became one of the pioneers of liturgical reform long before the Second Vatican Council. At his funeral on March 9, 1949, Samuel Cardinal Stritch praised the work of Fr. Laukemper. We remember Fr. Laukemper tonight as a reminder of the great tradition of St. Mary - Fremont Center, a tradition we continue to build upon today.
>
> Fr. Laukemper loved the liturgy, loved the spirit of the liturgy, and wanted his people to see how beautiful is the worship of God in the liturgy of the Church. He loved the sacred chant. He trained his choir. Everything about us here today proclaims this good pastor's efforts to try to bring his people to see what he saw when Mass was celebrated, and to call, as the Church wants us to call, all the sacred arts together to proclaim in the beautiful observances of the liturgy, something that is a worthy thing, as far as we can make it a worthy thing to offer to Almighty God.
>
> We build our churches, and we build our churches beautifully. And so, in love, we give God our beautiful churches. But our churches are just shells, and their beauty mocks unless, in our churches, the work of God takes place—the sacred liturgy.
>
> But I think that this great priest of God, whose death we mourn this morning, did a good thing in that he emphasized among us what can be done even in a small parish, where there are no great marbles, or no great stretch of arches, to bring the Church into the liturgy, and to bring the liturgy into the souls of the people.[3]

Lewinski resumed. "All that we have heard in some way defines who we are as a people of faith. While our individual experiences as Catholics may be quite diverse, what holds us together is the cross of Jesus. That cross will rise upward 100 feet as a testimony to this community's faith and solidarity in Christ. Let us now ask God's blessing upon this cross that will be placed on the steeple later this week." The assembly stood, and Lewinski prayed.

> Blessed are you, Lord God, Father all-holy,
> for your boundless love.
> The tree, once the source of shame and death for humankind,
> has become the cross of our redemption and life.
>
> When his hour had come to return to you in glory,
> the Lord Jesus, our King, our Priest, and our Teacher,
> freely mounted the scaffold of the cross
> and made it his royal throne,
> his altar of sacrifice, his pulpit of truth.

On the cross, lifted above the earth,
he triumphed over our age-old enemy.
Cloaked in his own blood,
he drew all things to himself.

On the cross, he opened his arms
and offered you his life:
The Sacrifice of the New Law
that gives to the sacraments their saving power.

On the cross,
he proved what he had prophesied:
the grain of wheat must die
to bring forth an abundant harvest.

Father,
we honor this cross
as the sign of our redemption.
May we reap the harvest of salvation
planted in pain by Christ Jesus.
May our sins be nailed to his cross,
the power of life released,
pride conquered, and weakness turned to strength.

As we prepare to place this cross above our church,
may it be our comfort in times of trouble,
our refuge in the face of danger,
our safeguard on life's journey,
until you welcome us to our heavenly home.

Then parishioners processed up the center aisle and individually venerated the cross. Lewinski sat, observing. When they had finished, he stood and recited the concluding prayer:

Almighty God,
you have built your Church from living stones.
We pray that as we place this cross
on the steeple of our new church,
we may be found ready
to live the mystery of the cross in our daily lives.
As we look forward with joy to the Day of Dedication,
we pray that you would renew our hearts,
strengthen our faith
and deepen our resolve to please you in all things.
We ask this through Christ our Lord. Amen.

Lewinski finished with, "I hope that as you look upon the cross, you will indeed see yourself as a very intimate part of the mystery of what that cross is all about. I hope you will stay afterward for the reception downstairs. Some wonderful goodies are prepared, and it is a time for fellowship. Also, we have available our own parish coloring book." The book was one of Lewinski's ways of engaging the children in the project. They were as much a part of the community as the adults while building a church for future generations.[4]

"The Lord be with you. May Almighty God bless you with this cross. May He continue to bless your families with peace and good health, and may He bring our parish to a wonderful day of dedication in, joy and hopefulness. May God bless you always, in the name of the Father and the Son and the Holy Spirit. Let us go forth in peace."

The choir sang a final hymn, and the service concluded.

In the first bulletin of 2002, Lewinski offered "Reflection #1." The topic was "church" as a building; and "Church" as a temple built of living stones. Both had always been a dual goal for Lewinski from the start of his mission at St. Mary. As a contemporary observed, "We are not a Church which has a mission, but rather a mission which has a Church."[5]

Lewinski apologized to those unable to find a seat for the Christmas Eve celebration. The fire department's prohibitions were observed for everyone's safety. The old church had experienced one Christmas fire in its history, which was quickly extinguished. A year hence, space would no longer be a problem.

In the bulletin a week later, Lewinski recalled:

> Our celebration around the cross on January 6th will have a special meaning for me as it marks my sixth anniversary as your pastor. It was on Epiphany Sunday in 1996 that I formally became pastor of St. Mary's.... It has been a wonderful, rewarding experience to shepherd the people of St. Mary's. I begin my second term of office as we look forward to a new church and pastoral offices. The future looks bright and promising.
> "Last Sunday's Prayer Around the Cross was a very moving service. In a ritual that was simple but rich, we began the transition into our new church by transforming the six-foot stainless steel cross into a symbol that spoke for our lives. I was moved by the way children and adults processed to the cross and reverenced the cross with a kiss, a touch, a genuflection, or a bow. Without words, we expressed what we believe and gave witness to what holds us together. I was so proud of St. Mary Parish. The faith of this community was shining brightly last Sunday.[6]

His "Reflection #2" spoke of the physical and spiritual journey between home and church. He recalled the intent behind the drive onto the campus and the walk into the church as he had described it to the Pastoral Council during their prior June tour.

The name of the long driveway off Erhart Rd. onto the new parish campus is called Emmaus Drive. It recalls the post-resurrection account (Luke 24: 13-35).

Each time we make our way to the church, we will be retracing the path of those two disciples on the road to Emmaus, believing that we, too, will encounter the Lord as we come to hear his word and break the Bread of Eucharist. After parking our cars, we will walk up the paved processional path that leads to the church's front doors. This offers a personal transition for us from all that we have been busy with back home to this gathering of God's Church in prayer. One might rightly say that the procession to the Altar begins when we leave our homes, travel up Emmaus Drive, and make our way up the processional walkway.

It is important that we come to the Altar with the proper disposition so that we can participate with all our mind and heart and be receptive to all that the Lord can do for us.[7]

On Thursday, January 10, 2002, a crew placed the steeple, also called the "spire," atop the roof. This brought the structure's highest point to 100 feet above the ground. Then, the cross blessed four days earlier was secured into the spire's tip.

If there was any doubt before, there could be no more. This structure was a church. For many of those present, it made worthwhile their hard work and sacrifice over the past six years.

It was a stunning achievement for those who had been at the parish when Lewinski arrived. Who could have known that the size of their campus would quadruple? In this rural farming community, what parishioner would claim they would execute a $10 million fundraising campaign? Who would have predicted a new church four times larger than in 1996, designed by a world-class architect? These would have seemed like foolish premonitions of an Old Testament prophet. "That's impossible" would have been an understandable response.

A full-color picture of the steeple being hoisted into position captioned "Crowning Glory," was featured on the Daily Herald's front page on January 11th. "Spiritual faith possesses no time limit," read the article. "But for the 100 parishioners who waited five hours for construction crews to place the towering steeple on top of the new $10 million St. Mary Fremont Center church, the wait was a test of patience."

The steeple raising was expected to occur at 9 a.m. but was delayed until about 2 p.m. while the construction crews made final adjustments. "The steeple is very important to us," Lewinski noted. "It's the symbol that everyone in the parish can identify with." Parishioners attending the unveiling said the event was something they had to see with their own eyes. "It's something that happens only once in a lifetime," said Grayslake resident Edward Swieszek.[8]

Lewinski's third Reflection, on January 20th, was about the doors to the Sanctuary. He wrote, "Standing in the narthex, where the community gathers and is able to greet one another, one sees the unusually large ceremonial doors that lead into the church proper. These imposing three-dimensional entry doors, crafted out of three different natural wood species, form the threshold between our ordinary daily activity and a place where heaven and earth meet. Think of the many important doors or thresholds through which you have walked and which led you into a new world. To walk through these doors is to enter into a realm where God resides in a special way."[9]

Lewinski reported Cardinal George had appointed him to St. Mary for a second term. This followed what the corporate world called a 360-degree performance appraisal.

"I participated," he wrote, "in an extensive review process facilitated by the Archdiocese. Approximately fifty parishioners were chosen randomly to offer their comments, observations, and evaluations of my ministry. The Archdiocesan Office of Ministerial Evaluation, the Episcopal Vicar and Dean, the Clergy Personnel Board, and Cardinal George reviewed all the reports. I found the review helpful as it affirmed my strengths and offered some direction for ongoing development."[10]

Meanwhile, they offered the opportunity to purchase paver stones for the garden on the Narthex's north side. Though a minor fundraiser, it gave parishioners a chance to literally memorialize a piece of the parish. The terrace would be an explorable record etched with memories. The pavers would be visible reminders in the coming decades of people who had acknowledged this significant time in the parish's history.[11]

Lewinski continued his series about the Rite of Dedication. It was two months away. Everyone deserved to understand the ceremony. Understanding the logistics was, in fact, something of a work in process for him. He acknowledged to the Pastoral Council in February the challenge of planning the choreography and liturgy in a space where they have never before celebrated anything.

Reflection #4 by Lewinski addressed the baptismal font's design. "When you walk through the ceremonial doors, you will find yourself before the baptismal font. Before we can come to the Lord's Table, the baptismal font calls us to conversion. Even long after our baptism, we routinely approach this font on the way to the altar to place our hand in the water and then consciously and deliberately sign ourselves in a gesture of baptismal re-commitment. When we die, they will carry our casket into

CROSS BLESSING

the church and stop at this font one last time to sprinkle our body with the water that holds the promise of our inheritance."[12]

Lewinski commented on the "positive and productive" Town Hall conducted on January 17th. One idea was a recommendation to change the Mass schedule because there is more space in the new church. A shortage of space had been a primary reason for building. The old church held just over 200, while the new one could seat almost 900.

Another concern was the ongoing use of the old church. Lewinski claimed it would continue as a worship space instead of being converted to meeting space. The old basement and the new facilities should provide the needed space going forward.

A third issue "was about the entry sign off Erhart Road onto Emmaus Drive, the roadway that leads to the new parking lot. It should be clear by now that the canonical title (official Church title) of our parish is "St. Mary of the Annunciation."[13]

A fourth item was dedicating the music room to a former pastor. "Father Laukemper was pastor of St. Mary's from 1927 to 1932. Under his leadership, a basement was dug out under the current church, and electric lights replaced the kerosene lamps. Father Laukemper was a man ahead of his time. He was one of the early pioneers of liturgical renewal in the United States. His love for the liturgy prompted him to teach parishioners about their role in the liturgy. He promoted a choir, changed German sermons into English, and became well-known beyond Chicago for his involvement in the renewal of the liturgy. He chaired the First National Liturgical Conference at Holy Name Cathedral in 1940. Because he died before he could see all his dreams realized (in 1949) at the Second Vatican Council, Fr. Laukemper never quite received the recognition he deserved.

"We are proud to claim him as one of St. Mary's pastors. We propose to name our new music room the 'Laukemper Room' to honor this great man and our precious heritage."[14]

In Reflection #5, Lewinski related the next step in the Rite of Dedication: a proclamation by Cardinal George followed by readings from scripture (Nehemiah 8: 1-10; 1 Peter 1: 17-21; and Luke 24: 13-35).

Reflection #6 mentioned the Litany of the Saints, the Solemn Prayer of Dedication, and the Anointing of the Altar and the Walls of the church. In his column, Lewinski commented, "The rhythm and discipline of Lent not only leads us to Easter this year but to a new church."

The bulletin posted a reminder that a month later, on March 16th, the cornerstone plaque would be installed on an outside wall.[15]

A photo of the new church's steel framework occupied the Daily Herald's front page on January 31st. An article accompanied it. "The drawing is starting to translate into reality," said the Rev. Ken Kiepura, St. Mary's associate pastor. "To see that steel superstructure, everything starts to take more shape. ... The whole idea of getting into a church that is designed for worship space is exciting for everyone," he said.[16]

Lewinski was always aware of the need to educate people before taking action. He also recognized the need for socialization. During a Pastoral Council meeting in January, he noted the need for social events and celebrations. It was important for a parish undergoing change like St. Mary's to ensure a continued feeling of community.

The parish conducted its third Gala, "Cornerstone to Our Future," on March 2, 2002. It was $5,000 more profitable than the previous year's. This event required far fewer people to produce and was more profitable on a dollar-per-worker basis than the annual Pork and Corn Roast. Not to mention it was immune to changes in weather and was air-conditioned. They planned the next Gala, a Mardi Gras ball, for March 1, 2003. Most attendees of prior Galas were looking forward to it.

Lewinski wanted all the artwork being considered for the church to be, like bread and wine, the work of human hands. During his national and international travels, he was always open to a source of artistic inspiration. He sometimes traveled several miles out of his way to satisfy his curiosity. His desire for artisan quality applied even to pieces that seemed ornamental and duplicated, such as the cross-shaped candle holders on the pillars in the sanctuary.

His Reflection #7 explained how four priests would assist the Cardinal during the blessing of the walls. "The priests will anoint the walls in twelve places. A cross will mark the place where each anointing will be made. On festive days, twelve candles will be lit as a reminder to us that the church is an image of the splendor of the heavenly city of Jerusalem. The anointed walls of the church signify that this building is given over entirely and perpetually to Christian worship."[17]

In Reflection #8, Lewinski wrote, "The Rite of Dedication makes an interesting point about the incensation. The incensation of the church building indicates that the dedication makes it a house of prayer, but the people of God are incensed first because they are the living temple in which each member is a spiritual altar."[18]

Lewinski explained the next part of the Rite of Dedication in Reflection #9. "The glowing light of the altar candle will be extended to twelve parish representatives who will each take a burning candle to one of the twelve crosses on the walls which were just anointed. This ceremonial lighting of the church reminds us of Christ, who is a light to the nations and whose brightness shines out in the Church and through it upon the whole human family."[19]

In Reflection #10, Lewinski noted the celebration of the Eucharist on the day of Dedication is no different than on any Sunday, except this is the first celebration in a new church. "From this day forward, it will be a house of prayer. The celebration of the sacrifice of the Mass is our most important act of worship. The assembly's seating around the altar gives witness to our role as active participants in the liturgy, an exercise of the priesthood of the faithful."[20]

Lewinski's Reflection #11 explained the transfer of the ciborium (bowl containing the consecrated hosts) to the Tabernacle in the Eucharistic Chapel. His next comments echoed his reminders to the trio of strangers who had challenged him during the July 1997 walk-through. "We reserve the Eucharist first of all so that we may take Communion to the sick and dying. We also reserve the Blessed Sacrament so that parishioners may have the opportunity of coming before the Eucharistic Presence for private prayer and adoration."[21]

In his column, Lewinski wrote about a ritual to honor the transition from the old church to the new.

> Beginning Easter Monday, April 1st, we will set up a Book of Memories in the old church. From April 1st to the day of the Dedication, we will encourage parishioners to stop into the old church for private prayer. Thank God for your memories of being part of St. Mary Parish. Express your gratitude to God for all that the 1889 place of worship has meant to you and your family. Write a prayer or share a memory in the Book of Memories. Let it be our communal journal. May it be a book of prayer we offer to God. This book will become part of our sacred history so that generations to come will know what was in our hearts as we prepared for the Dedication.[22]

The work that Lewinski had been doing with parishioner Ed Hendricks had resulted in an organized description of the church's features called "*A Walk Through the Church of St. Mary of the Annunciation at Fremont Center.*" It was used to train docents who would provide guided tours of the facility. On February 25th, a letter from Hendricks and Council member Jeanne Rutledge announced the first informational overview for volunteers to be held on March 11th. Critics could regard this exercise as an example of a pastor's ambitious pride. For Lewinski, however, it was another method of educating people about the significance of certain features and the reasoning behind them. He knew that people's experience of something is enriched by understanding it.

On Palm Sunday, Lewinski's column underscored the season's significance:

> I encourage you to make the effort to participate in the liturgies of the Triduum. This year, as we anticipate the Dedication of our church, the Triduum celebration takes on a special meaning. What we do in these Three Days of prayer and ritual will prepare us for a new beginning in a new sacred space. We are all busy people these days, but making the Triduum a priority is important for us individually and as a community.[23]

The front page article in *The Bell* in March, Issue #11, was "The Architecture of the New St. Mary Church" by Dirk Lohan, FAIA (Fellow of the American Institute of Architects). It was reprinted and shared in several ways during the upcoming months. Another article reviewed the significant accomplishments during the project. The narrative reinforced the parish's achievements. It recalled the many ways parishioners were able to be part of a historic undertaking.

The center spread featured photos of the steeple installation. Given the wind gusts and the number of observers, the decision to use a crane was a more prudent choice than a helicopter.

Another article outlined the parts of the Rite of Dedication of a Church, providing more insight. The "Q's from the Pews" had one answer to the questions, "Will the old church still be used? Will there be a new Mass schedule? Will there be child care? Will there be sufficient parking?" The answer was "Yes."

Another important question was: Will the elderly and physically challenged find it difficult to maneuver in the new church and pastoral center? The answer: no. Hallelujah!

One article's description of St. Mary's pastor sounded familiar. The pastor contributed greatly to the spiritual development of the congregation and enhancement of the liturgy. He was innovative, hard-working, and passionate about the liturgy. He began a choir; installed an organ; and was a liturgical reformer. He encouraged his flock to pray the Mass and actively participate. He celebrated the liturgy facing the congregation and introduced entrance and offertory processions.

This, however, was not Lewinski. It was Fr. Bernard Laukemper, pastor from 1927 to 1932—six decades prior. In honor of his visionary contributions, St. Mary's named the music room "The Laukemper Room."

One day, Lewinski would be similarly honored.

---

[1] Parish Archives. This and subsequent passages are from the ceremony's document titled "Prayer Around the Cross."

[2] When Morrissey arrived, Lewinski was just entering the seminary. The parish had about 150 households. By 1971, the number increased to 200, then to 300 by 1980. The growth continued during Fr. Keusal's terms from 1983-1995. —Gannon, p. 54.

[3] Cardinal Stritch's comments about Fr. Laukemper resemble those of Cardinal Cupich in 2017 when he stated "To worship in this church is to be in the presence of Fr. Ron Lewinski." He was referring to Lewinski's inspired influence on the art and design of the building.

[4] During the project, there were multiple efforts to involve the children via classroom visits, a coloring book of simplified drawings of the planned art and architecture, and surveys asking children for their opinions and ideas. Cultures see a new generation as a reason for hope. Some, like Native American communities, also gain insight from youth. Resources were precious and a tribe's survival was dependent on cooperation among all of its members. Whenever an important matter required consideration, the tribe would gather around the central fire to speak of what was in their hearts and to listen to the words and wisdom of others. Interestingly, even children had a place in the circle. Their voices were as respected as those of the elders. The tribal leadership knew that there were some things only young eyes could see.

[5] Hinohosa, Dr. Juan. Quoted in "Laity: rewrite life's script," *The New World*, May 17, 1998, p. 4. Hinohosa facilitated one of the Parish Council's formation meetings.

[6] Sunday bulletin, January 13, 2002, p. 3. Lewinski had earlier related during a Pastoral Council meeting the prior August that he had submitted his request for a second term.

[7] Ibid.

[8] Daily Herald, January 11, 2002, pp 1 & 13.

[9] Sunday bulletin, January 20, 2002, p. 1.

[10] Sunday bulletin, January 20, 2002, p. 3.

[11] Some of Lewinski's classmates also built churches. Fr. Bob Tonelli recalls building St. John the Evangelist in Streamwood, Illinois about the same time Lewinski was building St. Mary's. "Ron gave me an idea when we were building. They were about to lay the tile inside. He asked 'Have you thought about having the parishioners see it from the inside and have them write a prayer on the cement before they install the carpet and tile. That's one way for them to take ownership.' So we did that in March 2002. There was a phenomenal reaction. It is a once-in-a-lifetime experience. I watched these people—the children, parents, old people, whoever. After all the Masses were over, I went in at the end of the day, late at night, and I started reading the prayers. I was so overwhelmed that I was crying. These people let their faith shine through their prayers. They had made it their own. It was Ron's idea." —Tonelli, Bob. Personal conversation, February 2, 2022.

[12] Sunday bulletin, January 27, 2002, p. 1.

[13] Lewinski had observed the name on parish annual reports from the 1880s.

[14] Ibid., p. 3.

[15] Sunday bulletin, February 10, 2002, p. 3.

[16] Daily Herald, January 31, 2002, pp. 1 & 6.

[17] Sunday bulletin, February 17, 2002, p. 1.

[18] Sunday bulletin, February 24, 2002, p. 1.

[19] Sunday bulletin, March 3, 2002, p. 1.

[20] Sunday bulletin, March 10, 2002, p. 1.

[21] Sunday bulletin, March 17, 2002, p. 1.

[22] Sunday bulletin, March 17, 2002, p. 3.

[23] Sunday bulletin, March 25, 2002, p. 3.

CORNERSTONE DEDICATION

March 2002

They installed the cornerstone on March 16, 2002, at the church's southeast corner. Several dozen parishioners gathered on a sunny Saturday morning at the front entrance to the new church, near where the future bell tower would be located. The group might have been larger except for the weather. Despite blue skies and puffy clouds, it was quite brisk and windy. Most of the few dozen people attending—aged four to seventy—were bundled in gloves, scarves and winter coats. If their coat had a hood, it was up. Parents sheltered their children. The sun's warmth on exposed faces and hands vanished with each gust of wind.

Bishop Jerome Listecki, newly appointed Vicar for the area, presided. Lewinski and Deacon Bob Poletto assisted him. They were robed in white for the occasion. Fred Vipond and some choir members were present. Jim Richards and an assistant, from the construction firm, were on hand to secure the cornerstone into place. A portion of the concrete wall was exposed in the exterior brickwork, where the plaque would be cemented. Within it, another small cavity about four inches square was an oddity with no apparent use. Its function was, however, significant for Lewinski. He'd soon explain why.

Listecki extended his welcome. "It is a wonderful privilege to be here to bless this cornerstone because of its significance to this parish in so many different ways. It is a mark, and it is a tribute to the past and so many individuals who came in the dead of night to offer the sacrifice of the Mass with the priest and to establish a community here, going back to 1864. You can imagine the general spirit; they are, and they continue to be a witness to the presence of our Lord's community.

"It is a celebration of the present community here because of your accomplishments, pulling together under the direction of your pastor to build a beautiful church. It is a celebration of the work that can be accomplished when you join yourself to Christ: everything is possible through him. And it is a sign of hope for the future because it is a testimony to our world—a testimony to a world that needs witness, that needs to see his presence and people who believe in him and are dedicated to him, with the hope and understanding that this world will be touched directly by him, and our community and society will be changed by him. It is a hope that his presence will be here, making that statement for the future. Let us pray."

He turned to the prepared script held by an altar server. He read, "Lord, you built a holy Church and founded upon the apostles and Jesus Christ his cornerstone, grant that your people gathered here in your name may fear and love you and grow in the temple of your glory. May they always follow you until, with you at their head, they arrive at last in the heavenly city. We ask this through Jesus Christ our Lord. Amen."

Deacon Poletto read from the Acts of the Apostles (4:8-12). "Then Peter, filled with the Holy Spirit, answered them, Leaders of the people and elders: If we are being examined today about a good deed done to a cripple, namely, by what means he was saved, then all of you and all the people of Israel should know that it was in the name of Jesus Christ the Nazarean whom you crucified, whom God raised from the dead; in his name, this man stands before you healed. He is the stone rejected by you, the builders, which has become the cornerstone. There is no salvation through anyone else, nor is there any other name under heaven given to the human race by which we are to be saved."

Fred Vipond led the choir and chimes in a short hymn, after which Listecki read from the Gospel of St. Luke (6:46-49). "Why do you call me 'Lord' but not do what I command? I will show you what someone is like who comes to me, listens to my words, and acts on them. That one is like a person building a house, who dug deeply and laid the foundation on rock; when the flood came, the river burst against that house but could not shake it because it had been well built. But the one who listens and does not act is like a person who built a house on the ground without a foundation. When the river burst against it, it collapsed at once and was completely destroyed."

"When a bride prepares for a wedding," resumed Listecki, "usually everybody gathers around. They say you know what you need— something old, something borrowed, something new, something blue. Remember that? A lot of the brides here remember." Knowing chuckles from the ladies confirmed this.

"This," he said, pointing toward the church and the assembly, "is the bride of Christ. You listen to scripture. You listen to references. They talk about the Church being 'the bride of Christ.' So help to dedicate this bride this morning. Something old is not simply embodied in the parish tradition going back to 1864. Father Ron has something else to add."

He motioned toward Lewinski, who displayed a stone in his hand. Lewinski explained, "We led a parish group on pilgrimage to Israel two years ago. We brought back with us a stone from Nazareth. In addition to the plaque that we are putting up, we are going to put a piece of Nazareth into our church as well. So we will connect with an old tradition: the Annunciation of our namesake." He handed the stone to an altar server.

Listecki resumed his remarks. "So there is our old. Next, something borrowed." He paused. "Of course, there is a debt on the building." They returned laughter. *"Big debt."*

He hastened, remembering the chill. "We've got something old, something borrowed, and what is new? New is the church and the community that is called to celebrate it. As in the gospel, unless we build a foundation, it doesn't matter how beautiful the edifice is. The real spirit and soul of the Church is found right here," he motioned toward the people. "People who are dedicated and willing to work through Christ as community. Without you, the building is a museum piece; it is nothing more than artistic creation or an architectural design. This," he proclaimed, again pointing toward the crowd, "is the soul—literally the spirit of Jesus living in this community.

"Now, how about blue? Well, God provided that, if we look up to the heavens," he gestured toward a mostly blue sky with scattered puffs of clouds. "And some cold weather. Our hands are turning a little blue.

"So we have prepared our bride," he continued, hand outstretched touching the corner of the church, "to be the spouse of Christ in this community and a mother to care for her children, as God helps this family to grow and be nurtured and strengthened. As this area's new Vicar, I am privileged to bless this cornerstone."

Listecki and Lewinski then moved to the vacancy on the wall reserved for the cornerstone. As the bishop read the prepared text, Lewinski accepted the Nazarean stone from an altar server who had been holding it.

"Father," read Listecki, referring to the Almighty, "the prophet Daniel spoke of your son as a stone wondrously hewn from a mountain; the apostle Paul spoke of him as a stone firmly founded. Bless this foundation stone, this plaque to be laid in Christ's name. You appointed him the beginning and the end of all things. May the construction of this Stone and this Church continue to be brought to fulfillment in him, for He is Lord forever and ever. Amen."

He blessed the cornerstone with holy water. "With faith in Jesus Christ, we place this foundation stone plaque into the wall of this building that will soon become a house of prayer, a church for today and generations to come. May it become a holy place for word and sacrament, a source of grace to the glory of the Father, who with the Son and the Holy Spirit, lives and reigns forever and ever."

The assembly responded, "Amen." Next, the choir sang to the accompaniment of chimes while Richards and his assistant secured the

Nazarean stone into the niche. Then, they applied adhesive to the concrete before positioning the cornerstone plaque.

Listecki continued when they had finished. "Brothers and Sisters, now that we have placed this cornerstone plaque in the new church of St. Mary of the Annunciation, let us humbly pray to God."

Here Lewinski recited prayer verses interspersed with the assembly singing the refrain "Bless and watch over your Church, oh Lord."

"That God may transform into a living temple of his glory all whom he has gathered here and look upon Christ as the cornerstone of their faith; we pray to the Lord.

"That God in his power may overcome the sin and the division which separate his people so that they may ultimately worship as one; we pray to the Lord.

"That God may grant upon the bedrock of his Church the faith of all those who have undertaken the work of this building and those who have sacrificed to fund this work; we pray to the Lord.

"That those who are prevented from building places of worship may not grow discouraged, but continue to build witness to the Lord by conducting themselves as living temples of faith; we pray to the Lord.

"That God may embrace our parish with His love, cleanse us from all sin, and bring us to the day of dedication as a people renewed in faith; we pray to the Lord.

"Let us join the voice of the Church with that of Christ as we pray." Everyone joined him in the Lord's Prayer.

Then, Listecki continued, "God of love, we praise your holy name, for you have made us your temple by baptism and inspire us to build on earth churches dedicated to your worship. Look favorably upon the people of St. Mary of the Annunciation, for they have come with joy to celebrate this important stage in the building of their new church. Enable them to grow into the temple of your glory until shaped anew by your grace; they are gathered by your hand into your heavenly city. We ask this through Christ our Lord. Amen.

"The Lord be with you. May we bow our heads and pray for God's blessing."

Listecki concluded with a blessing, "Let us go forth in the peace of Christ," to which all responded, "Thanks be to God."

Immediately there was a joyful chorus of hand chimes and applause. Lewinski stepped forward to ensure the bishop received proper acknowledgment for presiding at the ceremony. "I want to thank Bishop Listecki for joining us this morning and ask you to keep him and his family in your prayers. His mother died about a day ago and will be buried on Monday. It was very generous and kind of the bishop to join us despite this great loss in his family. I know you will also keep his mother and him in your prayers. Thank you."

It was sad news on an otherwise joyous occasion, but it did not diminish the event's importance or impact. The bishop affirmed it. "A wonderful moment," he observed, referring to the dedication. He repeated, "A wonderful moment." There was grateful applause.

The crowd dispersed to return to the warmth of their cars and homes. Another milestone had been reached on the path to completion.

The first weekend of April was the last when the old church would be "*the* church" at St. Mary of the Annunciation. Lewinski wrote, "I arrived at St. Mary - Fremont Center in January 1996. Within weeks, I heard again and again that we would have to do something to plan for the parish's future. By June 1996, there was a consensus to build a new church to accommodate the growing population. Now, after six years of planning, designing, fundraising, and construction, we are ready to dedicate a new church to the Almighty in honor of St. Mary of the Annunciation. This will be our new spiritual home where we will hear God's Word, offer the Eucharist, and celebrate our life in Christ.

"The Dedication of a church is a highly significant event in the life of a local community. The very fact that there is a church to dedicate is an indication that there is a Church of living stones that praises God and serves God in this locality. The church building, then, is a reflection of a deeper mystery—the mystery of our solidarity in Christ.

"I am grateful to everyone who has helped to make this project such a grand success. The names are too many to print in one bulletin. And that's how it should be, because this project belongs to us all.

"As we celebrate the good news of this Easter Season, may the Risen Lord continue to bless our community and fill our hearts with joy and hope. And may St. Mary of the Annunciation, who has watched over our parish since 1864, continue to watch over the people who claim her as their loving patroness.

"Let us Celebrate!"[1]

---

[1] Sunday bulletin, April 7, 2002, p. 3.

DEDICATION DAY

April 14, 2002

The key wasn't working, and all eyes were upon him. It was supposed to unlock the doors from the narthex into the sanctuary. This moment was an essential part of the Dedication Ceremony. Its importance arose from the symbolism of opening the worship space to all, not simply unlocking a door. It was no ordinary lock, and these were no ordinary doors. But they almost hadn't come into existence at all, and they surely didn't materialize in a way Lewinski expected.

He had always envisioned a grand entryway. He had often spoken about a noble entrance to the church. He knew from the beginning they should be more than standard doors. They needed to serve a purpose beyond physical security. During a Town Hall, he claimed the great cathedrals' entries were ornate, obvious, and overstated. They identified the way into a church and prepared a visitor for a different psychological reality.

Proper doors transition from the ordinary, everyday world outside a church to the special and purposeful spiritual realm in a sanctuary. Lohan shared Lewinski's regard for the experience of sacredness inside a church. He mentioned it during the project and even years afterward.

Lewinski had spent countless hours during this journey from vision to reality, imagining many aspects of the building. The baptismal font, the altar, the chapel for devotion, and the art and design of the sanctuary. And these doors. He had commented on them during a tour he'd given the Pastoral Council the prior June. "The importance of doors in the architecture of our church," he had explained, "is that they are not just a utilitarian 'functional' thing. The doors have always had a very symbolic meaning.

"That's why even now—you are familiar with some rites—when we baptize an infant during the Mass, we greet the parents at the door, the symbolic entry point into the life of the church. At the time of our death, we are greeted there for one last time as we are brought through the portal of the church itself—the church building representative of the people of God. When you travel through Europe, you see great cathedrals. Some of those doors are magnificent, with saints and angels carved all around them. What you are about to enter is another world, a taste of paradise, an 'already' but 'not yet' kind of existence. So we hope to convey that with the doors themselves."

Lohan also had regard for the sacred. He had grown up in Germany and was familiar with classic cathedrals. During a Town Hall presentation, when the conceptual design was first introduced, Lohan remarked, "One thing we all know—particularly your committee and Father Ron have always requested—is that the entry door is prominent, special, and unique. I totally agree. There will be a doorway that will let you know that this is not a house but a special way to enter a sacred building."

The project faced ongoing constraints of quality, time, and cost. As often happens, more and more concessions were required. Time and quality were valued in this project. The parish expected neither to suffer serious compromise. Choosing contractors, securing bids, selecting trades, and monitoring progress were the reins on the horses of time and quality.

The third principle of project management, cost, was always the most at-risk. Even before the start, it was the biggest and most challenging unknown. As the Capital Campaign proceeded and the total pledge amount increased, concerns over cost decreased, but they could never disappear. One by one, aspects of the project came under scrutiny. The fundamental question was, "Is it needed, or just nice?" It is the same dilemma most families regularly face, regardless of their financial status. Even if something falls into the "needed" category (which still harbors a degree of wishful thinking), they apply further criteria to satisfy the wish while respecting the wallet. Is second- or third-best acceptable if we can't get the best? To what extent can we lower our expectations and still be satisfied after we make a decision? Gradually, they revised or eliminated things in the project to stay within budget.

Lewinski may have recalled how they decided to eliminate these eleven-foot-high doors as he attempted to unlock the door. The project had begun, and pledges from the Capital Campaign began accumulating. He'd allowed himself to imagine what those entrance doors might look like. In eager anticipation, he had even shared a sketch with groups during his construction tours.

There came a time, however, to review priorities. The doors Lewinski had dreamed about moved from "need" to "nice" and finally to "not at all." He understood that a less expensive alternative would have to be acceptable. But broken hearts don't readily embrace the restraints of practicality.

Whether Lewinski prayed for a miracle is unknown. One happened anyway. A parishioner heard about the cost of the doors not fitting within the project's remaining budget. Wondering if they could somehow help, the parishioner asked about the cost.

The parishioner told their spouse about the doors being removed from the plan and Lewinski's disappointment. They contemplated it, but, despite their eagerness to help, they decided it was beyond their ability.

Then they remembered a "rainy day" bank account they had established long ago. Maybe they could use that money and ask other parishioners to cover the rest. When they checked the account balance, they realized it would not cover a *portion* of the cost. They were astonished when they saw that the amount in the account matched the quoted price of the doors!

To the penny.

They interpreted this as an obvious indicator of action. Initially, they had thought they would someday use it for home improvements, a vacation, donations to charities, or any number of purposes. Now, no decision was needed. The doors Lewinski dreamed of were back in the plans.

A key in a working lock was naturally part of the plan, but it seemed to present a challenge on—of all times—dedication day. Surely, someone had been thoughtful enough to test it before this moment. The key was unique and could not be confused with any other. It could not possibly fit any other lock in the building.

Lewinski inserted the oversized key and turned it as far as possible. He tugged on the door. The lock remained secure. He realized the only alternative was to turn the key in the opposite direction. Perhaps because of its size, the key seemed to need several turns before reaching a stopping point. Again, he tugged. This time, there was movement. The entire effort took just seconds, but for Lewinski it seemed longer.

When he realized he'd unlocked the door, he gave an approving nod to Stan Zagula from the Planning Commission. Zagula unlatched the inner slides, which secured the doors at the top and bottom. He proudly opened both doors to a full 180-degree arc so they were flat against the wall separating the narthex from the sanctuary. The assembly could now enter the church for the first time.

Shortly before, many people had entered the narthex after parading from the old church. A steer and a handful of cows watched from across Erhart Road as the people processed from the old church past the original steeple bell toward the new church. They could see the high glass structure of the narthex glistening beyond the cemetery's crest. Their route was identical to the one from the groundbreaking ceremony two years prior. Like then, today was also a bright sunny day and, fortunately, the strong westerly wind was diminished.

IMAGE #23

DEDICATION DAY

A CROWD AWAITS THE ARRIVAL OF THE PROCESSION FROM THE
OLD CHURCH TO THE NEW CHURCH, SIMILAR TO THE PROCESSION
DURING THE GROUNDBREAKING CEREMONY TWO YEARS PRIOR.

People gathered in the crowded parking lot, waiting for the procession. Latecomers were walking or—with children—running down Emmaus Drive on their way to the ceremony. Everyone wanted to enter the narthex.

Inside, Cardinal George watched while the choir finished their entry hymn, "Sing to the Lord on High; rejoice and give thanks and praise, hallelujah hallelujah." The sound of the chorus in the glass-enclosed space was indeed remarkable. The Cardinal, Lewinski, and others waited as the remaining procession crowded into the Narthex.

"Dear Brothers and Sisters in Christ," began the Cardinal, "this is a day of great rejoicing. After years of planning and sacrifice, we come together as a community of faith to dedicate this church by offering within it the sacrifice of Jesus Christ. We will dedicate this church to the glory of God in honor of St. Mary of the Annunciation. This begins a new chapter in the history of this parish, which has served Fremont Township since 1864. May we open our hearts and minds to the future to which God calls us. May we always welcome God's word with faith, born in the one font of baptism and sustained at the one table of the Lord. May we become the living temple of spirit as we gather around this altar."

Wearing a powder blue suit and a white blouse, Ann Steffenhagen stepped forward. "Your Eminence, as a member of two of our founding families, I am deeply honored and very proud to be here. What we are celebrating today is the harvest of more than 138 years of living faith.

From the time our ancestors of German descent founded this parish to this day, St. Mary - Fremont Center has faithfully witnessed the Catholic faith. We have raised up, generation after generation, faithful disciples of Jesus Christ.

"So, on this special occasion, we want to say Thank You to those who have gone before us for the many sacrifices they have made on our behalf. For the past five years, we at St. Mary's have prayed, dreamed, planned, labored, and sacrificed with a view in mind of our future. As a representative of the parish community of St. Mary of the Annunciation, we now turn over to you—our Archbishop—the plans and drawings for our new church. They are a symbol of a community that has worked together in a creative spirit with mutual respect, sharing time, gifts, and talents, and inspired by the word of the angel Gabriel, 'for nothing is impossible with God.'"

Dirk Lohan then stepped forward, holding a large scroll in hand. "Your Eminence, it has been my privilege as the architect to have worked together in the last three years with this community and its pastor. On this beautiful day today, it is my honor to present to you the plans and drawings by Lohan Associates, which have been realized in this church." Applause echoed through the narthex.

Charles Metzler and two associates stepped forward. "Cardinal George, as General Contractor, we have diligently taken responsibility for erecting this house of worship. Together with all of the people of the Frederick Quinn Corporation, all the subcontractors, and workers, I am delighted to hand over to you the key to St. Mary of the Annunciation Church." The key was no normal key. It was a block of wood about 8" x 4" x 1." A metal part with teeth protruded from one end. The Cardinal accepted the key, passed it to Lewinski, and then shook hands with each man.

Cardinal George responded, "Thank you all for your hard work and sacrifice—the parish community in particular, and all those who have worked on creating a new house of worship, a new Catholic church."

Lewinski, with key in hand, went to unlock the doors as described earlier. Then, with the doors wide open, Cardinal George proclaimed words that undoubtedly originated in the mind of Lewinski: "Dear friends in Christ, grateful for the past and committed to the future, now as we pass through these doors with great rejoicing, we enter the house of the Lord."

Much musical fanfare accompanied the crowd following the Cardinal into the sanctuary. Few people knew how the doors they were passing had miraculously become a reality.

Inside, a few people seated themselves at assigned locations. Several minutes passed. The pews filled, and people overflowed along the side aisles and back into the narthex. Lewinski was indeed happy the team had planned that spacious area.

Cardinal George continued the ceremony from the baptismal font. "Brothers and sisters in Christ, in this solemn Rite of Dedication, let us ask the Lord our God to bless this water created by his hands. Water is a sign of our redemption, a reminder of our baptism, and a symbol of the cleansing of these walls and the altar of this church. May the instruments of catechumens who will be reborn in the waters of this bond find nourishment and strength in this community of faith. May the grace of God help us remain faithful members of his church, open to the spirit we have received."

After the Mass, a reception was held in the Narthex and meeting rooms. The dedication marked a unique and historic milestone in the parish's history. The experience of planning and executing the transition from old to new was remarkably similar to Lewinski's list published six years before the dedication (see "Preparing Vision" chapter).

Lewinski's column on the day of dedication expressed his heartfelt gratitude.

> What a joy it is to welcome Cardinal George to our parish on this day of our Dedication. With great solemnity, our Archbishop will preside over the ancient Rite of Dedication and consecrate the altar and walls of the church for the praise and glory of God.
>
> This occasion is a significant moment in the history of the parish. It reflects the life of a community that has grown from a small rural parish to a community with more than 1500 households. However, strong faith and the growing lay leadership in the parish are more important than the numbers. The diverse ministries at St. Mary are a testimony to a people committed to Christian service. As that circle of service grows ever wider, a sense of mission becomes all the more evident. At the heart of it, all is a rich communal prayer life rooted in the Eucharist. To dedicate this new church, then, is to acknowledge the living stones that are built up into a holy Church with Christ as the cornerstone.
>
> Today marks the completion of a six-year-long process of listening, observing, planning, designing, fundraising, constructing, educating, etc. For me personally, it has been the most demanding mission in my 30 years as a priest. It has been a great privilege and challenge to direct this process. Although the responsibility overwhelmed me at times, the support, encouragement, and hands-on help of so many parishioners inspired me and gave me the will to persevere. I am particularly grateful for the Planning Commission that has stayed with the task from beginning to end and for our pastoral staff that has been an enormous source of support. I've devoted myself wholeheartedly to this project and have grown inwardly. The intensity of this project, especially in the last two years, demanded a lot of my time. I have often felt badly that I was not giving all the time I wanted to other pastoral needs. But in the end, I knew I had a mission to fulfill for which I had to stay focused.

I feel humbled to have had the privilege and opportunity of directing the process of building a new church, pastoral center, and rectory. I am profoundly grateful to everyone who has played a role in bringing us to this day of Dedication. I am thankful for the generous contributors to the Capital Campaign and for all whose enthusiasm and prayers have helped us achieve our goals. While I may have directed the effort, it has truly been a community project.

As we begin a new chapter in our parish history today, I pray that our new church will soon feel like home. May our new facilities enable us, with God's help, to continue to be a strong and vibrant parish. Although we may be growing, we do not need to lose the spirit and values that have given St. Mary its unique identity. Let us praise God for all our blessings and rededicate ourselves for the future.

EPILOGUE

A New Beginning

The day after the new church's dedication, the local "Daily Herald"[1] carried a front-page article titled "*St. Mary's Parishioners Pack The Pews For First Service In New Church Building.*" The piece quoted pastor Ron Lewinski saying, "Some said early on that we could never do what we have accomplished today."

The article concluded on page ten. With what, in retrospect, seems providential, the same page carried a story[2] about another Catholic parish. It showed a picture of a priest who was recently installed there. He was the new pastor at St. Edna in nearby Arlington Heights, Illinois, and his name was Rev. Jerry Jacob. Twelve years later, Jerry Jacob succeeded Lewinski as pastor at St. Mary of the Annunciation.

The April 17, 2002 edition of the Daily Herald's "Neighbor" section featured almost an entire page devoted to pictures from the dedication. The story began, "It may look like a barn on the outside, but St. Mary of the Annunciation new facility near Mundelein is a monument to modern architecture."[3] It then described some of its features.

The April 25th issue of the local tri-city publication "News-Sun" showed a photo of Lewinski in the fifty-foot-high narthex. Titled "Designing Values," the article noted, "the new building is a harmonious addition to the landscape of disappearing corn and soybean fields. Its whitewashed exterior and the asymmetrical roof lines are an upscale complement to the barns and silos of the nearby dairy farm.

"'We didn't ask people what kind of church they wanted,' Lewinski said. 'We asked, what do you value? What is important in your life? What will it mean to gather in this space?'

"The main focus of the new St. Mary's is a bow to tradition. The long, high roof—reminiscent of the basilica shape—rises 50 feet and acts as a resplendent spine and support, uniting the building's sanctuary, Eucharistic Chapel, narthex, and pastoral offices."

The article ended by noting the parish's name had started as St. John the Baptist, changed to St. James, and finally, in the 1880s, it became St. Mary of the Annunciation. When Lewinski arrived in 1996, it was known as St. Mary at Fremont Center. While transforming the parish, he identified and restored the earlier name.[4]

✠

Subsequent to the dedication, the campus has served the parish well. The building's unique design strikes a noticeable profile, just as the little white church does . When the new church first opened, they offered tours. Docents familiar with the noteworthy characteristics guided visitors. In 2018, the parish revised the 16-year-old docent document to include changes that had occurred. Among them, information about the 48-rank pipe organ[5] (2,855 total pipes); a bell tower[6] housing four bells (including the original bell from the old church); a permanent outside bench memorial[7] to Lewinski; and commentary about shrines and other additions and modifications.

IMAGE #24

ORGAN DONATED BY THE FISHER FAMILY

HERE, THE CONSOLE IS TEMPORARILY POSITIONED IN FRONT OF THE ALTAR. SOME PIPES ARE VISIBLE THROUGH THE SLOTS IN THE WOODEN WALL THAT HIDES THE PIPE CHAMBER. (PHOTO FROM JUNE 22, 2008 ORGAN DEDICATION CEREMONY.)

IMAGE #25

BENCH FOR CONTEMPLATION

LEWINSKI WOULD OFTEN REST ON A HILLTOP BENCH AND
CONTEMPLATE THE CONSTRUCTION OF THE NEW FACILITIES
OCCURRING AT THE BOTTOM OF THE SLOPE.
(PICTURE TAKEN JULY 26, 2017, THE DAY OF HIS BURIAL.)

IMAGE #26

BENCH MEMORIAL

A NEW BENCH IS PART OF A BEAUTIFUL MEMORIAL TO LEWINSKI.
(CIRCA 2021)

Visitors comment on the unique worship space. It is a result of Lewinski's interpretation of the spirit of Vatican II and his collaboration with the architect. Concerns about sun, heat, and cold problems with glass construction were unfounded. The tall glass walls in the narthex achieve their goal of bringing the outside in. It has become a marvelous gathering area. They have used it for overflow seating, receptions, dinners, auctions, wakes, processions, and ceremonial functions.

Lewinski had once voiced concern about exiting the sanctuary and encountering a table of coffee and donuts during hospitality. They solved that by setting up the serving counter at the far end of the narthex. Adults have no trouble finding it; they follow the children.

The early conversations, campus walk-throughs, Town Halls, committee meetings, and various occasions at which parishioners and leadership could explore possibilities all contributed to creating a space reflecting the needs and values as the parish expressed them to the architect.

The old church couldn't accommodate the growing parish. It didn't have complete environmental control. The basement and the church above it shared the disadvantage of not being wheelchair accessible. These were overcome in the new building. It contains a sanctuary, narthex, and meeting rooms, all at ground level and conveniently accessible. The altar area has a ramp. The new church is fully accessible. Someone can move from their car in the parking lot to the altar in the church without encountering steps.

During a 1997 campus walk-through, Lewinski had stated a Eucharistic Chapel should be "accessible, reverent, beautiful, and inspiring." His remarks foresaw characteristics of the finished space, including a keypad-controlled entrance.

He had mentioned the benefit of having the choir, congregation, and presider situated during worship services so they could see each other. The design readily provides that, enabling the active involvement of everyone regardless of their role.

Lewinski observed that many churches decorative items during renovations after Vatican II. The construction of a new church enabled him to choose artwork, including hand-carved statues, original paintings, and hand-woven tapestries. His choices reflected a worldview encompassing different races and cultures. He commissioned pieces from various craftsmen in the United States, Italy, Spain, and South Africa.

The old church's confessional was small and cramped. A Reconciliation Chapel is a small comfortable room in the new church. The dialogue between the priest and penitent can be screened or face-to-face. Not by coincidence, a bronze relief depicting Zacchaeus[8] hangs on the wall next to the Chapel's door.

They also included a space that did not exist in the old facility. It is a small suite with a bathroom, closet, and sitting room. It serves well as a bride's room, an additional sacristy, and a private meeting room.

These features make the new church something the old church could never be. Lewinski, Lohan, and the parishioners' inspired work made all these things possible. Together, they wrote a significant new chapter in this parish's history. The sign at the entry onto Emmaus Drive from Erhart Road does identify St. Mary's as a Roman Catholic Community.

The economic downturn in 2002 impacted several parishioners. Existing ministries continued to evolve while new ones formed. Council member Tony Markiewicz established a Transition Ministry to aid those facing change in their work careers.

While Lewinski's image was that of a shepherd, his pastoral approach was to sow seeds and provide nourishment. He may have seemed satisfied when something flourished, but not because it was a seed that he had sown. Instead, he saw it as the spiritual growth of an individual. He fostered it in everyone.

Further economic challenges, especially during 2008, ended their hope of connecting to municipal water and sewer. Population growth continues, but far slower than the pace experienced during the parish's transformation. In 2022, the Wirtz family[9] announced plans to develop 700 acres east of the parish. Named "Ivanhoe Farms," this offered hope that city water and sewer would eventually come within reach.

They settled the mortgage for the new facility within twenty years. Per Mary Hall's comments at a 2001 Town Hall, they paid off the rectory within 15 years.

As for the Pork and Corn Roast and other fundraising challenges, some changes occurred. A second day—the preceding Saturday evening—became the focus for entertainment. This turned into another success.

The roomy and elegant narthex enabled daytime and evening events. Many guests often enjoy couple's dinners and Ladies' Tea. The parish conducted fewer, more targeted fundraisers to avoid "nickel and diming" people for money. The result was more infrequent but very profitable events like a silent auction (with wine tasting). It raised a respectable amount with much less effort than the Pork and Corn Roast.

"SummerFest" replaced the Pork and Corn Roast in 2014, the parish's 150th anniversary. It retained the food and entertainment portions but required less effort to produce.

They held a grand sesquicentennial celebration in 2014, featuring a series of live vignettes enacted by parishioners. *As the Bell Told*" was a historical review of the faith community's story based on parish records and the books by Wagner and Gannon.[10] The "play" was parishioner-written and required the same effort as any community theatre production. It testified to the love and effort the cast and crew devoted to it. Jon Matousek (who had studied theatre in college and was active with stage productions by the local community theatre group) directed it. Fred Vipond (Director of Music and Liturgy) directed the music and choir. Gary Gunther, who, together with his wife Rita, were longtime parishioners, was the Technical Director.

Both Lewinski and his successor, Fr. Jerry Jacob, attended.

In his January 2002 column, Lewinski mentioned naming a room in the parish's new Pastoral Center after a former pastor, Fr. Laukemper. After Lewinski's passing in 2017, the Joseph and Mary Retreat House (where he had briefly lived before coming to St. Mary's) named its conference room the "Lewinski Room."

The parish announced the March 2002 issue of *The Bell* would be the last before the dedication, but it became the final issue period. Lewinski titled his column "A Litany of Achievement." He remarked on his personal experience during the project.

> Every priest I know is ordained with the desire to be a parish priest. This means a desire to serve God's people in a pastoral setting, celebrating the sacraments, preaching, teaching and forming people in our Catholic tradition, sharing parishioners' moments of grief and joy, offering spiritual guidance, and forming communities of faith and action. Building a church is not usually included in that list of priestly responsibilities. So when a number of my colleagues heard I was being asked to build a church, they began to offer me their condolences. Some advised I move somewhere else. Others were afraid for my physical and mental health. Well, six years later, I'm still alive.
>
> What has this experience been like? Challenging, demanding, frustrating, inspiring, discouraging, time-consuming, worrisome, exciting, draining, rewarding…. You name it. I've experienced it. Truthfully, it has been a significant spiritual journey. I have had to grow and stretch in ways that I might otherwise not have. I have had to ask myself what is important about a parish, about a parish church, about our mission in the world. I've had to do some soul-searching regarding my own gifts and limitations. Raising funds has probably been the most difficult aspect about the whole process. But even raising funds exposed me to people whose generosity and good stewardship touched me deeply.
>
> Overall I have felt the true sense of mission in articulating a vision for the future and working together with you to provide for the needs of the Church in generations to come. This whole planning and building process has enabled me to get to know you better. In neighborhood pastoral visits, Town Hall meetings, consultations, committees, etc. I have seen your faith and dedication.

I wouldn't have the same affection for the parish I have now if we hadn't shared this long and tough challenge together

I've been inspired when you shared with me your hopes for St. Mary. I was moved when I saw you come forward to venerate the steeple cross on the day we blessed it. I've been pleased when you shared your experience of the Disciples in Mission that has helped to prepare you spiritually for the dedication. I believe we have grown a great deal over the past few years as we plan for the future.

As we dedicate our new church to the glory of God in honor of St. Mary of the Annunciation, I will be grateful, not simply because the major phase of this project will be over, but because of the many blessings that I have experienced through it all. I feel we are on the brink of a new tomorrow, a future filled with a lot of hope.

Thank you for the privilege of guiding this process to its completion as your pastor. Like a newly ordained priest who has dreams and visions for pastoral ministry, I, too, have dreams and visions of all that we can be and do together as God's Church in the future.

It's time to celebrate![11]

He ended his article by listing the project's impressive achievements. As always, Lewinski remained forward-looking and ready for whatever might come next. He would remain pastor until 2014, while simultaneously performing influential work for the Archdiocese and beyond.

Dirk Lohan continues his innovative work with his new company, Lohan Architecture PLLC. He has served on numerous not-for-profit boards, including the Great Books Foundation, the Adler Planetarium in Chicago, and the Board of Trustees of the Illinois Institute of Technology. For many years, he has been dedicated to helping children in the United States and around the world as Board Member and President of the SOS Children's Villages, Illinois and USA.[12]

---

[1] Daily Herald, April 15 2002, pp. 1 & 10.

[2] "Catholics Say Their Faith Not Shaken," Daily Herald, April 15, 2002, p 10.

[3] The Daily Herald, April 17, 2002, Section 5, pg. 1.

[4] News Sun, April 25, 2002, pp. 1 and 10.

[5] A gift of the Roger and Jacqueline Fisher family.

[6] Gifted by Ted and Tina Godek.

[7] Gift of Lino and Donna Cordoba.

[8] Zacchaeus means "innocent" in Hebrew. See also Luke 19:8.

[9] https://therealdeal.com/chicago/2022/11/28/wirtz-family-pitches-700-acre-ivanhoe-village-for-mundelein/ Nov. 28, 2002. Holdings of the Wirtz family include the Chicago Blackhawks, Breakthrough Beverage Group, the United Center in Rosemont, banks, and multiple real estate complexes.

[10] See the introduction of this book.

[11] The Bell, Vol. I, Issue 11, March, 2002, p. 3.

[12] Lohan Architecture PLLC, July, 2023. https://www.lohanarchitecture.com/dirk.

AFTERWORD

1947 - 2017

As I noted in the Introduction, this story is about Fr. Ron Lewinski's first six years at St. Mary of the Annunciation parish (1996-2002). Now I beg some forgiveness from you. I believe a brief review of his life will give a fuller perspective of the man and the priest.

He was baptized "Ronald John." As time passed, he earned nicknames from family, friends, and even "strangers." These included "Eeyore," "Ron the Baptist," "GD," "UR," and "Ithemba Lethu" ("Our Hope" in Zulu). A brief review of his varied life experiences follows.

Childhood

Lewinski was born on February 15, 1946. Even then, ahead of his time at the leading edge of the baby boomer generation. The country entered a new era of peace and prosperity. A prevailing attitude reflected gratitude for the peace following years of world war and national sacrifice.

During his childhood, he learned positive values at home and at school. In those days, the two reinforced each other. There was mutual consistency in behavioral and academic expectations.

A handful of television shows conveyed admirable values through entertainment via the popular 1950s superheroes like "Superman" and "Mighty Mouse." The television shows "Father Knows Best," "The Adventures of Ozzie and Harriet," "Leave it to Beaver," and "The Mickey Mouse Club" projected desirable family life and values. "The Magical World of Disney" and the New York World's Fair in 1963 offered fanciful recreation and hopeful predictions of better living.

Jack Benny, Jackie Gleason, Lucy and Desi, and other comedians assured viewers humor exists in almost any situation. Among these, Red Skelton was memorable for ending his show by extending a public blessing on national television with the phrase "Good night, and God bless!"

Notables such as (the now Venerable) Bishop Fulton J. Sheen and Billy Graham leveraged the new medium of television for their evangelization.

Lewinski became intrigued by the priesthood and impressed by the Mass at a young age. Every school day began with a priest, garbed in flowing robes and reciting mysterious but reverent-sounding words (in Latin) during Mass before classes began. As a child, he showed a curiosity and desire for meaning that drove his behavior later in life. A lifelong friend of Lewinski, Dr. Mike Zygmunt, shared these recollections of him:

> Probably around third or fourth grade, we started having more responsibility as altar boys. We'd volunteer for the more complex rituals like Christmas, Holy Week, Easter, etc. In the Church of the 1950s, we had many outdoor events: devotions to Mary, Easter, etc. We got involved in these things, and Ron, being more inquisitive about the liturgy and the entire process, used his skills and personality to make it more meaningful for people attending.
>
> We were intimidated by the monsignor, who was old and really set in his ways. It's like having a great-grandfather. When I look back, it is sad because those are the guys you want to talk with and learn from.
>
> Almost across the street from our church was a Russian Orthodox church. Ron and I were together a lot. When he'd walk from his house to church, he'd walk past my house. We had no school bus. After school, if we had time, or after a funeral, we'd visit different places.
>
> We went to this Russian Orthodox church and met the priest. He was heavily bearded, wore a black cassock, and used a crutch. We looked around the church, which was basically similar to ours, but there were different icons and different ornamentation. Well, we encountered some difficulty later because the nuns found out what we were doing.
>
> Remember how it was back then that if you went to a non-Catholic place of worship, you'd suffer God's wrath? So we'd go looking around. We'd walk in thinking a bolt of lightning would strike, but nothing happened. We found out we could enter the buildings without getting killed. So Ron and I, especially later when we had bikes—which increased our range of travel—went looking around at a few Protestant places. They had a totally different architecture and a more modern style of expression. Ron's eyes were opened by the different use of light and the settings.[1]

Lewinski seemed compelled to explore the tenets and traditions of his faith. He was ahead of his time, trying to learn about religious practices outside his church.

Youth

Like most of the nation, Lewinski—then in high school—experienced a two-week-long period of tension during the "Cuban Missile Crisis" in late 1962. He might well have wondered whether he'd live long enough to graduate. It seemed the fallout shelters they had prepared across the country, and the drills conducted by the Civil Defense, might prove their worth at any hour.

Less than a week before, Pope (now Saint) John XXIII—the "Good Pope"—convened the Second Vatican Council.[2] "Vatican II" had an immeasurable impact on the world, Catholics, and Lewinski. Whereas

Vatican I didn't even invite bishops from the United States, Vatican II extended an invitation worldwide, including women and non-Catholics.

"The Second Vatican Council was a turning point in terms of ecumenism. This resulted in a very robust effort to engage in dialogue with various Orthodox traditions, the Anglican Communion, Lutheran World Federation, World Methodist Conference, World Alliance of Reformed Churches, Baptist World Alliance, Disciples of Christ Pentecostals, Evangelicals and the Mennonites. All these dialogues continue because they are born out of the desire for unity…and out of the need for common witness."[3]

College/Seminary years
1964 -1972

Sometimes, despite feeling called to his vocation since childhood, Lewinski had doubts. Sr. Agnes Cunningham earned her doctorate in Sacred Theology at the Universite Catholoque de Lyon in France. Afterward, she became a theology instructor at Mundelein Seminary and one of the first nuns to work at a seminary. Cunningham related a story hinting at what would be a lifelong desire for affirmation by Lewinski.

> He had written a paper on Baptism in the Cappadocian Fathers. It was a very good paper, but I tended to give "A's" sparingly. Shortly after the grades had been registered, Ron came to me with a theology journal in his hand. Pointing to one article by a well-known theologian, Ron asked, "Sister, if you had read this article before you read my paper, would you still have given me a B+? I would like you to read the article and let me know, please."
>
> I agreed, took the journal, read the article and sent for Ron. "The grade I would have been obliged to give you," I said slowly, "would have been an A, perhaps even an A+. Your paper is far above what this author wrote. You know that once the grades have been registered, the Dean does not change them. I am very sorry."
>
> "I didn't want the grade to be changed," Ron answered. "I just wanted to know if I had understood the material I read."[4]

In 2017, Lewinski credited Sr. Agnes Cunningham and Sr. Elaine Marie Klugiewicz, for tremendously influencing him.

Sr. Cunningham recalled this expression of concern from Lewinski:

> At one of our first meetings, we were discussing an outstanding mid-term exam he had written. I encouraged him to continue this achievement. Ron said, "Sister, I wasn't sure I'd be coming to Mundelein. I had been told by one of my college professors that I was a 'dumb Polack' who would never amount to a good priest and that I might as well crop out rather than fail at Mundelein."
>
> "And why are you here?" I asked.

> Ron answered very seriously, "Sister, I have been convinced that God wants me to be a priest. If I had not been accepted at Mundelein, I would have known I was mistaken, but I was accepted. Sister, I want to be the best priest I can be for God."[5]

One of his lifetime practices during his priesthood was an annual one-week retreat at the Abbey of Gethsemani in Kentucky. Often, a friend would accompany him. Parishioner Veronica (Roni) Hertel, whose husband Joe sometimes accompanied Lewinski, recalls Lewinski's first encounter with the Abbey as she knows it:

> Fr. Ron was on a mission in the summer of 1968 with eleven other young adult men and women. They were with the Glenmary Missioners in Eastern Kentucky, working together to bring the Gospel to the rural, predominantly protestant neighbors. They went door to door, introducing themselves and offering Catholic liturgy and fellowship.
>
> He was discerning the priesthood, so he was introduced at a timely point in his life to the Trappist monks. He learned about their three pillars: labor, prayer and sacred scriptures. These are the foundation of his priesthood.
>
> After the long summer mission, he was returning by bus to Chicago when the driver talked about a beautiful Abbey in Kentucky [Gethsemani]. When they were getting close, Ron told the driver to drop him off. So he got off, walked up Monks Road in Trappist Kentucky to the Abbey, and fell in love with the place. Although he did not meet Thomas Merton, a world-renowned author and speaker, Merton's example influenced the priesthood of our beloved Fr. Ron.[6]

Similar to Merton's contemplative approach, St. Ignatius of Loyola offers a manner of knowing God and discerning one's vocation through *Spiritual Exercises*. The *Exercises* aim to help individuals move from a life experienced as confusion and disarray to a life of order and intentionality. Its purpose is to assist in finding God's will for life direction. Ignatius and Merton could agree "an individual experience of God will be a personal encounter that is conversational. This encounter happens in the context of dialogue." (Ignatius calls it "colloquy.") "What happens in the 'colloquy' between God and the individual is of paramount importance in the *Exercises* from start to finish."[7]

Another friend of Lewinski's, Pat Fahey, often accompanied him on retreat. Fahey recalls the impact the retreats had:

> After the evening meal, we would normally take a little walk out into the woods. We would spend maybe an hour just talking before coming back for the final hour. We'd talk about politics, church things, our families. He'd often talk about his own family, his sister, and his brother-in-law.
>
> Ron was kind of high-strung. He worried a lot about things. A retreat put him in a different frame of mind—relaxed him. Usually, we went during Spring break. It was wonderful—a beautiful time of the year down there. Ron and I

traveled to various monasteries. Ron traveled to different places worldwide, but he always came back to Gethsemani.[8]

Dr. Zygmunt offered insight into what he knew about the challenges in Lewinski's seminary days.

> Ron attempted to change things back in the old church so that people would have a feeling of what was being done instead of just the ritual. He disliked the idea that you went to church for an hour and then left. Some people would bring a prayer book or a rosary and not pay attention during the Mass. That's not what he was looking for.
>
> Ron often questioned the ritual and habit of events. He was careful with this. He learned how to communicate to try to get changes to occur without necessarily pushing buttons that would make people nervous. It is difficult to get past the concept of "We did it this way for a thousand years. Why do we have to change?" Changes can be really hard things to experience, especially when you're a young guy coming out of the seminary, feeling on top of the world, and you run into guys who try to stop you at every point.[9]

Vatican II was pivotal in the Church's history and Lewinski's life. It began in 1962 and ended in 1965 while he was in high school and entering college. By the time of his ordination, the Council's impact was taking effect. A classmate of Lewinski's, Fr. Bob Tonelli, recalled this about his seminary days with Lewinski.

> The motto by the early seventies was "Vatican II will not happen unless you make it happen." I single out the class of 1972 because we were prepared by the time we were ordained to make it happen.
>
> We were allowed to think, and we were also allowed to be creative. That was not true in pre-Vatican II days.
>
> Ron was very instrumental in helping us be better communicators and express ourselves and our spirituality when we prayed the Eucharistic prayer while facing the congregation. He was also instrumental in helping us understand the different parts of the Eucharistic prayer. We had a liturgy teacher, but Ron was so excited about this whole thing that he would be teaching us. He never "led classes," but he was definitely always talking about it. And we were too. We were excited. We were well prepared to go out and do our thing.
>
> Ron was part of that. He said, "we have to go out there and do it, guys," that kind of thing. Ron was very instrumental in that way.
>
> His attitude was more about looking to the future, not the past. That's what made him not just a great priest but a great person. Because he knew Church history, he knew how to be spiritual.[10]

Tonelli and others benefited from Lewinski's zeal. They experienced Vatican II through changes at the seminary. Fr. John Gorman, the new rector, became responsible for leading the change. Fr. Tonelli relates:

Msgr. John Gorman was a blessing to the seminary. He had become the rector after Vatican II. He knew what to do at the right moment. We had a rebellion in the seminary that few people know about. We boycotted classes in April 1967, I think for an entire week because we were so fed up with the teachers. Up to that time, we had nothing but Jesuits who had been in the seminary for thirty-some years. They were teaching the old theology; they weren't teaching anything new.

Of course, this was happening just as Fr. Gorman walks through the doors. He had to be a very understanding person—psychologically, how do you go through a reform movement in the seminary?

Gorman let go of all the Jesuit teachers and brought in new ones. He was also in favor of having women who were qualified to teach as well. So he brought in three nuns. Then he brought in Scripture scholars from Europe as well as other teachers from the U.S., including our own diocesan priests who already had credentials teaching theology. It was quite a mix of people. For the first time, we were getting introduced to theology that wasn't necessarily Catholic; we were introduced to Protestant theology because this was the ecumenical movement. We had to know about other philosophies that were out there.[11]

The priesthood before Vatican II was different from how the Council saw it in the future.[12] Lewinski felt God had called him to become a priest. But the priest Lewinski needed to become, by the time of his ordination, was a differently educated and empowered kind of priest than before.[13]

Fr. John Kartje, rector at Mundelein Seminary, stated, "Even before the Second Vatican Council, Chicago was always very forward-looking. There were English Masses in Chicago before the Council. I know Ron's love for liturgy was profound, so I've got to think that he was a real spearheader even at the seminary implementing those changes."[14]

Another of Lewinski's classmates, now Msgr. Pat Pollard, recalled:

It was devastating for some of the priests on the faculty. Ron and I both experienced it. Three of my spiritual directors not only quit the seminary but left the priesthood. It was a mistaken understanding of Vatican II. We lost tremendous numbers of people from the seminary, both students and priests, who did not know how to integrate what the Vatican was saying. It was a time of great turmoil.[15]

When Fr. John Gorman arrived as the seminary's new Rector, he'd recently earned his doctorate in clinical psychology. He replaced 90% of the instructors over a five-year period. Among the new instructors was Sr. Agnes Cunningham. Her teachings at the seminary had a lifelong impact on Lewinski and others. Pollard explained how John Gorman's reforming influence enabled Sr. Agnes' influence at a pivotal time:

If John Gorman hadn't been there, Sr. Agnes would never have been invited. Until 1966, there were only priests teaching. John was there from 1966 until the 1980s. His predecessor would never have allowed a layperson, and certainly not a woman, as an instructor.

She was a very balanced instructor. She searched for what the Council was trying to share. Her first course that I remember was Patristics—the Fathers of the Church. Ron never forgot that. Ron would go back and study Ignatius of Antioch and the other Fathers. That would come through later in his writings. Sister Agnes' influence was going back to the Fathers to see what they were saying. Then teach their basic understanding—otherwise, it would be lost in time.

Sr. Agnes referred to the footnotes in the Council documents. There were many footnotes, and Ron explored them to great length. There were quotations from Augustine, the Council of Trent, and other writings to show that the Council was not just some crazy people ranting in 1963. These are the things that Ron would pump into us. Ron realized that some of the impetus for Vatican II began a half-century earlier with some papers by theologians describing the Church in a different way.

The thing that sister Agnes beat into our heads is that sometimes the footnotes have more important information than the text they refer to. I think it is one of her key messages, and he certainly picked up on it, so he devoured every footnote.

In 1968, we officially received our Bachelor of Arts in Philosophy, and that was the last undergraduate degree issued by the University at St. Mary of the Lake. The University no longer issued Bachelor's degrees, only Masters and Doctorates. So we were in the last class to receive a Bachelor's degree.[16]

These descriptions of life at the seminary by Lewinski's classmates hint at how the Council's transforming influence rippled outward. Gorman replacing Jesuits with a diverse new faculty reflects a comment attributed to Saint John XXIII as the reason for convening the Second Vatican Council: "to throw open the windows of the Church to let in fresh air."[17]

Here is how Fr. (now Bishop) Gorman recalled those days from his perspective as rector:

[Prior to Vatican II, seminary life] was a very regimented kind of life. That's how everyone was judged—just by seminary life. The idea was that the seminary reflected the Church and the Church was in a really defensive mode due to the revolutions of the 16th and 17th centuries. So the Church was supposed to be "apart" from the world, and therefore the seminaries reflected that—being apart from the world physically and every other way.

We rarely got out of the building until after Christmas for a vacation. There was no contact with people.

It became clear that the Council changed the way the Church saw itself. Instead of being apart from the world, the Church began to see itself as in dialogue with, and of service to, the world. The word that Vatican II sent to seminaries was that the seminary should change and follow the mission of the Church.

The seminary building in the old days was a place of complete silence. Once you walked in, you would not talk. You were never allowed to visit a fellow seminarian's room. That's one of the things we changed. We opened up a corridor of ten men and would have meetings for sharing their experiences and for praying together. Therefore, the whole idea of being apart from each other was changed to being with and for each other. So they were no living longer apart from the world or apart from each other.

So there's a lot of change. Theology needed a pastoral dimension that the seminarians were going to serve in their parishes. Sacred Scripture was to be read according to modern literary expertise. We needed to have seminarians go out to live and serve at parishes. Consequently, for ordination, the input from parishes—what the people thought of him—was part of the evaluation of the seminarian.

That's the overall view of how and why these changes at the seminary took place: because the Church was changing.

Some of the faculty were older men, and they didn't like all the changes. We had a faculty meeting one time, and I said, according to Vatican II, we're not changing authority; we are changing the *way* authority is meant to be operative. The seminary before was encapsulated in fear: you wouldn't dare break a seminary rule. So now we loosened up the whole seminary, with students going out into parishes. I gave them the concept of "responsible freedom." That's exactly what they're going to have to be responsible for at the parish: how they handle their freedom. It was abused by some, and others came to realize what it means.[18]

Usually, individual seminarians don't attract attention. However, after ordination is when a priest is able—indeed, obliged—to employ his God-given gifts. During his formative years, it seems Lewinski—thinking about priesthood—was seeking his purpose. At the seminary, he found it. "There is danger if you lack purpose. You start listening to people who tell you what you want to hear."[19]

Those who knew Lewinski saw how he was constantly juggling multiple balls. He would engage with a purpose. No effort was too great. Pope John XXIII, who convened Vatican II, once wrote, "I am tormented by the disproportion between what I do and what remains to be done."[20]

Gorman recalls this about Lewinski:

After Ron was ordained, he became very important for the whole diocese in developing liturgy—how liturgy is meant to be part of a parish. He developed a lot of programs. We were all very much appreciative of what Ron did. He brought liturgy alive.[21]

Later in his career, Lewinski returned to the seminary as an adjunct instructor for Liturgy and the Sacraments. Fr. Kartje, a student of Lewinski's in 2002, was rector at the Seminary in 2018 when he recalled:

I saw that, during his mid and late career, he was very encouraging of seminarians to become engaged in their vocation. Even after he left St. Mary and was working with the Archdiocese, he was very involved here in terms of encouraging seminarians to go out and do things in the Archdiocese.

He was always giving me feedback, even after I became rector, based on his interactions with newly ordained priests: what he thought their strengths were and what he thought the seminary could pay more attention to. I'm sure that was very consistent with his attentiveness to his own formation and growth as a newly ordained priest.[22]

Lewinski's formation at the seminary, devotion to his studies, and zeal for learning formed the person he had felt he should be ever since his First Communion. One senses it from Thomas Merton's words, written when Lewinski was a toddler. "It is a tremendous thing, the economy of the Holy Ghost! When the Spirit of God finds a soul in which He can work, He uses that soul for any number of purposes: opens out before its eyes a hundred new directions, multiplying its work and its opportunities for the apostolate almost beyond belief and certainly far beyond the ordinary strength of a human being."[23]

Early pastoral work

St. Mary at Fremont Center became the first parish at which Lewinski had full responsibility as a pastor. However, his prior experience included working with various pastors, bishops, professionals, and laity. He had benefited, at his first parish assignment, from the freedom the pastor granted him. According to those who knew Pastor Joe Howard, he enabled Lewinski and the other priests to pursue their passions.

Vatican II, and its initiator, Pope John XXIII, left lifelong imprints on Lewinski. Shortly after John's first encyclical, he issued *Sacerdotii nostri primordia* (The Beginning of Our Priesthood) "to guide, inspire, and challenge Roman Catholic Priests." Priestly virtues that John inventories are preacher, catechist, teacher, and learner. Regarding catechesis, John harkens back to the Council of Trent, saying that the Council "pronounced the pastor's role of catechist to be a parish priest's first and greatest duty."[24]

The reforms from Vatican II energized Lewinski in his early days as a priest, especially those related to the Liturgy. "He would get upset about people being reluctant to change," recalled Sr. Corine Walsh, school principal at the time Lewinski joined St. Frances parish. "We told him to be patient. These kinds of changes take time."[25]

Lewinski's classmate, Fr. Bob Tonelli, recalls the early days of his and Lewinski's priesthood.

> We were doing a lot of adult education in the 1970s for the changes that were happening in the Church, and liturgy was one of them. We were trying to help people understand Vatican II. Some of them were leaving the Church because there was no Latin anymore. They didn't understand what this was really all about. It really took a lot for us younger guys to bring about this change.

The reason is because we were emphasizing really heavily the Eucharist, and people understanding the Mass better, and participation in it, and understanding Scripture. It is the first time Scripture is being read to them.

A lot of people weren't prepared because all they had was a Catechism. I grew up with a Catechism; if I had not gone to the seminary, I would never have learned all the other things.[26]

One of the changes most obvious to a congregation was celebrating the liturgy in the local vernacular. Until then, the tradition since 1570 had been Latin. Now the congregation could understand what the priest— facing them from the altar—was saying. The congregation's participation required more response from them. It was not just a ritual led by a presider with his back to the congregation; now a verbal exchange was occurring.

Fifty years after his ordination, Lewinski reflected on the impact of those changes on him:

I was ordained in 1972, and at that time there was enormous excitement about the Liturgy. I remember once saying to myself, 'Is *that* what we were praying [in Latin]?!' It was like a new discovery—it was exciting. I can remember shortly after being ordained, we celebrated Mass and the anointing of the sick. It was a *powerful* experience. So many people came up to me afterward. They were literally in tears. They were touched by the power of what had happened. So *that's* the excitement of what was happening because they could now understand it—a new discovery of a treasure that was there all along, but that now was unleashed to all of us to enjoy and celebrate.[27]

Before coming to St. Mary at Fremont Center, Lewinski had become a liturgical expert. Deacon Bob Poletto, who was friends with both Fr. Keusal and Fr. Lewinski, recalls:

He was such an expert in the liturgy. He was so sought after that you knew you had a guy who was at the top of his game, so to speak. He was sought out in the Archdiocese and around the world even, to come and talk as one of the top liturgists.

Most people thought he was a little uptight about liturgy. He *was* a stickler for correctness. He wanted it right. He knew what to do.[28]

A Father of the Rite of Christian Initiation of Adults (RCIA) (later renamed the Order of Christian Initiation—OCIA)

Beyond his liturgical expertise, Lewinski became well known for contributing to a process of welcoming people into the Christian community. This wasn't simply a matter of refining an existing process. He helped create the Rite of Christian Initiation of Adults. He became recognized as an expert. His involvement began during his seminary days, according to classmate Fr. Bob Tonelli:

> He definitely was a person who was very high-intensity. I remember our class really promoted RCIA wherever we went because of him—because *he* was promoting it to our class. We all got educated through *him* about how to do it. By the time we got ordained, he was already way ahead of the times of Vatican II regarding RCIA. He actually wrote articles about it at the seminary. His Master of Divinity thesis was on bringing back the process.
>
> That's why Ron was very instrumental in the nation by not only bringing it back but creating a way of approaching *how* we are going to welcome converts into the Church. That was his major work, you could say, as a priest in his early years. During RCIA's initial stages, Ron lectured bishops across the United States.
>
> Around 1974, the Cardinal allowed Chicago to become a guinea pig for the Vatican to resurrect the RCIA process, catechumens, and so on. Whenever we did the Rite of Election in the Cathedral, it just kept getting bigger and bigger. It was really tremendous how this blossomed eventually into his work, becoming part of the 1983 Code of Canon Law. Before Vatican II, non-Catholics who wanted to convert would go to a priest once a week for a year, and then the priest would let them know when they were ready to be baptized. But with RCIA, this became much more of an engaging process. Ron revived some of the rites that were from the early Church and incorporated them. That's how Chicago became the forerunner of RCIA. Basically, we have three categories of people: those who are going to be baptized, Protestants who are already baptized, and those who were never confirmed. It is about liturgy and a complete process for those who want to become Catholic.
>
> If it wasn't for Ron, I don't know if we would even be talking about RCIA.[29]

Lewinski combined his RCIA expertise with his deep understanding of liturgy to design a worship space at St. Mary's, bearing witness to Vatican II. Kathi Barrett, longtime Director of RCIA at the parish, notes:

> In the twenty years that I was in RCIA, I would take all the candidates and do a tour of the church. Ron was a liturgical master. He understood how the structure actually became part of the liturgy. A lot of churches have statues and all the things that they're supposed to have, but you don't see liturgy exactly the same as you see at St. Mary. Everything is part of the liturgy. That, to me, is an astounding thing.[30]

After Lewinski's death, Fr. Paul Turner, Director of the ODW office in Kansas City and a contemporary theologian, reflected on Lewinski:

> Ron worked on developing such ceremonies as the Rite of Welcoming, the Rite of Sending, the Call to Continuing Conversion, and the Penitential

Rite for candidates. These appear only in the U.S. edition, but they have been widely copied throughout the English-speaking world.

We have all sharpened our insights on initiation because of his patient work, clear explanations, challenging ideas, and faithful devotion. He has made us better professionals and persons.[31]

"Papal adviser"
1979

Lewinski's passion for welcoming people into the Church had become well known by 1979, just seven years after his ordination. That year, Lewinski lobbied for the Rite of Entrance, part of RCIA, to be performed by Pope (now St.) John Paul II. The planners scheduled the Pope to celebrate Mass in Chicago's Grant Park on October 5, 1979.[32] The ecumenical event was attended by people of all faiths and backgrounds, despite the Chicago Archdiocese having 2.4 million Catholics, the most of any Archdiocese in the U.S.

Sr. Madge Karecki, former President of Augustine College in Johannesburg and colleague of Lewinski's, recalled the circumstances as she knew them:

> Ron was very influential with his writing and speaking workshops, lectures, and other things about the RCIA. Before the Pope left for Chicago, Ron was trying to get them to incorporate the Rite of Initiation. When the Pope arrived, he said to Ron, "I have never done this." He continued, "I believe you can teach me the best way to do it." So Ron gratefully prepared the Holy Father for the Rite of Initiation that the Pope directed in Grant Park that day.[33]

Cardinal Cody oversaw the catechumens (individuals studying to become Christians) during the ceremony. The Pope performed the Rite before celebrating the Mass. Over 200,000 people attended. Lewinski lingered not far away, watching with great satisfaction.

Still, in 2014, despite Lewinski's dedication to RCIA since the early 1970s, he questioned how far the Church had progressed.

> The joyful experience of celebrating one of the rites of the catechumenate with the pope was memorable, but the pastoral implementation of the RCIA is far from complete. While it is common to find a notice about the RCIA in Sunday bulletins indicating that somehow the Rite has found its way into parish life, I'm not so sure that the pastoral vision upon which this Rite is based has continued to mature and develop. The call to conversion, the communal life, and mission still appear to be less attended to than concerns about catechetical content.... We might consider taking another look at our pastoral practice and renewing the vision that was so palatable when Pope John Paul II celebrated the Rite of Entrance into the Catechumenate in Chicago in 1979.[34]

Director, Office of Divine Worship (ODW)
1984 - 1994

Lewinski's decade at the Office of Divine Worship provided valuable practical experience while forging his personality and style. Fr. Gerard Broccolo, who had taught at the seminary, recalls ODW's genesis:

> Before the ODW, there was what they called the CCD office [responsible for teaching Christian Doctrine]. Fr. Ted Stone led it. He was very much into the liturgy in the aftermath of Vatican II. He and a lay couple, Tom and May Dore, were the pioneers in a lot of the early steps in liturgy reform and renewal after Vatican II for the Archdiocese of Chicago.
>
> I had gotten my degree in liturgy and was returning to the diocese. Then Ted Stone left the ministry, and Tom Dore died. Our auxiliary Bishop at the time and I decided to start an office for divine worship, and we hired Fr. Dan Coughlin as the first Director of ODW. I was working with Liturgy Training Publications, the unofficial publication arm of ODW at the time. I was called a consultant, and together with Fr. Dan we ran those two things.
>
> That was around 1970 to 1972. Somewhere in there, we decided we needed to expand more. Shortly thereafter, I was moving on and in 1977, we brought in Gabe Huck for LTP (Liturgy Training Publications). Dan Coughlin was getting ready to move on. He decided that one of the people he would hire to work at ODW was Ron Lewinski. So Dan hired Ron, who became Dan's protégé.[35]

Lewinski succeeded Fr. Dan Coughlin as Director, who later became the 59th Chaplain at the House of Representatives in Washington from 2000 to 2011. Coughlin was the first Roman Catholic Priest to serve in that position.[36] As Director, Lewinski managed a group of people responsible for helping parishes throughout the Chicago Archdiocese with matters of liturgy and catechesis. The parishes, who realized they could benefit from ODW as a single source of information and materials, actively sought the ODW's help. As word of ODW's success grew, other dioceses across the United States sought help as they sought to become self-sufficient.

Lewinski recruited Fr. Ronald Raab to the ODW in 1987. It happened on the eve of Raab's relocation from Colorado to California. Raab recounts the experience:

> At the beginning of June, I was in Colorado and had been assigned to a parish in Hayward, California. It was the day before I was supposed to leave. Everything was packed. I had all my stuff addressed to California. I was cleaning out the top drawer of my desk as last minute thing and the secretary walked in and said, "There's a Father Ron on the phone... it sounds very important."
>
> So I get on the phone, and it was Ron. He said, "I'd like to have you come interview for a job."

I said, "Ron, how did you know I was leaving?"

He said, "I didn't."

I said, "Had you called me the following day, I'd be gone already."
Actually, I was going back to Notre Dame for six weeks of summer school; but all my stuff was ready to be shipped to California the following day.

He said, "Well, don't do that. If you're coming to Notre Dame anyway, just come interview."

So I called the Provincial and explained. They said, well, okay, go interview. So I did. Later, the position in Hayward was filled. But at the end of summer school, I was called by the ODW in Chicago, and they said I had the job.[37]

Raab noted that the ODW still faced resistance, even two decades after Vatican II. Unwelcome change often makes progress difficult.

Gabe Huck served as Director of Liturgy Training Publications (LTP) in the Archdiocese of Chicago from 1977 until 2001. He authored and edited many books and articles with the help of LTP's staff. Huck recalled those days of Lewinski's influence:

Already when Vatican II did its work in the early 1960s, many in Chicago, on all levels, had been prepared over several decades and were ready to bring to their parishes the liturgical vision of the Council. Chicago parishes in the 1960s and early 1970s took on a leadership that shared the insight and renewal for parishes and their members all over the country. What would become Liturgy Training Publications grew from those pre-Council decades, and the post-Council leadership the Chicago church offered to dioceses and churches throughout the United States and beyond.

My part began with phone calls in 1977 from Ron Lewinski. We had become friends a few years before, both of us wanting this liturgical renewal to take hold throughout the churches. Ron encouraged the Chicago diocesan staff to keep alive their leadership in liturgy—and to enlarge their work. Then he invited me to come and meet these leaders in Chicago and apply to take on the periodicals and other publishing. And so it happened!

As LTP began to grow, a staff of two would eventually become a staff of 50 or more. Ron continued his pastoral work for the parishes he served, but he was also focusing on the gradual growth of what had come to be known as the Rite of Christian Initiation of Adults (RCIA). Through his articles and books we published at LTP, Ron's work would go far beyond the Chicago churches. He helped us start magazines about the RCIA. He was in much demand to speak of the RCIA in dioceses across the U.S. and beyond. The sense Ron had for the importance of this RCIA in the parishes was crucial. And he knew how to spread the news.

In the years Ron served as Director of Liturgy for the Chicago Archdiocese, he was able to share his insight and enthusiasm in many ways, including his writing for LTP's publications, always attentive to those next steps parishes needed to take in embracing the need for liturgy as the work of all the people.[38]

Sabbatical
1994-1995

Following his work at ODW and before coming to St. Mary's parish, Lewinski was Acting Director at what is now the Joseph and Mary Retreat House in Mundelein, next to the seminary he had once attended. During this time, Cardinal Bernardin granted him a one-year sabbatical. He visited several parishes to learn more about what made them "successful." He loved to travel, so it is not surprising that some parishes were outside the United States.

For Lewinski, according to Bishop Gerald Kicanas:

> Parish life and parish ministry were his interests both as a scholar and practitioner. He wanted to identify the factors that create a vibrant, active, and alive parish community. I was always impressed by Ron's passion for parish ministry, whether he was an Associate, or studying parishes, or eventually becoming pastor of a parish. So when there was discussion about who might be best to go to St. Mary's, he was certainly the front runner for that as someone who could take what he'd learned and implement it at St. Mary's. Ron was wholeheartedly embracing the Vatican II documents and trying to help people to see their value and the impact they would have on reenvisioning and enlivening the Church. I don't think in his mind there was any question about the significance of the documents and his efforts to try to implement those at St. Mary's.[39]

Pastor, St. Mary of the Annunciation
1996 - 2014

The Church's work is not achieved only by an institutional hierarchy. It needs the inspired actions of individual members who perform acts at an interpersonal level strengthened by Christ's instruction to "love one another." Lewinski achieved much as a pastor through his personal efforts; but also through empowered parishioners to whom he extended his support.

He was "active" in the sense he offered them his belief in their intent. He expressed his faith in their ability to move forward with his support but without relying on him. There was a "passive" aspect in his willingness to listen, his sincere desire to understand, and his ability to entrust others with a task for which he bore responsibility.

Thus a quarter-century of experience had been preparing Lewinski for his first pastorship. One may assume his lack of experience as a pastor was a disadvantage, yet it may have helped him. He'd been a Pastoral Associate. He'd been Director of the Office of Divine Worship in one of the largest Archdioceses in the United States. Beginning immediately after ordination, Lewinski worked to make the reforms of Vatican II meaningful to his parishioners. He lectured across the United States and overseas on Liturgy and on the RCIA. The articles he published were on a variety of topics. Besides the RCIA, he wrote about parish administration. During the sabbatical just prior to coming to St. Mary's, he had visited several parishes across the United States and overseas to determine what "makes a good parish." So, while not having held the formal title of "Pastor" by the time he arrived at St. Mary's, he had a broader and richer depth of experience than many pastors had.

One obvious difference parishioners at St. Mary's saw after Lewinski's arrival was his support for people—especially their ideas about creating ministries. It didn't mean people were free to do what they wanted, but the fact he would listen to proposals—and often agree with them—was a foreign attitude compared to the parish's prior experience.

Ideas didn't have to come from adults. One mother related the story of how her daughter made a pitch to Lewinski:

> Fr. Ron was trusting of the ministries. When my daughter, Elise, was in the sixth grade, we were interested in starting a "Challenge Club for Girls" at St. Mary's. It is a worldwide organization [that focuses on helping members develop apostolic hearts and function as Christian role models]. We went to see Fr. Ron. Elise did all the talking. She told Fr. Ron about the retreats she went on, the girls she met, and the positive experiences like the prayer card that she got with her prayer. If you're involved in this, you commit to praying a decade of the rosary every day, reading about a saint every day, etc. There are different things they do. She showed him these things, and she had her book of Saints there and was describing her experience. Afterward, he said, "Yes, that sounds fine." I just loved how he listened to this sixth-grader and was completely open and trusting that this would be a good thing for our parish.[40]

Lewinski's behavior in such situations reflects a comment by Mother Teresa; "You can do what I cannot. I can do what you cannot. Together, we can do great things."

Given the atmosphere of controversy after Vatican II, one could ask, as a seminarian, which style of priest Lewinski had in mind. The kind who wielded power, whether benevolent or otherwise, over the local parish? Or the kind that Vatican II advocated when he arrived at the seminary:

> With zeal and patience, pastors of souls must promote the liturgical instruction of the faithful and also their active participation in the liturgy both internally and externally, considering their age and condition, their way of life, and the standard of religious culture. By so doing, pastors will be fulfilling one of the chief duties of a faithful dispenser of the mysteries of God; and in this matter they must lead their flock not only in word but also by example.[41]

His life spent preparing for, and his performance as pastor at St. Mary's, demonstrated Lewinski's lifelong promotion of Vatican II reforms.

After his impactful first term (1996-2002), Lewinski continued to serve as pastor at St. Mary's for 12 more years. You might assume he'd rest for a while after transforming St. Mary parish. But it wasn't his style. He continued his work with Liturgy and RCIA in the U.S. and overseas.

In March 2005, during the Feast of the Good Shepherd, the parish presented him with a Good Shepherd statue. The same north Italian sculptor who had done other figures in the church carved it. The Good Shepherd's image had come to symbolize Lewinski.

He developed a program that would go Archdiocesan-wide in a few years. Called "Parish Transformation," it could be controversial because it examined some sensitive aspects of parish management. It reached over 200 parishes in the Archdiocese.

The front covers on the 2000 and 2004 parish directories are similar beyond coincidence. Both covers depict the church steeple. The earlier edition shows the old church steeple; the 2004 edition shows the new. These images portray the similarity in roofline and profile of the two structures from different angles. Trees and natural vegetation frame each picture in the foreground. The careful framing of the steeple between tree branches in each picture is evident. These covers are another example of Lewinski's way of connecting the old with the new. It was his manner not only during the project but as a lifetime practice.

President, ACTA Foundation
2007 - 2017

Lewinski's "world view" of the Church influenced his work at the ACTA (then known as Adult Catechetical Teaching Aids) Foundation.[42] According to their website, "The ACTA Foundation is dedicated to the promotion of creative efforts in adult catechesis. We support efforts to discover fresh approaches to adult catechesis, which integrate Christian doctrine with formation in Christian living."[43]

Founded by some Chicago Archdiocesan priests in 1957, it continues to promote catechetical initiatives and awards grants around the world for that purpose. As the Board's President, Lewinski helped review and approve grants. He'd often call recipients—anywhere in the world—to talk about their applications and plans.

Fr. Larry Dowling, President of the ACTA Foundation in 2022, recalls Lewinski's contribution:

My experience with Ron at both ACTA and the Archdiocese was that he was highly respected, very thoughtful, very innovative, and also good with follow-through. You don't often find many people who arrive with ideas and can actually put things into action. Ron was really good at that.... He was involved with a number of different initiatives on behalf of priests across the board; the term that is used is "he was a priest's priest." He was definitely supportive of his brother priests, and very generous sharing his wisdom and his time and his talent.... He did his very best to bring to fullness the gifts that God gave him.... He could challenge "the powers that be" when we as Christians were not being Christian. Ron had no problem doing that.... He had a gentle yet forceful approach to ministry, just being clear—and the clarity was rooted in faith and it was really evident in him.[44]

Another ACTA Foundation board member, Dr. Carole Eipers, recalled Lewinski this way:

Ron did a wonderful job running ACTA. We receive a lot of proposals. He brought wisdom and a bigger sense of Church. Some proposals were from some of the mission areas in Africa. Because of his travels, he could relate to the situation. So he would say he'd seen that this was a great need and we should consider a donation.[45]

His work at ACTA was yet another way he was promoting the Great Commission across the world.

Archdiocesan Dean (Vicar Forane)
2007 - 2017

The Bishop appoints this position after getting input from the priests at the parishes within the vicariate (a "regional territory" of parishes). Lewinski was well-equipped by this time for its responsibilities:

The vicar forane has the duty and office of vigilance and coordination over the apostolic and pastoral ministry of the clergy in his vicariate.

The vicar forane also has the duty of encouraging presbyters [priests] in his area to take part in educational opportunities offered to them, and may even be called upon to organize such gatherings. He is to further the spiritual development of the priests by encouraging them to attend days of recollection and retreats. He is to be vigilant and solicitous for their physical and material well-being, and in the defense of their rights. At the death of any priest in his vicariate, he is to take steps to safeguard the property and records of the parish.

The vicar forane makes sure that sacred functions are carried out according to established liturgical directives, and that the Blessed Sacrament is properly reserved in the churches of the vicariate.[46]

Lewinski performed these duties while pastor at St. Mary's, developing a significant "parish improvement process" that became "Parish Transformation," and continuing his work with RCIA.

President, Frassati Catholic Academy
2010 - 2015

The growth at St. Mary's predicted in the late 1990s suffered a blow with the 2001 recession and again with the 2008 economic downturn. Lewinski's dream of a new school was challenged. It became clear a different approach was needed at St. Mary's and other parishes. A campaign aimed at Phase II of the Masterplan began under the name of "Abundant Hope." Unfortunately, the "hope" was more abundant than the funds it needed.

St. Mary's joined with two other parishes in neighboring towns, Lake Zurich and Wauconda, to establish the Frassati Catholic Academy. Lewinski was named President. These additional responsibilities brought both success and angst for Lewinski. Conditions at St. Mary's school at one point resulted in a good deal of division between school parents. Lewinski was in the middle. He regretted it and apologized for whatever had happened, but several families left the parish because of it.[47]

Archdiocesan Pastoral Coordinator for Parish Transformation
2010 - 2016

Lewinski developed a passion for liturgy, baptism, and the Second Vatican Council during his seminary years. His work at the Office of Divine Worship, his assignments in the Archdiocese, and the sabbatical he took before becoming pastor at St. Mary's all informed his reformation of St. Mary's parish. Lewinski's ability to apply his pastoral perspective to both the local community and the broader Church showed a rare skill. Fr. Andrew Liaugminas, while Chaplain at Calvert House at the University of Chicago, observed:

> Fr. Ron had a truly intuitive sense of priestly ministry, pastoral liturgy, parish administration, and theological reflection, and was very gifted in each of these areas. While many priests may be gifted in one of these areas, and much fewer are gifted in multiple dimensions, for a priest to be strong in all of these areas is truly a rare skill set, and Fr. Ron had that rare and great combination of gifts, which he put fully to the service of his parish. In addition to that, he had a good sense of humor, the ability to be humble even though he was leading a large enterprise, and—importantly—the ability to celebrate each liturgy, deliver each homily, and give each talk as if he had just found the "pearl of great price" and were sharing this treasure for the first time.[48]

Lewinski's experience and missionary drive resulted in an Archdiocesan assessment process. It aimed to help parishes conduct a facilitated self-review for improvement. The Archdiocese trained a group of volunteers from various parishes as facilitators for the "Parish Transformation" process. Facilitators then spent about twelve days over a period of thirteen weeks with assigned parishes. Parish participants examined important areas of parish life and management. These included worship, finance, outreach, ministry, education, and others. It asked parishioners to question what the community stood for, what was important to them, and how they served those beyond their community. A facilitator led the parish in the introspective and assessment phase and helped them develop a plan through the use of a comprehensive template. A primary focus goal was to write a Mission Narrative.

The Narrative reflected the uniqueness of the parish community and the 'pearls' in its treasury of talent and service. Based on the Narrative, they developed Action Plans for things like Mission, School and Finance. They determined priorities and defined a timeline. The process utilized sound business paradigms such as objectives, action steps, timetables, and expected quantitative and qualitative results. All this was to help the parish understand itself and its place, strengthen it, and improve. It is akin to Strategic Planning in the business world.

Parish Transformation touched over 200 parishes in one of the largest and often the most influential Archdioceses in the United States.

Archdiocesan Coordinator for
Renew My Church
2016 - 2017

Parish Transformation didn't end Lewinski's influence in the Archdiocese. In 2016, Cardinal Cupich gave him a new responsibility as co-coordinator of another transforming program called "Renew My Church."[49] After Lewinski's death, the program continued under the leadership of Lewinski's co-coordinator, Fr. Peter Wojcik.

The mission imperatives of Renew My Church were to make disciples, build community, and inspire witness. Those, of course, are simplified descriptions of many complex activities needed to achieve them. Unfortunately, Lewinski died in 2017 when he and Fr. Wojcik were preparing to promote their offerings.

Fr. Wojcik, speaking about Lewinski's work on the "Parish Transformation" and "Renew My Church" programs, recalled Lewinski's visionary capacity: "Before anybody else in the Church, Ron already had an idea about how to do the renewal or how to initiate it. Now, we are able to do it; but I think it was in his mind and heart ten years before we thought about it at the diocese. Ron was already doing it."[50]

Fr. Wojcik recalled Lewinski's sense of humor and the sincerity Lewinski brought to his work.

> He was telling me a funny, and true, story in his office about a wedding incident. He said it with an accent and so much humor that I remember I was down on the carpet laughing.[51] (Also, he just loved Chinese food. He would get excited about it.) He always came up with some kind of humor.
>
> But he was very serious about our work. He would say, 'You know, Peter, we are like the two evangelizers, Cyril and Methodius.'
>
> He enjoyed the Holy Land big time. He enjoyed travel; he loved people and loved the experience. I remember we went to Rome together for one of the evangelization meetings, and we were actually able to meet the Holy Father. Ron was so excited about it. He was in front of me in line. He was just beaming while greeting the Holy Father. I was right behind him. They talked for a bit. One of the security people standing next to the Pope started pulling Ron ahead, and the Pope actually pulled Ron back to himself. That really brought so much joy to Ron. He was so grateful to the Pope for having a short conversation; it was just wonderful.[52]

Fr. Wojcik added, "The amazing thing about Ron was that you never knew what he was working on. He would drive an hour and a half to and from work in Chicago. Then at night, he was writing a book. I don't know how in the world he did it."[53]

✠

The proverb, "An idle mind is the devil's workshop," dates back to the fourth century when Lewinski's favorite Church Fathers wrote the texts that would impact his life. St. Benedict (c. 480-547) was a father of Western monasticism. Chapter 48 (of 73) in his "Rule" begins, "Idleness is the enemy of the soul." Satan can likely attest to that based on the frustration he must have experienced when trying to distract the mind of Fr. Ronald J. Lewinski. Benedict's "Rule" promoted manual labor as a distraction, but it seems Lewinski applied it to mental activity.

He valued contemplation as a method of strengthening one's humility. "In contemplation there is no embellishment of the ego at all."[54] He had frequent opportunity for deep prayer—such as during the Liturgy of the Hours[55] or when on retreat at the Abbey of Gethsemani. Filling the mind with various topics helps avoid idle moments and distractions.

Lewinski embodied an inclusive and shepherding spirit. It recalls a comment by Blase Cupich, then a Bishop, during his keynote address in April 2008 at Orlando, Florida: "… not only is the greater involvement of the laity through a sharing in their gifts not a threat to the ordained, it is the task of the ordained, who render 'tangible the actual work of Christ, the Head' to encourage and animate the laity to share those gifts for the good of all, including the ordained."[56] Lewinski's actions, beginning with his arrival at the parish, were a catalyst for bringing forth the gifts of those he shepherded.

Lewinski's experiences prior to his assignment at St. Mary's served him well as a pastor. Despite his vision of what could be, and his zeal to achieve it, he sometimes showed remarkable patience during the expansion project. His example is reminiscent of words in the Vatican II document *Sacrosanctum Concilium*. "Zeal" and "patience" seem like opposing virtues, but when properly combined, they catalyze progress. Without patience, zeal can become errant ambition. Without zeal, patience can cause the death of an idea. Lewinski showed how balancing the two— a tension of sorts—can produce remarkable results.

Many people regarded Lewinski as a close acquaintance or "member" of their family. He could relate in ways people would embrace. He possessed the ability to reflect the persona he perceived while retaining his own integrity. The fabric of connection he had with individuals arose from a commonality between them and himself. Each person regarded him somewhat differently than everyone else did. He was genuine in his relationships and never pretended to be someone else. The relationship's strength depended on mutual receptiveness.

Yet, few knew him in "totality." His considerable humility probably contributed to that. He was humble to a fault. Proper humility calls for a balance between unjustified boastfulness and repressed but justified pride. Sometimes, he could have been more assertive about his own achievements. The cynical joke, "It isn't arrogance if it is true," has a grounded parallel in "If it is worthy, it deserves recognition." Parishioners perceived him as a pastor, a persona different from Dean of the Vicariate, author, or instructor. One parishioner recalls accompanying Lewinski to events both inside and outside the parish:

> He was an experienced, successful guy; very well-spoken; took the time to listen; very well thought of. As Dean of the Vicariate, he was "in a different place" compared to a meeting at the school with the parents who had their own parochial views. A lot of times, Fr. Ron was a little bit bashful. Many people interpreted being bashful as being standoffish or aloof or something, which was crazy, but they didn't take time to know him. The people outside [of the parish] saw him entirely differently. I had seen him speak many different times at Archdiocesan events. He spoke all around the country. I remember going with him to New York and New Orleans. He was always "Mr. RCIA." That's who he was. Everybody spoke of him with reverence. I was at a meeting with Cardinal George in Chicago, and Fr. Ron had spoken to a thousand-plus people. They were all standing for Fr. Ron and applauding. Cardinal George came out and said, "I just want to say what a great priest—a humble priest. This is what a priest is." He went on and on about Fr. Ron. I thought, wow, it

would be nice for people in our parish to see this. Very few people ever got to see that side of him.[57]

Another parishioner recalled:

> Many people didn't really know Fr. Ron—they thought he was shy, they thought he was aloof. He was anything but, and I found that when I needed a confessor, he was very good.[58]

Fr. Don Senior, who passed in November 2022, was President Emeritus and Chancellor of the Catholic Theological Union (CTU) in Chicago and an internationally respected scripture scholar. He was also a board member at the ACTA Foundation, where Lewinski had been President. He recalled:

> It is important to note that the Archbishop gave him a number of important responsibilities beyond his role as pastor. He was down to earth, he wasn't a Goody Two Shoes or something like that. He saw flaws and inconsistencies, and wasn't afraid to express them; but he was not in any way a bitter man or caustic. I had the impression he was engaged, and realistically so. … He was open-minded, progressive—I would say—in his views. A really good priest who was trying to implement Vatican II and have a parish that was vibrant. I had thought of him as a very outstanding Chicago priest. He was well-known and respected by his peers as far as I could see. He was very knowledgeable. He was very amiable in the sense that he listened to what other people had to say when he had his own viewpoints. I know he was respected in other parts of the world."[59]

Many parishioners at St. Mary's remained unaware of Lewinski's "outside" activities.

> I never knew he was working on a book for RCIA. Do you know how I'd find out? We'd get brochures from LTP, which published his books. I'd be going through it, and I'd see something by Ron Lewinski, and I'd ask, "What's this? When did he write this?" He never even told me beforehand.[60]

Msgr. Pat Pollard shared this observation about Lewinski as a priest:

> Ron didn't relegate his life to just academic pursuits. e would help and teach at the seminary and instruct others. He was a great mentor to people who were touched by his competency. He wanted to be a parish priest and make it work. It's one of those things we can be proud of about Ron. He wanted all of his academic knowledge to be put to practical use. A bishop from Germany might come to talk with him. Ron could have kids in the school talk with him That's our Ron.
>
> Ron has always continued to study liturgy. There are some who are brilliant professors, but they can't get their heart into parish ministry. Whereas Ron could be sitting down and writing a pastoral theological paper for parish transformation—a real in-depth look at what a parish should be about. He

could write about how that could be part of every parish in the Archdiocese. That was the goal of the program called Parish Transformation. Next, he could put down his pen and be out at a parishioner's house relaxing around the barbecue pit.[61]

The first Christmas rituals in the new church in December 2002 were enjoyed by many thankful parishioners. After years of conducting Mass in the old church and the school gymnasium, there was finally a place to bring everyone together for Mass. Of course, Holy Days like Christmas and Easter ordinarily produce a larger financial collection than a regular Sunday service.

That year, parishioner generosity was noteworthy. Lewinski reported in his weekly bulletin column: "We can all be proud of the signs of good stewardship so evident in our Christmas collection, which was the highest recorded collection ever received in St. Mary's history."[62]

In the same column, Lewinski repeated his admiration for, and gratitude to, his parishioners:

"Let me also express my gratitude and that of the staff for the many cards and gifts that we received this holiday. Your kindness and thoughtfulness are a great support to us. I know that I can speak for the whole pastoral staff in saying there's no more wonderful community to serve than the people of St. Mary of the Annunciation."

Bishop John Gorman, former rector at Mundelein Seminary, reflects:

[Lewinski] was obviously very bright, and interested in liturgy and leadership. I think he had the ability to convince people by the integrity of his whole life, and the ability to respect other people with whom he was living, and share and engage in the work that he was committed to.

I had great respect for him. We were friends. I have respect for him as a student. Once he was ordained, he did so much for the Archdiocese.[63]

Another observation from Msgr. Pollard:

Ron wanted to get the message across "I am a parish priest at heart. Yes, I've been gifted with theological insight, yes I know how to read the ancient Fathers of the Church, and I can stand with academia like Sr. Agnes and talk about Cyril of Alexandria." At the same time, he could sit down with a parish council, the school board meeting, and the finance committee—you know, every part of the church at St. Mary's.

I was Director of Cemetery Services when the Order of Christian Funerals was revised. The full text of the Order was printed by LTP. Ron (then Director of ODW) and I sent it out to every parish with a letter we both signed. There were 375 issued. Ron and I repeated that again when the Roman Missal was edited, and LTP was granted permission to print it. We sent that out with a letter. Otherwise, we knew the pastors would not buy one; they would just continue to use the old book. In a very real sense, the renewal would never come to their parish until people heard the new word. It was all Ron's doing.[64]

In 2017, the seminary Lewinski had attended half a century earlier honored him. Rector Fr. John Kartje recalls the day he told Lewinski the news while Lewinski was sitting across the desk from him.

> One of my strongest memories of him was in this very office. It was here that I notified him [that he'd been awarded the "As Those Who Serve" award]. Just the emotion! He got choked up, and quiet, and tears welled up in his eyes. It was so powerful and beautiful—his humility and his love for this place and the Archdiocese of Chicago. As you know, he was involved in the universal Church in so many ways.[65]

About Lewinski as a priest, Fr. Kartje observed:

> He was an exemplary model of a parish priest, Father Ron never shirked tackling new projects and improving life for others. In many ways, he was also a servant to the entire Archdiocese and the Universal Church, most recently through his leadership with the Renew My Church program.[66]

During his acceptance speech, Lewinski advised seminarians:

> "Allow yourselves to be surprised. You've responded to the priesthood, but God will deliver you to the shores of your mission. Nearly all of my most meaningful experiences were things I didn't initiate, but they bore fruits beyond my prediction."[67]

The Catechism of the Catholic Church is a hefty 800+ pages. It is the "go-to" source for learning about Catholicism. They wrote it for an adult reader, so it is not suitable for educating children starting grade school.

When Lewinski began school, he and the other Catholic children of his era, studied "The Baltimore Catechism."[68] The parochial school version taught basic concepts in simple terms, establishing the relationship between God and His creations. Young Lewinski memorized the questions and answers.

Question: "Who made us?"
Answer: "God made us."
Question: "Who is God?"
Answer: "God is the Supreme Being, infinitely perfect, who made all things and keeps them in existence."
Question: "Why did God make us?"

Answer: "God made us to show forth His goodness and to share with us His everlasting happiness in heaven."

Question: "What must we do to gain the happiness of heaven?"

Answer: "To gain the happiness of heaven we must know, love, and serve God in this world."[69]

I can imagine St. Peter at Heaven's Gate, watching Lewinski approach with a somewhat apprehensive expression. "What," asks St. Peter in a firm but friendly tone, "did you do to warrant entrance into Heaven?"

Lewinski, looking directly at him, earnestly responds, "I tried to be the best priest I could be for God."

Somewhere, a bell chimes.

Lewinski was born into eternity on July 19, 2017. His funeral was on July 26 in the church he and his parishioners had built. It was standing room only. Over 130 ordained (bishops, priests, and deacons) attended. People arrived an hour early to get a seat—something normally seen only during Christmas and Easter services. The assembly overflowed from the sanctuary into the Narthex. Family, friends, and the nuns who Lewinski credited with having such an influence on him attended.

Cardinal Blase Cupich, presided. A seminarian Lewinski had mentored (now Fr.) Andrew Matijevic was Master of Ceremonies. Another former mentee, Fr. Andrew Liaugminas, then Chaplain at the University of Chicago, gave the homily. Scripture proclamations were made by Todd Williamson, Director of the Office of Divine Worship, and Jon Matousek, lector and an Archdiocesan facilitator for Parish Transformation.

During his comments, Cardinal Cupich proclaimed, "To worship in this church is to be in the presence of Father Ron Lewinski." Lewinski would be happy to hear those words, not because they praised him but because they acknowledged the hard work he, Lohan, and the parishioners had successfully completed.

A mother and her eight-year-old daughter in Italy once spent half an hour with Pope John XXIII. Afterward, the somewhat disappointed little girl claimed he seemed like an ordinary priest. Her mother explained simply, "he was just an ordinary priest who took his Christianity seriously."[70] I submit Lewinski's achievements show he, too, took his priesthood seriously.

He was buried, in his words, "in the sure and certain hope of the glorious resurrection." He rests in the cemetery between the old church and the new.

A fitting location for this pivotal pastor.

Please share your impressions, pro and con, by emailing
djkennebeck@emmaus-way.com

[1] Zygmunt, Mike. Personal conversation, November 24, 2018.

[2] It is called the 'second' because the First Vatican Council convened in 1869, four years after the parish was founded. It was the first Council since the Council of Trent three centuries earlier. Despite that gap, one of the twenty-one Cardinals invited to Vatican I claimed there was no need to hold a Council. Vatican I was interrupted by the Franco-Prussian war and was never resumed or even officially closed. —https://www.ewtn.com/catholicism/library/first-vatican-council-1505.

[3] Ross, Keum, Avtzi, Hewitt, ed. *Ecumenical Missiology: Changing Landscapes and New Conceptions of Mission*. Regnum Centenary Series, 2016.

[4] Cunningham, Agnes. From her letter *"Getting to Know Ron Lewinski,"* 2017.

[5] Ibid.

[6] Hertel, Veronica. Email to the author, August 21, 2022.

[7] Harman, Paul. "Vocation and the Spiritual Exercises of St. Ignatius of Loyola" in Haughey, p. 101.

[8] Fahey, Pat. Personal conversation, August 1, 2018.

[9] Ibid.

[10] Tonelli, Bob. Personal conversation, February 2, 2022.

[11] Ibid.

[12] "…it is not surprising that the Constitution, in Articles 214-19, becomes most insistent on the liturgical formation of priests. … 'Pastors themselves, in the first place,' should 'become thoroughly imbued with the spirit and power of the liturgy.'" —McNaspy, p. 49.

[13] See *Decree on Priestly Training, Optatam Totius*, October 28, 1965. —https://www.vatican.va/archive/hist_councils/ii_vatican_council/documents/vat-ii_decree_19651028_optatam-totius_en.html

[14] Kartje, John. Personal conversation, August 14, 2018.

[15] Pollard, Pat. Personal conversation, Sept. 23, 2021.

[16] Ibid.

[17] Confusion remains about the Pope's mention of "fresh air." Paul Collins in 2018 wrote, "Unfortunately, John XXIII probably never said that, which is sad because it is such a vivid image." —https://sharonkabel.com/post/windows/

[18] Gorman, John. Personal conversation, May 13, 2022.

[19] Catt, p. 3.

[20] Elliott, p. 144.

[21] Ibid.

[22] Kartje, John. Personal conversation, August 14, 2018.

[23] Merton, *Seven Storey*, p. 392.

[24] Tobin, p. 123.

[25] Walsh, Corine. Personal conversation, June 13, 2018.

[26] Tonelli, Bob. Personal conversation, February 2, 2022.

[27] Website Content. Liturgy Training Publications, Tribute Video, 2017. "Unleashed" refers to the Vatican II document *Sacrosanctum Concilium* which instructed that local vernacular could replace the Latin that had been in use for centuries. It did not, however, exclude Latin from use.

[28] Poletto, Bob. Personal conversation, May 3, 2022.

[29] Tonelli, Bob. Personal conversation. February 2 and May 4 2022.

[30] Barrett, Kathi. Personal conversation, May 3, 2018.

[31] Turner, Paul. *Fr. Ron: A Leader in Initiation*, p. 20.

[32] Pope John Paul II was ordained in 1946, the same year Lewinski was born.

[33] Karecki, Madge. Personal conversation, June 3, 2022.

[34] Lewinski, Ron. *The Rite of Acceptance with Pope John Paul II*, p. 19.

[35] Broccolo, Gerard. Personal conversation, June 3, 2022.

[36] Another of Lewinski's friends was Wilton Gregory. Gabe Huck recalls that Fr. Gregory, ordained a year after Lewinski in 1973, would sometimes help at the ODW offices. He would go on to become auxiliary bishop of Chicago and the first African American president of the U.S. Conference of Catholic Bishops (USCCB), before becoming the Archbishop of Washington D.C. In 2020, he was elevated to the rank of Cardinal, the first African American to hold that position. He, like Cardinal Cupich of Chicago, was named by Pope Francis as a delegate to a Synod in Rome in 2023.

[37] Raab, Ronald. Personal conversation, May 14, 2022.

[38] Huck, Gabe. Personal conversation, June 3, 2022.

[39] Kicanas, Gerald. Personal conversation, July 17, 2018.

[40] Payette, Kathy. Personal conversation, June 12 2019. The ministry lasted several years. Eventually mothers from the parish helped other parishes with their own Challenge Clubs.

[41] *Sacrosanctum Concilium*, C 19, from "Constitution on the Sacred Liturgy," Dec. 4, 1963.

[42] This is related to, but not the same as, ACTA Publishing ("A Commitment to All" Publications) in Chicago.

[43] https://www.actafoundation.org/

[44] Dowling, Larry. Personal conversation, June 8, 2022.

[45] Eipers, Carole. Personal conversation, June 13, 2022.

[46] https://www.encyclopedia.com/religion/encyclopedias-almanacs-transcripts-and-maps/vicar-forane. See also https://www.vatican.va/archive/cod-iuris-canonici/eng/documents/cic_lib2-cann460-572_en.html#CHAPTER_VII.

[47] A parishioner who knew Lewinski recalled: "I think he was starting to take some body blows, whether they were warranted or not. You could see him start to withdraw. He spoke at each Mass one weekend and got emotional. I know that he was sorry that he upset people; I don't think that he really ever meant to. It happens in a lot of leadership roles where you think you having things moving along; but the amount of energy you need is great, and there's a lot of nastiness. Suddenly all these accusations were flying around and he was very upset. I don't think he ever had any malice in his heart. Some people accosted him in the Narthex, or pulled their kids out of school, or made threats. He was like, what's going on? I think he loved a lot of people; but when you love people you can also be very heart-broken because people don't always love you back."

[48] Liaugminas, Andrew. Personal conversation, August 16, 2018.

[49] Williamson, Todd. "Ron spent his sabbatical time visiting parishes that were known for good liturgy. His whole purpose was to get profiles of how parishes can have a vibrant liturgical life. It is literally where we are now with "Renew My Church" here in Chicago. It is no wonder that Cardinal Cupich tapped Fr. Ron to be part of that." —Personal conversation, August 16, 2018.

[50] Wojcik, Peter. Personal conversation, March 22, 2022.

[51] The author knows of two humorous incidents involving Lewinski and weddings. The first occurred at a parish in a Chicago suburb that was mostly of Italian descent. Lewinski was counseling a woman engaged to be married. He wanted her to do something specific in preparation (exactly what isi unknown). Later, Lewinski's answered a knock on his door. A fellow asked if he was Father Lewinski. As soon as Lewinski confirmed that he was, the fellow punched him, sending Lewinski to the floor with a bloody nose. Lewinski often took joy in retelling the story about the woman's brother, while adopting an excellent Italian accent.

In another story, Lewinski had just finished a young couple's wedding in the late 1970s. One of the groomsmen walked up to Lewinski, shook his hand in congratulations, and handed him some "joints." Being occupied with greeting people, Lewinski casually put them in his pocket. Shortly, he realized that he was running late for an appointment and rushed to his car. He transferred the "doobies" to his glove compartment rather than tossing them on the road. On the way to his destination, a policeman stopped him for speeding. When the policeman asked for his title and registration, Lewinski opened the glove compartment only to have the marijuana fall out in open view of the policeman. After a few sputtered explanations from Lewinski, the policeman issued only a warning, confiscated the drugs, and cautioned him to slow down. We can presume the rest of the day went well for both Lewinski and the policeman.

[52] Wojcik, Pete. Ibid. Cyril and Methodius were brothers—known as "Apostles of the Slavs"—doing missionary work in the 9th century. They are credited with devising the Glagolitic alphabet, the first alphabet used to transcribe Old Church Slavonic.—https://en.wikipedia.org/wiki/Cyril_and_Methodius

[53] Ibid.

[54] Finley, p. 129.

[55] "The Liturgy of the Hours," also known as the "Divine Office" or the "Work of God" is the daily prayer of the Church, marking the hours of each day and sanctifying the day with prayer. — https://www.usccb.org/prayer-and-worship/liturgy-of-the-hours.
In this respect, it is similar to the five daily prayers in the Muslim faith. Formerly, the Liturgy of the Hours was practiced only by clergy, but it has become an increasingly common form of prayer among the laity. In Islamic tradition, however, *all* followers of the faith observe the daily prayer times. Perhaps accessibility to Liturgy of the Hours via tablet or cell phone (iBreviary is free for Apple and Android) will promote the practice among Catholic laity.

[56] Cupich, Blase. "The Emerging Models of Pastoral Leadership Project: The theological, Sacramental and Ecclesial Context" presentation at the National Ministry Summit in Orlando Florida, April 21, 2008. Cupich later became Cardinal and the ninth Archbishop of Chicago.

[57] Lyman, Robert. Personal conversation, September 10, 2019.

[58] Robinson, Jim. Parishioner Gathering on June 16, 2019.

[59] Senior, Don. Personal conversation, June 15, 2022.

[60] Barrett, Kathi. Personal conversation, May 3, 2018.

[61] Pollard, Pat. Personal conversation, September 23, 2021.

[62] Sunday bulletin, St. Mary of the Annunciation, January 5, 2003.

[63] Gorman, John. Personal conversation, May 13, 2022.

[64] Pollard, Pat. Personal conversation, September 23, 2021.
"The Order of Christian Funerals" document describes the Funeral Rites, primarily the Vigil, the Funeral Mass, and the Rite of Commitment. Lewinski's own funeral on July 26, 2017 was an excellent observation of the guidelines (although he apparently hadn't made any preparations for his own funeral). As testimony to Lewinski's reputation, it was attended by 139 ordained, and hundreds of lay people.

[65] Kartje, John. Personal conversation, August 14, 2018.
Lewinski was humble, but appreciative when his work was acknowledged. Similarly, he could become discouraged when he'd thought he'd done good work but it wasn't acknowledged. During a conversation on August 12, 2018, Sr. Elaine Marie (Lewinski's 2nd and 3rd grade teacher) shared her observation of him in school: "I think that he was so cooperative and he wanted to please people. If they were happy with his work, then he was thrilled about it and made more effort to produce. Not that he craved attention; but you could see the reaction in him when someone did praise his work, the satisfaction that his work was appreciated."

[66] Kartje, John. —https://usml.edu/father-ron-lewinski-dear-friend-beloved-parish-priest/. The "Renew My Church" program followed "Parish Transformation." Lewinski and Fr. Peter Wojcik led the program, beginning just before Lewinski's death in 2017.

[67] Ibid.

[68] Probably Fr. Michael McGuire's *The New Baltimore Catechism and Mass* or *Baltimore Catechism No. 1.*

[69] Ibid. p 14.

[70] Elliott, p. 137.

IMAGE GALLERY

The following pages contain additional images of people, places, or things that are mentioned in the text. See the "List of Images" at the front of this book for credits.

IMAGE #27

GOOD SHEPHERD STATUE

GIFTED BY THE PARISH TO LEWINSKI IN 2005.
IT WAS CARVED BY THE SAME ARTISAN WHO FASHIONED
STATUES IN THE CHURCH, INCLUDING MARY WITH THE INFANT JESUS.
AN IMAGE OF THE GOOD SHEPHERD HAD BECOME LEWINSKI'S
"BRAND." HE USED IT FOR PERSONAL NOTES, AND THE PARISH USED
IT FOR MATERIALS SUCH AS HIS FUNERAL PROGRAM IN 2017.

IMAGE #28

BELL AND BARN

LOOKING NORTH FROM THE OLD CHURCH
AN ORIGINAL BELL FROM 1367 HANGS IN A COPULA
IN FRONT OF THE OLD CHURCH ON THE
SOUTH SIDE OF ERHART ROAD. (CIRCA 2000)

IMAGE #29

CHURCH AND COWS

THE OLD CHURCH AS VIEWED FROM THE BARN
ON THE NORTH SIDE OF ERHART ROAD. (CIRCA 2000)

IMAGE #30

BEICHSTUHL (CONFESSOR'S CHAIR)

A CONFESSIONAL IN THE CHURCH SALEMER MUNSTER
SALEM, GERMANY (CIRCA 2018)

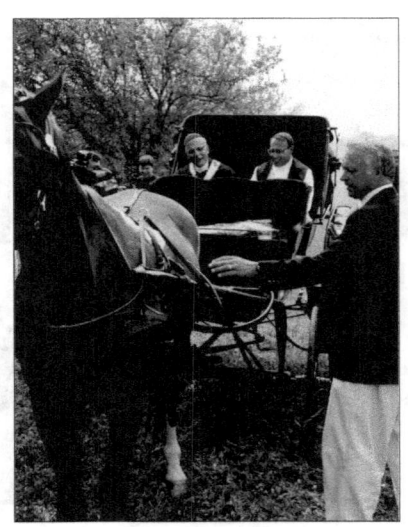

IMAGE #31

CARDINAL GEORGE AND FR. LEWINSKI

HORSE AND BUGGY AT THE PORK AND CORN ROAST
CARDINAL GEORGE AND FR. RON LEWINSKI (CIRCA 1998)

IMAGE #32

THE $60,000 DONUT

THE ROOFTOP BASE ("DONUT") FOR THE STEEPLE.
AT FIRST IT WAS MISTAKENLY CONSTRUCTED 8 FEET OFF-CENTER
BEFORE BEING RE-LOCATED (AT THE CONTRACTOR'S
EXPENSE) DIRECTLY ABOVE THE ALTAR.

IMAGE #33

BAPTISMAL FONT

DESIGN RENDERING OF THE IMMERSION FONT.

IMAGE #34

STEEPLE INSTALLATION

WORKERS INSTALL THE SPIRE ATOP THE CHURCH
(CIRCA 2002)

IMAGE #35

The Bells at St. Mary's

The bell tower near the narthex entrance
features a refurbished bell from 1867 (lowest)
which was previously housed in the
copula outside the old church.

IMAGE #36

CROSS FOR BAPTISMAL FONT

LEWINSKI ARRANGES TILES THAT WILL BE INLAID
ON THE BOTTOM OF THE BAPTISMAL FONT IN THE NEW CHURCH.
THE WORD "EAST" IS WRITTEN BY HIS LEFT HAND.
(CIRCA 2000)

TILES INSTALLED ON THE BOTTOM OF THE BAPTISMAL FONT.
(CIRCA 2002)

IMAGE #37

WEDDING FEAST AT CANA

A PAGE FROM THE CHILDREN'S COLORING BOOK DEPICTS
ONE OF THE THREE TAPESTRIES.
(CIRCA 2001)

IMAGE #38

PARTIAL TAPESTRY

ONE OF THREE TAPESTRIES BEING WOVEN IN SOUTH AFRICA.
THE WEAVER IS AT THE RIGHT SIDE OF THE PICTURE. THIS IS THE
BOTTOM HALF OF THE COMPLETED TAPESTRY SHOWN IN THE NEXT IMAGE.
(CIRCA 2001)

IMAGE #39

COMPLETED TAPESTRY

ONE OF THREE TAPESTRIES HUNG ON THE WALL ABOVE THE BAPTISMAL
FONT. EACH TAPESTRY DEPICTS ONE OF THE THREE EPIPHANIES.
(CIRCA 2002)

IMAGE #40

SANCTUARY DOORS

THE DOORS FROM THE NARTHEX TO THE SANCTUARY ARE
11 FEET HIGH AND WEIGH 500 POUNDS EACH.

IMAGE #41

LADIES' TEA IN THE NARTHEX

THE NARTHEX, WITH ITS TOWERING GLASS WALLS AND 50' CEILING,
PROVIDES A GRAND SPACE FOR SOCIAL OCCASIONS AS WELL AS
VISITATIONS AND CEREMONIAL ACTIVITIES.

IMAGE #42

A-MARY-CAN-GOTH C

SR. GAEL (PASTORAL ASSOCIATE) AND FR. RON (PASTOR)
IN AN HOMAGE TO GRANT WOOD'S "AMERICAN GOTHIC"
WHICH WAS PAINTED AT THE TIME THE 'OLD' CHURCH
(BACKGROUND, WITH MILK CANS ON THE STEPS)
WAS ELEVATED TO INSTALL A BASEMENT UNDER IT.
(PHOTO CIRCA 2000)

IMAGE #43

ALTAR PLATFORM AND ORGAN PIPE CAVITY

LEWINSKI EXPLAINS THE ALTAR AREA CONTAINING MOCK-UPS OF THE AMBO (LEFT), ALTAR (CENTER), AND PRESIDER'S CHAIR (RIGHT). ABOVE AND BEHIND THE ALTAR IS A ROOM-SIZED CAVITY FOR THE ORGAN PIPES.

FIRST ADVENT SERVICE. AFTER THE ORGAN PIPES ARE INSTALLED, THEY WILL BE VISIBLE IN THE HORIZONTAL SLOTS IN THE WALL BEHIND THE ALTAR.
(THE ADVENT WREATH HANGING IN THE FOREGROUND APPEARS TO BE PART OF THE CONICAL SPIRE ABOVE THE ALTAR BECAUSE OF THE CAMERA'S PERSPECTIVE.)

PERSONAL MANDALAS

"Mandala" is a Sanskrit word that translates to "circle" or "center." In Hindu and Buddhist traditions, mandalas typically are symmetrical designs, but they can also be asymmetrical and even free-hand drawings. They are usually circular in shape, the circle being divided into quarters, but sometimes they are square. Mandala-like images also appear in nature (think snowflakes or flowers).

During a Pastoral Council meeting, the group used personal mandalas to convey their thoughts and ideas about the parish to their team members. First, they drew their mandala. Each quadrant of the circle is a response to a specific question.

Then, individually, each participant interpreted their drawing for the others. The value of the mandala derives from the context of the meeting and the discussion rather than from the drawing. There was no need to share their mandala outside the meeting, but some drawings survived. They are shown here as an example of one of the various techniques employed to stimulate thinking and enhance team communication.

Unfortunately, the four questions for the mandalas on the next page did not survive. The meaning of the responses is now a matter of conjecture.

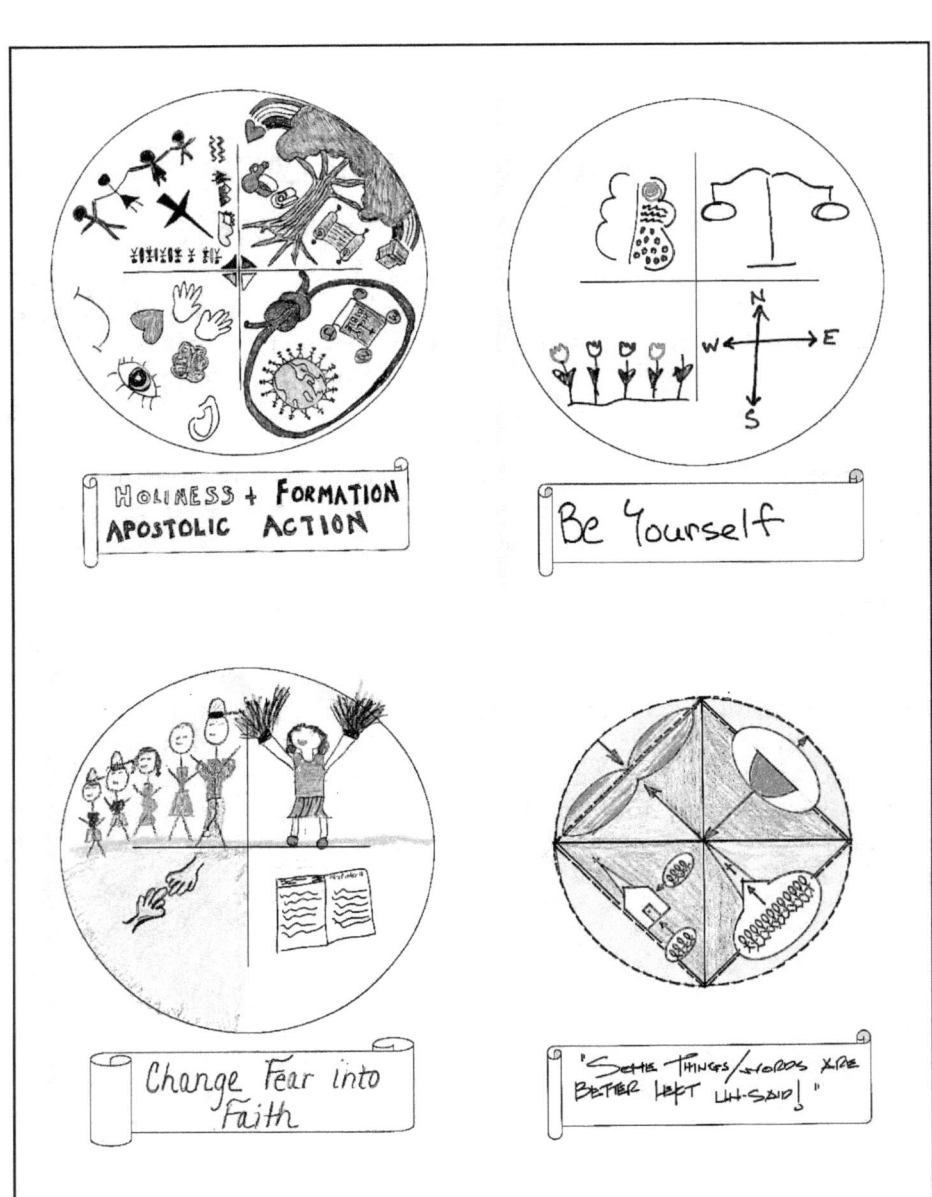

IMAGE #44

MANDALA DRAWINGS

THE NEXT BOOK

Get the companion volume to *The Pivotal Pastor!*

Remembering Ron Lewinski includes remembrances of a nationally known priest (Ron Lewinski) by over sixty individuals, both clergy and laity.

Fr. Lewinski passed in 2017 and had been a priest in the Chicago Archdiocese for 45 years. One contributor knew Lewinski for only a few hours, while others knew him for over six decades.

The book is edited by D.J. Kennebeck, author of *The Pivotal Pastor*. Ranging in length from two sentences to over four pages, each recollection provides insights into the pastor, priest, or man that the contributor knew.

The collage of verbal portraits gives perspectives on Lewinski's ambition, dedication, sincerity, visionary leadership, sensibility, zealousness, and humor. Contributors include a childhood friend, teachers, parishioners, and fellow clergy from newly ordained priests to Cardinal Blase Cupich, Archbishop of Chicago.

This book tells Lewinski's life story in its own way. The author has excluded page numbers and an index in favor of a Concordance. Thus the reader can identify topics unique to, or shared by, contributors regarding the man they individually knew.

Read excerpts starting after the index of this book.

BIBLIOGRAPHY

PRINT ARTICLES

Cupich, Blase. Keynote speech at the Emerging Models of Pastoral Leadership Project, *"Theological, Sacramental, and Ecclesial Context,"* Orlando FL, April 21 2008.

Krishnamurthy, Madhu. "St. Mary parishioners pack the pews for first service in new church building": Daily Herald, April 15 2002 pp 1, 10.

Lewinski, Ron. *The Reign of God – A Call to Conversion* (Association of Catholic Priests), p 5.

Manjoo, Farhad. "Snap Makes a Bet on the Cultural Supremacy of the Camera." *New York Times*, March 8, 2017. https://www.nytimes.com/2017/03/08/technology/snap-makes-a-bet-on-the-cultural-supremacy-of-the-camera.html.

Mead, Rebecca. "The Prophet of Dystopia." *New Yorker*, April 17, 2017.

Nadeau, Barbie. "The Vatican and Modern Art." *Newsweek*, Sept. 11, 2008.

Pai, Tanya. "The Squishy, Sugary History of Peeps." *Vox*, April 11, 2017.

Turner, Paul. "Fr. Ron: A Leader in Initiation." Liturgy Training Publications, *Pastoral Liturgy*, September/October 2017.

PERSONAL ARCHIVES

The "dialogue" that occurs in this story is derived from multiple sources including personal experience, writings of other people, public announcements, press articles, etc. One particular source upon which I drew heavily is video recordings which I'd personally made at the time of the event. Approximately two dozen of these recordings provided dialogue and informed the narrative.

PUBLIC DVDs

A Fremont Center Christmas (St. Mary of the Annunciation CD). Fred Vipond and musicians of St. Mary Parish. January 4, 2003. CD containing 21 recordings.

The Revolution of John XXIII: The Second Vatican Council (Ignatius Press, 2014) DVD 55 min.

BOOKS

Catechism of the Catholic Church. Libreria Editrice Vaticana, 2013.

Anonymous. *As crumbs that fall from the table: parables of minority and of real presence*, Emmanuel 97:326-29+ July-Aug.

Archdiocese of Chicago. *Tomorrow's Parish: Criteria for Planning Workbook*. Office of Research and Planning, 1997.

Archdiocese of Chicago. *Tomorrow's Parish: Guidebook for Planning*. Office of Research and Planning, 1997.

Abbott, Walter M., S.J., General Editor. *The Documents of Vatican II*. The America Press, 1966.

Appleby, R. Scott. *This is my body: how to understand the real presence*. U.S. Catholic 59:6+ July 1994.

Bausch, William J. *The Total Parish Manual*. Mystic, CT: 1994.

Bausch, William J. *The Parish of the Next Millennium*. Mystic, CT: 1998.

Bennett, William J. *The Book of Virtues*. Simon & Schuster, 1993.

Bennis, Warren. *On Becoming a Leader*. Addison-Wesley Publishing Co., 1989.

Bethel, Sheila Murray. *Making a difference: 12 qualities that make you a leader*. The Berkley Publishing Group, 1990.

Block, Peter. *Stewardship: choosing service over self-interest*. Berrett-Koehler Publishers, 1993.

Bridges, William. *Surviving corporate transition*. Bridges & Associates, 1993.

Bridges, William. *Managing Transitions: Making the Most of Change*. Addison-Wesley Publishing Co., 1991.

Brill, Peter L. & Worht, Richard. *The four levers of corporate change*. American Management Association, 1997.

Catt, Michael. *The Power of Purpose*. B&H Publishing, 2017.

Cummings, Thomas & Worley, Christopher. *Organizational Development and Change*, 5th Ed., West Publishing Co., 1993.

DeGeus, Arie. *The Living Company: Habits for survival in a turbulent business environment*. Boston: Harvard Business School Press, 1997.

DePree, Max. *Leadership is an Art*. Dell Publishing, 1997.

DeSiano, Frank and Boyack Kenneth. *Creating the Evangelizing Parish*. Paulist Press, 1993.

Dulles Avery. *Models of the Church*. Doubleday, 1987.

Elliott, Lawrence. *I Will Be Called John*. Reader's Digest Press, 1973.

Falardeau, Ernest. *The Eucharist and Spirituality*. Emmanuel 103:217-224, May 1997.

Finley, James. *Merton's Palace of Nowhere: A Search for God through Awareness of the True Self*. Ave Maria Press, 1978.

Flannery, Austin, Gen. Ed. Vatican II Vol. I, *The Conciliar and Post Conciliar Documents*. Costello Publishing Co., 1998.

Fortescue, Adrian. *The Greek Fathers: Their Lives and Writings*. Ignatius Press, 2007.

Fox, Matthew. *The Reinvention of Work: A New Vision of Livelihood for Our Time*. Harper, 1995.

Gannon, John. *Nothing is Impossible With God: The Story of St. Mary of the Annunciation*, 2014.

Gies, Frances and Joseph. *Cathedral, Forge and Waterwheel: Technology and Invention in the Middle Ages*. Harper Collins Publishers Inc, 1994.

Grazer, Brian, and Charles Fishman. *A Curious Mind: The Secret to a Bigger Life*. Simon & Schuster, 2015.

Greenleaf, Robert K. *Servant Leadership: A journey into the nature of legitimate power and greatness*. Paulist Press, 1977.

Guarino, Thomas G. *The Disputed Teachings of Vatican II*. William B. Eerdmans Publishing Co., 2018.

Hatch, Alden. *A Man Named John, The Life of Pope John XXIII*. Hawthorn Books Inc., 1963.

Haughey, John C., Editor. *Revisiting the Idea of Vocation*. The Catholic University of America Press, 2004.

Hauser, Richard J. *In His Spirit*. Beacon Publishing, 2011.

Heermann, Barry. *Building Team Spirit*. McGraw-Hill NY, 1997.

Hemrick, Eugene. *Habits of a Priestly Heart*. J.S. Paluch Company, Inc., 2009.

Horan, Ellamay. *A Catechism of Christian Doctrine; the Illustrated Revised Edition of the Baltimore Catechism No. 1*. W.H. Sadler Inc., 1944.

Hudson, Deal Wyatt. *Real Presence*. Crisis 16:6. , June, 1998.

Huebsch, Bill. *Vatican II in Plain English* – 3 volumes. Thomas More Publishing, 1997.

Kavanaugh, James. *A Modern Priest Looks at His Outdated Church*. Pocket Books, 1968

Kelly, J.N.D. *Early Christian Doctrines*. Harper Collins, 1978.

Klein, Eric & Izzo, John. B. *Awakening corporate soul: four paths to unleash the power of people at work*. Canada: Fairwinds Press, 1998.

Klein, Peter. *The Catholic Source Book*. Harcourt Religion Publishers, 2000.

Kline, Peter & Saunders, Bernard. *Ten Steps to a Learning Organization*. Great Ocean Publishers, 1993.

Kolp, Alan. *Traditions of spiritual guidance: the real presence a Quaker perspective on spiritual direction*. Way 33:240-247, July 1993.

LaMarsh, Jeanenne. *Changing the Way We Change: Gaining Control of Major Operational Change*. Addison-Wesley Pub. Co., 1995.

Legere, Thomas E. *Real Presence*. Emmanuel 94:510-511, Nov., 1988.

Legere, Thomas E. *Thoughts on the Run*. Winston Press, 1983.

Leman, Kevin. *The Birth Order Book*. Baker Publishing Group, 2009.

Lewinski, Ron. *An Introduction to the RCIA*. Liturgy Training Publications, 2017.

Lewinski, Ron. *Guide for Sponsors*. Liturgy Training Publications, 2008.

Lewinski, Ron. *Making Parish Policy*. Liturgy Training Publications, 1996.

Lewinski, Ron. *Welcoming the New Catholic*. Liturgy Training Publications, 1993.

Macy, Gary. *Treasures from the Storeroom: medieval religion and the eucharist*. The Liturgical Press, 1999.

Markham, Donna J. *Spiritlinking Leadership: Working through resistance to organizational change*. Paulist Press, 1999

McBrien, Richard P. *Catholicism*. HarperCollins, 1994.

McBrien, Richard P. *Responses to 101 Questions on the Church*. Paulist Press, 1996.

McGuire, Michael Fr. *The New Baltimore Catechism and Mass, No. 2 Official Revised Edition*. Benziger Brothers Inc., 1953.

McNaspy, C.J. *Our Changing Liturgy*. Hawthorn Books, 1966.

Meredith, Owen. *Parish Activities Handbook*. Twenty-Third Publications, 1996.

Merton, Thomas. *New Seeds of Contemplation*. New Directions Books, 2007.

Merton, Thomas. *The Seven Storey Mountain*. Harper Inc., 1998.

Merton, Thomas. *The Springs of Contemplation*. Farrar, Straus, Giroux, 1992.

Mitchell, Nathan D. *Who is at table?* Commonweal 122:10-15, Jan. 27, 1995.

Mize, Clay. *A Desperate God*. Thorn Hill Books, 2018.

Mize, Clay. *The Power of Humility*. Thorn Hill Books, 2013.

Myra, Harold and Shelley, Marshall. *The Leadership Secrets of Billy Graham*. Zondervan, 2005.

Olesen, Erik. *Mastering the Winds of Change*. HarperCollins Publishers, 1994.

Owen, Harrison. *Open Space Technology*. Berrett-Koehler Pub Inc., 1998.

Peck, M. Scott. *The Road Less Traveled*. Simon & Schuster, 1978.

Perkins-Reed, Marcia. *Thriving in Transition: effective living in times of change*. Simon & Schuster, 1996.

Rainer, Thom S. *Effective Evangelistic Churches.* Broadman and Holman Pub., 1996.

Rainer, Thom S. *Who Moved My Pulpit?* B&H Publishing, 2016.

Ratzinger, Joseph. *Introduction to Christianity*. Ignatius Press, 1968.

Reynolds, Maura. *Bring Christ's Real Presence to the Sick and Dying*. Today's Parish 13:16, April 1981.

Roberts, Andrew. *Churchill: Walking with Destiny*. Penguin Books, 2018.

Schmitt, Leonard. J. An untitled commemorative record of the history of St. Mary of the Annunciation produced at St. Mary of the Annunciation, 1964.

Senge, Peter M. *The Fifth Discipline: The Art and Practice of the Learning Organization*. Doubleday, 1990.

Smith, Zadie. *Swing Time*. Penguin Press, 2016.

Stone, Richard. *The Healing Art of Storytelling*. Hyperion, 1996.

Tobin, Greg, *The Good Pope*. Harper One, 2012.

USCCB: United States Conference of Catholic Bishops – Committee on the Liturgy. *Built of Living Stones: Art, Architecture, and Worship*. NCCB/USCC, Nov. 16, 2000.

Wagner, Tom. *Chronicle of St. Mary of the Annunciation*, 2014.

Warren, Michael. *Faith, Culture, and the Worshiping Community*. The Pastoral Press, 1993.

Weems Jr., Lovett H. *Church Leadership: Vision, Team, Culture and Integrity*. Abingdown Press, 1993.

Wheatley, Margaret J. *Leadership and the New Science: Learning About Organization from and Orderly Universe*. Berrett-Koehler Publishers Inc., 1992.

Whitehead, James D. and Whitehead, Evelyn Eaton. *The Emerging Laity: Returning Leadership to the Community of Faith*. Doubleday, 1988.

Wiltgen, Ralph M. *The Inside Story of Vatican II*. Charlotte, North Carolina: TAN Books, 2014.

Worgul, George S. Jr. *Imagination, ritual and eucharistic real presence*. Louvain Studies 9:198:210, Fall 1982.

ABOUT THE AUTHOR

David J. Kennebeck was a parishioner at St. Mary of the Annunciation parish from 1983 to 2015. He has an undergraduate degree from Western Illinois University and a Certificate in Pastoral Leadership from a Master in Leadership Studies at Lewis University in Romeoville, Illinois. He also has credentials in Project Management and has earned a certificate from Famous Writer's School in Connecticut.

While at St. Mary's of the Annunciation, he served on the Pastoral Council, the PR and Communications Committee, and various ministries. He created the parish's first website in 1998.

He and his wife are retired and enjoy visiting with family and friends. He welcomes comments, questions, and especially corrections.

IMAGE #45

LEFT TO RIGHT:
DIRK LOHAN, ARCHITECT
REVEREND RONALD J. LEWINSKI, PASTOR
ISABELLE AND DAVID KENNEBECK, PARISHIONERS
DEDICATION DAY AT ST. MARY OF THE ANNUNCIATION
APRIL 14, 2002

Contact the author at djkennebeck@emmaus-way.com

Remembering
Ron Lewinski

Remembrances of a
Pastor, Priest, Man
by
Clergy and Laity Who Knew Him

EXCERPTS FROM
Remembering Ron Lewinski
BEGIN HERE.

INTRODUCTION

This book evolved while I was researching and writing another book, "*The Pivotal Pastor.*" In a way, this is a companion volume to that book.

"*The Pivotal Pastor*" is my story about Fr. Ron Lewinski's first of three six-year terms (1996-2002) as Pastor at St. Mary of the Annunciation parish near Mundelein, IL. During that time, Ron transformed the parish from a "little country parish" into an active faith community by leading the community in an $11 million project and constructing a new church—designed by the world-class architect Dirk Lohan—that holds four times as many people as the old church (which was respectfully retained).

I was part of that experience and knew Fr. Ron Lewinski as a friend and pastor. But when beginning my inspired journey of writing about it, I needed to hear other perspectives about Ron. I collected most comments via interviews conducted over the phone or in person. Some people opted to submit written "content" instead.

As I was finishing "*The Pivotal Pastor,*" five years later, I realized that only a small percentage of the material that I'd collected was included in that book. When I read the unused content, I decided it deserved to be shared. This book is the result.

Why bother publishing the "leftover" material? After reading these memoirs, I think that will no longer be a question for you. I'll share some of my reasons.

First, in gratitude to the many people who generously shared their memories with the expectation that doing so would be fruitful.

Second, interesting and informative content gives a fuller portrait of the man people knew as Fr. Lewinski, or "Ron."

Third, I believe Ron Lewinski was one of the few truly "authentic" people one encounters during their life. He found his purpose in life and pursued it consistently and with integrity. He didn't do it for recognition; he was humble. He did not pursue material wealth, for surely he could have chosen other vocations to apply his gifts "profitably" for that purpose. He did not seek power; otherwise, he could have chosen a path within the Church's hierarchy. Instead, he amplified his gifts and allowed himself to become a voice of the Spirit, drawing forth the God-given uniqueness within others and fostering its development and expression. He was a vehicle for fueling the flame of others' lives.

This book would not exist without the contributions of everyone identified in the list of Contributors. Because the content didn't begin as an intentional collection of memoirs, the "tone" of the material varies from one contributor to another. I regard that as a diversity to be enjoyed.

Contributors to these memoirs range from someone who had only a few hours of conversation with Fr. Ron to others who knew him for over sixty years. The descriptions of Fr. Ron include commonly recognized traits: humor, authenticity, love for liturgy, humility, vision, and leadership. There is recognition of the paradox that he was an introvert who actively socialized. He was an intellectual who wrestled with religious theologies as readily as he did with a young teen who would later become an award-winning wrestler in college. Ron enjoyed swimming in community pools and backyard lakes, and was adept at navigating the hierarchies of clergy in the local and national church.

The reader may wonder why I begin the book with a reflection from Fr. Ron about taking a retreat. Well, I believe these memoirs deserve more than just a "reading." In fact, I suggest the reader not approach this book with the intent of reading "normally": from beginning to end. Instead, I propose the reader approach it in "pieces," choosing to read "chapters" sequentially or randomly, but perhaps never more than a handful at a time. Or, in the case of the longer chapters, perhaps one chapter at a time.

Each contributor's content, in its own chapter, warrants some degree of contemplation. The many people who have offered to share their perspectives of Fr. Ron should be acknowledged for their generosity. Reading with intentional patience will respect the spirit of their contribution. There are commonalities to be recognized, but the differences should be equally valued.

As I was assembling this collection, I would often regard it as a treasure of sorts. According to the author of one biography of Winston Churchill, there were, at the time this biographer wrote his book, already 1,000 other Churchill biographies. How could there be so many books about one person, and why add another to the list? After assembling this collection of memoirs, I believe the answer is that there are as many perspectives of someone or something as there are viewers. Each perspective is a special gem; a collection of gems is a treasure.

Certainly, there is value derived from simply reading an individual memoir. But I would like to think that the reader, by applying thoughtful intent, will dig past the surface value of a memoir and come to recognize meaning. What—a paragraph, a sentence, or perhaps even a phase or just a word—snags your attention? If you knew Ron Lewinski, what causes you to recognize a similarity to your own perspective, or presents a challenge that advocates for some change in your attitude? Spending time pondering these memoirs may help you recognize more of their value, just as time spent in contemplation during a retreat often produces lasting benefits that were not expected.

The contributors to this book are a fraction of those I initially approached. Some accepted my request to chat, some declined, and many didn't respond. I feel obliged to apologize to anyone who might wish they had been included as a contributor. I hope you'll recognize that Fr. Ron's connections were many, and there are practical restraints on my time and effort.

It has been my privilege to assemble this collection. I hope you find these "memoirs" insightful and sometimes even motivational. For those who knew Fr. Ron, be warned: some of this content may cause fond memories to surface. They did for me. —D.J. Kennebeck, Editor

EDITOR'S NOTES

Editor's Notes from *Remembering Ron Lewinski*

ARATA

~ "...The Wirtz's had land ..."—refers to Bill Wirtz and his family, owners of the Chicago Blackhawks, when the parish sought land for expansion in 1997.

~ "...'Moms and Tots' and sister Gael ..."—Sr. Gael Gensler was Pastoral Associate during the expansion. Growing the ministries was one of her responsibilities, which she did with great success.

BAILEY

~ "...*he had been leading RCIA...*"—Lewinski was one of the "Fathers" of The Rite of Christian Initiation of Adults (RCIA), having begun a lifelong relationship with it when it was in its infancy, even before he was ordained.

~ "... *Renew My Church* ..."—A process in the Chicago Archdiocese that seeks to make disciples, build community, and inspire witness—in light of people's Baptism and Confirmation—working with the Holy Spirit. An earlier process, "Parish Transformation," engaged parishes in a facilitated self-examination of their community.

BARRETT

~ "...*the right side looks and seems wider than the left side...*"—The reason for this appearance is because the sanctuary space, a large square, is bisected by a nave that is on a slightly diagonal axis instead of running parallel to the side walls in the middle of the space. This is an intentional design feature and causes the exterior roof to appear "crooked" when in fact, it is not.

BEHM

~ "...*doughnut-shaped base for the steeple...*"—The church steeple was designed to be placed directly over the altar in the sanctuary, thus Lewinski's insistence on the correct location of the doughnut hole. The steeple was originally intended to funnel light from the exterior down upon the altar, but architectural requirements thwarted the effect.

~ "...*a church with all that glass...*"—The 40-foot walls of the narthex, situated between the sanctuary and the pastoral center, are entirely glass. Gradually, the parishioners realized the architect had done other major projects using glass, including the Shedd Oceanarium and the Adler Planetarium in Chicago.

FR. GERARD BROCCOLO

~ "...the CCD office..."—Confraternity of Christian Doctrine. Related to Christian education, commonly using the Catechism. It is often used to refer to religious education in parochial schools and is also known as REP (Religious Education Program). The usage here refers to a precursor of what has become known as the Liturgy Office, which exists to support the Bishop of the diocese (in this case, the Archbishop of Chicago) and his parishes.

~ "...*Mundelein Seminary...*"—The seminary Fr. Lewinski attended and where he later taught in Mundelein, IL. The town's population grew from 21,000 in 1990 to 31,000 in 2000 and has not grown much since. Also known as the University of St. Mary of the Lake (USML), the seminary is named after George Cardinal Mundelein. In 1926, it hosted the XXVIII International Eucharistic Congress, which 800,000 people attended.

MSGR. JOHN CANARY

~ "...*the architect and the historical connections with Mies van der Rohe...*"—The architect of the new church at St. Mary's is Dirk Lohan, grandson of German-American architect Ludwig Mies van der Rohe (1886-1969), who is often associated with the phrases "less is more" and "God is in the details."

SR. AGNES CUNNINGHAM

~ "...*he came to appreciate his own baptism...*"—Lewinski regularly celebrated both his birthday (February 15) and his date of Baptism (March 3). One of his nicknames was "Ron the Baptist."

CARDINAL BLASE JOSEPH CUPICH

~ "...*Department of Parish Life and Formation...*"—This department initiated the Archdiocesan-wide process "Renew My Church" (RMC) that succeeded "Parish Transformation" which had impacted over 200 parishes in the Archdiocese. Lewinski's work with the RCIA substantially contributed to both programs.

BISHOP FRANZ-PETER TEBARTZ-VAN ELST

~ "...*saw the church illuminated...*"—From the beginning, Lewinski's design included an illuminated steeple representing a beacon "in an oasis." With the inclusion of the glass narthex, the building's illumination at night is even more striking.

~ "...*so many people at his funeral...*"—Fr. Lewinski's funeral on July 26, 2017, was presided over by Cardinal Cupich, several bishops, and over 120 ordained clergy (some from outside the Archdiocese and even outside the United States). The standing-room-only congregation overflowed from the sanctuary into the narthex.

FAHEY

~ "...*he would have missed Merton...*"—"Merton" refers to the monk Thomas Merton, an influential writer best known for his autobiographical account of conversion in 1948's "*The Seven Storey Mountain.*" Merton resided at the Abbey of Gethsemani, where Lewinski took annual retreats during his priesthood. Merton died in Bangkok in 1968, four years before Lewinski was ordained.

~ "...*they could turn part of it into a golf course...*"—A bit of irony in this story is that Mundelein Seminary, where Lewinski was ordained, boasts a golf course adjacent to the campus. The course occupies land that belonged to the Seminary. It was expanded to 18 holes in 1929 because Cardinal Mundelein's doctor told him he needed to walk more. Known as the Pine Meadow Golf Club, in 1986, it was named the Best New Public Course by Golf Magazine and has received numerous awards since, including one of America's top 25 Public Courses.

~ *"…resided in the parish where he worked…"*—Lewinski resided at different parishes over time but sometimes worked elsewhere, such as the ODW in Chicago.

SR. GAEL GENSLER

~ *"…after Mass at Diantha Hall …"*—Diantha Hall, named after a parishioner, is an expansion to the school—including a gym—that St. Mary's completed long before Lewinski's arrival. Soon after, he selected the gym for weekend services because it could hold twice as many people as the old church. This required parishioners to set up and tear down folding chairs and wooden platforms each weekend, which they did for five years until the new church was dedicated in 2002.

HERTEL

~ *"…in 2017 at St Theresa in Palatine…"*—Lewinski resided at St. Theresa in a Chicago suburb while working at the Archdiocese in Chicago. He passed in the rectory at St. Theresa on July 19, 2017.

~ *"…a box of gold tiles he wanted inlaid…"*— *"The Pivotal Pastor"* shows Lewinski arranging these tiles. A photo of the cross appears on the cover of this book.

BISHOP GERALD KICANAS

~ *"…something that could be valuable to other parishes…"*—This theme can actually be traced back to Lewinski's childhood as an altar server (See Zygmunt's remembrances.) It manifests at the seminary, during his sabbatical in 1994-1995, the application of his learnings to the St. Mary's expansion, and later Archdiocesan programs. In short, a vibrant liturgy was Ron's life-long pursuit.

SR. ELAINE MARIE KLUGIEWICZ

~ *"…one class for each grade at Pullman…"*—Though born in Hammond, IN, Lewinski's family moved, and he attended Assumption B.V.M. Elementary School in Chicago's South Side community known as Pullman.

~ *"…you could see the reaction in him…"*—Sr. Klugiewicz was probably the first to observe this trait of Lewinski's. Though humble and vocally self-critical, recognition by others provided Lewinski an inner satisfaction and motivation to achieve more.

LOHAN

~ *"…I first visited the Farnsworth House…"*—The Farnsworth House was designed and constructed by Ludwig Mies van der Rohe, Dirk Lohan's grandfather, after World War II. It is a 1,500-square-foot one-room weekend retreat in rural Plano, Illinois. Edith Farnsworth commissioned the steel and glass house, and is one of AIA Illinois' "25 must see" buildings.

~ *"…I went up to St. Mary parish and looked around…"*—While it doesn't seem unusual for an architect to explore, the belief by the project team is that Dirk Lohan was the only architectural candidate to "walk the site" and show a special interest in the potential of the project.

~ *"…the character of a big barn in terms of shape…"*—Some parishioners commented that an artist's rendering of the design reminded them of a corn crib between two pig pens. The critics apparently didn't recognize the irony in their comment. The parish had asked the architect to retain the rural nature of the farming community.

~ *"...hide it but make it audible..."*—The 2,800+ organ pipes at St. Mary's are installed in a room-sized alcove above and behind the altar. A wall of vertical wooden slats hides the pipes, except for a cutout on the right side which exposes some of the largest ones. Thus the visual appearance is ornamental without being distracting. Furthermore, the fabric behind the wood slats visually hides the pipes but allows the sound to penetrate the sanctuary. Thus, it is hidden but quite audible.

DEACON JOHN LUCAS

~ *"...It is truly a reflection of who he was..."*—This statement echoes one by Cardinal Cupich when, while presiding at Fr. Lewinski's Funeral Mass, stated, "To worship in this church is to be in the presence of Ron Lewinski."

LYMAN

~ *"...The ceremonial doors..."*—The story of these doors, which had been discarded from the plans until an act of Providence, is related in *"The Pivotal Pastor."*

MARKIEWICZ

~ *"...that is what happened..."*—The *"Pastoral Statement of US Catholic Bishops on Persons with Disabilities"* (rev. 1989) states: "Accessibility involves far more than physical alterations to parish buildings. Realistic provision must be made for Catholics with disabilities to participate fully in the Eucharist and other liturgical celebrations."

STOWE

~ *"...program for people with special needs called SPRED..."*—The Special Religious Development (SPRED) Program serves children and young adults with developmental disabilities such as Down syndrome, autism, and learning disabilities.

THOMPSON

~ *"...Another book [by Merton] was about contemplation..."*—Likely *"The Springs of Contemplation"* or perhaps *"New Seeds of Contemplation."*

FR. BOB TONELLI

~ *"...not music that the older people adapted to..."*—As an example, a 1993 survey at St. Mary's showed that nearly 80% of parishioners over the age of 65 preferred only organ music. During Lewinski's pastorship, instruments were expanded from organ and piano to include french horn, harp, violin, trombone, trumpet, tuba, guitar, flute, handbells, and tambourine.

~ *"...people don't understand: this is an American thing..."*—in *"The Pivotal Pastor,"* the chapter "In the Dark" describes Lewinski confronting this misperception.

~ *"...Ron had asked if I had ever seen the Basilica of St. Clement..."*—"Clement" is the name of Lewinski's father.

~ *"...We needed an idea about how we could say farewell to the old church..."*—St. John's parish was fortunate to convert their old church into a Parish Center. Soon after arriving at St. Mary's parish, Lewinski promised that the old church would not be grazed. He made this promise without knowing how the parish would be able to grow within the limited confines of the existing campus. He had faith they would find a way. The old church continues to be a house of worship on the parish campus.

SR. CORINE WALSH

~ *"...Liturgy of the Hours..."*—Another of the contributors mentioned that Fr. Ron would be the first to recommend that everyone pray the Liturgy of the Hours. It is available in book form and the app "iBreviary" for tablets and phones.

~ *"...what he was doing and how he did it..."*—This refers to the $11 million expansion project Lewinski led during his first term at St. Mary parish. Over the course of six years, the number of households doubled, ministries quadrupled, and a new church was built that holds four times more than the old one.

WASHBURN

~ *"...an abbey that really had an effect on the committee..."*—This is St. Procopius Abbey in Lisle, IL. Early in the project, a team of parishioners accompanied Lewinski during visits to locations that could provide ideas and inspiration about what a future St. Mary's parish might look like.

~ *"...the altar and an adjoining backdrop..."*—see LOHAN, "make it audible."

JIM WOJCIK

~ *"...the entire parish should go through the RCIA process..."*—Although there is a "process," Lewinski's approach to RCIA was to enable someone to pursue it as inspired by the Holy Spirit rather than as a rigid curriculum with pre-defined beginning and ending points.

FR. PETER WOJCIK

~ *"...somebody interrupting a wedding..."*—See also Howard Fischer's "Vigil" comments.

ZAGULA

~ *"...the "why" behind everything..."*—These questions are addressed in *"The Pivotal Pastor,"* as well as in a document at St. Mary's parish office, which docents use for guided tours of the facility.

Contributors to *Remembering Ron Lewinski*

Mike & Kathleen Arata
Parishioners
David & Jean Bailey
Former Parishioners
Kathi & Tony Barrett
Parishioners
Ken Behm
Parishioner
Fr. Britto Berchmans
Friend of Fr. Ron
Fr. Gerard Broccolo
Former professor at Mundelein Seminary
Angela Bujan
Former Parishioner
Msgr. John Canary
Former Archdiocesan Vicar General
of the Chicago Archdiocese
Diane Ciesielski
Fr. Ron's sister
Paul Ciesielski
Nephew of Fr. Ron
Sr. Agnes Cunningham
Former Patristics instructor at Mundelein Seminary
Cardinal Blase Joseph Cupich
Archbishop of Chicago
Fr. Larry Dowling
Board President of the ACTA Foundation
Carole Eipers
National Catechetical Advisor for
William H. Sadler Inc.
Bishop Franz-PeterTebartz-van Elst
Curia-Bishop in the Vatican
Pat* & Donna Fahey
Friends of Fr. Ron
Fr. Robert Fedek
Priest Secretary to Cardinal Cupich
Deacon Howard Fischer
Director of Parish Operations
at St. Mary of the Annunciation

Roger Fisher
Parishioner
John Gannon
Former parishioner
Sr. Gael Gensler
Former Pastoral Associate at St. Mary's parish
Bishop John Gorman
Former Rector at Mundelein Seminary
Cardinal Wilton Daniel Gregory
Archbishop of Washington D.C.
Ed Hendricks
Former parishioner
Joe & Veronica Hertel
Parishioners
Gabe Huck
Former Director of Liturgy Training Publications
Steve Janco
Former associate of Fr. Ron
Sr. Madge Karecki*
Former President of.
St. Augustine College in Johannesburg
Fr. John Kartje
Rector/President at the
University of St. Mary of the Lake
Bishop Gerald Kicanas
Bishop EmeritusTucson Diocese
Sr. Elaine Marie Klugiewicz
Fr. Ron's 2nd and 3rd grade teacher
Ed & Laura Kuderna
Former Parishioners
Fr. Andrew Liaugminas
Priest of the Archdiocese of Chicago
Dirk LohanFAIA
Architect of the 'new' church at St. Mary's
Deacon John Lucas*
Friend of Fr. Ron
Bob Lyman
Parishioner
Anthony Markiewicz
Parishioner
Fr. Andrew Matijevic
Associate Pastor at Holy Name CathedralChicago

Jon & Sue Matousek
Parishioners
Chris Needler
Author and friend of Diane Ciesielski
Kathy Payette
Parishioner
Deacon Bob Poletto
Deacon at St. Mary's parish
Msgr. Pat Pollard
Classmate of Fr. Ron
Janice Powell
Parishioner
Fr. Ronald Raab
Friend of Fr. Ron
John Riggio
Parishioner
Jim & Holly Robinson
Parishioners
James Scavone
Former Director of Liturgy and Music
at St. Mary's parish
Fr. Don Senior*
Columnist, Scholar, President Emeritus of CTU
Dave & Jill Stowe
Former parishioners
Dan & Amy Thompson
Parishioners
Fr. Bob Tonelli
Classmate of Fr. Ron
Victoria Tufano
Editor at Liturgy Training Publications
Fr. Paul Turner
Dir. of the Office of Divine Worship
for the Diocese of Kansas City-St. Joseph
Sr. Corine Walsh
Former Principal of the school at
St. Frances of Rome
Dan Washburn
Parishioner
Todd Williamson
Director of the Office for Divine Worship
in the Chicago Archdiocese

Jim Wojcik*
Former parishioner at St. Frances of Rome
Fr. Peter Wojcik
Associate of Fr. Ron
Stan Zagula
Parishioner
Jack & Linda Zucco
Parishioners
Dr. Mike Zygmunt
A Lifelong friend of Fr. Ron

* Deceased prior to publication

*"USML", "University of St. Mary of the Lake", and
"Mundelein Seminary" refer to the same institution.*

ORDER

THE PIVOTAL PASTOR
ISBN: 979-8-9866668-0-8 (PAPERBACK)

AND

REMEMBERING RON LEWINSKI
ISBN: 979-8-9866668-7-7 (PAPERBACK)

FROM

WWW.EMMAUS-WAY.COM*
AMAZON
BARNES & NOBLE
BAM
AND OTHER BOOKSELLERS

*ONLY THE PUBLISHER, EMMAUS WAY, OFFERS
MATCHING BOOKMARKS AND COPIES
INSCRIBED AND SIGNED BY THE AUTHOR

A PDF VERSION OF THIS BOOK, WITH COLOR IMAGES,
IS AVAILABLE FROM WWW.EMMAUS-WAY.COM